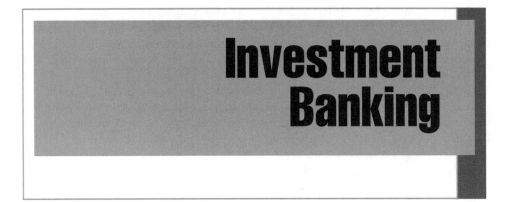

Founded in 1807, John Wiley & Sons is the oldest independent publishing company in the United States. With offices in North America, Europe, Australia, and Asia, Wiley is globally committed to developing and marketing print and electronic products and services for our customers' professional and personal knowledge and understanding.

The Wiley Finance series contains books written specifically for finance and investment professionals as well as sophisticated individual investors and their financial advisors. Book topics range from portfolio management to e-commerce, risk management, financial engineering, valuation, and financial instrument analysis, as well as much more.

For a list of available titles, please visit our Web site at www.WileyFinance.com.

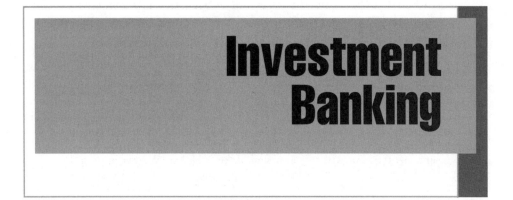

Investment Banking

*Valuation, Leveraged Buyouts,
and Mergers & Acquisitions*

JOSHUA ROSENBAUM

JOSHUA PEARL

WILEY

John Wiley & Sons, Inc.

Published by John Wiley & Sons, Inc., Hoboken, New Jersey.
Published simultaneously in Canada.

For general information on our other products and services or for technical support, please contact our Customer Care Department within the United States at (800) 762-2974, outside the United States at (317) 572-3993 or fax (317) 572-4002.

Wiley also publishes its books in a variety of electronic formats. Some content that appears in print may not be available in electronic books. For more information about Wiley products, visit our web site at www.wiley.com.

Library of Congress Cataloging-in-Publication Data:

Rosenbaum, Joshua, 1971–
    Investment banking : valuation, leveraged buyouts, and mergers & acquisitions /
Joshua Rosenbaum, Joshua Pearl.
        p. cm. — (Wiley finance series)
    Includes bibliographical references and index.
    ISBN 978-0-470-44220-3 (cloth)
    1. Investment banking.   2. Valuation.   3. Leveraged buyouts.   4. Consolidation and
merger of corporations.   I. Pearl, Joshua, 1981–   II. Title.
    HG4534.R67 2009
    332.6'6068—dc22

                                                                                    2008049819

Printed in the United States of America.

10 9 8

Contents

PART TWO

Leveraged Buyouts

CHAPTER 4

Leveraged Buyouts   161

PART THREE

Mergers & Acquisitions

About the Authors

JOSHUA ROSENBAUM is a Managing Director at UBS Investment Bank in the Global Industrial Group. He originates, structures, and advises on M&A, corporate finance, and capital markets transactions. Previously, he worked at the International Finance Corporation, the direct investment division of the World Bank. He received his AB from Harvard and his MBA with Baker Scholar honors from Harvard Business School.

JOSHUA PEARL is a Director at UBS Investment Bank in Leveraged Finance. He originates, structures, and executes leveraged loan and high yield bond financings, as well as leveraged buyouts and restructurings. Previously, he worked at Moelis & Company in Capital Markets and Deutsche Bank in Leveraged Finance. He received his BS in Business from Indiana University's Kelley School of Business.

CONTACT THE AUTHORS

Please feel free to contact Joshua Rosenbaum and Joshua Pearl with any questions, comments, or suggestions for future editions at **josh@investmentbankingbook.com**.

Foreword

Mark Twain, long known for his critical views of formal education, once wisely noted: "I never let my schooling interfere with my education."

Twain's one-liner strikes at the core of investment banking, where deals must be lived before proper knowledge and understanding can be obtained. Hard time must be spent doing deals, with complexities in valuation, terms, and negotiations unique to every situation. The truly great firms and dealmakers have become so by developing cultures of apprenticeship that transfer knowledge and creativity from one generation to the next. The task of teaching aspiring investment bankers and finance professionals has been further complicated by the all-consuming nature of the trade, as well as its constantly evolving art and science.

Therefore, for me personally, it's exciting to see Joshua Rosenbaum and Joshua Pearl take the lead in training a new generation of investment bankers. Their work in documenting valuation and deal process in an accessible manner is a particularly important contribution as many aspects of investment banking cannot be taught, even in the world's greatest universities and business schools. Rosenbaum and Pearl provide aspiring—and even the most seasoned—investment bankers with a unique real-world education inside Wall Street's less formal classroom, where deals come together at real-time speed.

The school of hard knocks and of learning-by-doing, which was Twain's classroom, demands strong discipline and sound acumen in the core fundamentals of valuation. It requires applying these techniques to improve the quality of deals for all parties, so that dealmakers can avoid critical and costly mistakes, as well as unnecessary risks. My own 35 plus years of Wall Street education has clearly demonstrated that valuation is at the core of investment banking. Any banker worth his salt must possess the ability to properly value a business in a structured and defensible manner. This logic and rationale must inspire clients and counterparties alike, while spurring strategic momentum and comprehension into the art of doing the deal.

Rosenbaum and Pearl succeed in providing a systematic approach to addressing a critical issue in any M&A, IPO, or investment situation—namely, how much is a business or transaction worth. They also put forth the framework for helping approach more nuanced questions such as how much to pay for the business and how to get the deal done. Due to the lack of a comprehensive written reference material on valuation, the fundamentals and subtlety of the trade are often passed on orally from banker-to-banker on a case-by-case basis. In codifying the art and science of investment banking, the authors convert this oral history into an accessible framework by bridging the theoretical to the practical with user-friendly, step-by-step approaches to performing primary valuation methodologies.

Many seasoned investment bankers commonly lament the absence of relevant and practical "how-to" materials for newcomers to the field. The reality is that most financial texts on valuation and M&A are written by academics. The few books written by practitioners tend to focus on dramatic war stories and hijinks, rather than the nuts-and-bolts of the techniques used to get deals done. Rosenbaum and Pearl fill this heretofore void for practicing and aspiring investment bankers and finance professionals. Their book is designed to prove sufficiently accessible to a wide audience, including those with a limited finance background.

It is true that we live in uncertain and volatile times—times that have destroyed or consumed more than a few of the most legendary Wall Street institutions. However, one thing will remain a constant in the long-term—the need for skilled finance professionals with strong technical expertise. Companies will always seek counsel from experienced and independent professionals to analyze, structure, negotiate, and close deals as they navigate the market and take advantage of value-creating opportunities. Rosenbaum and Pearl promulgate a return to the fundamentals of due diligence and the use of well-founded realistic assumptions governing growth, profitability, and approach to risk. Their work toward instilling the proper skill set and mindset in aspiring generations of Wall Street professionals will help establish a firm foundation for driving a brighter economic future.

JOSEPH R. PERELLA
Chairman and CEO, Perella Weinberg Partners

Acknowledgments

We are deeply indebted to the numerous colleagues and peers who provided invaluable guidance, input, and hard work to help make this book possible.

Our book could not have been completed without the sage advice and enthusiasm of **Steve Momper**, Director of Darden Business Publishing at the University of Virginia. Steve believed in our book from the beginning and supported throughout the entire process. Most importantly, he introduced us to our publisher, John Wiley & Sons, Inc.

Special thanks to **Ryan Drook, Joseph Meisner, Michael Lanzarone, Joseph Bress, Benjamin Hochberg, James Paris**, and **Peter M. Goodson** for their insightful editorial contributions. As top-notch professionals in investment banking and private equity, their expertise and practical guidance proved invaluable. Many thanks to **Eric Leicht, Greg Pryor, Steven Sherman, Mark Gordon, Jennifer DiNucci**, and **Ante Vucic** for their exhaustive work in assisting with the legal nuances of our book. As partners at the nation's leading corporate law firms, their oversight helped ensure the accuracy and timeliness of the content.

We'd like to thank the outstanding team at Wiley. **Bill Falloon**, our acquisition editor, was always accessible and the consummate professional. He never wavered in his vision and support, and provided strong leadership throughout the entire process. **Joan O'Neil**, our publisher, impressed upon us the capabilities of the Wiley franchise and championed our book both internally and externally. **Alla Spivak**, our marketing coordinator, helped us realize our vision through her creativity and foresight. **Meg Freeborn, Mary Daniello**, and **Brigitte Coulton** (of Aptara), our production team, facilitated a smooth editorial process. **Skyler Balbus**, our associate editor, worked diligently to ensure all the ancillary details were addressed.

We also want to express immeasurable gratitude to our families and friends for their encouragement, support, and sacrifice during the weekends and holidays that ordinarily would have been dedicated to them.

This book could not have been completed without the efforts and reviews of the following individuals:

Mark Adler, *Piper Jaffray*

Kenneth Ahern, *University of Michigan, Ross School of Business*

Marc Auerbach, *Standard & Poor's/Leveraged Commentary & Data*

Carliss Baldwin, *Harvard Business School*

Kyle Barker, *UBS Investment Bank*

Ronnie Barnes, *Royal Bank of Scotland*

Joshua Becker, *Stockwell Capital*

Joseph Bress, *The Carlyle Group*

Thomas Cole, *HSBC Securities*

Aswath Damodaran, *New York University, Stern School of Business*

Thomas Davidoff, *University of California Berkeley, Haas School of Business*

Victor Delaglio, *Deutsche Bank*

Jennifer Fonner DiNucci, *Cooley Godward Kronish LLP*

Wojciech Domanski, *MidOcean Partners*

Ryan Drook, *Deutsche Bank*

Chris Falk, *Florida State University – Panama City*

Heiko Freitag, *GSO Capital Partners*

Mark Funk, *EVP & CFO, Mobile Mini, Inc.*

Andrew Gladston, *UBS Investment Bank*

Peter D. Goodson, *University of California Berkeley, Haas School of Business and Columbia Business School*

Peter M. Goodson, *Fortress Investment Group*

Mark Gordon, *Wachtell, Lipton, Rosen & Katz*

Gary Gray, *Pennsylvania State University, Smeal School of Business*

David Haeberle, *Indiana University, Kelley School of Business*

John Haynor, *UBS Investment Bank*

Milwood Hobbs, *Goldman Sachs*

Benjamin Hochberg, *Lee Equity Partners, LLC*

Alec Hufnagel, *Kelso & Company*

Jon Hugo, *Deutsche Bank*

Roger Ibbotson, *Yale School of Management*

Cedric Jarrett, *Deutsche Bank*

John Joliet, *UBS Investment Bank*

Tamir Kaloti, *Deutsche Bank*

Michael Kamras, *Credit Suisse*

Kenneth Kim, *State University of New York at Buffalo, School of Management*

Eric Klar, *MNC Partners, LLC*

Kenneth Kloner, *UBS Investment Bank*

Philip Konnikov, *UBS Investment Bank*

Alex Lajoux, *National Association of Corporate Directors, Coauthor of "The Art of M&A" Series*

Ian Lampl

Michael Lanzarone, CFA, *Barclays Capital*

Eu-Han Lee, *Indus Capital Advisors (HK) Ltd.*

Franky Lee, *Deutsche Bank*

Eric Leicht, *White & Case LLP*

Jay Lurie, *Macquarie Capital*

David Mayhew, *Deutsche Bank*

Coley McMenamin, *Banc of America Securities*

Joseph Meisner, *UBS Investment Bank*

Steve Momper, *University of Virginia, Darden Business Publishing*

Kirk Murphy, *Benchmark Capital*

Joshua Neren

Paul Pai, *Deutsche Bank*

James Paris

Dan Park, *Deutsche Bank*

Gregory Pryor, *White & Case LLP*

David Ross, *Deutsche Bank*

Ashish Rughwani, *Dominus Capital*

David Sanford, *UBS Investment Bank*

Arnold Schneider, *Georgia Tech College of Management*

Mustafa Singaporewalla

Steven Sherman, *Shearman & Sterling LLP*

Andrew Shogan

Emma Smith, *Deutsche Bank*

David Spalding, *Dartmouth College*

Andrew Steinerman, *JP Morgan*

Matthew Thomson

Robb Tretter, *Bracewell & Giuliani LLP*

John Tripodoro, *Cahill Gordon & Reindel LLP*

Ante Vucic, *Wachtell, Lipton, Rosen & Katz*

Jack Whalen, *Kensico Capital*

Supplemental Materials

VALUATION MODELS

The model templates (and completed versions) for the valuation methodologies discussed in this book are available in Microsoft Excel format at **www.wiley .com/go/investmentbanking**—password:wiley09. They will be updated for new accounting standards, as appropriate. The completed models match the input and output pages for the respective valuation methodologies. The company names and financial data in the models are completely illustrative. The website contains the following files:

Model Templates

- Comparable Companies_Template.xls
- Precedent Transactions_Template.xls
- DCF Analysis_Template.xls
- LBO Analysis_Template.xls

Completed Models

- Comparable Companies_Completed.xls
- Precedent Transactions_Completed.xls
- DCF Analysis_Completed.xls
- LBO Analysis_Completed.xls

Note: When opening the models in Microsoft Excel, please ensure that you perform the following procedure: in the main toolbar select Tools, select Options, select the "Calculation" tab, select Manual, select Iteration, and set "Maximum iterations:" to 1000 (also see Chapter 3, Exhibit 3.30). The model templates on the website are formatted with yellow shading and blue font to denote manual input cells. Black font denotes formula cells. In the text, however, gray shading is used to denote manual input cells, where possible. For Chapter 5: LBO Analysis, please reference the electronic version to view manual input and formula cells.

INSTRUCTOR TEACHING AIDS

To accompany the chapters, we have included a test bank of over 300 questions and answers for classroom and other instructional use. The test bank can be accessed by instructors in Microsoft Word format at **www.wiley.com/go/investmentbanking**. The test bank is also available in interactive format to facilitate online testing. The website includes the following files:

- Chapter 1_Comparable Companies Analysis_Q&A.doc
- Chapter 2_Precedent Transactions Analysis_Q&A.doc
- Chapter 3_Discounted Cash Flow Analysis_Q&A.doc
- Chapter 4_Leveraged Buyouts_Q&A.doc
- Chapter 5_Leveraged Buyout Analysis_Q&A.doc
- Chapter 6_M&A Sale Process_Q&A.doc

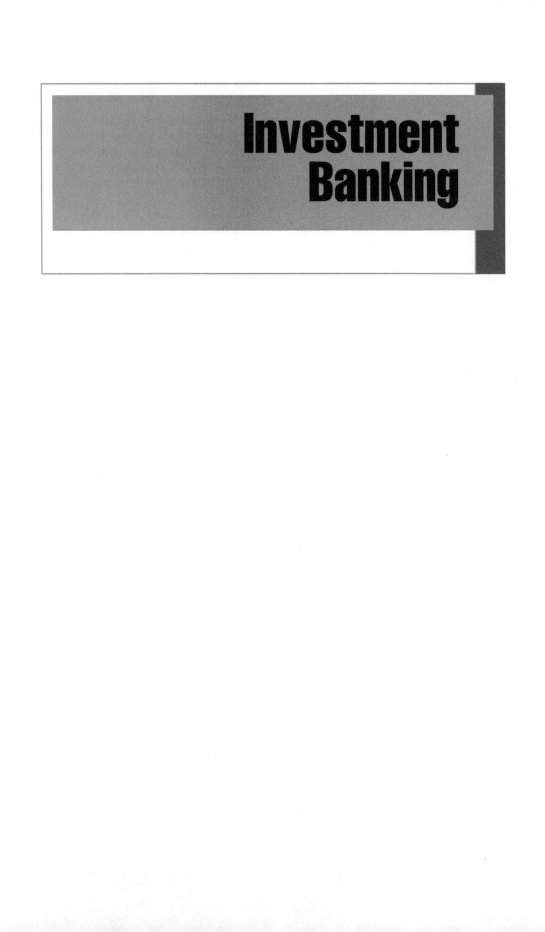

Investment Banking

Introduction

In the constantly evolving world of finance, a solid technical foundation is an essential tool for success. Due to the fast-paced nature of this world, however, no one has been able to take the time to properly codify the lifeblood of the corporate financier's work—namely, valuation. We have responded to this need by writing the book that we wish had existed when we were trying to break into Wall Street. *Investment Banking: Valuation, Leveraged Buyouts, and Mergers & Acquisitions* is a highly accessible and authoritative book written by investment bankers that explains how to perform the valuation work at the core of the financial world. This book fills a noticeable gap in contemporary finance literature, which tends to focus on theory rather than practical application.

In the aftermath of the subprime mortgage crisis and ensuing credit crunch, the world of finance is returning to the fundamentals of valuation and critical due diligence for mergers & acquisitions (M&A), capital markets, and investment opportunities. This involves the use of more realistic assumptions governing approach to risk as well as a wide range of valuation drivers, such as expected financial performance, discount rates, multiples, leverage levels, and financing terms. While valuation has always involved a great deal of "art" in addition to time-tested "science," the artistry is perpetually evolving in accordance with market developments and conditions. In this sense, our book is particularly topical—in addition to detailing the technical fundamentals behind valuation, we infuse practical judgment skills and perspective to help guide the science.

The genesis for this book stemmed from our personal experiences as students seeking to break into Wall Street. As we both independently went through the rigorous process of interviewing for associate and analyst positions at investment banks and other financial firms, we realized that our classroom experience was a step removed from how valuation and financial analysis is performed in real world situations. This was particularly evident during the technical portion of the interviews, which is often the differentiator for recruiters trying to select among dozens of qualified candidates.

Faced with this reality, we searched in vain for a practical how-to guide on the primary valuation methodologies used on Wall Street. At a loss, we resorted to compiling bits and pieces from various sources and ad hoc conversations with friends and contacts already working in investment banking. Needless to say, we didn't feel as prepared as we would have liked. While we were fortunate enough to secure job offers, the process left a deep impression on us. In fact, we continued to refine the comprehensive preparatory materials we had created as students, which served as the foundation for this book.

Once on Wall Street, we both went through mandatory training consisting of crash courses on finance and accounting, which sought to teach us the skill set

1

necessary to become effective investment bankers. Months into the job, however, even the limitations of this training were revealed. Actual client situations and deal complexities, combined with evolving market conditions, accounting guidelines, and technologies stretched our knowledge base and skills. In these situations, we were forced to consult with senior colleagues for guidance, but often the demands of the job left no one accessible in a timely manner. Given these realities, it is difficult to overstate how helpful a reliable handbook based on years of "best practices" and deal experience would have been.

Consequently, we believe this book will prove invaluable to those individuals seeking or beginning careers on Wall Street—from students at undergraduate universities and graduate schools to "career changers" looking to break into finance. For working professionals, this book is also designed to serve as an important reference material. Our experience has demonstrated that given the highly specialized nature of many finance jobs, there are noticeable gaps in skill sets that need to be addressed. Furthermore, many professionals seek to continuously brush up on their skills as well as broaden and refine their knowledge base. This book will also be highly beneficial for trainers and trainees at Wall Street firms, both within the context of formal training programs and informal on-the-job training.

Our editorial contributors from private equity firms and hedge funds have also identified the need for a practical valuation handbook for their investment professionals and key portfolio company executives. Many of these professionals come from a consulting or operational background and do not have a finance pedigree. Furthermore, the vast majority of buy-side investment firms do not have in-house training programs and rely heavily upon on-the-job training. This book will serve as a helpful reference guide for individuals joining, or seeking jobs at, these institutions.

This book also provides essential tools for professionals at corporations, including members of business development, finance, and treasury departments. These specialists are responsible for corporate finance, valuation, and transaction-related deliverables on a daily basis. They also work with investment bankers on various M&A transactions (including leveraged buyouts (LBOs) and related financings), as well as initial public offerings (IPOs), restructurings, and other capital markets transactions. Similarly, this book is intended to provide greater context for the legions of attorneys, consultants, and accountants focused on M&A, corporate finance, and other transaction advisory services.

Given the increasing globalization of the financial world, this book is designed to be sufficiently universal for use outside of North America. Our work on cross-border transactions—including in rapidly developing markets such as Asia, Latin America, Russia, and India—has revealed a tremendous appetite for skilled resources throughout the globe. Therefore, this book fulfills an important need as a valuable training material and reliable handbook for finance professionals in these markets.

STRUCTURE OF THE BOOK

This book focuses on the primary valuation methodologies currently used on Wall Street, namely comparable companies analysis, precedent transactions analysis, discounted cash flow analysis, and leveraged buyout analysis. These methodologies are used to determine valuation for public and private companies within the context of M&A transactions, LBOs, IPOs, restructurings, and investment decisions. They also form the cornerstone for valuing companies on a standalone basis, including an assessment of whether a given public company is overvalued or undervalued. Using a step-by-step, how-to approach for each methodology, we build a chronological knowledge base and define key terms, financial concepts, and processes throughout the book. We also provide context for the various valuation methodologies through a comprehensive overview of the fundamentals of LBOs and an organized M&A sale process, including key participants, financing sources and terms, strategies, milestones, and legal and marketing documentation.

This body of work builds on our combined experience on a multitude of transactions, as well as input received from numerous investment bankers, investment professionals at private equity firms and hedge funds, attorneys, corporate executives, peer authors, and university professors. By drawing upon our own transaction and classroom experience, as well as that of a broad network of professional and professorial sources, we bridge the gap between academia and industry as it relates to the practical application of finance theory. The resulting product is accessible to a wide audience—including those with a limited finance background—as well as sufficiently detailed and comprehensive to serve as a primary reference tool and training guide for finance professionals.

This book is organized into three primary parts, as summarized below.

Part One: Valuation (Chapters 1–3)

Part One focuses on the three most commonly used methodologies that serve as the core of a comprehensive valuation toolset—comparable companies analysis (Chapter 1), precedent transactions analysis (Chapter 2), and discounted cash flow analysis (Chapter 3). Each of these chapters employs a user-friendly, how-to approach to performing the given valuation methodology while defining key terms, detailing various calculations, and explaining advanced financial concepts.

At the end of each chapter, we use our step-by-step approach to determine a valuation range for an illustrative target company, ValueCo Corporation ("ValueCo"), in accordance with the given methodology. The Base Case set of financials for ValueCo that forms the basis for our valuation work throughout the book is provided in Exhibits I.I to I.III. In addition, all of the valuation models and output pages used in this book are accessible in electronic format on our website, **www.wiley.com/go/investmentbanking**.

Chapter 1: Comparable Companies Analysis Chapter 1 provides an overview of comparable companies analysis ("comparable companies" or "trading comps"), one of the primary methodologies used for valuing a given focus company, division, business, or collection of assets ("target"). Comparable companies provides a market benchmark against which a banker can establish valuation for a private company or analyze the value of a public company at a given point in time. It has a broad range of applications, most notably for various M&A situations, IPOs, restructurings, and investment decisions.

The foundation for trading comps is built upon the premise that similar companies provide a highly relevant reference point for valuing a given target as they share key business and financial characteristics, performance drivers, and risks. Therefore, valuation parameters can be established for the target by determining its relative positioning among peer companies. The core of this analysis involves selecting a universe of comparable companies for the target. These peer companies are benchmarked against one another and the target based on various financial statistics and ratios. Trading multiples—which utilize a measure of value in the numerator and an operating metric in the denominator—are then calculated for the universe. These multiples provide a basis for extrapolating a valuation range for the target.

Chapter 2: Precedent Transactions Analysis   Chapter 2 focuses on precedent transactions analysis ("precedent transactions" or "transaction comps") which, like comparable companies, employs a multiples-based approach to derive an implied valuation range for a target. Precedent transactions is premised on multiples paid for comparable companies in prior transactions. It has a broad range of applications, most notably to help determine a potential sale price range for a company, or part thereof, in an M&A or restructuring transaction.

The selection of an appropriate universe of comparable acquisitions is the foundation for performing precedent transactions. The best comparable acquisitions typically involve companies similar to the target on a fundamental level. As a general rule, the most recent transactions (i.e., those that have occurred within the previous two to three years) are the most relevant as they likely took place under similar market conditions to the contemplated transaction. Potential buyers and sellers look closely at the multiples that have been paid for comparable acquisitions. As a result, bankers and investment professionals are expected to know the transaction multiples for their sector focus areas.

Chapter 3: Discounted Cash Flow Analysis   Chapter 3 discusses discounted cash flow analysis ("DCF analysis" or the "DCF"), a fundamental valuation methodology broadly used by investment bankers, corporate officers, academics, investors, and other finance professionals. The DCF has a wide range of applications, including valuation for various M&A situations, IPOs, restructurings, and investment decisions. It is premised on the principle that a target's value can be derived from the present value of its projected *free cash flow* (FCF). A company's projected FCF is derived from a variety of assumptions and judgments about its expected future financial performance, including sales growth rates, profit margins, capital expenditures, and net working capital requirements.

The valuation implied for a target by a DCF is also known as its *intrinsic value*, as opposed to its market value, which is the value ascribed by the market at a given point in time. Therefore, a DCF serves as an important alternative to market-based valuation techniques such as comparable companies and precedent transactions, which can be distorted by a number of factors, including market aberrations (e.g., the post-subprime credit crunch). As such, a DCF plays a valuable role as a check on the prevailing market valuation for a publicly traded company. A DCF is also critical when there are limited (or no) "pure play" peer companies or comparable acquisitions.

Part Two: Leveraged Buyouts (Chapters 4 & 5)

Part Two focuses on leveraged buyouts, which comprised a large part of the capital markets and M&A landscape in the mid-2000s. This was due to the proliferation of private investment vehicles (e.g., private equity firms and hedge funds) and their considerable pools of capital, as well as structured credit vehicles (e.g., collateralized debt obligations). We begin with a discussion in Chapter 4 of the fundamentals of LBOs, including an overview of key participants, characteristics of a strong LBO candidate, economics of an LBO, exit strategies, and key financing sources and terms. Once this framework is established, we apply our step-by-step how-to approach in Chapter 5 to construct a comprehensive LBO model and perform an LBO analysis for ValueCo. LBO analysis is a core tool used by bankers and private equity professionals alike to determine financing structure and valuation for leveraged buyouts.

Chapter 4: Leveraged Buyouts   Chapter 4 provides an overview of the fundamentals of leveraged buyouts. An LBO is the acquisition of a target using debt to finance a large portion of the purchase price. The remaining portion of the purchase price is funded with an equity contribution by a financial sponsor ("sponsor"). In this chapter, we provide an overview of the economics of LBOs and how they are used to generate returns for sponsors. We also dedicate a significant portion of Chapter 4 to a discussion of LBO financing sources, particularly the various debt instruments and their terms and conditions.

LBOs are used by sponsors to acquire a broad range of businesses, including both public and private companies, as well as their divisions and subsidiaries. Generally speaking, companies with stable and predictable cash flows as well as substantial assets represent attractive LBO candidates. However, sponsors tend to be flexible investors provided the expected returns on the investment meet required thresholds. In an LBO, the disproportionately high level of debt incurred by the target is supported by its projected FCF and asset base, which enables the sponsor to contribute a small equity investment relative to the purchase price. This, in turn, enables the sponsor to realize an acceptable return on its equity investment upon exit, typically through a sale or IPO of the target.

Chapter 5: LBO Analysis   Chapter 5 removes the mystery surrounding LBO analysis, the core analytical tool used to assess financing structure, investment returns, and valuation in leveraged buyout scenarios. These same techniques can also be used to assess refinancing opportunities and restructuring alternatives for corporate issuers. LBO analysis is a more complex methodology than those previously discussed as it requires specialized knowledge of financial modeling, leveraged debt capital markets, M&A, and accounting. At the center of LBO analysis is a financial model, which is constructed with the flexibility to analyze a given target under multiple financing structures and operating scenarios.

As with the methodologies discussed in Part One, LBO analysis is an essential component of a comprehensive valuation toolset. On the debt financing side, LBO analysis is used to help craft a viable financing structure for the target on the basis of its cash flow generation, debt repayment, credit statistics, and investment returns over the projection period. Sponsors work closely with financing providers (e.g., investment banks) to determine the preferred financing structure for a particular transaction. In an M&A advisory context, LBO analysis provides the basis for determining an implied valuation range for a given target in a potential LBO sale based on achieving acceptable returns.

Part Three: Mergers & Acquisitions (Chapter 6)

Part Three focuses on the key process points and stages for running an effective M&A sale process, the medium whereby companies are bought and sold in the marketplace. This discussion serves to provide greater context for the topics discussed earlier in the book as theoretical valuation methodologies are tested based on what a buyer will actually pay for a business or collection of assets. We also describe how valuation analysis is used to frame the seller's price expectations, set guidelines for the range of acceptable bids, evaluate offers received, and, ultimately, guide negotiations of the final purchase price.

Chapter 6: M&A Sale Process   The sale of a company, division, business, or collection of assets is a major event for its owners (shareholders), management, employees, and other stakeholders. It is an intense, time-consuming process with high stakes, usually spanning several months. Consequently, the seller typically hires an investment bank ("sell-side advisor") and its team of trained professionals to ensure that key objectives are met—namely an optimal mix of value maximization, speed of execution, and certainty of completion, among other deal-specific considerations. Prospective buyers also often hire an investment bank ("buy-side advisor") to perform valuation work, interface with the seller, and conduct negotiations, among other critical tasks.

The sell-side advisor is responsible for identifying the seller's priorities from the onset and crafts a tailored sale process accordingly. From an analytical perspective, a sell-side assignment requires a comprehensive valuation of the target using those methodologies discussed in this book. Perhaps the most basic decision, however, relates to whether to run a broad or targeted auction, or pursue a negotiated sale. Generally, an auction requires more upfront organization, marketing, process points, and resources than a negotiated sale with a single party. Consequently, Chapter 6 focuses primarily on the auction process.

VALUECO SUMMARY FINANCIAL INFORMATION

Exhibits I.I through I.III display the historical and projected financial information for ValueCo. These financials—as well as the various valuation multiples, financing terms, and other financial statistics discussed throughout the book—are purely illustrative and designed to represent normalized economic and market conditions.

EXHIBIT 1.1 ValueCo Summary Historical Operating Data

($ in millions)

ValueCo Summary Historical Operating Data				
	Fiscal Year Ending December 31			LTM
	2005A	2006A	2007A	9/30/2008A
Sales	**$780.0**	**$850.0**	**$925.0**	**$977.8**
% growth	*NA*	*9.0%*	*8.8%*	*NA*
Cost of Goods Sold	471.9	512.1	555.0	586.7
Gross Profit	**$308.1**	**$337.9**	**$370.0**	**$391.1**
% margin	*39.5%*	*39.8%*	*40.0%*	*40.0%*
Selling, General & Administrative	198.9	214.6	231.3	244.4
EBITDA	**$109.2**	**$123.3**	**$138.8**	**$146.7**
% margin	*14.0%*	*14.5%*	*15.0%*	*15.0%*
Depreciation & Amortization	15.6	17.0	18.5	19.6
EBIT	**$93.6**	**$106.3**	**$120.3**	**$127.1**
% margin	*12.0%*	*12.5%*	*13.0%*	*13.0%*
Capital Expenditures	15.0	18.0	18.5	19.6
% sales	*1.9%*	*2.1%*	*2.0%*	*2.0%*

Note: For modeling purposes (e.g., DCF analysis and LBO analysis), D&A is broken out separately from COGS & SG&A as its own line item.

EXHIBIT 1.II ValueCo Summary Projected Operating Data

($ in millions)

ValueCo Summary Projected Operating Data						
	Fiscal Year Ending December 31					
	2008E	2009E	2010E	2011E	2012E	2013E
Sales	**$1,000.0**	**$1,080.0**	**$1,144.8**	**$1,190.6**	**$1,226.3**	**$1,263.1**
% growth	*8.1%*	*8.0%*	*6.0%*	*4.0%*	*3.0%*	*3.0%*
Cost of Goods Sold	600.0	648.0	686.9	714.4	735.8	757.9
Gross Profit	**$400.0**	**$432.0**	**$457.9**	**$476.2**	**$490.5**	**$505.2**
% margin	*40.0%*	*40.0%*	*40.0%*	*40.0%*	*40.0%*	*40.0%*
Selling, General & Administrative	250.0	270.0	286.2	297.6	306.6	315.8
EBITDA	**$150.0**	**$162.0**	**$171.7**	**$178.6**	**$183.9**	**$189.5**
% margin	*15.0%*	*15.0%*	*15.0%*	*15.0%*	*15.0%*	*15.0%*
Depreciation & Amortization	20.0	21.6	22.9	23.8	24.5	25.3
EBIT	**$130.0**	**$140.4**	**$148.8**	**$154.8**	**$159.4**	**$164.2**
% margin	*13.0%*	*13.0%*	*13.0%*	*13.0%*	*13.0%*	*13.0%*
Capital Expenditures	20.0	21.6	22.9	23.8	24.5	25.3
% sales	*2.0%*	*2.0%*	*2.0%*	*2.0%*	*2.0%*	*2.0%*

EXHIBIT I.III   ValueCo Summary Historical Balance Sheet Data

($ in millions)

ValueCo Summary Historical Balance Sheet Data					
	Fiscal Year Ending December 31			As of	FYE
	2005A	2006A	2007A	9/30/2008A	2008E
Cash and Cash Equivalents	$22.6	$11.9	$14.0	$7.9	$25.0
Accounts Receivable	123.2	141.1	152.6	161.3	165.0
Inventories	94.6	104.0	115.6	122.2	125.0
Prepaid and Other Current Assets	7.1	8.5	9.3	9.8	10.0
Total Current Assets	**$247.5**	**$265.5**	**$291.5**	**$301.3**	**$325.0**
Property, Plant and Equipment, net	649.0	650.0	650.0	650.0	650.0
Goodwill and Intangible Assets	175.0	175.0	175.0	175.0	175.0
Other Assets	75.0	75.0	75.0	75.0	75.0
Total Assets	**$1,146.5**	**$1,165.5**	**$1,191.5**	**$1,201.3**	**$1,225.0**
Accounts Payable	65.2	66.0	69.4	73.3	75.0
Accrued Liabilities	69.9	83.2	92.5	97.8	100.0
Other Current Liabilities	15.6	20.4	23.1	24.4	25.0
Total Current Liabilities	**$150.7**	**$169.6**	**$185.0**	**$195.6**	**$200.0**
Total Debt	450.0	400.0	350.0	300.0	300.0
Other Long-Term Liabilities	25.0	25.0	25.0	25.0	25.0
Total Liabilities	**$625.7**	**$594.6**	**$560.0**	**$520.6**	**$525.0**
Noncontrolling Interest	-	-	-	-	-
Shareholders' Equity	520.8	570.9	631.5	680.7	700.0
Total Liabilities and Equity	**$1,146.5**	**$1,165.5**	**$1,191.5**	**$1,201.3**	**$1,225.0**

Comparable Companies Analysis

Comparable companies analysis ("comparable companies" or "trading comps") is one of the primary methodologies used for valuing a given focus company, division, business, or collection of assets ("target"). It provides a market benchmark against which a banker can establish valuation for a private company or analyze the value of a public company at a given point in time. Comparable companies has a broad range of applications, most notably for various mergers & acquisitions (M&A) situations, initial public offerings (IPOs), restructurings, and investment decisions.

The foundation for trading comps is built upon the premise that similar companies provide a highly relevant reference point for valuing a given target due to the fact that they share key business and financial characteristics, performance drivers, and risks. Therefore, the banker can establish valuation parameters for the target by determining its relative positioning among peer companies. The core of this analysis involves selecting a universe of comparable companies for the target ("comparables universe"). These peer companies are benchmarked against one another and the target based on various financial statistics and ratios. Trading multiples are then calculated for the universe, which serve as the basis for extrapolating a valuation range for the target. This valuation range is calculated by applying the selected multiples to the target's relevant financial statistics.

While valuation metrics may vary by sector, this chapter focuses on the most widely used trading multiples. These multiples—such as enterprise value-to-earnings before interest, taxes, depreciation, and amortization (EV/EBITDA) and price-to-earnings (P/E)—utilize a measure of value in the numerator and a financial statistic in the denominator. While P/E is the most broadly recognized in circles outside Wall Street, multiples based on enterprise value are widely used by bankers because they are independent of capital structure and other factors unrelated to business operations (e.g., differences in tax regimes and certain accounting policies).

Comparable companies analysis is designed to reflect "current" valuation based on prevailing market conditions and sentiment. As such, in many cases it is more relevant than *intrinsic valuation* analysis, such as discounted cash flow analysis (see Chapter 3). At the same time, market trading levels may be subject to periods of irrational investor sentiment that skew valuation either too high or too low. Furthermore, no two companies are exactly the same, so assigning a valuation based on the trading characteristics of similar companies may fail to accurately capture a given company's true value.

As a result, trading comps should be used in conjunction with the other valuation methodologies discussed in this book. A material disconnect between the derived valuation ranges from the various methodologies might be an indication that key assumptions or calculations need to be revisited. Therefore, when performing trading comps (or any other valuation/financial analysis exercise), it is imperative to diligently footnote key sources and assumptions both for review and defense of conclusions.

This chapter provides a highly practical, step-by-step approach to performing trading comps consistent with how this valuation methodology is performed in real world applications (see Exhibit 1.1). Once this framework is established, we walk through an illustrative comparable companies analysis using our target company, ValueCo (see Introduction for reference).

EXHIBIT 1.1   Comparable Companies Analysis Steps

Step I.   Select the Universe of Comparable Companies
Step II.   Locate the Necessary Financial Information
Step III.   Spread Key Statistics, Ratios, and Trading Multiples
Step IV.   Benchmark the Comparable Companies
Step V.   Determine Valuation

SUMMARY OF COMPARABLE COMPANIES ANALYSIS STEPS

- **Step I. Select the Universe of Comparable Companies.** The selection of a universe of comparable companies for the target is the foundation for performing trading comps. While this exercise can be fairly simple and intuitive for companies in certain sectors, it can prove challenging for others whose peers are not readily apparent. To identify companies with similar business and financial characteristics, it is first necessary to gain a sound understanding of the target.

  As a starting point, the banker typically consults with peers or senior colleagues to see if a relevant set of comparable companies already exists internally. If beginning from scratch, the banker casts a broad net to review as many potential comparable companies as possible. This broader group is eventually narrowed, and then typically further refined to a subset of "closest comparables." A survey of the target's public competitors is generally a good place to start identifying potential comparable companies.

- **Step II. Locate the Necessary Financial Information.** Once the initial comparables universe is determined, the banker locates the financial information necessary to analyze the selected comparable companies and calculate ("spread"[1]) key financial statistics, ratios, and trading multiples (see Step III). The primary data for calculating these metrics is compiled from various sources, including a

---

[1]The notion of "spreading" refers to performing calculations in a spreadsheet program such as Microsoft Excel.

company's SEC filings,[2] consensus research estimates, equity research reports, and press releases, as well as financial information services.

- **Step III. Spread Key Statistics, Ratios, and Trading Multiples.** The banker is now prepared to spread key statistics, ratios, and trading multiples for the comparables universe. This involves calculating market valuation measures such as enterprise value and equity value, as well as key income statement items, such as EBITDA and net income. A variety of ratios and other metrics measuring profitability, growth, returns, and credit strength are also calculated at this stage. Selected financial statistics are then used to calculate trading multiples for the comparables.

    As part of this process, the banker needs to employ various financial concepts and techniques, including the calculation of *last twelve months* (LTM)[3] financial statistics, *calendarization* of company financials, and adjustments for *non-recurring items*. These calculations are imperative for measuring the comparables accurately on both an absolute and relative basis (see Step IV).

- **Step IV. Benchmark the Comparable Companies.** The next level of analysis requires an in-depth examination of the comparable companies in order to determine the target's relative ranking and closest comparables. To assist in this task, the banker typically lays out the calculated financial statistics and ratios for the comparable companies (as calculated in Step III) alongside those of the target in spreadsheet form for easy comparison (see Exhibits 1.53 and 1.54). This exercise is known as "benchmarking."

    Benchmarking serves to determine the relative strength of the comparable companies versus one another and the target. The similarities and discrepancies in size, growth rates, margins, and leverage, for example, among the comparables and the target are closely examined. This analysis provides the basis for establishing the target's relative ranking as well as determining those companies most appropriate for framing its valuation. The trading multiples are also laid out in a spreadsheet form for benchmarking purposes (see Exhibits 1.2 and 1.55). At this point, it may become apparent that certain outliers need to be eliminated or that the comparables should be further tiered (e.g., on the basis of size, sub-sector, or ranging from closest to peripheral).

- **Step V. Determine Valuation.** The trading multiples of the comparable companies serve as the basis for deriving a valuation range for the target. The banker typically begins by using the means and medians for the relevant trading multiples (e.g., EV/EBITDA) as the basis for extrapolating an initial range. The high and low multiples for the comparables universe provide further guidance in terms of a potential ceiling or floor. The key to arriving at the tightest, most appropriate range, however, is to rely upon the multiples of the closest comparables as guideposts. Consequently, only a few carefully selected companies

---

[2]The Securities and Exchange Commission (SEC) is a federal agency created by the Securities Exchange Act of 1934 that regulates the U.S. securities industry. SEC filings can be located online at www.sec.gov.

[3]The sum of the prior four quarters of a company's financial performance, also known as trailing twelve months (TTM).

EXHIBIT 1.2 Comparable Companies Analysis—Trading Multiples Output Page

ValueCo Corporation
Comparable Companies Analysis
($ in millions, except per share data)

Company	Ticker	Current Share Price	% of 52-wk. High	Equity Value	Enterprise Value	Enterprise Value / LTM Sales	2008E Sales	2009E Sales	LTM EBITDA	2008E EBITDA	2009E EBITDA	LTM EBIT	2008E EBIT	2009E EBIT	LTM EBITDA Margin	Total Debt / EBITDA	Price / LTM EPS	2008E EPS	2009E EPS	LT EPS Growth
Tier I: Large-Cap																				
Vucic Brands	VUC	$70.00	83%	$8,829	$14,712	1.7x	1.6x	1.4x	8.5x	7.8x	7.2x	10.0x	9.3x	8.5x	20%	3.2x	14.6x	13.6x	12.5x	16%
Pearl Corp.	PRL	22.00	81%	8,850	11,323	0.9x	0.8x	0.8x	7.0x	6.7x	6.3x	8.4x	8.0x	7.4x	13%	2.3x	12.7x	12.1x	11.3x	13%
Spalding Co.	SLD	57.00	76%	7,781	8,369	1.0x	1.0x	0.9x	7.4x	7.1x	6.5x	8.6x	8.3x	7.6x	14%	0.9x	14.0x	13.4x	12.3x	14%
Leicht & Co.	LCT	85.00	82%	7,456	9,673	1.2x	1.1x	1.1x	7.6x	7.1x	6.7x	9.5x	8.9x	8.4x	16%	1.9x	14.2x	13.3x	12.5x	11%
Drook Corp.	DRK	78.25	74%	5,034	6,161	0.9x	0.9x	0.8x	7.0x	6.6x	6.2x	8.4x	7.9x	7.4x	13%	1.9x	12.4x	11.7x	11.0x	10%
Mean						1.1x	1.1x	1.0x	7.5x	7.1x	6.6x	9.0x	8.5x	7.9x	15%	2.0x	13.6x	12.8x	11.9x	13%
Median						1.0x	1.0x	0.9x	7.4x	7.1x	6.5x	8.6x	8.3x	7.6x	14%	1.9x	14.0x	13.3x	12.3x	13%
Tier II: Mid-Cap																				
Goodson Corp.	GDS	$44.00	79%	$4,368	$5,534	0.9x	0.9x	0.9x	7.0x	6.8x	6.6x	9.0x	8.9x	8.6x	13%	1.6x	13.7x	13.5x	13.1x	13%
The DiNucci Group	TDG	29.85	71%	3,772	5,202	0.8x	0.8x	0.7x	6.7x	6.4x	6.1x	11.5x	11.0x	10.4x	12%	2.4x	17.5x	17.1x	16.1x	15%
Pryor, Inc.	PRI	42.80	78%	3,484	4,764	1.1x	1.1x	1.0x	7.3x	6.9x	6.4x	9.0x	8.9x	8.3x	16%	2.4x	13.4x	12.7x	11.8x	14%
Adler Industries	ADL	47.00	82%	2,600	3,149	0.8x	0.8x	0.7x	6.7x	6.3x	5.9x	9.7x	9.2x	8.6x	12%	1.2x	15.2x	14.4x	13.4x	11%
Lanzarone International	LNZ	28.50	81%	1,750	2,139	0.9x	0.9x	0.8x	7.2x	6.7x	6.3x	8.5x	8.0x	7.4x	13%	1.7x	13.3x	12.5x	11.6x	15%
Mean						0.9x	0.9x	0.8x	6.9x	6.6x	6.3x	9.6x	9.2x	8.7x	13%	1.9x	14.6x	14.0x	13.2x	14%
Median						0.9x	0.9x	0.8x	7.0x	6.7x	6.3x	9.4x	8.9x	8.6x	13%	1.7x	13.7x	13.5x	13.1x	14%
Tier III: Small-Cap																				
Lajoux Global	LJX	$15.00	83%	$1,050	$1,650	0.9x	0.9x	0.8x	7.1x	6.8x	6.4x	8.3x	8.0x	7.5x	13%	3.1x	12.6x	12.1x	11.3x	13%
Momper Corp.	MOMP	20.00	80%	1,000	1,500	1.1x	1.0x	0.9x	7.0x	6.7x	6.3x	8.6x	8.1x	7.5x	15%	2.6x	11.8x	11.1x	10.0x	15%
McMenamin & Co.	MCM	16.50	78%	630	705	1.2x	1.2x	1.1x	7.3x	7.1x	6.6x	10.1x	9.8x	9.1x	17%	2.6x	19.9x	19.3x	17.9x	14%
Trip Co.	TRIP	11.25	78%	321	441	0.9x	0.9x	0.8x	6.7x	6.5x	6.1x	9.1x	8.7x	8.2x	14%	2.1x	15.6x	15.0x	14.0x	12%
Paris Industries	PRS	10.25	73%	156	192	0.5x	0.5x	0.5x	5.5x	5.3x	5.0x	9.1x	8.9x	8.3x	10%	3.8x	14.3x	14.0x	13.1x	10%
Mean						0.9x	0.9x	0.8x	6.7x	6.5x	6.0x	9.0x	8.7x	8.1x	14%	2.8x	14.8x	14.3x	13.3x	13%
Median						0.9x	0.9x	0.8x	7.0x	6.7x	6.3x	9.1x	8.7x	8.2x	14%	2.6x	14.3x	14.0x	13.1x	13%
Overall																				
Mean						1.0x	1.0x	0.9x	7.0x	6.7x	6.3x	9.2x	8.8x	8.2x	14%	2.3x	14.3x	13.7x	12.8x	13%
Median						0.9x	0.9x	0.8x	7.0x	6.7x	6.3x	9.1x	8.9x	8.3x	13%	2.3x	14.0x	13.4x	12.5x	13%
High						1.7x	1.6x	1.4x	8.5x	7.8x	7.2x	11.5x	11.0x	10.4x	20%	3.8x	19.9x	19.3x	17.9x	16%
Low						0.5x	0.5x	0.5x	5.5x	5.3x	5.0x	8.3x	7.9x	7.4x	10%	0.9x	11.8x	11.1x	10.0x	10%

Source: Company filings, Bloomberg, Consensus Estimates
Note: Last twelve months data based on September 30, 2008. Estimated annual financial data based on a calendar year.

may serve as the ultimate basis for valuation, with the broader group serving as additional reference points. As this process involves as much "art" as "science," senior bankers are typically consulted for guidance on the final decision. The chosen range is then applied to the target's relevant financial statistics to produce an implied valuation range.

STEP I. SELECT THE UNIVERSE OF COMPARABLE COMPANIES

The selection of a universe of comparable companies for the target is the foundation for performing trading comps. In order to identify companies with similar business and financial characteristics, it is first necessary to gain a sound understanding of the target. At its base, the methodology for determining comparable companies is relatively intuitive. Companies in the same sector (or, preferably, "sub-sector") with similar size tend to serve as good comparables. While this can be a fairly simple exercise for companies in certain sectors, it may prove challenging for others whose peers are not readily apparent.

For a target with no clear, publicly traded comparables, the banker seeks companies outside the target's core sector that share business and financial characteristics on some fundamental level. For example, a medium-sized manufacturer of residential windows may have limited or no truly direct publicly traded peers in terms of products, namely companies that produce windows. If the universe is expanded to include companies that manufacture building products, serve homebuilders, or have exposure to the housing cycle, however, the probability of locating companies with similar business drivers is increased. In this case, the list of potential comparables could be expanded to include manufacturers of related building products such as decking, roofing, siding, doors, and cabinets.

Study the Target

The process of learning the in-depth "story" of the target should be exhaustive as this information is essential for making decisions regarding the selection of appropriate comparable companies. Toward this end, the banker is encouraged to read and study as much company- and sector-specific material as possible. *The actual selection of comparable companies should only begin once this research is completed.*

For targets that are public registrants,[4] annual (10-K) and quarterly (10-Q) SEC filings, consensus research estimates, equity and fixed income research reports, press releases, earnings call transcripts, investor presentations,[5] and corporate

---

[4]Public or publicly traded companies refer to those listed on a public stock exchange where their shares can be traded. Public filers ("public registrants"), however, may include privately held companies that are issuers of public debt securities and, therefore, subject to SEC disclosure requirements.

[5]Presentations at investment conferences or regular performance reports, typically posted on a company's corporate website. Investor presentations may also be released for significant M&A events or as part of Regulation FD requirements. They are typically posted on the company's corporate website under "Investor Relations" and filed in an 8-K.

websites provide key business and financial information. Private companies present a greater challenge as the banker is forced to rely upon sources such as corporate websites, sector research reports, news runs, and trade journals for basic company data. Public competitors' SEC filings, research reports, and investor presentations may also serve as helpful sources of information on private companies. In an organized M&A sale process[6] for a private company, however, the banker is provided with detailed business and financial information on the target (see Chapter 6).

Identify Key Characteristics of the Target for Comparison Purposes

A simple framework for studying the target and selecting comparable companies is shown in Exhibit 1.3. This framework, while by no means exhaustive, is designed to determine commonality with other companies by profiling and comparing key business and financial characteristics.

EXHIBIT 1.3   Business and Financial Profile Framework

Business Profile	Financial Profile
■ Sector	■ Size
■ Products and Services	■ Profitability
■ Customers and End Markets	■ Growth Profile
■ Distribution Channels	■ Return on Investment
■ Geography	■ Credit Profile

Business Profile

Companies that share core business characteristics tend to serve as good comparables. These core traits include sector, products and services, customers and end markets, distribution channels, and geography.

Sector

Sector refers to the industry or markets in which a company operates (e.g., chemicals, consumer products, healthcare, industrials, and technology). A company's sector can be further divided into sub-sectors, which facilitates the identification of the target's closest comparable. Within the industrials sector, for example, there are numerous sub-sectors, such as aerospace and defense, automotive, building products, metals and mining, and paper and packaging. For companies with distinct business divisions, the segmenting of comparable companies by sub-sector may be critical for valuation.

   A company's sector conveys a great deal about its key drivers, risks, and opportunities. For example, a cyclical sector such as oil & gas will have dramatically different earnings volatility than consumer staples. On the other hand, cyclical or highly fragmented sectors may present growth opportunities that are unavailable to companies in more stable or consolidated sectors. The proper identification and

---

[6]A process through which a target is marketed to prospective buyers, typically run by an investment banking firm. See Chapter 6: M&A Sale Process for additional information.

classification of the target's sector and sub-sector is an essential step toward locating comparable companies.

Products and Services

A company's products and services are at the core of its business model. Accordingly, companies that produce similar products or provide similar services typically serve as good comparables. Products are commodities or value-added goods that a company creates, produces, or refines. Examples of products include computers, lumber, oil, prescription drugs, and steel. Services are acts or functions performed by one entity for the benefit of another. Examples of common services include banking, installation, lodging, logistics, and transportation. Many companies provide both products and services to their customers, while others offer one or the other. Similarly, some companies offer a diversified product and/or service mix, while others are more focused.

Customers and End Markets

Customers A company's customers refer to the purchasers of its products and services. Companies with a similar customer base tend to share similar opportunities and risks. For example, companies supplying automobile manufacturers abide by certain manufacturing and distribution requirements, and are subject to the automobile purchasing cycles and trends.

The quantity and diversity of a company's customers are also important. Some companies serve a broad customer base while others may target a specialized or niche market. While it is generally positive to have low customer concentration from a risk management perspective, it is also beneficial to have a stable customer core to provide visibility and comfort regarding future revenues.

End Markets A company's end markets refer to the broad underlying markets into which it sells its products and services. For example, a plastics manufacturer may sell into several end markets, including automotive, construction, consumer products, medical devices, and packaging. End markets need to be distinguished from customers. For example, a company may sell into the housing end market, but to retailers or suppliers as opposed to homebuilders.

A company's performance is generally tied to economic and other factors that affect its end markets. A company that sells products into the housing end market is susceptible to macroeconomic factors that affect the overall housing cycle, such as interest rates and unemployment levels. Therefore, companies that sell products and services into the same end markets generally share a similar performance outlook, which is important for determining appropriate comparable companies.

Distribution Channels

Distribution channels are the avenues through which a company sells its products and services to the end user. As such, they are a key driver of operating strategy, performance, and, ultimately, value. Companies that sell primarily to the wholesale channel, for example, often have significantly different organizational and cost structures than those selling directly to retailers or end users. Selling to a superstore or value retailer requires a physical infrastructure, sales force, and logistics that may be unnecessary for serving the professional or wholesale channels.

Some companies sell at several levels of the distribution chain, such as wholesale, retail, and direct-to-customer. A flooring manufacturer, for example, may distribute its products through selected wholesale distributors and retailers, as well as directly to homebuilders and end users.

Geography

Companies that are based in (and sell to) different regions of the world often differ substantially in terms of fundamental business drivers and characteristics. These may include growth rates, macroeconomic environment, competitive dynamics, path(s)-to-market, organizational and cost structure, and potential opportunities and risks. Such differences—which result from local demographics, economic drivers, regulatory regimes, consumer buying patterns and preferences, and cultural norms—can vary greatly from country to country and, particularly, from continent to continent. Consequently, there are often valuation disparities for similar companies in different global regions or jurisdictions.[7] Therefore, in determining comparable companies, bankers tend to group U.S.-based (or focused) companies in a separate category from European- or Asian-based companies even if their basic business models are the same.

For example, a banker seeking comparable companies for a U.S. retailer would focus primarily on U.S. companies with relevant foreign companies providing peripheral guidance. This geographic grouping is slightly less applicable for truly global industries such as oil and aluminum, for example, where domicile is less indicative than global commodity prices and market conditions. Even in these instances, however, valuation disparities by geography are often evident.

Financial Profile

Key financial characteristics must also be examined both as a means of understanding the target and identifying the best comparable companies.

Size

Size is typically measured in terms of market valuation (e.g., equity value and enterprise value), as well as key financial statistics (e.g., sales, gross profit, EBITDA, EBIT, and net income). Companies of similar size in a given sector are more likely to have similar multiples than companies with significant size discrepancies. This reflects the fact that companies of similar size are also likely to be analogous in other respects (e.g., economies of scale, purchasing power, pricing leverage, customers, growth prospects, and the trading liquidity of their shares in the stock market).

Consequently, differences in size often map to differences in valuation. Hence, the comparables are often tiered based on size categories. For example, companies with under $5 billion in equity value (or enterprise value, sales) may be placed in one group and those with greater than $5 billion in a separate group. This tiering, of course, assumes a sufficient number of comparables to justify organizing the universe into sub-groups.

---

[7]Other factors, such as the local capital markets conditions, including volume, liquidity, transparency, shareholder base, and investor perceptions, as well as political risk, also contribute to these disparities.

Profitability

A company's profitability measures its ability to convert sales into profit. Profitability ratios ("margins") employ a measure of profit in the numerator, such as gross profit, EBITDA, EBIT, or net income, and sales in the denominator.[8] As a general rule, for companies in the same sector, higher profit margins translate into higher valuations, all else being equal. Consequently, determining a company's relative profitability versus its peers' is a core component of the benchmarking analysis (see Step IV).

Growth Profile

A company's growth profile, as determined by its historical and estimated future financial performance, is an important driver of valuation. Equity investors reward high growth companies with higher trading multiples than slower growing peers. They also discern whether the growth is primarily organic or acquisition-driven, with the former generally viewed as preferable. In assessing a company's growth profile, historical and estimated future growth rates for various financial statistics (e.g., sales, EBITDA, and earnings per share (EPS)) are examined at selected intervals. For mature public companies, EPS growth rates are typically more meaningful. For early stage or emerging companies with little or no earnings, however, sales or EBITDA growth trends may be more relevant.

Return on Investment

Return on investment (ROI) measures a company's ability to provide earnings (or returns) to its capital providers. ROI ratios employ a measure of profitability (e.g., EBIT, NOPAT,[9] or net income) in the numerator and a measure of capital (e.g., invested capital, shareholders' equity, or total assets) in the denominator. The most commonly used ROI metrics are return on invested capital (ROIC), return on equity (ROE), and return on assets (ROA). Dividend yield, which measures the dividend payment that a company's shareholders receive for each share owned, is another type of return metric.

Credit Profile

A company's credit profile refers to its creditworthiness as a borrower. It is typically measured by metrics relating to a company's overall debt level ("leverage") as well as its ability to make interest payments ("coverage"), and reflects key company- and sector-specific benefits and risks. Moody's Investors Service (Moody's), Standard & Poor's (S&P), and Fitch Ratings (Fitch) are the three primary independent credit rating agencies that provide formal assessments of a company's credit profile.

---

[8]Depending on the sector, profitability may be measured on a per unit basis (e.g., per ton or pound).

[9]Net operating profit after taxes, also known as tax-effected EBIT or earnings before interest after taxes (EBIAT).

Screen for Comparable Companies

Once the target's basic business and financial characteristics are researched and understood, the banker uses various resources to screen for potential comparable companies. At the initial stage, the focus is on identifying companies with a similar business profile. While basic financial information (e.g., sales, enterprise value, or equity value) should be assessed early on, more detailed financial benchmarking is performed in Step IV.

Investment banks generally have established lists of comparable companies by sector containing relevant multiples and other financial data, which are updated on a quarterly basis and for appropriate company-specific actions. Often, however, the banker needs to start from scratch. In these cases, an examination of the target's public competitors is usually the best place to begin. Competitors generally share key business and financial characteristics and are susceptible to similar opportunities and risks. Public companies typically discuss their primary competitors in their 10-Ks, annual proxy statement (DEF14A),[10] and, potentially, in investor presentations. Furthermore, equity research reports, especially those known as *initiating coverage*,[11] often explicitly list the research analyst's views on the target's comparables and/or primary competitors. For private targets, public competitors' 10-Ks, proxy statements, investor presentations, research reports, and broader industry reports are often helpful sources.

An additional source for locating comparables is the proxy statement for a relatively recent M&A transaction in the sector ("merger proxy"),[12] as it contains excerpts from a *fairness opinion*. As the name connotes, a fairness opinion opines on the "fairness" of the purchase price and deal terms offered by the acquirer from a financial perspective (see Chapter 6). The fairness opinion is supported by a detailed overview of the methodologies used to perform a valuation of the target, typically including comparable companies, precedent transactions, DCF analysis, and LBO analysis, if applicable.[13] The trading comps excerpt from the fairness opinion generally provides a list of the comparable companies used to value the M&A target as well as the selected range of multiples used in the valuation analysis.

The banker may also screen for companies that operate in the target's sector using SIC or NAICS codes.[14] Subscription financial information services, such as those offered by Capital IQ, FactSet, and Thomson Reuters, provide comprehensive

---

[10] A company's annual proxy statement typically provides a suggested peer group of companies that is used for benchmarking purposes.

[11] An initiating coverage equity research report refers to the first report published by an equity research analyst beginning coverage on a particular company. This report often provides a comprehensive business description, sector analysis, and commentary.

[12] A solicitation of shareholder votes in a business combination initially filed under SEC Form PREM14A (preliminary merger proxy statement) and then DEFM14A (definitive merger proxy statement).

[13] Not all companies are LBO candidates. See Chapter 4: Leveraged Buyouts for an overview of the characteristics of strong LBO candidates.

[14] Standard Industrial Classification (SIC) is a system established by the U.S. government for classifying the major business operations of a company with a numeric code. Some bankers use the newer North American Industry Classification System (NAICS) codes in lieu of SIC codes. The SEC, however, still uses SIC codes.

company databases with SIC/NAICS code information. This type of screen is typically used either to establish a broad initial universe of comparables or to ensure that no potential companies have been overlooked. Sector reports published by the credit rating agencies (e.g., Moody's, S&P, and Fitch) may also provide helpful lists of peer companies.

In addition to the aforementioned, senior bankers are perhaps the most valuable resources for determining the comparables universe. Given their sector knowledge and familiarity with the target, a brief conversation is usually sufficient for them to provide the junior banker with a strong starting point. Toward the end of the process—once the junior banker has done the legwork to craft and refine a robust list of comparables—a senior banker often provides the finishing touches in terms of more nuanced additions or deletions.

At this stage of the process, there may be sufficient information to eliminate certain companies from the group or tier the selected companies by size, business focus, or geography, for example.

STEP II. LOCATE THE NECESSARY FINANCIAL INFORMATION

This section provides an overview of the relevant sources for locating the necessary financial information to calculate key financial statistics, ratios, and multiples for the selected comparable companies (see Step III). The most common sources for public company financial data are SEC filings (such as 10-Ks, 10-Qs, and 8-Ks), as well as earnings announcements, investor presentations, equity research reports, consensus estimates, press releases, and selected financial information services. A summary list of where to locate key financial data is provided in Exhibit 1.4.

In trading comps, valuation is driven on the basis of both historical performance (e.g., LTM financial data) and expected future performance (e.g., consensus estimates for future calendar years). Depending on the sector and point in the cycle, however, financial projections tend to be more meaningful. Estimates for forward-year financial performance are typically sourced from consensus estimates (First Call or IBES)[15] as well as individual company equity research reports. In the context of an M&A or debt capital raising transaction, by contrast, more emphasis is placed on LTM financial performance. LTM financial information is calculated on the basis of data obtained from a company's public filings (see Exhibits 1.24 and 1.25).

SEC Filings: 10-K, 10-Q, 8-K, and Proxy Statement

As a general rule, the banker uses SEC filings to source historical financial information for comparable companies. This financial information is used to determine historical sales, gross profit, EBITDA, EBIT, and net income (and EPS) on both an annual and LTM basis. SEC filings are also the primary source for other key financial items

---

[15] First Call and Institutional Brokers' Estimate System (IBES) provide consensus analyst estimates for thousands of publicly traded companies. Both First Call and IBES are owned by Thomson Reuters.

such as balance sheet data, capital expenditures ("capex"), basic shares outstanding, stock options/warrants data, and information on non-recurring items. SEC filings can be obtained through numerous mediums, including a company's corporate website (typically through an "Investor Relations" link) as well as EDGAR[16] and other financial information services.

10-K (Annual Report)   The 10-K is an annual report filed with the SEC by a public registrant that provides a comprehensive overview of the company and its prior year performance.[17] It is required to contain an exhaustive list of disclosure items including, but not limited to, a detailed business description, management, discussion & analysis (MD&A),[18] audited financial statements[19] and supplementary data, outstanding debt detail, basic shares outstanding, and stock options/warrants data. It also contains an abundance of other pertinent information about the company and its sector, such as business segment detail, customers, end markets, competition, insight into material opportunities (and challenges and risks), significant recent events, and acquisitions.

10-Q (Quarterly Report)   The 10-Q is a quarterly report filed with the SEC by a public registrant that provides an overview of the most recent quarter and year-to-date (YTD) period.[20] It is less comprehensive than the 10-K, but provides financial statements as well as MD&A relating to the company's financial performance for the most recent quarter and YTD period versus the prior year periods.[21] The 10-Q also provides the most recent share count information and may also contain the most recent stock options/warrants data. For detailed financial information on a company's final quarter of the fiscal year, the banker refers to the 8-K containing the fourth quarter earnings press release that usually precedes the filing of the 10-K.

8-K (Current Report)   The 8-K, or current report, is filed by a public registrant to report the occurrence of *material* corporate events or changes ("triggering event") that are of importance to shareholders or security holders.[22] For the purposes of

---

[16]The Electronic Data Gathering, Analysis, and Retrieval (EDGAR) system performs automated collection, validation, indexing, acceptance, and forwarding of submissions by companies and others who are required to file forms with the SEC.

[17]The deadline for the filing of the 10-K ranges from 60 to 90 days after the end of a company's fiscal year depending on the size of its public float.

[18]A section in a company's 10-K and 10-Q that provides a discussion and analysis of the prior reporting period's financial performance. It also contains forward-looking information about the possible future effects of known and unknown events, conditions, and trends.

[19]The financial statements in a 10-K are audited and certified by a Certified Public Accountant (CPA) to meet the requirements of the SEC.

[20]The deadline for the filing of the 10-Q ranges from 40 to 45 days after the end of a company's fiscal quarter depending on the size of its public float. The 10-K, instead of the 10-Q, is filed after the end of a company's fiscal fourth quarter.

[21]The financial statements in a company's 10-Q are reviewed by a CPA, but not audited.

[22]Depending on the particular triggering event, the 8-K is typically filed within four business days after occurrence.

preparing trading comps, key triggering events include, but are not limited to, earnings announcements, entry into a definitive purchase/sale agreement,[23] completion of an acquisition or disposition of assets, capital markets transactions, and Regulation FD disclosure requirements.[24] The corresponding 8-Ks for these events often contain important information necessary to calculate a company's updated financial statistics, ratios, and trading multiples that may not be reflected in the most recent 10-K or 10-Q (see "Adjustments for Recent Events").

Proxy Statement A proxy statement is a document that a public company sends to its shareholders prior to a shareholder meeting containing material information regarding matters on which the shareholders are expected to vote. It is also filed with the SEC on Schedule 14A. For the purposes of spreading trading comps, the annual proxy statement provides a basic shares outstanding count that may be more recent than that contained in the latest 10-K or 10-Q. As previously discussed, the annual proxy statement also typically contains a suggested peer group for benchmarking purposes.

Equity Research

Research Reports Equity research reports provide individual analyst estimates of future company performance, which may be used to calculate forward-looking multiples. They generally include estimates of sales, EBITDA and/or EBIT, and EPS for future quarters and the future two- or three-year period (on an annual basis). More comprehensive reports provide additional estimated financial information from the research analyst's model, including key items from the income statement, balance sheet, and cash flow statement. These reports may also provide segmented financial projections, such as sales and EBIT at the business division level.

Equity research reports often provide commentary on non-recurring items and recent M&A and capital markets transactions, which are helpful for determining *pro forma* adjustments and normalizing financial data. They may also provide helpful sector and market information, as well as explicitly list the research analyst's view on the company's comparables universe. Initiating coverage research reports tend to be more comprehensive than normal interim reports. As a result, it is beneficial to mine these reports for financial, market, and competitive insights. Research reports can be located through various subscription financial information services such as FactSet, OneSource, and Thomson Reuters.

Consensus Estimates Consensus research estimates for selected financial statistics are widely used by bankers as the basis for calculating forward-looking trading multiples in trading comps. As previously discussed, the primary sources for consensus

---

[23] The legal contract between a buyer and seller detailing the terms and conditions of an M&A transaction. See Chapter 6: M&A Sale Process for additional information.

[24] Regulation FD (Fair Disclosure) provides that when a public filer discloses material non-public information to certain persons, as defined by the SEC, it must make public disclosure of that information typically through the filing of an 8-K.

estimates are First Call and IBES, which can be located through Bloomberg, FactSet, and Thomson Reuters, among other financial information services. The banker typically chooses one source or the other so as to maintain consistency throughout the analysis.[25]

Press Releases and News Runs

A company issues a press release when it has something important to report to the public. Standard press releases include earnings announcements, declaration of dividends, and management changes, as well as M&A and capital markets transactions. Earnings announcements, which are accompanied by the filing of an 8-K, are typically issued prior to the filing of a 10-K or 10-Q. Therefore, the banker relies upon the financial data provided in the earnings announcement to update trading comps in a timely manner. A company may also release an investor presentation to accompany its quarterly earnings call, which may be helpful in readily identifying key financial data and obtaining additional color and commentary. In the event that certain financial information is not provided in the earnings press release, the banker must wait until the filing of the 10-K or 10-Q for complete information. A company's press releases and recent news articles are available on its corporate website as well as through Bloomberg, Factiva, LexisNexis, and Thomson Reuters, among others.

Financial Information Services

As discussed throughout this section, financial information services are a key source for obtaining SEC filings, research reports, consensus estimates, and press releases, among other items. They are also the primary source for current and historical company share price information, which is essential for calculating equity value and determining a company's current share price as a percentage of its 52-week high. Financial information services, such as Bloomberg, may also be sourced to provide information on a company's credit ratings. If practical, however, we suggest sourcing credit ratings directly from the official Moody's, S&P, and Fitch websites to ensure accurate and up-to-date information.[26]

Summary of Financial Data Primary Sources

Exhibit 1.4 provides a summary of the primary sources used to obtain the necessary financial information to perform trading comps.

---

[25] Once a given consensus estimates source is selected, it is important to screen individual estimates for obsolescent data and outliers. For example, if a company has recently made a transformative acquisition, some analysts may have revised their estimates accordingly, while others may have not. Bloomberg and other sources allow the banker to view individual estimates (and the date when they were posted), which allows for the identification and removal of inconsistent estimates as appropriate.

[26] Access to these websites requires a subscription.

EXHIBIT 1.4   Summary of Financial Data Primary Sources

Information Item	Source
Income Statement Data	
Sales Gross Profit EBITDA[a] EBIT Net Income / EPS	Most recent 10-K, 10-Q, 8-K, Press Release
Research Estimates	First Call or IBES, individual equity research reports
Balance Sheet Data	
Cash Balance Debt Balances Shareholders' Equity	Most recent 10-K, 10-Q, 8-K, Press Release
Cash Flow Statement Data	
Depreciation & Amortization Capital Expenditures	Most recent 10-K, 10-Q, 8-K, Press Release
Share Data	
Basic Shares Outstanding	10-K, 10-Q, or Proxy Statement, whichever is most recent
Options and Warrants Data	10-K or 10-Q, whichever is more recent
Market Data	
Share Price Data	Financial information service
Credit Ratings	Rating agencies' websites, Bloomberg

[a] As a non-GAAP (generally accepted accounting principles) financial measure, EBITDA is not reported on a public filer's income statement. It may, however, be disclosed as supplemental information in the company's public filings.

STEP III. SPREAD KEY STATISTICS, RATIOS, AND TRADING MULTIPLES

Once the necessary financial information for each of the comparables has been located, it is entered into an input page (see Exhibit 1.5).[27] This sample input page

---

[27] For modeling/data entry purposes, manual inputs are typically formatted in blue font, while formula cells (calculations) are in black font (electronic versions of our models are available on our website, www.wiley.com/go/investmentbanking). In this book, we use darker shading to denote manual input cells.

EXHIBIT 1.5 Sample Comparable Company Input Page

Company A (NYSE:AAA)
Input Page
($ in millions, except per share data)

General Information

Company Name	Company A
Ticker	AAA
Stock Exchange	NYSE
Fiscal Year Ending	Dec-31
Moody's Corporate Rating	NA
S&P Corporate Rating	NA
Predicted Beta	1.00
Marginal Tax Rate	38.0%

Selected Market Data

Current Price	1/0/1900	NA
% of 52-week High		
52-week High Price	1/0/1900	
52-week Low Price	1/0/1900	
Dividend Per Share (MRQ)		
Fully Diluted Shares Outstanding		
Equity Value		
Plus: Total Debt		
Plus: Preferred Stock		
Plus: Noncontrolling Interest		
Less: Cash and Cash Equivalents		
Enterprise Value		

Trading Multiples

	LTM 9/30/2008	NFY 2008E	NFY+1 2009E
EV/Sales	NA	NA	NA
Metric	NA	NA	NA
EV/EBITDA	NA	NA	NA
Metric	NA	NA	NA
EV/EBIT	NA	NA	NA
Metric	NA	NA	NA
P/E	NA	NA	NA
Metric	NA	NA	NA

LTM Return on Investment Ratios

Return on Invested Capital	
Return on Equity	
Return on Assets	
Implied Annual Dividend Per Share	NA

LTM Credit Statistics

Debt/Total Capitalization	
Total Debt/EBITDA	
Net Debt/EBITDA	
EBITDA/Interest Expense	
(EBITDA-capex)/Interest Expense	
EBIT/Interest Expense	

Growth Rates

	Sales	EBITDA	EPS
Historical			
1-year			
2-year CAGR			
Estimated			
1-year			
2-year CAGR			
Long-term			

Reported Income Statement

		Fiscal Year Ending December 31			Prior Stub	Current Stub	LTM
	2005A	2006A	2007A		9/30/2007	9/30/2008	9/30/2008
Sales							NA
COGS							NA
Gross Profit							NA
SG&A							NA
Other Expense / (Income)							NA
EBIT							NA
Interest Expense							NA
Pre-tax Income							NA
Income Taxes							NA
Noncontrolling Interest							NA
Preferred Dividends							NA
Net Income	NA	NA	NA		NA	NA	NA
Effective Tax Rate	NA	NA	NA		NA	NA	NA
Weighted Avg. Diluted Shares							
Diluted EPS	NA	NA	NA		NA	NA	NA

Adjusted Income Statement

Reported Gross Profit							NA
Non-recurring Items in COGS							NA
Adj. Gross Profit	NA	NA	NA		NA	NA	NA
% margin							
Reported EBIT							NA
Non-recurring Items in COGS							NA
Other Non-recurring Items							NA
Adjusted EBIT	NA	NA	NA		NA	NA	NA
% margin							
Depreciation & Amortization							NA
Adjusted EBITDA	NA	NA	NA		NA	NA	NA
% margin							
Reported Net Income							NA
Non-recurring Items in COGS							NA
Other Non-recurring Items							NA
Non-operating Non-rec. Items							NA
Tax Adjustment							NA
Adjusted Net Income	NA	NA	NA		NA	NA	NA
% margin							
Adjusted Diluted EPS							NA

Cash Flow Statement Data

Depreciation & Amortization							NA
% sales	NA	NA	NA		NA	NA	NA
Capital Expenditures							NA
% sales	NA	NA	NA		NA	NA	NA

Business Description

[to come]

Balance Sheet Data

	2007A	9/30/2008
Cash and Cash Equivalents		
Accounts Receivable		
Inventories		
Prepaids and Other Current Assets		
Total Current Assets		
Property, Plant and Equipment, net		
Goodwill and Intangible Assets		
Other Assets		
Total Assets		
Accounts Payable		
Accrued Liabilities		
Other Current Liabilities		
Total Current Liabilities		
Total Debt		
Other Long-Term Liabilities		
Total Liabilities		
Noncontrolling Interest		
Preferred Stock		
Shareholders' Equity		
Total Liabilities and Equity		
Balance Check	0.000	0.000

Calculation of Fully Diluted Shares Outstanding

Basic Shares Outstanding	
Plus: Shares from In-the-Money Options	
Less: Shares Repurchased	
Net New Shares from Options	
Plus: Shares from Convertible Securities	
Fully Diluted Shares Outstanding	

Options/Warrants

Tranche	Number of Shares	Exercise Price	In-the-Money Shares	Proceeds
Tranche 1				
Tranche 2				
Tranche 3				
Tranche 4				
Tranche 5				
Total				

Convertible Securities

	Amount	Conversion Price	Conversion Ratio	New Shares
Issue 1				
Issue 2				
Issue 3				
Issue 4				
Issue 5				
Total				

Notes

(1) [to come]
(2) [to come]
(3) [to come]
(4) [to come]

is designed to assist the banker in calculating the key financial statistics, ratios, and multiples for the comparables universe.[28] The input page data, in turn, feeds into output sheets that are used to benchmark the comparables (see Exhibits 1.53, 1.54, and 1.55).

In the pages that follow, we discuss the financial data displayed on the sample input sheet, as well as the calculations behind them. We also describe the mechanics for calculating LTM financial statistics, calendarizing company financials, and adjusting for non-recurring items and recent events.

Calculation of Key Financial Statistics and Ratios

In this section, we outline the calculation of key financial statistics, ratios, and other metrics in accordance with the financial profile framework introduced in Step I.

- Size (Market Valuation: equity value and enterprise value; and Key Financial Data: sales, gross profit, EBITDA, EBIT, and net income)

- Profitability (gross profit, EBITDA, EBIT, and net income margins)

- Growth Profile (historical and estimated growth rates)

- Return on Investment (ROIC, ROE, ROA, and dividend yield)

- Credit Profile (leverage ratios, coverage ratios, and credit ratings)

Size: Market Valuation

Equity Value   Equity value ("market capitalization") is the value represented by a given company's basic shares outstanding plus "in-the-money" stock options,[29] warrants,[30] and convertible securities—collectively, "fully diluted shares outstanding." It is calculated by multiplying a company's current share price[31] by its fully diluted shares outstanding (see Exhibit 1.6).

---

[28]This template should be adjusted as appropriate in accordance with the specific company/sector (see Exhibit 1.33).

[29]Stock options are granted to employees as a form of non-cash compensation. They provide the right to buy (call) shares of the company's common stock at a set price ("exercise" or "strike" price) during a given time period. Employee stock options are subject to vesting periods that restrict the number of shares available for exercise according to a set schedule. They become eligible to be converted into shares of common stock once their vesting period expires ("exercisable"). An option is considered "in-the-money" when the underlying company's share price surpasses the option's exercise price.

[30]A warrant is a security typically issued in conjunction with a debt instrument that entitles the purchaser of that instrument to buy shares of the issuer's common stock at a set price during a given time period. In this context, warrants serve to entice investor interest (usually as a detachable equity "sweetener") in riskier classes of securities such as non-investment grade bonds and mezzanine debt, by providing an increase to the security's overall return.

[31]For trading comps, the banker typically uses the company's share price as of the prior day's close as the basis for calculating equity value and trading multiples.

EXHIBIT 1.6   Calculation of Equity Value

When compared to other companies, equity value only provides a measure of relative size. Therefore, for insight on absolute and relative market performance—which is informative for interpreting multiples and framing valuation—the banker looks at the company's current share price as a percentage of its 52-week high. This is a widely used metric that provides perspective on valuation and gauges current market sentiment and outlook for both the individual company and its broader sector. If a given company's percentage is significantly out of line with that of its peers, it is generally an indicator of company-specific (as opposed to sector-specific) issues. For example, a company may have missed its earnings guidance or underperformed versus its peers over the recent quarter(s). It may also be a sign of more entrenched issues involving management, operations, or specific markets.

Calculation of Fully Diluted Shares Outstanding   A company's fully diluted shares are calculated by adding the number of shares represented by its in-the-money options, warrants, and convertibles securities to its basic shares outstanding.[32] A company's most recent basic shares outstanding count is typically sourced from the first page of its 10-K or 10-Q (whichever is most recent). In some cases, however, the latest proxy statement may contain more updated data and, therefore, should be used in lieu of the 10-K or 10-Q. The most recent stock options/warrants information is obtained from a company's latest 10-K or, in some cases, the 10-Q.

The incremental shares represented by a company's in-the-money options and warrants are calculated in accordance with the treasury stock method (TSM). Those shares implied by a company's in-the-money convertible and equity-linked securities are calculated in accordance with the if-converted method or net share settlement (NSS), as appropriate.

Options and Warrants—The Treasury Stock Method   The TSM assumes that all tranches of in-the-money options and warrants are exercised at their weighted average strike price with the resulting option proceeds used to repurchase outstanding

---

[32]Investment banks and finance professionals may differ as to whether they use "outstanding" or "exercisable" in-the-money options and warrants in the calculation of fully diluted shares outstanding when performing trading comps. For conservatism (i.e., assuming the most dilutive scenario), many firms employ all outstanding in-the-money options and warrants as opposed to just exercisable as they represent future claims against the company.

shares of stock at the company's current share price. In-the-money options and warrants are those that have an exercise price lower than the current market price of the underlying company's stock. As the strike price is lower than the current market price, the number of shares repurchased is less than the additional shares outstanding from exercised options. This results in a net issuance of shares, which is dilutive.

In Exhibit 1.7 we provide an example of how to calculate fully diluted shares outstanding using the TSM.

EXHIBIT 1.7 Calculation of Fully Diluted Shares Outstanding Using the Treasury Stock Method

As shown in Exhibit 1.7, the 5 million options are in-the-money as the exercise price of $18.00 is lower than the current share price of $20.00. This means that the holders of the options have the right to buy the company's shares at $18.00 and sell them at $20.00, thereby realizing the $2.00 differential. Under the TSM, it is assumed that the $18.00 of potential proceeds received by the company is used to repurchase shares that are currently trading at $20.00. Therefore, the number of shares repurchased is 90% ($18.00 / $20.00) of the options, or 4.5 million shares in total (90% × 5 million). To calculate net new shares, the 4.5 million shares repurchased are subtracted from options of 5 million, resulting in 0.5 million. These new shares are added to the company's basic shares outstanding to derive fully diluted shares of 100.5 million.

Convertible and Equity-Linked Securities Outstanding convertible and equity-linked securities also need to be factored into the calculation of fully diluted shares outstanding. Convertible and equity-linked securities bridge the gap between traditional debt and equity, featuring characteristics of both. They include a broad range of instruments, such as traditional cash-pay convertible bonds, convertible hybrids, perpetual convertible preferred, and mandatory convertibles.[33]

---

[33] While the overall volume of issuance for convertible and equity-linked securities is less than that for straight debt instruments, they are relatively common in certain sectors.

This section focuses on the traditional cash-pay convertible bond as it is the most "plain-vanilla" structure. A cash-pay convertible bond ("convert") represents a straight debt instrument and an embedded equity call option that provides for the convert to be exchanged into a defined number of shares of the issuer's common stock under certain circumstances. The value of the embedded call option allows the issuer to pay a lower coupon than a straight debt instrument of the same credit. The strike price of the call option ("conversion price"), which represents the share price at which equity would be issued to bondholders if the bonds were converted, is typically set at a premium to the company's underlying share price at the time of issuance.

For the purposes of performing trading comps, to calculate fully diluted shares outstanding, it is standard practice to first determine whether the company's outstanding converts are in-the-money, meaning that the current share price is above the conversion price. In-the-money cash-pay converts are converted into additional shares in accordance with either the if-converted method or net share settlement, as applicable. Out-of-the-money converts, by contrast, remain treated as debt. Proper treatment of converts requires a careful reading of the relevant footnotes in the company's 10-K or prospectus for the security.

If-Converted Method   In accordance with the if-converted method, when performing trading comps, in-the-money converts are converted into additional shares by dividing the convert's amount outstanding by its conversion price.[34] Once converted, the convert is treated as equity and included in the calculation of the company's equity value. The equity value represented by the convert is calculated by multiplying the new shares outstanding from conversion by the company's current share price. Accordingly, the convert must be excluded from the calculation of the company's total debt.

As shown in Exhibit 1.8, as the company's current share price of $20.00 is greater than the conversion price of $15.00, we determine that the $150 million convert is in-the-money. Therefore the convert's amount outstanding is simply divided by the conversion price to calculate new shares of 10 million ($150 million / $15.00). The new shares from conversion are then added to the company's basic shares outstanding of 100 million and net new shares from in-the-money options of 0.5 million to calculate fully diluted shares outstanding of 110.5 million.

The conversion of in-the-money converts also requires an upward adjustment to the company's net income to account for the foregone interest expense payments associated with the coupon on the convert. This amount must be tax-effected before being added back to net income. Therefore, while conversion is typically EPS dilutive due to the additional share issuance, net income is actually higher on a pro forma basis.

---

[34]For GAAP reporting purposes (e.g., for EPS and fully diluted shares outstanding), the if-converted method requires issuers to measure the dilutive impact of the security through a two-test process. First, the issuer needs to test the security as if it were debt on its balance sheet, with the stated interest expense reflected in net income and the underlying shares omitted from the share count. Second, the issuer needs to test the security as if it were converted into equity, which involves excluding the interest expense from the convert in net income and including the full underlying shares in the share count. Upon completion of the two tests, the issuer is required to use the more dilutive of the two methodologies.

EXHIBIT 1.8 Calculation of Fully Diluted Shares Outstanding Using the If-Converted Method

($ in millions, except per share data; shares in millions)

Assumptions	
Stock	
Current Share Price	$20.00
Basic Shares Outstanding	100.0
Convertible	
Amount Outstanding	$150.0
Conversion Price	$15.00

If-Converted		
Amount Outstanding	$150.0	= Amount Outstanding / Conversion Price
/ Conversion Price	$15.00	= $150.0 million / $15.0
Incremental Shares	**10.0**	Calculated in Exhibit 1.7
Plus: Basic Shares Outstanding	100.0	= New Shares from Conversion
Plus: Net New Shares from Options	0.5	+ Net New Shares from Options
Fully Diluted Shares Outstanding	**110.5**	+ Basic Shares Outstanding
		= 10.0 million + 0.5 million + 100.0 million

Net Share Settlement For converts issued with a net share settlement accounting feature,[35] the issuer is permitted to satisfy the face (or accreted) value of an in-the-money convert with cash upon conversion. Only the value represented by the excess of the current share price over the conversion price is assumed to be settled with the issuance of additional shares,[36] which results in less share issuance. This serves to limit the dilutive effects of conversion by affording the issuer TSM accounting treatment.

As shown in Exhibit 1.9, the if-converted method results in incremental shares of 10 million shares, while NSS results in incremental shares of only 2.5 million. The NSS calculation is conducted by first multiplying the number of underlying shares in the convert of 10 million by the company's current share price of $20.00 to determine the implied conversion value of $200 million. The $50 million spread between the conversion value and par ($200 million − $150 million) is then divided by the current share price to determine the number of incremental shares from conversion of 2.5 million ($50 million / $20.00).[37] The $150 million face value of the convert

---

[35] Effective for fiscal years beginning after December 15, 2008, the Financial Accounting Standards Board (FASB) put into effect new guidelines for NSS accounting. These changes effectively bifurcate an NSS convert into its debt and equity components, resulting in higher reported interest expense due to the higher imputed cost of debt. However, the new guidelines do not change the calculation of shares outstanding in accordance with the TSM. Therefore, one should consult with a capital markets specialist for accounting guidance on in-the-money converts with NSS features.

[36] The NSS feature may also be structured so that the issuer can elect to settle the excess conversion value in cash.

[37] As the company's share price increases, the amount of incremental shares issued also increases as the spread between conversion and par value widens.

remains treated as debt due to the fact that the issuer typically has the right to settle this amount in cash.

EXHIBIT 1.9   Incremental Shares from If-Converted Versus Net Share Settlement

($ in millions, except per share data; shares in millions)

If-Converted	
Amount Outstanding	$150.0
/ Conversion Price	$15.00
Incremental Shares	**10.0**
Incremental Shares – If-Converted	**10.0**

Net Share Settlement	
Amount Outstanding	$150.0
/ Conversion Price	$15.00
Incremental Shares	**10.0**
x Current Share Price	$20.00
Total Value of Convert	**$200.0**
Less: Par Value of Amount Outstanding	(150.0)
Excess Over Par Value	**$50.0**
/ Current Share Price	$20.00
Incremental Shares – NSS	**2.5**

= Excess Over Par Value / Current Share Price
= $50.0 million / $20.00

= Total Value of Convert - Par Value of Amt. Out.
= $200.0 million - $150.0 million

= Incremental Shares x Current Share Price
= 10.0 million x $20.00

= Amount Outstanding / Conversion Price
= $150.0 million / $15.00

Enterprise Value   Enterprise value ("total enterprise value" or "firm value") is the sum of all ownership interests in a company and claims on its assets from both debt and equity holders. As the graphic in Exhibit 1.10 depicts, it is defined as equity value + total debt + preferred stock + noncontrolling interest[38] – cash and cash equivalents. The equity value component is calculated on a fully diluted basis.

EXHIBIT 1.10   Calculation of Enterprise Value

Enterprise Value	=	Equity Value	+	Total Debt	+	Preferred Stock	+	Noncontrolling Interest	–	Cash and Cash Equivalents

Theoretically, enterprise value is considered independent of capital structure, meaning that changes in a company's capital structure do not affect its enterprise value. For example, if a company raises additional debt that is held on the balance sheet as cash, its enterprise value remains constant as the new debt is offset by the increase in cash (i.e., net debt remains the same, see Scenario I in Exhibit 1.11).

---

[38]Formerly known as "minority interest," noncontrolling interest is a significant, but non-majority, interest (less than 50%) in a company's voting stock by another company or an investor. Effective for fiscal years beginning after December 15, 2008, FAS 160 changed the accounting and reporting for minority interest, which is now called noncontrolling interest and can be found in the shareholders' equity section of a company's balance sheet. On the income statement, the noncontrolling interest holder's share of income is subtracted from net income.

Similarly, if a company issues equity and uses the proceeds to repay debt, the incremental equity value is offset by the decrease in debt on a dollar-for-dollar basis (see Scenario II in Exhibit 1.11).[39] Therefore, these transactions are enterprise value neutral.

EXHIBIT 1.11 Effects of Capital Structure Changes on Enterprise Value

($ in millions)

Scenario I: Issuance of Debt				
	Actual **2007**	**Adjustments** **+**	**-**	**Pro forma** **2007**
Equity Value	$750.0			$750.0
Plus: Total Debt	250.0	100.0		350.0
Plus: Preferred Stock	35.0			35.0
Plus: Noncontrolling Interest	15.0			15.0
Less: Cash and Cash Equivalents	(50.0)		(100.0)	(150.0)
Enterprise Value	**$1,000.0**			**$1,000.0**

($ in millions)

Scenario II: Issuance of Equity to Repay Debt				
	Actual **2007**	**Adjustments** **+**	**-**	**Pro forma** **2007**
Equity Value	$750.0	100.0		$850.0
Plus: Total Debt	250.0		(100.0)	150.0
Plus: Preferred Stock	35.0			35.0
Plus: Noncontrolling Interest	15.0			15.0
Less: Cash and Cash Equivalents	(50.0)			(50.0)
Enterprise Value	**$1,000.0**			**$1,000.0**

In both Scenario I and II, enterprise value remains constant despite a change in the company's capital structure. Hence, similar companies would be expected to have consistent enterprise value multiples despite differences in capital structure. One notable exception concerns highly leveraged companies, which may trade at a discount relative to their peers due to the perceived higher risk of financial distress[40] and potential constraints to growth.

Size: Key Financial Data

- **Sales** (or revenue) is the first line item, or "top line," on an income statement. Sales represents the total dollar amount realized by a company through the sale of its products and services during a given time period. Sales levels and trends are a key factor in determining a company's relative positioning among its peers. All else being equal, companies with greater sales volumes tend to

---

[39]These illustrative scenarios ignore financing fees associated with the debt and equity issuance as well as potential breakage costs associated with the repayment of debt. See Chapter 4: Leveraged Buyouts for additional information.

[40]Circumstances whereby a company is unable or struggles to meet its credit obligations, typically resulting in business disruption, insolvency, or bankruptcy. As the perceived risk of financial distress increases, equity value generally decreases accordingly.

benefit from scale, market share, purchasing power, and lower risk profile, and are often rewarded by the market with a premium valuation relative to smaller peers.

- **Gross Profit,** defined as sales less cost of goods sold (COGS),[41] is the profit earned by a company after subtracting costs directly related to the production of its products and services. As such, it is a key indicator of operational efficiency and pricing power, and is usually expressed as a percentage of sales for analytical purposes (gross profit margin, see Exhibit 1.12). For example, if a company sells a product for $100.00, and that product costs $60.00 in materials, manufacturing, and direct labor to produce, then the gross profit on that product is $40.00 and the gross profit margin is 40%.

- **EBITDA** (earnings before interest, taxes, depreciation and amortization) is an important measure of profitability. As EBITDA is a non-GAAP financial measure and typically not reported by public filers, it is generally calculated by taking EBIT (or operating income/profit as often reported on the income statement) and adding back the depreciation and amortization (D&A) as sourced from the cash flow statement.[42] EBITDA is a widely used proxy for operating cash flow as it reflects the company's total cash operating costs for producing its products and services. In addition, EBITDA serves as a fair "apples-to-apples" means of comparison among companies in the same sector because it is free from differences resulting from capital structure (i.e., interest expense) and tax regime (i.e., tax expense).

- **EBIT** (earnings before interest and taxes) is often the same as reported operating income, operating profit, or income from operations[43] on the income statement found in a company's SEC filings. Like EBITDA, EBIT is independent of tax regime and serves as a useful metric for comparing companies with different capital structures. It is, however, less indicative as a measure of operating cash flow than EBITDA because it includes non-cash D&A expense. Furthermore, D&A reflects discrepancies among different companies in capital spending and/or depreciation policy as well as acquisition histories (amortization).

- **Net income** ("earnings" or the "bottom line") is the residual profit after all of a company's expenses have been netted out. Net income can also be viewed as the earnings available to equity holders once all of the company's obligations have been satisfied (e.g., to suppliers, vendors, service providers, employees, utilities, lessors, lenders, state and local treasuries). Wall Street tends to view net income on a per share basis (i.e., EPS).

---

[41]COGS, as reported on the income statement, may include or exclude D&A depending on the filing company. If D&A is excluded, it is reported as a separate line item on the income statement.

[42]In the event a company reports D&A as a separate line item on the income statement (i.e., broken out separately from COGS and SG&A), EBITDA can be calculated as sales less COGS less SG&A.

[43]EBIT may differ from operating income/profit due to the inclusion of income generated outside the scope of a company's ordinary course business operations ("other income").

Profitability

- **Gross profit margin** ("gross margin") measures the percentage of sales remaining after subtracting COGS (see Exhibit 1.12). It is driven by a company's direct cost per unit, such as materials, manufacturing, and direct labor involved in production. These costs are typically largely variable, as opposed to corporate overhead which is more fixed in nature.[44] Companies ideally seek to increase their gross margin through a combination of improved sourcing/procurement of raw materials and enhanced pricing power, as well as by improving the efficiency of manufacturing facilities and processes.

EXHIBIT 1.12   Gross Profit Margin

- **EBITDA** and **EBIT margin** are accepted standards for measuring a company's operating profitability (see Exhibit 1.13). Accordingly, they are used to frame relative performance both among peer companies and across sectors.

EXHIBIT 1.13   EBITDA and EBIT Margin

- **Net income margin** measures a company's overall profitability as opposed to its operating profitability (see Exhibit 1.14). It is net of interest expense and, therefore, affected by capital structure. As a result, companies with similar operating margins may have substantially different net income margins due to differences in leverage. Furthermore, as net income is impacted by taxes, companies with similar operating margins may have varying net income margins due to different tax rates.

EXHIBIT 1.14   Net Income Margin

---

[44] *Variable* costs change depending on the volume of goods produced and include items such as materials, direct labor, transportation, and utilities. *Fixed* costs remain more or less constant regardless of volume and include items such as lease expense, advertising and marketing, insurance, corporate overhead, and administrative salaries. These costs are usually captured in the SG&A (or equivalent) line item on the income statement.

Growth Profile

A company's growth profile is a critical value driver. In assessing a company's growth profile, the banker typically looks at historical and estimated future growth rates as well as compound annual growth rates (CAGRs) for selected financial statistics (see Exhibit 1.15).

EXHIBIT 1.15   Historical and Estimated Diluted EPS Growth Rates

		Fiscal Year Ending December 31					
	2005A	**2006A**	**2007A**	**CAGR ('05 - '07)**	**2008E**	**2009E**	**CAGR ('07 - '09)**
Diluted EPS	$1.00	$1.15	$1.30	14.0%	$1.50	$1.65	12.7%
% growth		15.0%	13.0%		15.4%	10.0%	
Long-Term Growth Rate							12.0%

= (Ending Value / Beginning Value) ^ (1 / Ending Year - Beginning Year) - 1
= ($1.30 / $1.00) ^ (1 / (2007 - 2005)) - 1

Source: Consensus Estimates

Historical annual EPS data is typically sourced directly from a company's 10-K or a financial information service that sources SEC filings. As with the calculation of any financial statistic, historical EPS must be adjusted for non-recurring items to be meaningful. The data that serves as the basis for a company's projected 1-year, 2-year, and long-term[45] EPS growth rates is generally obtained from consensus estimates.

Return on Investment

- **Return on invested capital (ROIC)** measures the return generated by all capital provided to a company. As such, ROIC utilizes a pre-interest earnings statistic in the numerator, such as EBIT or tax-effected EBIT (also known as NOPAT or EBIAT) and a metric that captures both debt and equity in the denominator (see Exhibit 1.16). The denominator is typically calculated on an average basis (e.g., average of the balances as of the prior annual and most recent periods).

EXHIBIT 1.16   Return on Invested Capital

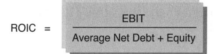

$$ROIC = \frac{EBIT}{\text{Average Net Debt} + \text{Equity}}$$

- **Return on equity (ROE)** measures the return generated on the equity provided to a company by its shareholders. As a result, ROE incorporates an earnings metric net of interest expense, such as net income, in the numerator and average shareholders' equity in the denominator (see Exhibit 1.17). ROE is an important indicator of performance as companies are intently focused on shareholder returns.

---

[45]Represents a three-to-five-year estimate of annual EPS growth, as reported by equity research analysts.

EXHIBIT 1.17 Return on Equity

$$ROE = \frac{\text{Net Income}}{\text{Average Shareholders' Equity}}$$

- **Return on assets (ROA)** measures the return generated by a company's asset base, thereby providing a barometer of the asset efficiency of a business. ROA typically utilizes net income in the numerator and average total assets in the denominator (see Exhibit 1.18).

EXHIBIT 1.18 Return on Assets

$$ROA = \frac{\text{Net Income}}{\text{Average Total Assets}}$$

- **Dividend yield** is a measure of returns to shareholders, but from a different perspective than earnings-based ratios. Dividend yield measures the annual dividends per share paid by a company to its shareholders (which can be distributed either in cash or additional shares), expressed as a percentage of its share price. Dividends are typically paid on a quarterly basis and, therefore, must be annualized to calculate the implied dividend yield (see Exhibit 1.19).[46] For example, if a company pays a quarterly dividend of $0.05 per share ($0.20 per share on an annualized basis) and its shares are currently trading at $10.00, the dividend yield is 2% (($0.05 × 4 payments) / $10.00).

EXHIBIT 1.19 Implied Dividend Yield

$$\text{Implied Dividend Yield} = \frac{\text{Most Recent Quarterly Dividend Per Share} \times 4}{\text{Current Share Price}}$$

Credit Profile

Leverage Leverage refers to a company's debt level. It is typically measured as a multiple of EBITDA (e.g., debt-to-EBITDA) or as a percentage of total capitalization (e.g., debt-to-total capitalization). Both debt and equity investors closely track a company's leverage as it reveals a great deal about financial policy, risk profile, and capacity for growth. As a general rule, the higher a company's leverage, the higher its risk of financial distress due to the burden associated with greater interest expense and principal repayments.

---

[46]Not all companies choose to pay dividends to their shareholders.

■ **Debt-to-EBITDA** depicts the ratio of a company's debt to its EBITDA, with a higher multiple connoting higher leverage (see Exhibit 1.20). It is generally calculated on the basis of LTM financial statistics. There are several variations of this ratio, including total debt-to-EBITDA, senior secured debt-to-EBITDA, net debt-to-EBITDA, and total debt-to-(EBITDA less capex). As EBITDA is typically used as a rough proxy for operating cash flow, this ratio can be viewed as a measure of how many years of a company's cash flows are needed to repay its debt.

EXHIBIT 1.20 Leverage Ratio

■ **Debt-to-total capitalization** measures a company's debt as a percentage of its total capitalization (debt + preferred stock + noncontrolling interest + equity) (see Exhibit 1.21). This ratio can be calculated on the basis of book or market values depending on the situation. As with debt-to-EBITDA, a higher debt-to-total capitalization ratio connotes higher debt levels and risk of financial distress.

EXHIBIT 1.21 Capitalization Ratio

$$\text{Debt-to-Total Capitalization} = \frac{\text{Debt}}{\text{Debt} + \text{Preferred Stock} + \text{Noncontrolling Interest} + \text{Equity}}$$

Coverage Coverage is a broad term that refers to a company's ability to meet ("cover") its interest expense obligations. Coverage ratios are generally comprised of a financial statistic representing operating cash flow (e.g., LTM EBITDA) in the numerator and LTM interest expense in the denominator. There are several variations of the coverage ratio, including EBITDA-to-interest expense, (EBITDA less capex)-to-interest expense, and EBIT-to-interest expense (see Exhibit 1.22). Intuitively, the higher the coverage ratio, the better positioned the company is to meet its debt obligations and, therefore, the stronger its credit profile.

EXHIBIT 1.22 Interest Coverage Ratio

Credit Ratings   A credit rating is an assessment[47] by an independent rating agency of a company's ability and willingness to make full and timely payments of amounts due on its debt obligations. Credit ratings are typically required for companies seeking to raise debt financing in the capital markets as only a limited class of investors will participate in a corporate debt offering without an assigned credit rating on the new issue.[48]

The three primary credit rating agencies are Moody's, S&P, and Fitch. Nearly every public debt issuer receives a rating from Moody's, S&P, and/or Fitch. Moody's uses an alphanumeric scale, while S&P and Fitch both use an alphabetic system combined with pluses (+) and minuses (−) to rate the creditworthiness of an issuer. The ratings scales of the primary rating agencies are shown in Exhibit 1.23.

EXHIBIT 1.23   Ratings Scales of the Primary Rating Agencies

	Moody's	S&P	Fitch	Definition
Investment Grade	Aaa	AAA	AAA	Highest Quality
	Aa1	AA+	AA+	
	Aa2	AA	AA	Very High Quality
	Aa3	AA−	AA−	
	A1	A+	A+	
	A2	A	A	High Quality
	A3	A−	A−	
	Baa1	BBB+	BBB+	
	Baa2	BBB	BBB	Medium Grade
	Baa3	BBB−	BBB−	
Non-Investment Grade	Ba1	BB+	BB+	
	Ba2	BB	BB	Speculative
	Ba3	BB−	BB−	
	B1	B+	B+	
	B2	B	B	Highly Speculative
	B3	B−	B−	
	Caa1	CCC+	CCC+	
	Caa2	CCC	CCC	Substantial Risk
	Caa3	CCC−	CCC−	
	Ca	CC	CC	
	C	C	C	Extremely Speculative /
	-	D	D	Default

Supplemental Financial Concepts and Calculations

Calculation of LTM Financial Data   U.S. public filers are required to report their financial performance on a quarterly basis, including a full year report filed at the end

---

[47]Ratings agencies provide opinions, but do not conduct audits.

[48]Ratings are assessed on the issuer (corporate credit ratings) as well as on the individual debt instruments (facility ratings).

of the fiscal year. Therefore, in order to measure financial performance for the most recent annual or LTM period, the company's financial results for the previous four quarters are summed. This financial information is sourced from the company's most recent 10-K and 10-Q, as appropriate. As previously discussed, however, prior to the filing of the 10-Q or 10-K, companies typically issue a detailed earnings press release in an 8-K with the necessary financial data to help calculate LTM performance. Therefore, it may be appropriate to use a company's earnings announcement to update trading comps on a timely basis.

As the formula in Exhibit 1.24 illustrates, LTM financials are typically calculated by taking the full prior fiscal year's financial data, adding the YTD financial data for the current year period ("current stub"), and then subtracting the YTD financial data from the prior year ("prior stub").

EXHIBIT 1.24   Calculation of LTM Financial Data

In the event that the most recent quarter is the fourth quarter of a company's fiscal year, then no LTM calculations are necessary as the full prior fiscal year (as reported) serves as the LTM period. Exhibit 1.25 shows an illustrative calculation for a given company's LTM sales for the period ending 9/30/08.

EXHIBIT 1.25   Calculation of LTM 9/30/08 Sales

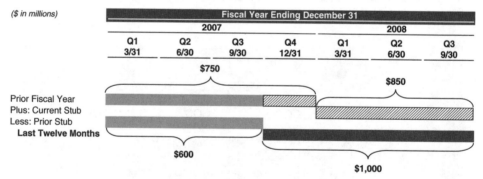

Calendarization of Financial Data   The majority of U.S. public filers report their financial performance in accordance with a fiscal year (FY) ending December 31, which corresponds to the calendar year (CY) end. Some companies, however, report on a different schedule (e.g., a fiscal year ending April 30). Any variation in fiscal year ends among comparable companies must be addressed for benchmarking purposes. Otherwise, the trading multiples will be based on financial data for different periods and, therefore, not truly "comparable."

To account for variations in fiscal year ends among comparable companies, each company's financials are adjusted to conform to a calendar year end in order to produce a "clean" basis for comparison, a process known as "calendarization." This is a relatively straightforward algebraic exercise, as illustrated by the formula in

Exhibit 1.26, used to calendarize a company's fiscal year sales projection to produce a calendar year sales projection.[49]

EXHIBIT 1.26 Calendarization of Financial Data

Next Calendar Year (CY) Sales $= \dfrac{(\text{Month \#}) \times (\text{FYA Sales})}{12} + \dfrac{(12 - \text{Month \#}) \times (\text{NFY Sales})}{12}$

Note: "Month #" refers to the month in which the company's fiscal year ends (e.g. the Month # for a company with a fiscal year ending April 30 would be 4). FYA = fiscal year actual and NFY = next fiscal year.

Exhibit 1.27 provides an illustrative calculation for the calendarization of a company's calendar year 2008 estimated (E) sales, assuming a fiscal year ending April 30.

EXHIBIT 1.27 Calendarization of Sales

Adjustments for Non-Recurring Items To assess a company's financial performance on a "normalized" basis, it is standard practice to adjust reported financial data for non-recurring items, a process known as "scrubbing" or "sanitizing" the financials. Failure to do so may lead to the calculation of misleading ratios and multiples, which, in turn, may produce a distorted view of valuation. These adjustments involve the add-back or elimination of one-time charges and gains, respectively, to create a more indicative view of ongoing company performance. Typical charges include those incurred for restructuring events (e.g., store/plant closings and headcount reduction), losses on asset sales, changes in accounting principles, inventory write-offs, goodwill impairment, extinguishment of debt, and losses from litigation settlements, among others. Typical benefits include gains from asset sales, favorable litigation settlements, and tax adjustments, among others.

Non-recurring items are often described in the MD&A section and financial footnotes in a company's public filings (e.g., 10-K and 10-Q) and earnings announcements. These items are often explicitly depicted as "non-recurring," "extraordinary," "unusual," or "one-time." Therefore, the banker is encouraged to comb electronic

---

[49]If available, quarterly estimates should be used as the basis for calendarizing financial projections.

versions of the company's public filings and earnings announcements using word searches for these adjectives. Often, non-recurring charges or benefits are explicitly broken out as separate line items on a company's reported income statement and/or cash flow statement. Research reports can be helpful in identifying these items, while also providing color commentary on the reason they occurred.

In many cases, however, the banker must exercise discretion as to whether a given charge or benefit is non-recurring or part of normal business operations. This determination is sometimes relatively subjective, further compounded by the fact that certain events may be considered non-recurring for one company, but customary for another. For example, a generic pharmaceutical company may find itself in court frequently due to lawsuits filed by major drug manufacturers related to patent challenges. In this case, expenses associated with a lawsuit should not necessarily be treated as non-recurring because these legal expenses are a normal part of ongoing operations. While financial information services such as Capital IQ provide a breakdown of recommended adjustments that can be helpful in identifying potential non-recurring items, ultimately the banker should exercise professional judgment.

When adjusting for non-recurring items, it is important to distinguish between pre-tax and after-tax amounts. For a pre-tax restructuring charge, for example, the full amount is simply added back to calculate adjusted EBIT and EBITDA. To calculate adjusted net income, however, the pre-tax restructuring charge needs to be tax-effected[50] before being added back. Conversely, for after-tax amounts, the disclosed amount is simply added back to net income, but must be "grossed up" at the company's tax rate (t) (i.e., divided by $(1 - t)$) before being added back to EBIT and EBITDA.

Exhibit 1.28 provides an illustrative income statement for the fiscal year 2007 as it might appear in a 10-K. Let's assume the corresponding notes to these financials mention that the company recorded one-time charges related to an inventory write-down ($5 million pre-tax) and restructuring expenses from downsizing the sales force ($10 million pre-tax). Provided we gain comfort that these charges are truly non-recurring, we would need to normalize the company's earnings statistics accordingly for these items in order to arrive at adjusted EBIT, EBITDA, and diluted EPS.

As shown in Exhibit 1.29, to calculate adjusted EBIT and EBITDA, we add back the full pre-tax charges of $5 million and $10 million ($15 million in total). This provides adjusted EBIT of $150 and adjusted EBITDA of $200 million. To calculate adjusted net income and diluted EPS, however, the tax expense on the incremental $15 million pre-tax earnings must be subtracted. Assuming a 40% marginal tax rate, we calculate tax expense of $6 million and additional net income of $9 million

---

[50]In the event the SEC filing footnotes do not provide detail on the after-tax amounts of such adjustments, the banker typically uses the marginal tax rate. The marginal tax rate for U.S. corporations is the rate at which a company is required to pay federal, state, and local taxes. The highest federal corporate income tax rate for U.S. corporations is 35%, with state and local taxes typically adding another 2% to 5% or more (depending on the state). Most public companies disclose their federal, state and local tax rates in their 10-Ks in the notes to their financial statements.

EXHIBIT 1.28   Reported Income Statement

($ in millions, except per share data)

Income Statement	
	Reported 2007
Sales	**$1,000.0**
Cost of Goods Sold	625.0
Gross Profit	**$375.0**
Selling, General & Administrative	230.0
Restructuring Charges	10.0
Operating Income (EBIT)	**$135.0**
Interest Expense	35.0
Pre-tax Income	**$100.0**
Income Taxes	40.0
Net Income	**$60.0**
Weighted Avg. Diluted Shares	30.0
Diluted EPS	$2.00

($15 million – $6 million). The $9 million is added to reported net income, resulting in adjusted net income of $69 million. We then divide the $69 million by weighted average diluted shares outstanding of 30 million to calculate adjusted diluted EPS of $2.30.

EXHIBIT 1.29   Adjusted Income Statement

($ in millions, except per share data)

Income Statement	Reported 2007	Adjustments +	Adjustments –	Adjusted 2007	
Sales	**$1,000.0**			**$1,000.0**	
Cost of Goods Sold	625.0		(5.0)	620.0	Inventory write-down
Gross Profit	**$375.0**			**$380.0**	
Selling, General & Administrative	230.0			230.0	
Restructuring Charges	10.0		(10.0)	-	Restructuring charge related to severance from downsizing the sales force
Operating Income (EBIT)	**$135.0**			**$150.0**	
Interest Expense	35.0			35.0	
Pre-tax Income	**$100.0**			**$115.0**	
Income Taxes	40.0	6.0		46.0	= (Inventory write-down + Restructuring charge) x Marginal Tax Rate = ($5.0 million + $10.0 million) x 40.0%
Net Income	**$60.0**			**$69.0**	
Operating Income (EBIT)	$135.0	15.0		$150.0	
Depreciation & Amortization	50.0			50.0	D&A is typically sourced from a company's cash flow statement although it is sometimes broken out on the income statement
EBITDA	**$185.0**			**$200.0**	
Weighted Avg. Diluted Shares	30.0			30.0	
Diluted EPS	$2.00			$2.30	

$15.0 million add-back of total non-recurring items

Adjustments for Recent Events   In normalizing a company's financials, the banker must also make adjustments for recent events, such as M&A transactions, financing activities, conversion of convertible securities, stock splits, or share repurchases in between reporting periods. Therefore, prior to performing trading comps, the banker checks company SEC filings (e.g., 8-Ks, registration statements/prospectuses[51]) and press releases since the most recent reporting period to determine whether the company has announced such activities.

For a recently announced M&A transaction, for example, the company's financial statements must be adjusted accordingly. The balance sheet is adjusted for the effects of the transaction by adding the purchase price financing (including any refinanced or assumed debt), while the LTM income statement is adjusted for the target's incremental sales and earnings. Equity research analysts typically update their estimates for a company's future financial performance promptly following the announcement of an M&A transaction. Therefore, the banker can use updated consensus estimates in combination with the pro forma balance sheet to calculate forward-looking multiples.[52]

Calculation of Key Trading Multiples

Once the key financial statistics are spread, the banker proceeds to calculate the relevant trading multiples for the comparables universe. While various sectors may employ specialized or sector-specific valuation multiples (see Exhibit 1.33), the most generic and widely used multiples employ a measure of market valuation in the numerator (e.g., enterprise value, equity value) and a universal measure of financial performance in the denominator (e.g., EBITDA, net income). For enterprise value multiples, the denominator employs a financial statistic that flows to <u>both</u> debt and equity holders, such as sales, EBITDA, and EBIT. For equity value (or share price) multiples, the denominator must be a financial statistic that flows <u>only</u> to equity holders, such as net income (or diluted EPS). Among these multiples, EV/EBITDA and P/E are the most common.

The following sections provide an overview of the more commonly used equity value and enterprise value multiples.

Equity Value Multiples

Price-to-Earnings Ratio / Equity Value-to-Net Income Multiple The P/E ratio, calculated as current share price divided by diluted EPS (or equity value divided by net income), is the most widely recognized trading multiple. Assuming a constant share count, the P/E ratio is equivalent to equity value-to-net income. These ratios can also

---

[51] A registration statement/prospectus is a filing prepared by an issuer upon the registration/issuance of public securities, including debt and equity. The primary SEC forms for registration statements are S-1, S-3, and S-4; prospectuses are filed pursuant to Rule 424. When a company seeks to register securities with the SEC, it must file a registration statement. Within the registration statement is a preliminary prospectus. Once the registration statement is deemed effective, the company files the final prospectus as a 424 (includes final pricing and other key terms).

[52] As previously discussed, however, the banker needs to confirm beforehand that the estimates have been updated for the announced deal prior to usage. Furthermore, certain analysts may only update NFY estimates on an "as contributed" basis for the incremental earnings from the transaction for the remainder of the fiscal year (as opposed to adding a pro forma full year of earnings).

be viewed as a measure of how much investors are willing to pay for a dollar of a company's current or future earnings. P/E ratios are typically based on forward-year EPS[53] (and, to a lesser extent, LTM EPS) as investors are focused on future growth. Companies with higher P/Es than their peers tend to have higher earnings growth expectations.

The P/E ratio is particularly relevant for mature companies that have a demonstrated ability to consistently grow earnings. However, while the P/E ratio is broadly used and accepted, it has certain limitations. For example, it is not relevant for companies with little or no earnings as the denominator in these instances is *de minimus*, zero, or even negative. In addition, as previously discussed, net income (and EPS) is net of interest expense and, therefore, dependent on capital structure. As a result, two otherwise similar companies in terms of size and operating margins can have substantially different net income margins (and consequently P/E ratios) due to differences in leverage. Similarly, accounting discrepancies, such as for depreciation or taxes, can also produce meaningful disparities in P/E ratios among comparable companies.

The two formulas for calculating the P/E ratio (both equivalent, assuming a constant share count) are shown in Exhibit 1.30.

EXHIBIT 1.30   Equity Value Multiples

$$\frac{\text{Share Price}}{\text{Diluted EPS}} \qquad \frac{\text{Equity Value}}{\text{Net Income}}$$

Enterprise Value Multiples   Given that enterprise value represents the interests of both debt and equity holders, it is used as a multiple of unlevered financial statistics such as sales, EBITDA, and EBIT. The most generic and widely used enterprise value multiples are EV/EBITDA, EV/EBIT, and EV/sales (see Exhibits 1.31 and 1.32). As with P/E ratios, enterprise value multiples tend to focus on forward estimates in addition to LTM statistics for framing valuation.

Enterprise Value-to-EBITDA and Enterprise Value-to-EBIT Multiples   EV/EBITDA serves as a valuation standard for most sectors. It is independent of capital structure and taxes, as well as any distortions that may arise from differences in D&A among different companies. For example, one company may have spent heavily on new machinery and equipment in recent years, resulting in increased D&A for the current and future years, while another company may have deferred its capital spending until a future period. In the interim, this situation would produce disparities in EBIT margins between the two companies that would not be reflected in EBITDA margins.

For the reasons outlined above, as well as potential discrepancies due to acquisition-related amortization, EV/EBIT is less commonly used than EV/EBITDA. However, EV/EBIT may be helpful in situations where D&A is unavailable (e.g., when valuing divisions of public companies) or for companies with high capex.

---

[53]Generally, the earnings for the next two calendar years.

EXHIBIT 1.31 Enterprise Value-to-EBITDA and Enterprise Value-to-EBIT

$$\frac{\text{Enterprise Value}}{\text{EBITDA}} \qquad \frac{\text{Enterprise Value}}{\text{EBIT}}$$

Enterprise Value-to-Sales Multiple EV/sales is also used as a valuation metric, although it is typically less relevant than the other multiples discussed. Sales may provide an indication of size, but it does not necessarily translate into profitability or cash flow generation, both of which are key value drivers. Consequently, EV/sales is used largely as a sanity check on the earnings-based multiples discussed above.

In certain sectors, however, as well as for companies with little or no earnings, EV/sales may be relied upon as a meaningful reference point for valuation. For example, EV/sales may be used to value an early stage technology company that is aggressively growing sales, but has yet to achieve profitability.

EXHIBIT 1.32 Enterprise Value-to-Sales

$$\frac{\text{Enterprise Value}}{\text{Sales}}$$

Sector-Specific Multiples Many sectors employ specific valuation multiples in addition to, or instead of, the traditional metrics previously discussed. These multiples use an indicator of market valuation in the numerator and a key sector-specific financial, operating, or production/capacity statistic in the denominator. Selected examples are shown in Exhibit 1.33.

EXHIBIT 1.33 Selected Sector-Specific Valuation Multiples

Valuation Multiple	Sector
Enterprise Value /	
Access Lines/Fiber Miles/Route Miles	■ Telecommunications
Broadcast Cash Flow ("BCF")	■ Media ■ Telecommunications
Earnings Before Interest Taxes, Depreciation, Amortization, and Rent Expense ("EBITDAR")	■ Casinos ■ Restaurants ■ Retail
Earnings Before Interest Taxes, Depreciation, Depletion, Amortization, and Exploration Expense ("EBITDAX")	■ Natural Resources ■ Oil & Gas
Population ("POP")	■ Telecommunications
Production/Capacity (in units)	■ Metals & Mining ■ Natural Resources ■ Oil & Gas ■ Paper and Forest Products
Reserves	■ Metals & Mining ■ Natural Resources ■ Oil & Gas
Subscriber	■ Media ■ Telecommunications
Square Footage	■ Real Estate ■ Retail
Equity Value (Price) /	
Book Value (per share)	■ Financial Institutions ■ Homebuilders
Cash Available for Distribution (per share)	■ Real Estate
Discretionary Cash Flow (per share)	■ Natural Resources
Funds from Operations ("FFO") (per share)	■ Real Estate
Net Asset Value (NAV) (per share)	■ Financial Institutions ■ Real Estate

STEP IV. BENCHMARK THE COMPARABLE COMPANIES

Once the initial universe of comparable companies is selected and key financial statistics, ratios, and trading multiples are spread, the banker is set to perform benchmarking analysis. Benchmarking centers on analyzing and comparing each of the comparable companies with one another and the target. The ultimate objective is to determine the target's relative ranking so as to frame valuation accordingly. While the entire universe provides a useful perspective, the banker typically hones in on a selected group of closest comparables as the basis for establishing the target's implied valuation range. The closest comparables are generally those most similar to the target in terms of business and financial profile.

We have broken down the benchmarking exercise into a two-stage process. First, we benchmark the key financial statistics and ratios for the target and its comparables in order to establish relative positioning, with a focus on identifying the closest or "best" comparables and noting potential outliers. Second, we analyze and compare the trading multiples for the peer group, placing particular emphasis on the best comparables.

Benchmark the Financial Statistics and Ratios

The first stage of the benchmarking analysis involves a comparison of the target and comparables universe on the basis of key financial performance metrics. These metrics, as captured in the financial profile framework outlined in Steps I and III, include measures of size, profitability, growth, returns, and credit strength. They are core value drivers and typically translate directly into relative valuation.

The results of the benchmarking exercise are displayed on spreadsheet output pages that present the data for each company in an easy-to-compare format (see Exhibits 1.53 and 1.54). These pages also display the mean, median, maximum (high), and minimum (low) for the universe's selected financial statistics and ratios.

A thoughtful benchmarking analysis goes beyond a quantitative comparison of the comparables' financial metrics. In order to truly assess the target's relative strength, the banker needs to have a strong understanding of each comparable company's story. For example, what are the reasons for the company's high or low growth rates and profit margins? Is the company a market leader or laggard, gaining or losing market share? Has the company been successful in delivering upon announced strategic initiatives or meeting earnings guidance? Has the company announced any recent M&A transactions or significant ownership/management changes? The ability to interpret these issues, in combination with the above-mentioned financial analysis, is critical to assessing the performance of the comparable companies and determining the target's relative position.

Benchmark the Trading Multiples

The trading multiples for the comparables universe are also displayed on a spreadsheet output page for easy comparison and analysis (see Exhibit 1.55). This enables the banker to view the full range of multiples and assess relative valuation for each of the comparable companies. As with the financial statistics and ratios, the means, medians, highs, and lows for the range of multiples are calculated and displayed, providing a preliminary reference point for establishing the target's valuation range.

Once the trading multiples have been analyzed, the banker conducts a further refining of the comparables universe. Depending on the resulting output, it may become apparent that certain outliers need to be excluded from the analysis or that the comparables should be further tiered (e.g., on the basis of size, sub-sector, or ranging from closest to peripheral). The trading multiples for the best comparables are also noted as they are typically assigned greater emphasis for framing valuation.

STEP V. DETERMINE VALUATION

The trading multiples for the comparable companies serve as the basis for deriving an appropriate valuation range for the target. The banker typically begins by using the means and medians of the most relevant multiple for the sector (e.g., EV/EBITDA or P/E) to extrapolate a defensible range of multiples. The high and low multiples of the comparables universe provide further guidance. The multiples of the best comparables, however, are typically relied upon as guideposts for selecting the tightest, most appropriate range.

Consequently, as few as two or three carefully selected comparables often serve as the ultimate basis for valuation, with the broader group providing reference points. Hence, the selected multiple range is typically tighter than that implied by simply taking the high and low multiples for the universe. As part of this exercise, the banker must also determine which period financial data is most relevant for calculating the trading multiples. Depending on the sector, point in the business cycle, and comfort with consensus estimates, the comparable companies may be trading on the basis of LTM, one-year forward, or even two-year forward financials.

As shown in the illustrative example in Exhibit 1.34, the target has three closest comparables that trade in the range of approximately 6.0x to 7.0x 2008E EBITDA, versus a high/low range of 5.0x to 8.0x, a mean of 6.5x and a median of 6.4x.

EXHIBIT 1.34   Selected Enterprise Value-to-EBITDA Multiple Range

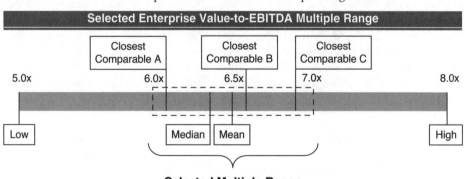

The selected multiple range is then applied to the target's appropriate financial statistics to derive an implied valuation range.

Valuation Implied by EV/EBITDA

Exhibit 1.35 demonstrates how a given EV/EBITDA multiple range translates into an implied range for enterprise value, equity value, and share price. For these calculations, we assume net debt[54] of $500 million and fully diluted shares outstanding of 100 million.[55]

EXHIBIT 1.35   Valuation Implied by EV/EBITDA

($ in millions, except per share data)

EBITDA	Financial Metric	Multiple Range	Implied Enterprise Value	Less: Net Debt	Implied Equity Value	Fully Diluted Shares	Implied Share Price
LTM	$200	6.50x – 7.50x	$1,300 – $1,500	(500)	$800 – $1,000	100	$8.00 – $10.00
2008E	215	6.00x – 7.00x	1,290 – 1,505	(500)	790 – 1,005	100	$7.90 – $10.05
2009E	230	5.50x – 6.50x	1,265 – 1,495	(500)	765 – 995	100	$7.65 – $9.95

At a 6.0x to 7.0x multiple range for 2008E EBITDA, the endpoints are multiplied by the target's 2008E EBITDA of $215 million to produce an implied enterprise value range of $1,290 million to $1,505 million.

To calculate implied equity value, we subtract net debt of $500 million from enterprise value, which results in a range of $790 million to $1,005 million. For public companies, the implied equity value is then divided by fully diluted shares outstanding to yield implied share price. Dividing the endpoints of the equity value range by fully diluted shares outstanding of 100 million provides an implied share price range of $7.90 to $10.05. The same methodology can then be performed using the selected multiple range for EV/LTM EBITDA and EV/2009E EBITDA.

Valuation Implied by P/E

Exhibits 1.36 and 1.37 demonstrate how the P/E ratio translates into implied share price and enterprise value ranges. As with the example in Exhibit 1.35, we assume net debt of $500 million and a static fully diluted shares outstanding count of 100 million.

Implied Share Price   For a public company, the banker typically begins with net income and builds up to implied equity value. The implied equity value is then divided by fully diluted shares outstanding to calculate implied share price. A P/E multiple range of 11.0x to 14.0x 2008E net income, for example, yields an implied equity value of $825 million to $1,050 million when multiplied by the target's 2008E net income of $75 million. Dividing this range by fully diluted shares outstanding of 100 million produces an implied share price range of $8.25 to $10.50.

---

[54] "Net debt" is often defined to include all obligations senior to common equity.

[55] For illustrative purposes, we assume that the number of fully diluted shares outstanding remains constant for each of the equity values presented. As discussed in Chapter 3: Discounted Cash Flow Analysis, however, assuming the existence of stock options, the number of fully diluted shares outstanding as determined by the TSM is dependent on share price, which in turn is dependent on equity value and shares outstanding (see Exhibit 3.31). Therefore, the target's fully diluted shares outstanding and implied share price vary in accordance with its amount of stock options and their weighted average exercise price.

EXHIBIT 1.36   Valuation Implied by P/E – Share Price

($ in millions, except per share data)

Net Income	Financial Metric	Multiple Range		Implied Equity Value		Fully Diluted Shares	Implied Share Price	
LTM	$70	12.00x	– 15.00x	$840	– $1,050	100	$8.40	– $10.50
2008E	75	11.00x	– 14.00x	825	– 1,050	100	$8.25	– $10.50
2009E	80	10.00x	– 13.00x	800	– 1,040	100	$8.00	– $10.40

Implied Enterprise Value   To calculate an implied enterprise value range using the assumptions above, the same P/E multiple range of 11.0x to 14.0x is multiplied by 2008E net income of $75 million to produce an implied equity value range of $825 to $1,050 million. Net debt of $500 million is added to the low and high endpoints of the implied equity value range to calculate an implied enterprise value range of $1,325 million to $1,550 million.

EXHIBIT 1.37   Valuation Implied by P/E – Enterprise Value

($ in millions)

Net Income	Financial Metric	Multiple Range		Implied Equity Value		Plus: Net Debt	Implied Enterprise Value	
LTM	$70	12.00x	– 15.00x	$840	– $1,050	500	$1,340	– $1,550
2008E	75	11.00x	– 14.00x	825	– 1,050	500	1,325	– 1,550
2009E	80	10.00x	– 13.00x	800	– 1,040	500	1,300	– 1,540

As a final consideration, it is necessary to analyze the extrapolated valuation range for the target and test the key assumptions and conclusions. The banker should also compare the valuation derived from comparable companies to other methodologies, such as precedent transactions, DCF analysis, and LBO analysis (if applicable). Significant discrepancies may signal incorrect assumptions, misjudgment, or even mathematical error, thereby prompting the banker to re-examine the inputs and assumptions used in each technique. Common errors in trading comps typically involve the inclusion or over-emphasis of inappropriate comparable companies, incorrect calculations (e.g., fully diluted equity value, enterprise value, LTM financial data, or calendarization), as well as the failure to accurately scrub the financials for non-recurring items and recent events.

KEY PROS AND CONS

Pros

- *Market-based* – information used to derive valuation for the target is based on actual public market data, thereby reflecting the market's growth and risk expectations, as well as overall sentiment

- *Relativity* – easily measurable and comparable versus other companies

- *Quick and convenient* – valuation can be determined on the basis of a few easy-to-calculate inputs

- *Current* – valuation is based on prevailing market data, which can be updated on a daily (or intraday) basis

Cons

- *Market-based* – valuation that is completely market-based can be skewed during periods of irrational exuberance or bearishness

- *Absence of relevant comparables* – "pure play" comparables may be difficult to identify or even non-existent, especially if the target operates in a niche sector, in which case the valuation implied by trading comps may be less meaningful

- *Potential disconnect from cash flow* – valuation based on prevailing market conditions or expectations may have significant disconnect from the valuation implied by a company's projected cash flow generation (e.g., DCF analysis)

- *Company-specific issues* – valuation of the target is based on the valuation of other companies, which may fail to capture target-specific strengths, weaknesses, opportunities, and risks

ILLUSTRATIVE COMPARABLE COMPANIES ANALYSIS FOR VALUECO

The following section provides a detailed, step-by-step example of how comparable companies analysis is used to establish a valuation range using our illustrative target company, ValueCo. As discussed in the Introduction, we assume that ValueCo is a private company and that the financial statistics and valuation multiples throughout the book represent normalized economic and market conditions.

Step I. Select the Universe of Comparable Companies

Study the Target Our first task was to learn ValueCo's "story" in as much detail as possible so as to provide a frame of reference for locating comparable companies. As ValueCo is a private company, for the purposes of this exercise we assumed that it is being sold through an organized M&A sale process (see Chapter 6). Therefore, we were provided with substantive information on the company, its sector, products, customers, competitors, distribution channels, and end markets, as well as historical financial performance and projections. We sourced this information from the confidential information memorandum (CIM, see Exhibit 6.5), management presentation (see Exhibit 6.6), and data room (see Exhibit 6.7).[56]

Identify Key Characteristics of the Target for Comparison Purposes This exercise involved examining ValueCo's key business and financial characteristics in accordance with the framework outlined in Exhibit 1.3, which provided us with a systematic approach for identifying companies that shared key similarities with ValueCo.

Screen for Comparable Companies Our search for comparable companies began by examining ValueCo's public competitors, which we initially identified by perusing the CIM as well as selected industry reports. We then searched through equity research reports on these public competitors for the analysts' views on comparable companies, which provided us with additional companies to evaluate. We also reviewed the proxy statements for recent M&A transactions involving companies in ValueCo's sector, and found ideas for additional comparable companies from the enclosed fairness opinion excerpts. To ensure that no potential comparables were missed, we screened companies using SIC/NAICS codes corresponding to ValueCo's sector.

These sources provided us with enough information to create a solid initial list of comparable companies (see Exhibit 1.38). We also compiled summary financial information using data downloaded from a financial information service in order to provide a basic understanding of their financial profiles.

---

[56] See Chapter 6: M&A Sale Process for an overview of the key documents and sources of information in an organized sale process.

EXHIBIT 1.38 List of Comparable Companies

($ in millions)

List of Comparable Companies					
Company	Ticker	Business Description	Equity Value	Enterprise Value	LTM Sales
Vucic Brands	VUC	Manufactures and sells home and hardware products including cabinetry, faucets, plumbing accessories, windows, and doors	$8,829	$14,712	$8,670
Pearl Corp.	PRL	Manufactures and distributes building products in North America and internationally, including roofing, siding, and windows	8,850	11,323	12,750
Spalding Co.	SLD	Manufactures and distributes paints, coatings, brushes, and related products to professional, industrial, commercial, and retail customers	7,781	8,369	8,127
Leicht & Co.	LCT	Designs, manufactures, and sells floor covering products for residential and commercial applications	7,456	9,673	8,109
Drook Corp.	DRK	Manufactures and markets power tools and accessories, hardware, and doors in the United States and Europe	5,034	6,161	6,708
Goodson Corp.	GDS	Manufactures and markets gypsum, ceiling systems, cabinets, and doors	4,368	5,534	6,125
The DiNucci Group	TDG	Produces residential and commercial building materials, glass fiber reinforcements, and other similar materials for composite systems	3,772	5,202	6,489
Pryor, Inc.	PRI	Designs, manufactures, and markets tools, diagnostics, construction equipment, and engineered products, primarily in the United States and Europe	3,484	4,764	4,223
Adler Industries	ADL	Manufactures and sells roofing and siding products primarily in the United States	2,600	3,149	3,895
Lanzarone International	LNZ	Designs and manufactures a wide variety of products for commercial and residential heating, ventilation, and air conditioning	1,750	2,139	2,286
Lajoux Global	LJX	Manufactures a range of products for residential heating, ventilation, air conditioning, and refrigeration markets in the United States and Europe	1,050	1,650	1,775
Momper Corp.	MOMP	Manufactures, distributes, and installs home improvement and building products	1,000	1,500	1,415
McMenamin & Co.	MCM	Manufactures and markets a variety of building products, including screw fastening systems, stainless steel fasteners, and venting systems	630	705	571
Trip Co.	TRIP	Manufactures and distributes composite products primarily for residential and commercial decking and railing applications in North America	321	441	486
Paris Industries	PRS	Manufactures and supplies residential windows, doors, and other accessories	156	192	352

Step II. Locate the Necessary Financial Information

In Step II, we set out to locate the financial information necessary to spread the key financial statistics and ratios for each of the companies that we identified as being comparable to ValueCo. For Momper Corp. ("Momper"), one of ValueCo's closest comparables, for example, this information was obtained from its most recent SEC filings, consensus estimates, and equity research. Additional financial information was sourced from financial information services.

10-K and 10-Q We used Momper's most recent 10-K and 10-Q for the periods ending December 31, 2007, and September 30, 2008, respectively, as the primary sources for historical financial information. Specifically, these filings provided us with the prior year annual as well as current and prior year YTD financial statistics necessary to calculate LTM data. They also served as sources for the most recent basic shares outstanding count, options/warrants data, and balance sheet and cash flow statement information. The MD&A and notes to the financials were key for identifying non-recurring items (see Exhibit 1.47).

Earnings Announcement and Earnings Call Transcript   We read through the most recent earnings announcement and earnings call transcript to gain further insight on Momper's financial performance and outlook.

8-K/Press Releases   We confirmed via a search of Momper's corporate website that there were no intra-quarter press releases, 8-Ks, or other SEC filings disclosing new M&A, capital markets, or other activities since the filing of its most recent 10-Q that would affect the relevant financial statistics.

Consensus Estimates and Equity Research   Consensus estimates formed the basis for the 2008E and 2009E income statement inputs, namely sales, EBITDA, EBIT, and EPS. We also read individual equity research reports for further color on factors driving Momper's growth expectations as well as insights on non-recurring items.

Financial Information Service   We used a financial information service to source Momper's closing share price on December 15, 2008 (the day we performed the analysis), as well as its 52-week high and low share price data.

Moody's and S&P Websites   We obtained Momper's, Moody's, and S&P credit ratings from the respective credit rating agencies' websites.

Step III. Spread Key Statistics, Ratios, and Trading Multiples

After locating the necessary financial information for the selected comparable companies, we created input sheets for each company, as shown in Exhibit 1.39 for Momper. These input sheets link to the output pages used for benchmarking the comparables universe (see Exhibits 1.53, 1.54, and 1.55).

Below, we walk through each section of the input sheet in Exhibit 1.39.

General Information   In the "General Information" section of the input page, we entered various basic company data (see Exhibit 1.40). Momper Corp., ticker symbol MOMP, is a U.S.-based company that is listed on the NASDAQ. Momper reports its financial results based on a fiscal year ending December 31 and has corporate credit ratings of Ba2 and BB as rated by Moody's and S&P, respectively. Momper's predicted levered beta is 1.25, as sourced from Barra (see Chapter 3). We also determined a marginal tax rate of 38% from Momper's tax rate disclosures in its 10-K.

Selected Market Data   Under "Selected Market Data," we entered Momper's share price information as well as the most recent quarterly (MRQ) dividend paid of $0.10 per share (as sourced from the latest 10-Q, see Exhibit 1.41). Momper's share price was $20.00 as of market close on December 15, 2008, representing 80% of its 52-week high. As the trading multiples benchmarking output page shows (see Exhibit 1.55), this percentage is consistent with that of most of the comparables, which indicates that the market expects Momper to perform roughly in line with its peers.

EXHIBIT 1.39 Input Page for Momper Corp.

Momper Corp. (NasdaqNM:MOMP)
Input Page
($ in millions; except per share data)

General Information

Company Name	Momper Corp.
Ticker	MOMP
Stock Exchange	NasdaqNM
Fiscal Year Ending	Dec-31
Moody's Corporate Rating	Ba2
S&P Corporate Rating	BB
Predicted Beta	1.25
Marginal Tax Rate	38.0%

Selected Market Data

Current Price	12/15/2006	$20.00
% of 52-week High		80.0%
52-week High Price	7/21/2008	25.00
52-week Low Price	4/4/2008	16.00
Dividend Per Share (MRQ)		0.10
Fully Diluted Shares Outstanding		50.000
Equity Value		$1,000.0
Plus: Total Debt		550.0
Plus: Preferred Stock		-
Plus: Noncontrolling Interest		-
Less: Cash and Cash Equivalents		(50.0)
Enterprise Value		$1,500.0

Trading Multiples

	LTM 9/30/2008	NFY 2008E	NFY+1 2009E
EV/Sales	1.1x	1.0x	0.9x
Metric	$1,415.0	$1,475.0	$1,600.0
EV/EBITDA	7.0x	6.7x	6.3x
Metric	$215.0	$225.0	$240.0
EV/EBIT	8.6x	8.1x	7.5x
Metric	$175.0	$185.0	$200.0
P/E	11.8x	11.1x	10.0x
Metric	$1.70	$1.80	$2.00

LTM Return on Investment Ratios

Return on Invested Capital	15.8%
Return on Equity	14.6%
Return on Assets	6.1%
Implied Annual Dividend Yield	2.0%

LTM Credit Statistics

Total Debt / Total Capitalization	47.8%
Total Debt / EBITDA	2.6x
Net Debt / EBITDA	2.3x
EBITDA / Interest Expense	5.7x
(EBITDA-capex) / Interest Expense	4.9x
EBIT / Interest Expense	4.6x

Growth Rates

	Sales	Adj. EBITDA	Adj. EPS
Historical			
1-year	8.0%	8.1%	17.2%
2-year CAGR	8.3%	7.5%	17.6%
Estimated			
1-year	9.3%	12.5%	17.1%
2-year CAGR	8.9%	9.5%	14.1%
Long-term			15.0%

Reported Income Statement

	Fiscal Year Ending December 31			Prior Stub 9/30/2007	Current Stub 9/30/2008	LTM 9/30/2008
	2005A	2006A	2007A			
Sales	$1,150.0	$1,250.0	$1,350.0	$1,000.0	$1,065.0	$1,415.0
COGS	760.0	825.0	875.0	660.0	700.0	915.0
Gross Profit	$390.0	$425.0	$475.0	$340.0	$365.0	$500.0
SG&A	250.0	275.0	300.0	220.0	255.0	335.0
Other Expense / (Income)	-	-	-	-	-	-
EBIT	$140.0	$150.0	$175.0	$120.0	$110.0	$165.0
Interest Expense	45.0	40.0	38.5	30.0	29.4	37.9
Pre-tax Income	$95.0	$110.0	$136.5	$90.0	$80.6	$127.1
Income Taxes	36.1	41.8	51.9	34.2	30.6	48.3
Noncontrolling Interest	-	-	-	-	-	-
Preferred Dividends	-	-	-	-	-	-
Net Income	$58.9	$68.2	$84.6	$55.8	$50.0	$78.8
Effective Tax Rate	38.0%	38.0%	38.0%	38.0%	38.0%	38.0%
Weighted Avg. Diluted Shares	53.0	52.0	51.0	51.0	50.0	50.0
Diluted EPS	$1.11	$1.31	$1.66	$1.09	$1.00	$1.56

Adjusted Income Statement

	2005A	2006A	2007A	Prior Stub 9/30/2007	Current Stub 9/30/2008	LTM 9/30/2008
Reported Gross Profit	$390.0	$425.0	$475.0	$340.0	$365.0	$500.0	
Non-recurring Items in COGS	-	-	(10.0)	-	8.0	8.0	(1)
Adj. Gross Profit	$390.0	$425.0	$475.0	$340.0	$373.0	$508.0	
% margin	33.9%	34.0%	35.2%	34.0%	35.0%	35.9%	
Reported EBIT	$140.0	$150.0	$175.0	$120.0	$110.0	$165.0	
Non-recurring Items in COGS	-	-	(10.0)	-	8.0	8.0	
Other Non-recurring Items	-	-	-	-	12.0	2.0	(2), (3)
Adjusted EBIT	$140.0	$150.0	$165.0	$120.0	$130.0	$175.0	
% margin	12.2%	12.0%	12.2%	12.0%	12.2%	12.4%	
Depreciation & Amortization	33.0	35.0	35.0	30.0	35.0	40.0	
Adjusted EBITDA	$173.0	$185.0	$200.0	$150.0	$165.0	$215.0	
% margin	15.0%	14.8%	14.8%	15.0%	15.5%	15.2%	
Reported Net Income	$58.9	$68.2	$84.6	$55.8	$50.0	$78.8	
Non-recurring Items in COGS	-	-	(10.0)	-	8.0	8.0	
Other Non-recurring Items	-	-	-	-	12.0	2.0	
Non-operating Non-rec. Items	-	-	-	-	-	-	
Tax Adjustment	-	-	3.8	-	(7.6)	(3.8)	
Adjusted Net Income	$58.9	$68.2	$78.4	$55.8	$62.4	$85.0	
% margin	5.1%	5.5%	5.8%	5.6%	5.9%	6.0%	
Adjusted Diluted EPS	$1.11	$1.31	$1.54	$1.09	$1.25	$1.70	

Cash Flow Statement Data

	2005A	2006A	2007A	Prior Stub 9/30/2007	Current Stub 9/30/2008	LTM 9/30/2008
Depreciation & Amortization	33.0	35.0	35.0	30.0	35.0	40.0
% sales	2.9%	2.8%	2.6%	3.0%	3.3%	2.8%
Capital Expenditures	25.0	27.5	29.0	22.0	23.0	30.0
% sales	2.2%	2.2%	2.1%	2.2%	2.2%	2.1%

Notes

(1) In Q2 2008, Momper Corp. recorded a $8 million pre-tax inventory valuation charge related to product obsolescence (see Q2 2008 10-Q MD&A, page 14).
(2) In Q4 2007, Momper Corp. realized a $10 million pre-tax gain on the sale of a non-core business (see 2007 10-K MD&A, page 45).
(3) In Q3 2008, Momper Corp. recognized $12 million of pre-tax restructuring costs in connection with downsizing the sales force (see Q3 2008 10-Q MD&A, page 15).

Business Description

Manufactures, distributes, and installs home improvement and building products

Balance Sheet Data

	2007A	9/30/2008
Cash and Cash Equivalents	$25.0	$50.0
Accounts Receivable	250.0	275.0
Inventories	200.0	217.0
Prepaids and Other Current Assets	35.0	30.0
Total Current Assets	$510.0	$572.0
Property, Plant and Equipment, net	205.0	193.0
Goodwill and Intangible Assets	600.0	600.0
Other Assets	45.0	40.0
Total Assets	$1,360.0	$1,405.0
Accounts Payable	95.0	110.0
Accrued Liabilities	85.0	95.0
Other Current Liabilities	15.0	20.0
Total Current Liabilities	$195.0	$225.0
Total Debt	575.0	550.0
Other Long-Term Liabilities	25.0	30.0
Total Liabilities	$795.0	$805.0
Noncontrolling Interest	-	-
Preferred Stock	-	-
Shareholders' Equity	565.0	600.0
Total Liabilities and Equity	$1,360.0	$1,405.0
Balance Check	0.000	0.000

Calculation of Fully Diluted Shares Outstanding

Basic Shares Outstanding	48.500
Plus: Shares from In-the-Money Options	2.750
Less: Shares Repurchased	(1.250)
Net New Shares from Options	1.500
Plus: Shares from Convertible Securities	-
Fully Diluted Shares Outstanding	50.000

Options/Warrants

Tranche	Number of Shares	Exercise Price	In-the-Money Shares	Proceeds
Tranche 1	1.250	$5.00	1.250	$6.3
Tranche 2	1.000	10.00	1.000	10.0
Tranche 3	0.500	17.50	0.500	8.8
Tranche 4	0.250	30.00	-	-
Tranche 5	-	-	-	-
Total	3.000		2.750	$25.0

Convertible Securities

	Amount	Conversion Price	Conversion Ratio	New Shares
Issue 1				
Issue 2				
Issue 3				
Issue 4				
Issue 5				
Total				

EXHIBIT 1.40   General Information Section

General Information	
Company Name	Momper Corp.
Ticker	MOMP
Stock Exchange	NasdaqNM
Fiscal Year Ending	Dec-31
Moody's Corporate Rating	Ba2
S&P Corporate Rating	BB
Predicted Beta	1.25
Marginal Tax Rate	*38.0%*

This section also calculates equity value and enterprise value once the appropriate basic shares outstanding count, options/warrants data, and most recent balance sheet data is entered (see Exhibits 1.42, 1.43, 1.44, and 1.45).

EXHIBIT 1.41   Selected Market Data Section

Selected Market Data			
Current Price	12/15/2008	$20.00	← = Closing Share Price on December 15, 2008
% of 52-week High		*80.0%*	← = Closing Share Price / 52-week High Price
52-week High Price	7/21/2008	25.00	
52-week Low Price	4/4/2008	16.00	
Dividend Per Share (MRQ)		0.10	
Fully Diluted Shares Outstanding		-	
Equity Value		**-**	
Plus: Total Debt		-	
Plus: Preferred Stock		-	
Plus: Noncontrolling Interest		-	
Less: Cash and Cash Equivalents		-	
Enterprise Value		**-**	

Calculation of Fully Diluted Shares Outstanding   Momper's most recent basic shares outstanding count is 48.5 million, as sourced from the first page of its latest 10-Q. We searched recent press releases and SEC filings to ensure that no stock splits, follow-on offerings, or major share buybacks, for example, took place following the most recent 10-Q filing. We also confirmed that Momper does not have convertible securities outstanding. However, Momper has several tranches of options, which must be reflected in the calculation of fully diluted shares in accordance with the TSM.

As shown in Exhibit 1.42 under the "Options/Warrants" heading, Momper has four tranches of options, each consisting of a specified number of shares and corresponding weighted average exercise price. The first tranche, for example, represents a group of options collectively owning the right to buy 1.25 million shares at a weighted average exercise price of $5.00. This tranche is deemed in-the-money given that Momper's current share price of $20.00 is above the weighted average strike price. The exercise of this tranche generates proceeds of $6.25 million (1.25 million × $5.00), which are assumed to repurchase Momper shares at the current share price of $20.00.

EXHIBIT 1.42 Calculation of Fully Diluted Shares Outstanding Section

Calculation of Fully Diluted Shares Outstanding					
Basic Shares Outstanding				48.500	= Total In-the-Money Shares
Plus: Shares from In-the-Money Options				2.750	
Less: Shares Repurchased				(1.250)	= Total Options Proceeds / Current Share Price
Net New Shares from Options				1.500	= $25 million / $20.00
Plus: Shares from Convertible Securities				-	
Fully Diluted Shares Outstanding				50.000	

Options/Warrants

Tranche	Number of Shares	Exercise Price	In-the-Money Shares	Proceeds	
Tranche 1	1.250	$5.00	1.250	$6.3	= IF(Weighted Average Strike Price < Current Share Price, display Number of Shares, otherwise display 0)
Tranche 2	1.000	10.00	1.000	10.0	= IF($5.00 < $20.00, 1.250, 0)
Tranche 3	0.500	17.50	0.500	8.8	
Tranche 4	0.250	30.00	-	-	
Tranche 5	-	-	-	-	
Total	3.000		2.750	$25.0	= IF(In-the-Money Shares > 0, then In-the-Money Shares x Weighted Average Strike Price, otherwise display 0)

= IF(1.250 > 0, 1.250 x $5.00, 0)

Convertible Securities

	Amount	Conversion Price	Conversion Ratio	New Shares
Issue 1	-	-	-	-
Issue 2	-	-	-	-
Issue 3	-	-	-	-
Issue 4	-	-	-	-
Issue 5	-	-	-	-
Total				-

We utilized this same approach for the other tranches of options. The fourth tranche, however, has a weighted average exercise price of $30.00 (above the current share price of $20.00) and was therefore identified as out-of-the-money. Consequently, these options were excluded from the calculation of fully diluted shares outstanding.

In aggregate, the 2.75 million shares from the in-the-money options generate proceeds of $25 million. At Momper's current share price of $20.00, these proceeds are used to repurchase 1.25 million shares ($25 million/$20.00). The repurchased shares are then subtracted from the 2.75 million total in-the-money shares to provide net new shares of 1.5 million, as shown under the net new shares from options line item in Exhibit 1.42. These incremental shares are added to Momper's basic shares to calculate fully diluted shares outstanding of 50 million.

Equity Value The 50 million fully diluted shares outstanding output feeds into the "Selected Market Data" section, where it is multiplied by Momper's current share price of $20.00 to produce an equity value of $1,000 million (see Exhibit 1.43). This calculated equity value forms the basis for calculating enterprise value.

Balance Sheet Data In the "Balance Sheet Data" section, we entered Momper's balance sheet data for the prior fiscal year ending 12/31/07 and the most recent quarter ending 9/30/08, as sourced directly from its 10-Q (see Exhibit 1.44).

Enterprise Value We used selected balance sheet data, specifically total debt and cash, together with the previously calculated equity value to determine Momper's enterprise value. As shown in Exhibit 1.45, Momper had $550 million of total debt outstanding and cash and cash equivalents of $50 million as of 9/30/08. The net debt

EXHIBIT 1.43   Equity Value

Selected Market Data		
Current Price	12/15/2008	$20.00
% of 52-week High		*80.0%*
52-week High Price	7/21/2008	25.00
52-week Low Price	4/4/2008	16.00
Dividend Per Share (MRQ)		0.10
Fully Diluted Shares Outstanding		50.000
Equity Value		**$1,000.0**

= Current Share Price x Fully Diluted Shares Outstanding
= $20.00 x 50.0 million

EXHIBIT 1.44   Balance Sheet Data Section

Balance Sheet Data		
	2007A	**9/30/2008**
Cash and Cash Equivalents	$25.0	$50.0
Accounts Receivable	250.0	275.0
Inventories	200.0	217.0
Prepaids and Other Current Assets	35.0	30.0
Total Current Assets	**$510.0**	**$572.0**
Property, Plant and Equipment, net	205.0	193.0
Goodwill and Intangible Assets	600.0	600.0
Other Assets	45.0	40.0
Total Assets	**$1,360.0**	**$1,405.0**
Accounts Payable	95.0	110.0
Accrued Liabilities	85.0	95.0
Other Current Liabilities	15.0	20.0
Total Current Liabilities	**$195.0**	**$225.0**
Total Debt	575.0	550.0
Other Long-Term Liabilities	25.0	30.0
Total Liabilities	**$795.0**	**$805.0**
Noncontrolling Interest	-	-
Preferred Stock	-	-
Shareholders' Equity	565.0	600.0
Total Liabilities and Equity	**$1,360.0**	**$1,405.0**
Balance Check	*0.000*	*0.000*

balance of $500 million was added to equity value of $1,000 million to produce an enterprise value of $1,500 million.

Reported Income Statement   In the "Reported Income Statement" section, we entered the historical income statement items directly from Momper's most recent 10-K and 10-Q. The LTM column automatically calculates Momper's LTM financial data on the basis of the prior annual year, and the prior and current year stub inputs (see Exhibit 1.46).

EXHIBIT 1.45 Enterprise Value

Selected Market Data		
Current Price	12/15/2008	$20.00
% of 52-week High		80.0%
52-week High Price	7/21/2008	25.00
52-week Low Price	4/4/2008	16.00
Dividend Per Share (MRQ)		0.10
Fully Diluted Shares Outstanding		50.000
Equity Value		**$1,000.0**
Plus: Total Debt		550.0
Plus: Preferred Stock		-
Plus: Noncontrolling Interest		-
Less: Cash and Cash Equivalents		(50.0)
Enterprise Value		**$1,500.0**

= Equity Value + Total Debt - Cash
= $1,000.0 million + $550.0 million - $50.0 million

EXHIBIT 1.46 Reported Income Statement Section

Reported Income Statement				Prior Stub	Current Stub	LTM
	Fiscal Year Ending December 31			9/30/2007	9/30/2008	9/30/2008
	2005A	2006A	2007A			
Sales	$1,150.0	$1,250.0	$1,350.0	$1,000.0	$1,065.0	$1,415.0
COGS	760.0	825.0	875.0	660.0	700.0	915.0
Gross Profit	$390.0	$425.0	$475.0	$340.0	$365.0	$500.0
SG&A	250.0	275.0	300.0	220.0	255.0	335.0
Other Expense / (Income)	-	-	-	-	-	-
EBIT	$140.0	$150.0	$175.0	$120.0	$110.0	$165.0
Interest Expense	45.0	40.0	38.5	30.0	29.4	37.9
Pre-tax Income	$95.0	$110.0	$136.5	$90.0	$80.6	$127.1
Income Taxes	36.1	41.8	51.9	34.2	30.6	48.3
Noncontrolling Interest	-	-	-	-	-	-
Preferred Dividends	-	-	-	-	-	-
Net Income	$58.9	$68.2	$84.6	$55.8	$50.0	$78.8
Effective Tax Rate	38.0%	38.0%	38.0%	38.0%	38.0%	38.0%
Weighted Avg. Diluted Shares	53.0	52.0	51.0	51.0	50.0	50.0
Diluted EPS	$1.11	$1.31	$1.66	$1.09	$1.00	$1.56

= Prior Fiscal Year + Current Stub - Prior Stub
= $1,350.0 million + $1,065.0 million - $1,000.0 million

Adjusted Income Statement After entering the reported income statement, we made adjustments in the "Adjusted Income Statement" section, as appropriate, for those items we determined to be non-recurring (see Exhibit 1.47), namely:

- $10 million pre-tax gain on the sale of a non-core business in Q4 2007

- $8 million pre-tax inventory valuation charge in Q2 2008 related to product obsolescence

- $12 million pre-tax restructuring charge in Q3 2008 related to severance costs

As the adjustments for non-recurring items relied on judgment, we carefully footnoted our assumptions and sources.

EXHIBIT 1.47   Adjusted Income Statement Section

| Inventory valuation charge ("write-off") |
| Gain on sale of non-core business ("asset sale") | Restructuring charge |

Adjusted Income Statement				Prior Stub	Current Stub	LTM
	Fiscal Year Ending December 31			9/30/2007	9/30/2008	9/30/2008
	2005A	**2006A**	**2007A**			
Reported Gross Profit	$390.0	$425.0	$475.0	$340.0	$365.0	$500.0	
Non-recurring Items in COGS	-	-	-	-	8.0	8.0	(1)
Adj. Gross Profit	**$390.0**	**$425.0**	**$475.0**	**$340.0**	**$373.0**	**$508.0**	
% margin	*33.9%*	*34.0%*	*35.2%*	*34.0%*	*35.0%*	*35.9%*	
Reported EBIT	$140.0	$150.0	$175.0	$120.0	$110.0	$165.0	
Non-recurring Items in COGS	-	-	-	-	8.0	8.0	
Other Non-recurring Items	-	-	(10.0)	-	12.0	2.0	(2), (3)
Adjusted EBIT	**$140.0**	**$150.0**	**$165.0**	**$120.0**	**$130.0**	**$175.0**	
% margin	*12.2%*	*12.0%*	*12.2%*	*12.0%*	*12.2%*	*12.4%*	
Depreciation & Amortization	33.0	35.0	35.0	30.0	35.0	40.0	
Adjusted EBITDA	**$173.0**	**$185.0**	**$200.0**	**$150.0**	**$165.0**	**$215.0**	
% margin	*15.0%*	*14.8%*	*14.8%*	*15.0%*	*15.5%*	*15.2%*	
Reported Net Income	$58.9	$68.2	$84.6	$55.8	$50.0	$78.8	
Non-recurring Items in COGS	-	-	-	-	8.0	8.0	
Other Non-recurring Items	-	-	(10.0)	-	12.0	2.0	
Non-operating Non-rec. Items	-	-	-	-	-	-	
Tax Adjustment	-	-	3.8	-	(7.6)	(3.8)	
Adjusted Net Income	**$58.9**	**$68.2**	**$78.4**	**$55.8**	**$62.4**	**$85.0**	
% margin	*5.1%*	*5.5%*	*5.8%*	*5.6%*	*5.9%*	*6.0%*	
Adjusted Diluted EPS	$1.11	$1.31	$1.54	$1.09	$1.25	$1.70	

Notes
(1) In Q2 2008, Momper Corp. recorded a $8 million pre-tax inventory valuation charge related to product obsolescence (see Q2 2008 10-Q MD&A, page 14).
(2) In Q4 2007, Momper Corp. realized a $10 million pre-tax gain on the sale of a non-core business (see 2007 10-K MD&A, page 45).
(3) In Q3 2008, Momper Corp. recognized $12 million of pre-tax restructuring costs in connection with downsizing the sales force (see Q3 2008 10-Q MD&A, page 15).

= Negative adjustment for pre-tax gain on asset sale x Marginal tax rate
= - ($10.0) million x 38.0%

= Add-back for pre-tax inventory and restructuring charges x Marginal tax rate
= - ($8.0 million + $12.0 million) x 38.0%

As shown in Exhibit 1.47, we entered the $8 million non-recurring product obsolescence charge as an add-back in the non-recurring items in COGS line item under the "Current Stub 9/30/2008" column heading; we also added back the $12 million restructuring charge in the other non-recurring items line under the "Current Stub 9/30/2008" column. The $10 million gain on asset sale, on the other hand, was backed out of reported earnings (entered as a negative value) under the "2007A" column. These calculations resulted in adjusted LTM EBIT and EBITDA of $175 million and $215 million, respectively.

To calculate LTM adjusted net income after adding back the full non-recurring charges of $8 million and $12 million, respectively, and subtracting the full $10.0 million gain on sale amount, we made tax adjustments in the tax adjustment line item. These adjustments were calculated by multiplying each full amount by Momper's marginal tax rate of 38%. This resulted in adjusted net income and diluted EPS of $85 million and $1.70, respectively.

The adjusted financial statistics then served as the basis for calculating the various LTM profitability ratios, credit statistics, and trading multiples used in the benchmarking analysis (see Exhibits 1.53, 1.54, and 1.55).

Cash Flow Statement Data Momper's historical D&A and capex were entered directly into the input page as they appeared in its 10-K and 10-Q (see Exhibit 1.48).

EXHIBIT 1.48 Cash Flow Statement Data Section

Cash Flow Statement Data						
	Fiscal Year Ending December 31			Prior Stub	Current Stub	LTM
	2005A	2006A	2007A	9/30/2007	9/30/2008	9/30/2008
Depreciation & Amortization	33.0	35.0	35.0	30.0	35.0	40.0
% sales	2.9%	2.8%	2.6%	3.0%	3.3%	2.8%
Capital Expenditures	25.0	27.5	29.0	22.0	23.0	30.0
% sales	2.2%	2.2%	2.1%	2.2%	2.2%	2.1%

LTM Return on Investment Ratios

Return on Invested Capital For ROIC, we calculated 15.8% by dividing Momper's LTM 9/30/08 adjusted EBIT of $175 million (as calculated in Exhibit 1.47) by the sum of its average net debt and shareholders' equity balances for the periods ending 12/31/07 and 9/30/08 (see Exhibit 1.49).

Return on Equity For ROE, we calculated 14.6% by dividing Momper's LTM 9/30/08 adjusted net income of $85 million (as calculated in Exhibit 1.47) by its average shareholders' equity balance for the periods ending 12/31/07 and 9/30/08 (($565 million + $600 million) / 2).

Return on Assets For ROA, we calculated 6.1% by dividing Momper's LTM 9/30/08 adjusted net income of $85 million by its average total assets for the periods ending 12/31/07 and 9/30/08 (($1,360 million + $1,405 million) / 2).

Dividend Yield To calculate dividend yield, we annualized Momper's dividend payment of $0.10 per share for the most recent quarter (see Exhibit 1.41), which implied an annual dividend payment of $0.40 per share. We checked recent press releases to ensure there were no changes in dividend policy after the filing of the 10-Q. The implied annualized dividend payment of $0.40 per share was then divided by Momper's current share price of $20.00 to calculate an implied annual dividend yield of 2%.

LTM Credit Statistics

Debt-to-Total Capitalization For debt-to-total capitalization, we divided Momper's total debt of $550 million as of 9/30/08 by the sum of its total debt and

EXHIBIT 1.49 LTM Return on Investment Ratios Section

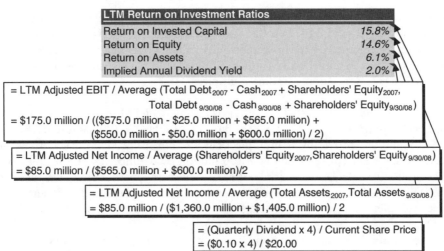

LTM Return on Investment Ratios	
Return on Invested Capital	*15.8%*
Return on Equity	*14.6%*
Return on Assets	*6.1%*
Implied Annual Dividend Yield	*2.0%*

= LTM Adjusted EBIT / Average (Total Debt$_{2007}$ - Cash$_{2007}$ + Shareholders' Equity$_{2007}$,
Total Debt$_{9/30/08}$ - Cash$_{9/30/08}$ + Shareholders' Equity$_{9/30/08}$)
= \$175.0 million / ((\$575.0 million - \$25.0 million + \$565.0 million) +
(\$550.0 million - \$50.0 million + \$600.0 million) / 2)

= LTM Adjusted Net Income / Average (Shareholders' Equity$_{2007}$, Shareholders' Equity$_{9/30/08}$)
= \$85.0 million / (\$565.0 million + \$600.0 million)/2

= LTM Adjusted Net Income / Average (Total Assets$_{2007}$, Total Assets$_{9/30/08}$)
= \$85.0 million / (\$1,360.0 million + \$1,405.0 million) / 2

= (Quarterly Dividend x 4) / Current Share Price
= (\$0.10 x 4) / \$20.00

shareholders' equity for the same period (\$550 million + \$600 million). This provided a debt-to-total capitalization ratio of 47.8% (see Exhibit 1.50).

Total Debt-to-EBITDA For total debt-to-EBITDA, we divided Momper's total debt of \$550 million by its LTM 9/30/08 adjusted EBITDA of \$215 million. This provided a total leverage multiple of 2.6x (2.3x on a net debt basis).

EBITDA-to-Interest Expense For EBITDA-to-interest expense, we divided Momper's LTM 9/30/08 adjusted EBITDA of \$215 million by its interest expense of \$37.9 million for the same period. This provided a ratio of 5.7x. We also calculated Momper's (EBITDA – capex)-to-interest expense and EBIT-to-interest expense ratios at 4.9x and 4.6x, respectively.

EXHIBIT 1.50 LTM Credit Statistics Section

LTM Credit Statistics	
Total Debt / Total Capitalization	47.8%
Total Debt / EBITDA	2.6x
Net Debt / EBITDA	2.3x
EBITDA / Interest Expense	5.7x
(EBITDA-capex) / Interest Expense	4.9x
EBIT / Interest Expense	4.6x

= Total Debt$_{9/30/08}$ / (Total Debt$_{9/30/08}$ + Shareholders' Equity$_{9/30/08}$)
= \$550.0 million / (\$550.0 million + \$600.0 million)

= Total Debt$_{9/30/08}$ / LTM Adjusted EBITDA
= \$550.0 million / \$215.0 million

= (Total Debt$_{9/30/08}$ - Cash$_{9/30/08}$) / LTM Adjusted EBITDA
= (\$550.0 million - \$50.0 million) / \$215.0 million

= LTM Adjusted EBITDA / LTM Interest Expense
= \$215.0 million / \$37.9 million

Trading Multiples

In the "Trading Multiples" section, we entered consensus estimates for Momper's 2008E and 2009E sales, EBITDA, EBIT, and EPS (see Exhibit 1.51). These estimates, along with the calculated enterprise and equity values, were used to calculate forward trading multiples. Momper's LTM adjusted financial data is also linked to this section and used to calculate trailing trading multiples.

Enterprise Value Multiples For enterprise value-to-LTM EBITDA, we divided Momper's enterprise value of $1,500 million by its LTM 9/30/08 adjusted EBITDA of $215 million, providing a multiple of 7.0x. For EV/2008E EBITDA, we divided the same enterprise value of $1,500 million by Momper's 2008E EBITDA of $225 million to calculate a multiple of 6.7x. This same methodology was used for EV/2009E EBITDA as well as for the trailing and forward sales and EBIT enterprise value multiples.

Price-to-Earnings Ratio The approach for calculating P/E mirrors that for EV/EBITDA. We divided Momper's current share price of $20.00 by its LTM, 2008E, and 2009E EPS of $1.70, $1.80, and $2.00, respectively. These calculations provided P/E ratios of 11.8x, 11.1x, and 10.0x, respectively.

EXHIBIT 1.51 Trading Multiples Section

Trading Multiples			
	LTM 9/30/2008	NFY 2008E	NFY+1 2009E
EV/Sales	1.1x	1.0x	0.9x
Metric	$1,415.0	$1,475.0	$1,600.0
EV/EBITDA	7.0x	6.7x	6.3x
Metric	$215.0	$225.0	$240.0
EV/EBIT	8.6x	8.1x	7.5x
Metric	$175.0	$185.0	$200.0
P/E	11.8x	11.1x	10.0x
Metric	$1.70	$1.80	$2.00

= Enterprise Value / LTM Sales
= $1,500.0 million / $1,415.0 million

= Enterprise Value / 2008E EBITDA
= $1,500.0 million / $225.0 million

= Current Share Price / 2009E EPS
= $20.00 / $2.00

Growth Rates

In the "Growth Rates" section, we calculated Momper's historical and estimated growth rates for sales, EBITDA, and EPS for various periods. For historical data, we used the adjusted income statement financials from Exhibit 1.47. As shown in Exhibit 1.52, Momper's EPS grew 17.2% from 2006 to 2007 (1-year historical growth) and at a 17.6% CAGR from 2005 to 2007 (2-year historical compounded growth).

For the forward growth rates, we used consensus estimates from the "Trading Multiples" section. On a forward year basis, Momper's expected EPS growth rate for 2007A to 2008E is 17.1%, with an expected 2007A to 2009E CAGR of 14.1%. We sourced Momper's long-term EPS growth rate of 15%, which is based on equity research analysts' estimates, from consensus estimates.

EXHIBIT 1.52 Growth Rates Section

Growth Rates			
	Sales	Adj. EBITDA	Adj. EPS
Historical			
1-year	8.0%	8.1%	17.2%
2-year CAGR	8.3%	7.5%	17.6%
Estimated			
1-year	9.3%	12.5%	17.1%
2-year CAGR	8.9%	9.5%	14.1%
Long-term			15.0%

= 2008E Sales / 2007A Sales - 1
= $1,475.0 million / $1,350.0 million - 1

= (2009E EBITDA / 2007A Adjusted EBITDA) ^ (1 / (2009 - 2007)) - 1
= ($240.0 million / $200.0 million) ^ (1 / 2) - 1

Step IV. Benchmark the Comparable Companies

After completing Steps I to III, we were prepared to perform the benchmarking analysis for ValueCo.

The first two benchmarking output pages focused on the comparables' financial characteristics, enabling us to determine ValueCo's relative position among its peers for key value drivers (see Exhibits 1.53 and 1.54). This benchmarking analysis, in combination with a review of key business characteristics (outlined in Exhibit 1.3), also enabled us to identify ValueCo's closest comparables—in this case, Lajoux Global, Momper Corp., and McMenamin & Co. These closest comparables were instrumental in helping to frame the ultimate valuation range.

Similarly, the benchmarking analysis allowed us to identify outliers, such as Vucic Brands and Paris Industries, which were determined to be less relevant due to their size and profitability. In this case, we did not eliminate the outliers altogether. Rather, we elected to group the comparable companies into three tiers based on size—Large-Cap, Mid-Cap, and Small-Cap. The companies in the "Mid-Cap" and "Small-Cap" groups are closer in size and other business and financial characteristics to ValueCo and, therefore, more relevant in our view. The companies in the "Large-Cap" group, however, provided further perspective as part of a more thorough analysis.

We used the output page in Exhibit 1.55 to analyze and compare the trading multiples for ValueCo's comparables. As previously discussed, financial performance typically translates directly into valuation (i.e., the top performers tend to receive a premium valuation to their peers, with laggards trading at a discount). Therefore, we

EXHIBIT 1.53 ValueCo Corporation: Benchmarking Analysis – Financial Statistics and Ratios, Page 1

ValueCo Corporation

Benchmarking Analysis – Financial Statistics and Ratios, Page 1

($ in millions, except per share data)

Company	Ticker	Market Valuation		LTM Financial Statistics					LTM Profitability Margins				Growth Rates						
		Equity Value	Enterprise Value	Sales	Gross Profit	EBITDA	EBIT	Net Income	Gross Profit (%)	EBITDA (%)	EBIT (%)	Net Income (%)	Sales Hist. 1-year	Sales Est. 1-year	EBITDA Hist. 1-year	EBITDA Est. 1-year	EPS Hist. 1-year	EPS Est. 1-year	EPS Est. LT
ValueCo Corporation	NA	NA	NA	$978	$372	$147	$127	$66	38%	15%	13%	7%	9%	8%	13%	8%	NA	NA	NA
Tier I: Large-Cap																			
Vucic Brands	VUC	$8,829	$14,712	$8,670	$3,468	$1,739	$1,474	$603	40%	20%	17%	7%	11%	10%	11%	10%	13%	13%	16%
Pearl Corp.	PRL	8,850	11,323	12,750	4,335	1,607	1,352	695	34%	13%	11%	5%	9%	7%	9%	7%	8%	9%	13%
Spalding Co.	SLD	7,781	8,369	8,127	3,007	1,138	975	557	37%	14%	12%	7%	9%	6%	9%	6%	8%	6%	14%
Leicht & Co.	LCT	7,456	9,673	8,109	2,879	1,281	1,014	525	36%	16%	13%	6%	9%	9%	9%	9%	8%	10%	11%
Drook Corp.	DRK	5,034	6,161	6,708	2,415	885	738	407	36%	13%	11%	6%	10%	7%	9%	6%	10%	7%	10%
Mean									37%	15%	13%	6%	9%	8%	9%	8%	9%	9%	13%
Median									36%	14%	12%	6%	9%	7%	9%	7%	8%	9%	13%
Tier II: Mid-Cap																			
Goodson Corp.	GDS	$4,368	$5,534	$6,125	$2,144	$796	$613	$318	35%	13%	10%	5%	15%	7%	15%	7%	14%	8%	13%
The DiNucci Group	TDG	3,772	5,202	6,489	2,271	779	454	213	35%	12%	7%	3%	10%	7%	10%	7%	1%	10%	15%
Pryor, Inc.	PRI	3,484	4,764	4,223	1,563	657	507	261	37%	16%	12%	6%	10%	9%	13%	13%	10%	5%	14%
Adler Industries	ADL	2,600	3,149	3,895	1,441	471	323	171	37%	12%	8%	4%	7%	8%	7%	8%	7%	9%	11%
Lanzarone International	LNZ	1,750	2,139	2,286	846	299	252	131	37%	13%	11%	6%	8%	7%	9%	8%	9%	7%	15%
Mean									36%	13%	10%	5%	10%	8%	11%	9%	8%	8%	14%
Median									37%	13%	10%	5%	10%	7%	10%	8%	7%	8%	14%
Tier III: Small-Cap																			
Lajoux Global	LJX	$1,050	$1,650	$1,775	$641	$232	$198	$83	36%	13%	11%	5%	10%	8%	14%	9%	26%	11%	13%
Momper Corp.	MOMP	1,000	1,500	1,415	508	215	175	85	36%	15%	12%	6%	8%	9%	8%	13%	17%	17%	15%
McMenamin & Co.	MCM	630	705	571	221	97	70	32	39%	17%	12%	6%	5%	9%	10%	10%	9%	9%	14%
Trip Co.	TRIP	321	441	486	170	66	49	21	35%	14%	10%	4%	13%	9%	13%	9%	13%	16%	12%
Paris Industries	PRS	156	192	352	106	35	21	11	30%	10%	6%	3%	5%	8%	5%	8%	4%	7%	10%
Mean									35%	14%	10%	5%	8%	9%	10%	10%	14%	12%	13%
Median									36%	14%	11%	5%	8%	9%	10%	9%	13%	11%	13%
Overall																			
Mean									36%	14%	11%	5%	9%	8%	10%	9%	10%	9%	13%
Median									36%	13%	11%	6%	9%	8%	9%	8%	9%	9%	13%
High									40%	20%	17%	7%	15%	10%	15%	13%	26%	17%	16%
Low									30%	10%	6%	3%	5%	6%	5%	6%	1%	5%	10%

Source: Company filings, Bloomberg, Consensus Estimates

Note: Last twelve months data based on September 30, 2008. Estimated annual financial data based on a calendar year.

ValueCo Corporation
Benchmarking Analysis – Financial Statistics and Ratios, Page 2
($ in millions, except per share data)

Company	Ticker	FYE	General Information Predicted Beta	Return on Investment ROIC (%)	ROE (%)	ROA (%)	Implied Div. Yield (%)	LTM Leverage Ratios Debt / Tot. Cap. (%)	Debt / EBITDA (x)	Net Debt / EBITDA (x)	LTM Coverage Ratios EBITDA / Int. Exp. (x)	EBITDA - Cpx / Int. Exp. (x)	EBIT / Int. Exp. (x)	Credit Ratings Moody's	S&P
ValueCo Corporation	NA	Dec-31	NA	13%	10%	6%	NA	31%	2.0x	2.0x	7.2x	6.2x	6.2x	NA	NA
Tier I: Large-Cap															
Vucic Brands	VUC	Dec-31	1.05	13%	11%	4%	2%	49%	3.2x	3.1x	4.3x	3.7x	3.7x	Baa2	BBB
Pearl Corp.	PRL	Dec-31	0.95	19%	14%	6%	4%	42%	2.3x	1.5x	7.0x	5.8x	5.9x	Baa2	BBB+
Spalding Co.	SLD	Sep-30	1.15	23%	15%	8%	4%	22%	0.9x	0.5x	14.8x	12.4x	12.6x	A3	A-
Leicht & Co.	LCT	Dec-31	1.25	16%	13%	6%	NA	36%	1.9x	1.7x	7.7x	6.7x	6.1x	Baa3	BBB-
Drook Corp.	DRK	Dec-31	1.10	20%	17%	6%	2%	40%	1.9x	1.3x	10.9x	9.7x	9.1x	Baa2	BBB
Mean			1.10	18%	14%	6%	3%	38%	2.0x	1.6x	8.9x	7.6x	7.5x		
Median			1.10	19%	14%	6%	3%	40%	1.9x	1.5x	7.7x	6.7x	6.1x		
Tier II: Mid-Cap															
Goodson Corp.	GDS	Dec-31	1.35	17%	12%	6%	NA	33%	1.6x	1.5x	8.0x	4.9x	6.1x	Ba1	BB+
The DiNucci Group	TDG	Apr-30	1.23	12%	9%	3%	NA	43%	2.4x	1.8x	7.0x	4.7x	4.1x	Ba1	BBB-
Pryor, Inc.	PRI	Dec-31	1.15	19%	16%	6%	3%	49%	2.4x	1.9x	7.6x	7.0x	5.9x	Baa3	BBB-
Adler Industries	ADL	Dec-31	1.11	12%	8%	4%	NA	20%	1.2x	1.2x	10.0x	7.5x	6.8x	Baa1	BBB+
Lanzarone International	LNZ	Dec-31	1.08	19%	13%	6%	2%	34%	1.7x	1.3x	7.5x	5.8x	6.3x	Ba1	BB+
Mean			1.18	16%	12%	5%	2%	36%	1.9x	1.5x	8.0x	6.0x	5.9x		
Median			1.15	17%	12%	6%	2%	34%	1.7x	1.5x	7.6x	5.8x	6.1x		
Tier III: Small-Cap															
Lajoux Global	LJX	Dec-31	1.35	15%	13%	5%	NA	51%	3.1x	2.6x	3.7x	3.2x	3.1x	B1	B+
Momper Corp.	MOMP	Dec-31	1.25	16%	15%	6%	2%	48%	2.6x	2.3x	5.7x	4.9x	4.6x	Baa2	BB
McMenamin & Co.	MCM	Dec-31	1.19	17%	9%	5%	2%	42%	2.1x	0.8x	5.2x	3.7x	2.0x	Baa2	BB
Trip Co.	TRIP	Jan-31	0.85	14%	9%	5%	NA	37%	2.1x	1.8x	4.3x	3.5x	3.2x	Baa3	BB-
Paris Industries	PRS	Dec-31	1.15	8%	5%	3%	NA	39%	3.8x	1.0x	10.1x	4.5x	6.1x	NA	NA
Mean			1.16	14%	10%	5%	2%	43%	2.8x	1.7x	5.8x	4.0x	3.8x		
Median			1.19	15%	9%	5%	2%	42%	2.6x	1.8x	5.2x	3.7x	3.2x		
Overall															
Mean			1.15	16%	12%	5%	3%	39%	2.3x	1.6x	7.6x	5.9x	5.7x		
Median			1.15	16%	13%	6%	2%	40%	2.3x	1.5x	7.5x	4.9x	5.9x		
High			1.35	23%	17%	8%	4%	51%	3.8x	3.1x	14.8x	12.4x	12.6x		
Low			0.85	8%	5%	3%	2%	20%	0.9x	0.5x	3.7x	3.2x	2.0x		

Source: Company filings, Bloomberg, Consensus Estimates

EXHIBIT 1.55 ValueCo Corporation: Comparable Companies Analysis – Trading Multiples Output Page

ValueCo Corporation
Comparable Companies Analysis
($ in millions, except per share data)

Company	Ticker	Current Share Price	% of 52-wk. High	Equity Value	Enterprise Value	EV / LTM Sales	EV / 2008E Sales	EV / 2009E Sales	EV / LTM EBITDA	EV / 2008E EBITDA	EV / 2009E EBITDA	EV / LTM EBIT	EV / 2008E EBIT	EV / 2009E EBIT	LTM EBITDA Margin	Total Debt / EBITDA	Price / LTM EPS	Price / 2008E EPS	Price / 2009E EPS	LT EPS Growth
Tier I: Large-Cap																				
Vucic Brands	VUC	$70.00	83%	$8,829	$14,712	1.7x	1.6x	1.4x	8.5x	7.8x	7.2x	10.0x	9.3x	8.5x	20%	3.2x	14.6x	13.6x	12.5x	16%
Pearl Corp.	PRL	22.00	81%	8,850	11,323	0.9x	0.8x	0.8x	7.0x	6.7x	6.3x	8.4x	8.0x	7.4x	13%	2.3x	12.7x	12.1x	11.3x	13%
Spalding Co.	SLD	57.00	76%	7,781	8,369	1.0x	1.0x	0.9x	7.4x	7.1x	6.5x	8.6x	8.3x	7.6x	14%	0.9x	14.0x	13.4x	12.3x	14%
Leicht & Co.	LCT	85.00	82%	7,456	9,673	1.2x	1.1x	1.1x	7.6x	7.1x	6.7x	9.5x	8.9x	8.4x	16%	1.9x	14.2x	13.3x	12.5x	11%
Drook Corp.	DRK	78.25	74%	5,034	6,161	0.9x	0.9x	0.8x	7.0x	6.6x	6.2x	8.4x	7.9x	7.4x	13%	1.9x	12.4x	11.7x	11.0x	10%
Mean						1.1x	1.1x	1.0x	7.5x	7.1x	6.6x	9.0x	8.5x	7.9x	15%	2.0x	13.6x	12.8x	11.9x	13%
Median						1.0x	1.0x	0.9x	7.4x	7.1x	6.5x	8.6x	8.3x	7.6x	14%	1.9x	14.0x	13.3x	12.3x	13%
Tier II: Mid-Cap																				
Goodson Corp.	GDS	$44.00	79%	$4,368	$5,534	0.9x	0.9x	0.9x	7.0x	6.8x	6.6x	9.0x	8.9x	8.6x	13%	1.6x	13.7x	13.5x	13.1x	13%
The DiNucci Group	TDG	29.85	71%	3,772	5,202	0.8x	0.8x	0.7x	6.7x	6.4x	6.1x	11.5x	11.0x	10.4x	12%	2.4x	17.5x	17.1x	16.1x	15%
Pryor, Inc.	PRI	42.80	78%	3,484	4,764	1.1x	1.1x	1.0x	7.3x	6.9x	6.4x	9.4x	9.2x	8.3x	16%	2.4x	13.4x	12.7x	11.8x	14%
Adler Industries	ADL	47.00	82%	2,600	3,149	0.8x	0.8x	0.7x	6.7x	6.3x	5.9x	9.7x	9.2x	8.6x	12%	1.2x	15.2x	14.4x	13.4x	11%
Lanzarone International	LNZ	28.50	81%	1,750	2,139	0.9x	0.9x	0.8x	7.2x	6.7x	6.3x	8.5x	8.0x	7.4x	13%	1.7x	13.3x	12.5x	11.6x	15%
Mean						0.9x	0.9x	0.8x	6.9x	6.6x	6.3x	9.6x	9.2x	8.7x	13%	1.9x	14.6x	14.0x	13.2x	14%
Median						0.9x	0.9x	0.8x	7.0x	6.7x	6.3x	9.4x	8.9x	8.6x	13%	1.7x	13.7x	13.5x	13.1x	14%
Tier III: Small-Cap																				
Lajoux Global	LJX	$15.00	83%	$1,050	$1,650	0.9x	0.9x	0.8x	7.1x	6.8x	6.4x	8.3x	8.0x	7.5x	13%	3.1x	12.6x	12.1x	11.3x	13%
Momper Corp.	MOMP	20.00	80%	1,000	1,500	1.1x	1.0x	0.9x	7.0x	6.7x	6.3x	8.6x	8.1x	7.5x	15%	2.6x	11.8x	11.1x	10.0x	15%
McMenamin & Co.	MCM	16.50	78%	630	705	1.2x	1.2x	1.1x	7.3x	7.1x	6.6x	10.1x	9.8x	9.1x	17%	2.6x	19.9x	19.3x	17.9x	14%
Trip Co.	TRIP	11.25	78%	321	441	0.9x	0.9x	0.8x	6.7x	6.5x	6.1x	9.1x	8.7x	8.2x	14%	2.1x	15.6x	15.0x	14.0x	12%
Paris Industries	PRS	10.25	73%	156	192	0.5x	0.5x	0.5x	5.5x	5.3x	5.0x	9.1x	8.9x	8.3x	10%	3.8x	14.3x	14.0x	13.1x	10%
Mean						0.9x	0.9x	0.8x	6.7x	6.5x	6.0x	9.0x	8.7x	8.1x	14%	2.8x	14.8x	14.3x	13.3x	13%
Median						0.9x	0.9x	0.8x	7.0x	6.7x	6.3x	9.1x	8.7x	8.2x	14%	2.6x	14.3x	14.0x	13.1x	13%
Overall																				
Mean						1.0x	1.0x	0.9x	7.0x	6.7x	6.3x	9.2x	8.8x	8.2x	14%	2.3x	14.3x	13.7x	13.2x	13%
Median						0.9x	0.9x	0.8x	7.0x	6.7x	6.3x	9.1x	8.9x	8.3x	13%	2.3x	14.0x	13.4x	13.1x	13%
High						1.7x	1.6x	1.4x	8.5x	7.8x	7.2x	11.5x	11.0x	10.4x	20%	3.8x	19.9x	19.3x	17.9x	16%
Low						0.5x	0.5x	0.5x	5.5x	5.3x	5.0x	8.3x	7.9x	7.4x	10%	0.9x	11.8x	11.1x	10.0x	10%

Source: Company filings, Bloomberg, Consensus Estimates
Note: Last twelve months data based on September 30, 2008. Estimated annual financial data based on a calendar year.

focused on the multiples for ValueCo's closest comparables as the basis for framing valuation.

Step V. Determine Valuation

The means and medians for the Mid-Cap and Small-Cap comparables universe helped establish an initial valuation range for ValueCo, with the highs and lows providing further perspective. We also looked to the Large-Cap comparables for peripheral guidance. To fine-tune the range, however, we focused on those comparables deemed closest to ValueCo in terms of business and financial profile—namely, Lajoux Global, Momper Corp., and McMenamin & Co., as well as Adler Industries and Lanzarone International to a lesser extent.

Companies in ValueCo's sector tend to trade on the basis of forward EV/EBITDA multiples. Therefore, we framed our valuation of ValueCo on the basis of the forward EV/EBITDA multiples for its closest comparables, selecting ranges of 6.25x to 7.25x 2008E EBITDA, and 5.75x to 6.75x 2009E EBITDA. We also looked at the implied valuation based on a range of 6.5x to 7.5x LTM EBITDA.

EXHIBIT 1.56 ValueCo Corporation: Implied Valuation Range – Enterprise Value

ValueCo Corporation
Implied Valuation Range
($ in millions, LTM 9/30/2008)

EBITDA	Metric	Multiple Range			Implied Enterprise Value		
LTM	$146.7	6.50x	–	7.50x	$953.3	–	$1,100.0
2008E	150.0	6.25x	–	7.25x	937.5	–	1,087.5
2009E	162.0	5.75x	–	6.75x	931.5	–	1,093.5

The chosen multiple ranges in Exhibit 1.56 translated into an implied enterprise value range of approximately $932 million to $1,100 million. This implied valuation range is typically displayed in a format such as that shown in Exhibit 1.57 (known as a "football field") for eventual comparison against other valuation methodologies, which we discuss in the following chapters.

EXHIBIT 1.57 ValueCo Football Field Displaying Comparable Companies

($ in millions)

Comparable Companies

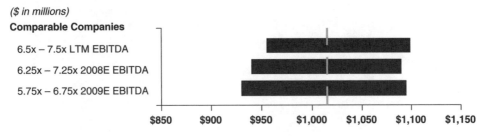

6.5x – 7.5x LTM EBITDA		
6.25x – 7.25x 2008E EBITDA		
5.75x – 6.75x 2009E EBITDA		

$850 $900 $950 $1,000 $1,050 $1,100 $1,150

Precedent Transactions Analysis

Precedent transactions analysis ("precedent transactions" or "transaction comps"), like comparable companies analysis, employs a multiples-based approach to derive an implied valuation range for a given company, division, business, or collection of assets ("target"). It is premised on multiples paid for comparable companies in prior M&A transactions. Precedent transactions has a broad range of applications, most notably to help determine a potential sale price range for a company, or part thereof, in an M&A transaction or restructuring.

The selection of an appropriate universe of comparable acquisitions is the foundation for performing precedent transactions. This process incorporates a similar approach to that for determining a universe of comparable companies. The best comparable acquisitions typically involve companies similar to the target on a fundamental level (i.e., sharing key business and financial characteristics such as those outlined in Chapter 1, see Exhibit 1.3).

As with trading comps, it is often challenging to obtain a robust universe of truly comparable acquisitions. This exercise may demand some creativity and perseverance on the part of the banker. For example, it is not uncommon to consider transactions involving companies in different, but related, sectors that may share similar end markets, distribution channels, or financial profiles. As a general rule, the most recent transactions (i.e., those that have occurred within the previous two to three years) are the most relevant as they likely took place under similar market conditions to the contemplated transaction. In some cases, however, older transactions may be appropriate to evaluate if they occurred during a similar point in the target's business cycle or macroeconomic environment.

Under normal market conditions, transaction comps tend to provide a higher multiple range than trading comps for two principal reasons. First, buyers generally pay a "control premium" when purchasing another company. In return for this premium, the acquirer receives the right to control decisions regarding the target's business and its underlying cash flows. Second, strategic buyers often have the opportunity to realize synergies, which supports the ability to pay higher purchase prices. Synergies refer to the expected cost savings, growth opportunities, and other financial benefits that occur as a result of the combination of two businesses.

Potential acquirers look closely at the multiples that have been paid for comparable acquisitions. As a result, bankers and investment professionals are expected to know the transaction multiples for their sector focus areas. As in Chapter 1, this chapter employs a step-by-step approach to performing precedent transactions, as shown in Exhibit 2.1, followed by an illustrative analysis for ValueCo.

71

EXHIBIT 2.1   Precedent Transactions Analysis Steps

Step I.   Select the Universe of Comparable Acquisitions
Step II.   Locate the Necessary Deal-Related and Financial Information
Step III. Spread Key Statistics, Ratios, and Transaction Multiples
Step IV.   Benchmark the Comparable Acquisitions
Step V.   Determine Valuation

SUMMARY OF PRECEDENT TRANSACTIONS ANALYSIS STEPS

- **Step I. Select the Universe of Comparable Acquisitions.** The identification of a universe of comparable acquisitions is the first step in performing transaction comps. This exercise, like determining a universe of comparable companies for trading comps, can often be challenging and requires a strong understanding of the target and its sector. As a starting point, the banker typically consults with peers or senior colleagues to see if a relevant set of comparable acquisitions already exists internally. In the event the banker is starting from scratch, we suggest searching through M&A databases, examining the M&A history of the target and its comparable companies, and reviewing merger proxies of comparable companies for lists of selected comparable acquisitions disclosed in the fairness opinions. Equity and fixed income research reports for the target (if public), its comparable companies, and overall sector may also provide lists of comparable acquisitions, including relevant financial data (for reference purposes only).

  As part of this process, the banker seeks to learn as much as possible regarding the specific circumstances and deal dynamics of each transaction. This is particularly important for refining the universe and, ultimately, honing in on the "best" comparable acquisitions.

- **Step II. Locate the Necessary Deal-Related and Financial Information.** This section focuses on the sourcing of deal-related and financial information for M&A transactions involving both public and private companies. Locating information on comparable acquisitions is invariably easier for transactions involving public companies (including private companies with publicly registered debt securities) due to SEC disclosure requirements. For competitive reasons, however, public acquirers sometimes safeguard these details and only disclose information that is required by law or regulation. For M&A transactions involving private companies, it is often difficult—and sometimes impossible—to obtain complete (or any) financial information necessary to determine their transaction multiples.

- **Step III. Spread Key Statistics, Ratios, and Transaction Multiples.** Once the relevant deal-related and financial information has been located, the banker is prepared to spread each selected transaction. This involves entering the key transaction data relating to purchase price, form of consideration, and target financial statistics into an input page, where the relevant multiples for each transaction are calculated. The key multiples used for precedent transactions mirror those used for comparable companies (e.g., enterprise value-to-EBITDA and equity value-to-net income). As with comparable companies, certain sectors may also rely on additional or other metrics to derive valuation (see Chapter 1, Exhibit 1.33). The notable difference is that multiples for precedent transactions often reflect a premium paid by the acquirer for control and potential synergies. In addition, multiples for precedent transactions are typically calculated on the basis of actual LTM financial statistics (available at the time of deal announcement).

- **Step IV. Benchmark the Comparable Acquisitions.** As with trading comps, the next level of analysis involves an in-depth study of the selected comparable acquisitions so as to identify those most relevant for valuing the target. As part of this benchmarking analysis, the banker examines the key financial statistics and ratios for the acquired companies, with an eye toward those most comparable to the target. Output pages, such as those shown in Exhibits 1.53 and 1.54 in Chapter 1, facilitate this analysis. Other relevant deal circumstances and dynamics are also examined.

  The transaction multiples for each selected acquisition are linked to an output sheet where they can be easily benchmarked against one another and the broader universe (see Exhibit 2.2). Each precedent transaction is closely examined as part of the final refining of the universe, with the best comparable transactions identified and obvious outliers eliminated. Ultimately, an experienced sector banker is consulted to help determine the final universe.

- **Step V. Determine Valuation.** In precedent transactions, the multiples of the selected comparable acquisitions universe are used to derive an implied valuation range for the target. The banker typically uses the mean and median multiples from the universe as a guide to establish a preliminary valuation range for the target, with the high and low ends also serving as reference points. These calculations often serve as the precursor for a deeper level of analysis whereby the banker uses the multiples from the most relevant transactions to anchor the ultimate valuation range. Often, the banker focuses on as few as two or three of the most similar transactions. Once an experienced banker is consulted to finalize the chosen multiples range, the endpoints are multiplied by the target's appropriate LTM financial statistics to produce an implied valuation range. As with trading comps, the target's implied valuation range is then given a sanity check and compared to the output from other valuation methodologies.

EXHIBIT 2.2 Transaction Multiples Output Page

ValueCo Corporation
Precedent Transactions Analysis
($ in millions)

Date Announced	Acquirer	Target	Transaction Type	Purchase Consideration	Equity Value	Enterprise Value	Enterprise Value / LTM Sales	LTM EBITDA	LTM EBIT	LTM EBITDA Margin	Equity Value / LTM Net Income	Premiums Paid Days Prior to Unaffected 1	7	30
11/3/2008	Pearl Corp.	Rosenbaum Industries	Public / Public	Cash	$1,700	$2,000	1.5x	8.0x	9.1x	18%	13.6x	30%	27%	33%
10/30/2008	Goodson Corp.	Schneider & Co.	Public / Public	Cash / Stock	932	1,232	1.2x	7.6x	8.7x	16%	13.9x	29%	32%	31%
6/22/2008	Leicht & Co.	ParkCo	Public / Private	Cash	650	875	1.1x	7.1x	8.1x	15%	12.0x	NA	NA	NA
4/15/2008	Pryor, Inc.	Bress Products	Public / Public	Stock	1,301	1,326	1.6x	8.5x	12.5x	19%	14.4x	29%	36%	34%
10/1/2007	The Hochberg Group	Whalen Inc.	Sponsor / Private	Cash	225	330	1.3x	7.7x	9.2x	17%	13.3x	NA	NA	NA
8/8/2007	Cole Manufacturing	Gordon Inc.	Public / Public	Stock	2,371	2,796	1.4x	8.0x	10.7x	18%	17.7x	33%	31%	36%
7/6/2007	Eu-Han Capital	Rughwani International	Sponsor / Public	Cash	1,553	2,233	1.2x	7.5x	9.3x	15%	12.4x	38%	42%	43%
11/9/2006	The Meisner Group	Kamras Brands	Sponsor / Public	Cash	916	936	1.2x	7.3x	8.3x	16%	13.1x	34%	35%	36%
6/21/2006	Domanski Capital	Neren Industries	Sponsor / Public	Cash	1,248	1,798	1.0x	7.2x	8.3x	13%	16.0x	35%	37%	39%
3/20/2006	Lanzarone International	Falk & Sons	Public / Private	Cash	360	530	0.9x	6.5x	8.1x	14%	10.6x	NA	NA	NA
Mean							1.2x	7.5x	9.2x	16%	13.7x	33%	34%	36%
Median							1.2x	7.5x	8.9x	16%	13.4x	33%	35%	36%
High							1.6x	8.5x	12.5x	19%	17.7x	36%	42%	43%
Low							0.9x	6.5x	8.1x	13%	10.6x	29%	27%	31%

Source: Company filings

STEP I. SELECT THE UNIVERSE OF COMPARABLE ACQUISITIONS

The identification of a universe of comparable acquisitions is the first step in performing transaction comps. This exercise, like determining a universe of comparable companies for trading comps, can often be challenging and requires a strong understanding of the target and its sector. Investment banks generally have internal M&A transaction databases containing relevant multiples and other financial data for focus sectors, which are updated as appropriate for newly announced deals. Often, however, the banker needs to start from scratch.

When practical, the banker consults with peers or senior colleagues with first-hand knowledge of relevant transactions. Senior bankers can be helpful in establishing the basic landscape by identifying the key transactions in a given sector. Toward the end of the screening process, an experienced banker's guidance is beneficial for the final refining of the universe.

Screen for Comparable Acquisitions

The initial goal when screening for comparable acquisitions is to locate as many potential transactions as possible for a relevant, recent time period and then further refine the universe. Below are several suggestions for creating an initial list of comparable acquisitions.

- Search M&A databases such as SDC Platinum,[1] which allows for the screening of M&A transactions through multiple search criteria, including SIC/NAICS codes, transaction size, form of consideration, time period, and geography, among others

- Examine the target's M&A history and determine the multiples it has paid and received for the purchase and sale, respectively, of its businesses

- Revisit the target's universe of comparable companies (as determined in Chapter 1) and examine the M&A history of each comparable company

- Search merger proxies for comparable acquisitions as they typically contain excerpts from fairness opinion(s) that cite a list of selected transactions analyzed by the financial advisor(s)

- Review equity and fixed income research reports for the target (if public), its comparable companies, and sector as they may provide lists of comparable acquisitions, including relevant financial data (for reference purposes only)

Examine Other Considerations

Once an initial set of comparable acquisitions is selected, it is important for the banker to gain a better understanding of the specific circumstances and context

---

[1] Thomson Reuters SDC Platinum™ is a financial transactions database that provides detailed information on new issuances, M&A, syndicated loans, private equity, and more. Additional dedicated M&A transaction applications include Capital IQ and FactSet Mergerstat, both of which are subscription services.

for each transaction. Although these factors generally do not change the list of comparable acquisitions to be examined, understanding the "story" behind each transaction helps the banker better interpret the multiple paid, as well as its relevance to the target being valued. This next level of analysis involves examining factors such as market conditions and deal dynamics.

Market Conditions   Market conditions refer to the business and economic environment, as well as the prevailing state of the capital markets, at the time of a given transaction. They must be viewed within the context of specific sectors and cycles (e.g., housing, steel, and technology). These conditions directly affect availability and cost of acquisition financing and, therefore, influence the price an acquirer is willing, or able, to pay. They also affect buyer and seller confidence with respect to undertaking a transaction.

For example, at the height of the technology bubble in the late 1990s and early 2000s, many technology and telecommunications companies were acquired at unprecedented multiples. Equity financing was prevalent during this period as companies used their stock, which was valued at record levels, as acquisition currency. Boardroom confidence was also high, which lent support to contemplated M&A activity. After the bubble burst and market conditions adjusted, M&A activity slowed dramatically and companies changed hands for fractions of the multiples seen just a couple of years earlier. The multiples paid for companies during this period quickly became irrelevant for assessing value in the following era.

Similarly, during the record low-rate debt financing environment of the mid-2000s, acquirers (financial sponsors, in particular) were able to support higher than historical purchase prices due to the market's willingness to supply abundant and inexpensive debt with favorable terms. In the ensuing credit crunch that began during the second half of 2007, however, debt financing became scarce and expensive, thereby dramatically changing value perceptions. As a result, the entire M&A landscape changed, including the volume of deals and buyers' perspectives on valuation.

Deal Dynamics   Deal dynamics refer to the specific circumstances surrounding a given transaction. For example:

- Was the acquirer a strategic buyer or a financial sponsor?

- What were the buyer's and seller's motivations for the transaction?

- Was the target sold through an *auction process* or *negotiated sale*? Was the nature of the deal *friendly* or *hostile*?

- What was the purchase consideration (i.e., mix of cash and stock)?

This information can provide insight into factors that may have impacted the price paid by the acquirer.

Strategic Buyer vs. Financial Sponsor   Traditionally, strategic buyers have been able to pay higher purchase prices than financial sponsors due to their potential ability to realize synergies from the transaction, among other factors, including lower cost of capital and return thresholds. During periods of robust credit markets, such as the mid-2000s, however, sponsors were able to place higher leverage on targets and, therefore, compete more effectively with strategic buyers on purchase price. In the ensuing credit crunch, the advantage shifted back to strategic buyers as only the strongest and most creditworthy companies were able to source acquisition financing.

Motivations Buyer and seller motivations may also play an important role in interpreting purchase price. For example, a strategic buyer may "stretch" to pay a higher price for an asset if there are substantial synergies to be realized and/or the asset is critical to its strategic plan ("scarcity value"). Similarly, a financial sponsor may be more aggressive on price if synergies can be realized by combining the target with an existing portfolio company. From the seller's perspective, motivations may also influence purchase price. A corporation in need of cash that is selling a non-core business, for example, may prioritize speed of execution, certainty of completion, and other structural considerations, which may result in a lower valuation than a pure value maximization strategy.

Sale Process and Nature of the Deal The type of sale process and nature of the deal should also be examined. For example, auctions, whereby the target is shopped to multiple prospective buyers, are designed to maximize competitive dynamics with the goal of producing the best offer at the highest possible price. Hostile situations, whereby the target actively seeks alternatives to a proposed takeover by a particular buyer, may also produce higher purchase prices. In a *merger of equals* transaction premised on partnership, on the other hand, both sides may forego a premium as they collectively participate in the upside (e.g., growth and synergies) over time.

Purchase Consideration The use of stock as a meaningful portion of the purchase consideration tends to result in a lower valuation (measured by multiples and premiums paid) than for an all-cash transaction. The primary explanation for this occurrence is that when target shareholders receive stock, they retain an equity interest in the combined entity and, therefore, expect to share in the upside (driven by growth and realizing synergies). Target shareholders also maintain the opportunity to obtain a control premium at a later date through a future sale of the company. As a result, target shareholders may require less upfront compensation than for an all-cash transaction in which they are unable to participate in value creation opportunities that result from combining the two companies.

STEP II. LOCATE THE NECESSARY DEAL-RELATED AND FINANCIAL INFORMATION

This section focuses on the sourcing of key deal-related and financial information for M&A transactions involving both public and private targets. Locating information on comparable acquisitions is invariably easier for transactions involving public targets (including private companies with publicly registered debt securities) due to SEC disclosure requirements.

For M&A transactions involving private targets, the availability of sufficient information typically depends on whether public securities were used as the acquisition financing. In many cases, it is often challenging and sometimes impossible to obtain complete (or any) financial information necessary to determine the transaction multiples in such deals. For competitive reasons, even public acquirers may safeguard these details and only disclose information that is required by law or regulation. Nonetheless, the resourceful banker conducts searches for information on private transactions via news runs and various databases. In some cases, these searches yield enough data to determine purchase price and key target financial statistics; in other cases, there simply may not be enough relevant information available.

Below, we grouped the primary sources for locating the necessary deal-related and financial information for spreading comparable acquisitions into separate categories for public and private targets.

Public Targets

Proxy Statement   In a one-step merger transaction,[2] the target obtains approval from its shareholders through a vote at a shareholder meeting. Prior to the vote, the target provides appropriate disclosure to the shareholders via a proxy statement. The proxy statement contains a summary of the background and terms of the transaction, a description of the financial analysis underlying the fairness opinion(s) of the financial advisor(s), a copy of the definitive purchase/sale agreement ("definitive agreement"), and summary and pro forma financial data (if applicable, depending on the form of consideration). As such, it is a primary source for locating key information used to spread a precedent transaction. The proxy statement is filed with the SEC under the codes PREM14A (preliminary) and DEFM14A (definitive).

In the event that a public acquirer is issuing new shares in excess of 20% of its pre-deal shares outstanding to fund the purchase consideration,[3] it will also need to file a proxy statement for its shareholders to vote on the proposed transaction. In addition, a registration statement to register the offer and sale of shares must be filed with the SEC if no exemption from the registration requirements is available.[4]

Schedule TO/Schedule 14D-9   In a tender offer, the acquirer offers to buy shares directly from the target's shareholders.[5] As part of this process, the acquirer mails an Offer to Purchase to the target's shareholders and files a Schedule TO. In response to the tender offer, the target files a Schedule 14D-9 within ten business days of

---

[2] An M&A transaction for public targets where shareholders approve the deal at a formal shareholder meeting pursuant to relevant state law. See Chapter 6: M&A Sale Process for additional information.

[3] The requirement for a shareholder vote in this situation arises from the listing rules of the New York Stock Exchange and the Nasdaq Stock Market. If the amount of shares being issued is less than 20% of pre-deal levels, or if the merger consideration consists entirely of cash or debt, the acquirer's shareholders are typically not entitled to vote on the transaction.

[4] When both the acquirer and target are required to prepare proxy and/or registration statements, they typically combine the statements in a joint disclosure document.

[5] A tender offer is an offer to purchase shares for cash. An acquirer can also effect an exchange offer, pursuant to which the target's shares are exchanged for shares of the acquirer.

commencement. The Schedule 14D-9 contains a recommendation from the target's board of directors to the target's shareholders on how to respond to the tender offer, typically including a fairness opinion. The Schedule TO and the Schedule 14D-9 include the same type of information with respect to the terms of the transaction as set forth in a proxy statement.

Registration Statement/Prospectus (S-4, 424B)   When a public acquirer issues shares as part of the purchase consideration for a public target, the acquirer is typically required to file a registration statement/prospectus in order for those shares to be freely tradeable by the target's shareholders. Similarly, if the acquirer is issuing public debt securities (or debt securities intended to be registered)[6] to fund the purchase, it must also file a registration statement/prospectus. The registration statement/prospectus contains the terms of the issuance, material terms of the transaction, and purchase price detail. It may also contain acquirer and target financial information, including on a pro forma basis to reflect the consummation of the transaction (if applicable, depending on the materiality of the transaction).[7]

Schedule 13E-3   Depending on the nature of the transaction, a "going private"[8] deal may require enhanced disclosure. For example, in an LBO of a public company where an "affiliate" (such as a senior company executive or significant shareholder) is part of the buyout group, the SEC requires broader disclosure of information used in the decision-making process on a Schedule 13E-3. Disclosure items on Schedule 13E-3 include materials such as presentations to the target's board of directors by its financial advisor(s) in support of the actual fairness opinion(s).

8-K   In addition to the SEC filings mentioned above, key deal information can be obtained from the 8-K that is filed upon announcement of the transaction. Generally, a public target is required to file an 8-K within four business days of the transaction announcement. In the event a public company is selling a subsidiary or division that is significant in size, the parent company typically files an 8-K upon announcement of the transaction. Public acquirers are also required to file an 8-K upon announcement for material transactions.[9] A private acquirer does not need to file an 8-K as it is not

---

[6]Debt securities are typically sold to qualified institutional buyers (QIBs) through a private placement under Rule 144A of the Securities Act of 1933 initially, and then registered with the SEC within one year after issuance so that they can be traded on an open exchange. This is done to expedite the sale of the debt securities as SEC registration, which involves review of the registration statement by the SEC, can take several weeks or months. Once the SEC review of the documentation is complete, the issuer conducts an exchange offer pursuant to which investors exchange the unregistered bonds for registered bonds.

[7]A joint proxy/registration statement typically incorporates the acquirer's and target's applicable 10-K and 10-Q by reference as the source for financial information.

[8]A company "goes private" when it engages in certain transactions that have the effect of delisting its shares from a public stock exchange. In addition, depending on the circumstances, a publicly held company may no longer be required to file reports with the SEC when it reduces the number of its shareholders to fewer than 300.

[9]Generally, an acquisition is required to be reported in an 8-K if the assets, income, or value of the target comprise 10% or greater of the acquirer's. Furthermore, for larger transactions

subject to the SEC's disclosure requirements. When filed in the context of an M&A transaction, the 8-K contains a brief description of the transaction, as well as the corresponding press release and definitive agreement as exhibits.

The press release filed upon announcement typically contains a summary of the deal terms, transaction rationale, and a description of the target and acquirer. In the event there are substantial changes to the terms of the transaction following the original announcement, the banker uses the 8-K for the final announced deal (and enclosed press release) as the basis for calculating the deal's transaction multiples. This is a relatively common occurrence in competitive situations where two or more parties enter into a bidding war for a target.

10-K and 10-Q   The target's 10-K and 10-Q are the primary sources for locating the information necessary to calculate its relevant LTM financial statistics, including adjustments for non-recurring items and significant recent events. The most recent 10-K and 10-Q for the period ending prior to the announcement date typically serve as the source for the necessary information to calculate the target's LTM financial statistics and balance sheet data. In some cases, the banker may use a filing after announcement if the financial information is deemed more relevant. The 10-K and 10-Q are also relied upon to provide information on the target's shares outstanding and options/warrants.[10]

Equity and Fixed Income Research   Equity and fixed income research reports often provide helpful deal insight, including information on pro forma adjustments and expected synergies. Furthermore, research reports typically provide color on deal dynamics and other circumstances.

Private Targets

A private target (i.e., a non-public filer) is not required to publicly file documentation in an M&A transaction as long as it is not subject to SEC disclosure requirements. Therefore, the sourcing of relevant information on private targets depends on the type of acquirer and/or acquisition financing.

When a public acquirer buys a private target (or a division/subsidiary of a public company), it may be required to file certain disclosure documents. For example, in the event the acquirer is using public securities as part of the purchase consideration for a private target, it is required to file a registration statement/prospectus. Furthermore, if the acquirer is issuing shares in excess of 20% of its pre-deal shares, a proxy statement is filed with the SEC and mailed to its shareholders so they can evaluate the proposed transaction and vote. As previously discussed, regardless of the type of financing, the acquirer files an 8-K upon announcement and completion of material transactions.

---

where assets, income, or value of the target comprise 20% or greater of the acquirer's, the acquirer must file an 8-K containing historical financial information on the target and pro forma financial information within 75 days of the completion of the acquisition.

[10]The proxy statement may contain more recent share count information than the 10-K or 10-Q.

For LBOs of private targets, the availability of necessary information depends on whether public debt securities (typically high yield bonds) are issued as part of the financing. In this case, the S-4 contains the relevant data on purchase price and target financials to spread the precedent transaction.

Private acquirer/private target transactions (including LBOs) involving non-public financing are the most difficult transactions for which to obtain information because there are no SEC disclosure requirements. In these situations, the banker must rely on less formal sources for deal information, such as press releases and news articles. These news pieces can be found by searching a company's corporate website as well as through information services such as Bloomberg, Factiva, LexisNexis, and Thomson Reuters. The banker should also search relevant sector-specific trade journals for potential disclosures. Any information provided on these all-private transactions, however, relies on discretionary disclosure by the parties involved. As a result, in many cases it is impossible to obtain even basic deal information that can be relied upon, thus precluding these transactions from being used to derive valuation.

Summary of Primary SEC Filings in M&A Transactions

Exhibit 2.3 provides a list of key SEC filings that can be used to source relevant deal-related data and target financial information for performing precedent transactions. In general, if applicable, the definitive proxy statement or tender offer document should serve as the primary source for deal-related data.

Exhibit 2.4 provides an overview of the sources for transaction information in public and private company transactions.

STEP III. SPREAD KEY STATISTICS, RATIOS, AND TRANSACTION MULTIPLES

Once the relevant deal-related and financial information has been located, the banker is prepared to spread each selected transaction. This involves entering the key transaction data relating to purchase price, form of consideration, and target financial statistics into an input page, such as that shown in Exhibit 2.5, where the relevant multiples for each transaction are calculated. An input sheet is created for each comparable acquisition, which, in turn, feeds into summary output sheets used for the benchmarking analysis. In the pages that follow, we explain the financial data displayed on the input page and the calculations behind them.

Calculation of Key Financial Statistics and Ratios

The process for spreading the key financial statistics and ratios for precedent transactions is similar to that outlined in Chapter 1 for comparable companies (see Exhibits 1.53 and 1.54). Our focus for this section, therefore, is on certain nuances for calculating equity value and enterprise value in precedent transactions, including under different purchase consideration scenarios. We also discuss the analysis of premiums paid and synergies.

EXHIBIT 2.3 Primary SEC Filings in M&A Transaction—U.S. Issuers

SEC Filings	Description
Proxy Statements and Other Disclosure Documents	
PREM14A/DEFM14A	Preliminary/definitive proxy statement relating to an M&A transaction
PREM14C/DEFM14C[a]	Preliminary/definitive information statement relating to an M&A transaction
Schedule 13E-3	Filed to report going private transactions initiated by certain issuers or their affiliates
Tender Offer Documents	
Schedule TO	Filed by an acquirer upon commencement of a tender offer
Schedule 14D-9	Recommendation from the target's board of directors on how shareholders should respond to a tender offer
Registration Statement/Prospectus	
S-4	Registration statement for securities issued in connection with a business combination or exchange offer. May include proxy statement of acquirer and/or public target
424B	Prospectus
Current and Periodic Reports	
8-K	When filed in the context of an M&A transaction, used to disclose a material acquisition or sale of the company or a division/subsidiary
10-K and 10-Q	Target company's applicable annual and quarterly reports

[a] In certain circumstances, an *information statement* is sent to shareholders instead of a proxy statement. This occurs if one or more shareholders comprise a majority and can approve the transaction via a written consent, in which case a shareholder vote is not required. An information statement generally contains the same information as a proxy statement.

Equity Value Equity value ("equity purchase price" or "offer value") for public targets in precedent transactions is calculated in a similar manner as that for comparable companies. However, it is based on the announced offer price per share as opposed to the closing share price on a given day. To calculate equity value for public M&A targets, the offer price per share is multiplied by the target's fully diluted shares outstanding at the given offer price. For example, if the acquirer offers the target's shareholders $20.00 per share and the target has 50 million fully diluted shares outstanding (based on the TSM at that price), the equity purchase price would

EXHIBIT 2.4   Transaction Information by Target Type

Information Item	Target Type	
	Public	Private
Announcement Date	■ 8-K / Press Release	■ Acquirer 8-K / Press Release ■ News Run
Key Deal Terms[a]	■ 8-K / Press Release ■ Proxy ■ Schedule TO ■ 14D-9 ■ Registration Statement / Prospectus (S-4, 424B) ■ 13E-3	■ Acquirer 8-K / Press Release ■ Acquirer Proxy ■ Registration Statement / Prospectus (S-4, 424B) ■ M&A Database ■ News Run ■ Trade Publications
Target Description and Financial Data	■ Target 10-K / 10-Q ■ 8-K ■ Proxy ■ Registration Statement / Prospectus (S-4, 424B) ■ 13E-3	■ Acquirer 8-K ■ Acquirer Proxy ■ Registration Statement / Prospectus (S-4, 424B) ■ M&A Database ■ News Run ■ Trade Publications
Target Historical Share Price Data	■ Financial Information Service	NA

[a]Should be updated for amendments to the definitive agreement or a new definitive agreement for a new buyer.

be $1,000 million ($20.00 × 50 million). In those cases where the acquirer purchases less than 100% of the target's outstanding shares, equity value must be grossed up to calculate the implied equity value for the entire company.

In calculating fully diluted shares for precedent transactions, all outstanding in-the-money options and warrants are converted at their weighted average strike prices regardless of whether they are exercisable or not.[11] As with the calculation of fully diluted shares outstanding for comparable companies, out-of-the money options and warrants are not assumed to be converted. For convertible and equity-linked securities, the banker must determine whether they are in-the-money and perform conversion in accordance with the terms and *change of control* provisions as detailed in the registration statement/prospectus.

---

[11]Assumes that all unvested options and warrants vest upon a change of control (which typically reflects actual circumstances) and that no better detail exists for strike prices than that mentioned in the 10-K or 10-Q.

EXHIBIT 2.5 Precedent Transactions Input Page Template

Acquisition of Target by Acquirer
Input Page
($ in millions, except per share data)

General Information

	Target
Ticker	TRGT
Fiscal Year Ending	Jan-00
Marginal Tax Rate	-

	Acquirer
Ticker	ACQR
Fiscal Year Ending	Jan-00

Date Announced	1/0/1900
Date Effective	1/0/1900
Transaction Type	NA
Purchase Consideration	NA

Calculation of Equity and Enterprise Value

Offer Price per Share

Cash Offer Price per Share	-
Stock Offer Price per Share	-
Exchange Ratio	-
Acquirer Share Price	-
Offer Price per Share	-

Fully Diluted Shares Outstanding	-
Implied Equity Value	-

Implied Enterprise Value	
Plus: Total Debt	-
Plus: Preferred Stock	-
Plus: Noncontrolling Interest	-
Less: Cash and Cash Equivalents	-
Implied Enterprise Value	-

LTM Transaction Multiples

EV/Sales	NA
Metric	-
EV/EBITDA	NA
Metric	-
EV/EBIT	NA
Metric	-
P/E	NA
Metric	-

Premiums Paid

	Premium
Transaction Announcement	NA
1 Day Prior	

Unaffected Share Price	
1 Day Prior	NA
7 Days Prior	NA
30 Days Prior	NA

Source Documents

	Period	Date Filed
Target 10-K		1/0/1900
Target 10-Q	1/0/1900	1/0/1900
Target 8-K		1/0/1900
Target DEFM14A		1/0/1900
Acquirer 424B		1/0/1900
Acquirer 8-K		1/0/1900

Reported Income Statement

	FYE 1/0/1900	Prior Stub 1/0/1900	Current Stub 1/0/1900	LTM 1/0/1900
Sales				
COGS				
Gross Profit				
SG&A				
Other Expense / (Income)				
EBIT				
Interest Expense				
Pre-Tax Income				
Income Taxes				
Noncontrolling Interest				
Preferred Dividends				
Net Income				
Effective Tax Rate	NA	NA	NA	NA
Weighted Avg. Diluted Shares				
Diluted EPS	NA	NA	NA	NA

Adjusted Income Statement

	FYE	Prior Stub	Current Stub	LTM
Reported Gross Profit				
Non-recurring Items in COGS				
Adjusted Gross Profit				
% margin	NA	NA	NA	NA
Reported EBIT				
Non-recurring Items in COGS				
Other Non-recurring Items				
Adjusted EBIT				
% margin	NA	NA	NA	NA
Depreciation & Amortization				
Adjusted EBITDA				
% margin	NA	NA	NA	NA
Reported Net Income				
Non-recurring Items in COGS				
Other Non-recurring Items				
Non-operating Non-rec. Items				
Tax Adjustment				
Adjusted Net Income				
% margin	NA	NA	NA	NA
Adjusted Diluted EPS	NA	NA	NA	NA

Cash Flow Statement Data

	FYE	Prior Stub	Current Stub	LTM
Depreciation & Amortization				
% sales	NA	NA	NA	NA
Capital Expenditures				
% sales	NA	NA	NA	NA

Target Description

[to come]

Acquirer Description

[to come]

Comments

[to come]

Calculation of Fully Diluted Shares Outstanding

Basic Shares Outstanding	-
Plus: Shares from In-the-Money Options	-
Less: Shares Repurchased from Option Proceeds	-
Net New Shares from Options	-
Plus: Shares from Convertible Securities	-
Fully Diluted Shares Outstanding	-

Options/Warrants

Tranche	Number of Shares	Exercise Price	In-the-Money Shares	Proceeds
Batch 1			-	-
Batch 2			-	-
Batch 3			-	-
Batch 4			-	-
Batch 5			-	-
Total			-	-

Convertible Securities

	Amount	Conversion Price	Conversion Ratio	New Shares
Issue 1			-	-
Issue 2			-	-
Issue 3			-	-
Issue 4			-	-
Issue 5			-	-
Total				-

Notes

(1) [to come]
(2) [to come]
(3) [to come]
(4) [to come]
(5) [to come]

For M&A transactions in which the target is private, equity value is simply enterprise value less any assumed/refinanced net debt.

Purchase Consideration   Purchase consideration refers to the mix of cash, stock, and/or other securities that the acquirer offers to the target's shareholders. In some cases, the form of consideration can affect the target shareholders' perception of the value embedded in the offer. For example, some shareholders may prefer cash over stock as payment due to its guaranteed value. On the other hand, some shareholders may prefer stock compensation in order to participate in the upside potential of the combined companies. Tax consequences and other issues may also play a decisive role in guiding shareholder preferences.

The three primary types of consideration for a target's equity are all-cash, stock-for-stock, and cash/stock mix.

All-Cash Transaction   As the term implies, in an all-cash transaction, the acquirer makes an offer to purchase all or a portion of the target's shares outstanding for cash (see Exhibit 2.6). This makes for a simple equity value calculation by multiplying the cash offer price per share by the number of fully diluted shares outstanding. Cash represents the cleanest form of currency and certainty of value for all shareholders. However, receipt of such consideration typically triggers a taxable event as opposed to the exchange or receipt of shares of stock, which, if structured properly, is not taxable until the shares are eventually sold.

EXHIBIT 2.6   Press Release Excerpt for All-Cash Transaction

> CLEVELAND, Ohio – June 30, 2008 – AcquirerCo and TargetCo today announced the two companies have entered into a definitive agreement for AcquirerCo to acquire the equity of TargetCo, a publicly held company, in an all-cash transaction at a price of approximately $1.0 billion, or $20.00 per share. The acquisition is subject to TargetCo shareholder and regulatory approvals and other customary closing conditions, and is expected to close in the fourth quarter of 2008.

Stock-for-Stock Transaction   In a stock-for-stock transaction, the calculation of equity value is based on either a *fixed exchange ratio* or a *floating exchange ratio* ("fixed price"). The exchange ratio is calculated as offer price per share divided by the acquirer's share price. A fixed exchange ratio, which is more common than a fixed price structure, is a ratio of how many shares of the acquirer's stock are exchanged for each share of the target's stock. In a floating exchange ratio, the number of acquirer shares exchanged for target shares fluctuates so as to ensure a fixed value for the target's shareholders.

Fixed Exchange Ratio   A fixed exchange ratio defines the number of shares of the acquirer's stock to be exchanged for each share of the target's stock. As per Exhibit 2.7, if AcquirerCo agrees to exchange one half share of its stock for every one share of TargetCo stock, the exchange ratio is 0.5.

EXHIBIT 2.7 Press Release Excerpt for Fixed Exchange Ratio Structure

CLEVELAND, Ohio – June 30, 2008 – AcquirerCo has announced a definitive agreement to acquire TargetCo in an all stock transaction valued at $1.0 billion. Under the terms of the agreement, which has been approved by both boards of directors, TargetCo stockholders will receive, at a fixed exchange ratio, 0.50 shares of AcquirerCo common stock for every share of TargetCo common stock. Based on AcquirerCo's stock price on June 27, 2008, of $40.00, this represents a price of $20.00 per share of TargetCo common stock.

For precedent transactions, offer price per share is calculated by multiplying the exchange ratio by the share price of the acquirer, typically one day prior to announcement (see Exhibit 2.8).

EXHIBIT 2.8 Calculation of Offer Price per Share and Equity Value in a Fixed Exchange Ratio Structure

In a fixed exchange ratio structure, the offer price per share (value to target) moves in line with the underlying share price of the acquirer. The amount of the acquirer's shares received, however, is constant (see Exhibit 2.9). For example, assuming TargetCo has 50 million fully diluted shares outstanding, it will receive 25 million shares of AcquirerCo stock. The shares received by the target and the respective ownership percentages for the acquirer and target remain fixed regardless

EXHIBIT 2.9 Fixed Exchange Ratio – Value to Target and Shares Received of share price movement between execution of the definitive agreement ("signing") and transaction close (assuming no structural protections for either the acquirer or target, such as a *collar*).[12]

Following a deal's announcement, the market immediately starts to assimilate the publicly disclosed information. In response, the target's and acquirer's share prices begin to trade in line with the market's perception of the transaction.[13] Therefore, the target assumes the risk of a decline in the acquirer's share price, but preserves the potential to share in the upside, both immediately and over time. The fixed exchange ratio is more commonly used than the floating exchange ratio as it "links" both parties' share prices, thereby enabling them to share the risk (or opportunity) from movements post-announcement.

Floating Exchange Ratio   A floating exchange ratio represents the set dollar amount per share that the acquirer has agreed to pay for each share of the target's stock in the form of shares of the acquirer's stock. As per Exhibit 2.10, TargetCo shareholders will receive $20.00 worth of AcquirerCo shares for each share of TargetCo stock they own.

EXHIBIT 2.10   Press Release Excerpt for Floating Exchange Ratio Structure

CLEVELAND, Ohio – June 30, 2008 – AcquirerCo and TargetCo today announced the execution of a definitive agreement pursuant to which AcquirerCo will acquire TargetCo for stock. Pursuant to the agreement, TargetCo stockholders will receive $20.00 of AcquirerCo common stock for each share of TargetCo common stock they hold. The number of AcquirerCo shares to be issued to TargetCo stockholders will be calculated based on the average closing price of AcquirerCo common stock for the 30 trading days immediately preceding the third trading day before the closing of the transaction.

In a floating exchange ratio structure, as opposed to a fixed exchange ratio, the dollar offer price per share (value to target) is set and the number of shares exchanged fluctuates in accordance with the movement of the acquirer's share price (see Exhibit 2.11).

The number of shares to be exchanged is typically based on an average of the acquirer's share price for a specified time period prior to transaction close. This structure presents target shareholders with greater certainty in terms of value received as the acquirer assumes the full risk of a decline in its share price (assuming no structural protections for the acquirer). In general, a floating exchange ratio is used when the acquirer is significantly larger than the target. It is justified in these cases on the basis that while a significant decline in the target's business does not materially impact the value of the acquirer, the reciprocal is not true.

---

[12]In a fixed exchange ratio deal, a collar can be used to guarantee a certain range of prices to the target's shareholders. For example, a target may agree to a $20.00 offer price per share based on an exchange ratio of 1:2, with a collar guaranteeing that the shareholders will receive no less than $18.00 and no more than $22.00, regardless of how the acquirer's shares trade between signing and closing.

[13]Factors considered by the market when evaluating a proposed transaction include strategic merit, economics of the deal, synergies, and likelihood of closing.

EXHIBIT 2.11   Floating Exchange Ratio – Value to Target and Shares Received

Cash and Stock Transaction   In a cash and stock transaction, the acquirer offers a combination of cash and stock as purchase consideration (see Exhibit 2.12).

EXHIBIT 2.12   Press Release Excerpt for Cash and Stock Transaction

> CLEVELAND, Ohio – June 30, 2008 – AcquirerCo and TargetCo announced today that they signed a definitive agreement whereby AcquirerCo will acquire TargetCo for a purchase price of approximately $1.0 billion in a mix of cash and AcquirerCo stock. Under the terms of the agreement, which was unanimously approved by the boards of directors of both companies, TargetCo stockholders will receive $10.00 in cash and 0.25 shares of AcquirerCo common stock for each outstanding TargetCo share. Based AcquirerCo's closing price of $40.00 on June 27, 2008, AcquirerCo will issue an aggregate of approximately 12.5 million shares of its common stock and pay an aggregate of approximately $500.0 million in cash in the transaction.

The cash portion of the offer represents a fixed value per share for target shareholders. The stock portion of the offer can be set according to either a fixed or floating exchange ratio. The calculation of offer price per share and equity value in a cash and stock transaction (assuming a fixed exchange ratio) is shown in Exhibit 2.13.

EXHIBIT 2.13   Calculation of Offer Price per Share and Equity Value in a Cash and Stock Transaction

Enterprise Value   Enterprise value ("transaction value") is the total value offered by the acquirer for the target's equity interests, as well as the assumption or refinancing

of the target's net debt. It is calculated for precedent transactions in the same manner as for comparable companies, comprising the sum of equity, net debt, preferred stock, and noncontrolling interest. Exhibit 2.14 illustrates the calculation of enterprise value, with equity value calculated as offer price per share (the sum of the target's "unaffected" share price and premium paid, see "Premiums Paid") multiplied by the target's fully diluted shares outstanding.

EXHIBIT 2.14   Calculation of Enterprise Value

Calculation of Key Transaction Multiples

The key transaction multiples used in transaction comps mirror those used for trading comps. Equity value, as represented by the offer price for the target's equity, is used as a multiple of net income (or offer price per share as a multiple of diluted EPS) and enterprise value (or transaction value) is used as a multiple of EBITDA, EBIT, and to a lesser extent sales. In precedent transactions, these multiples are typically higher than those in trading comps due to the premium paid for control and/or synergies.

Multiples for precedent transactions are typically calculated on the basis of actual LTM financial statistics available at the time of announcement. The full projections that an acquirer uses to frame its purchase price decision are generally not public and subject to a confidentiality agreement.[14] Therefore, while equity research may offer insights into future performance for a public target, identifying the actual projections that an acquirer used when making its acquisition decision is typically not feasible. Furthermore, buyers are often hesitant to give sellers full credit for projected financial performance as they assume the risk for realization.

As previously discussed, whenever possible, the banker sources the information necessary to calculate the target's LTM financials directly from SEC filings and other public primary sources. As with trading comps, the LTM financial data needs to be adjusted for non-recurring items and recent events in order to calculate clean multiples that reflect the target's normalized performance.

---

[14]Legal contract between a buyer and seller that governs the sharing of confidential company information. See Chapter 6: M&A Sale Process for additional information. In the event the banker performing transaction comps is privy to non-public information regarding one of the selected comparable acquisitions, the banker must refrain from using that information in order to maintain client confidentiality.

Equity Value Multiples

Offer Price per Share-to-LTM EPS / Equity Value-to-LTM Net Income   The most broadly used equity value multiple is the P/E ratio, namely offer price per share divided by LTM diluted earnings per share (or equity value divided by LTM net income, see Exhibit 2.15).

EXHIBIT 2.15   Equity Value Multiples

Enterprise Value Multiples

Enterprise Value-to-LTM EBITDA, EBIT, and Sales   As in trading comps, enterprise value is used in the numerator when calculating multiples for financial statistics that apply to both debt and equity holders. The most common enterprise value multiples are shown in Exhibit 2.16, with EV/LTM EBITDA being the most prevalent. As discussed in Chapter 1, however, certain sectors may rely on additional or other metrics to drive valuation (see Exhibit 1.33).

EXHIBIT 2.16   Enterprise Value Multiples

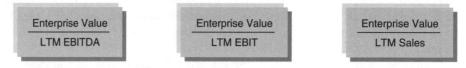

Premiums Paid   The *premium paid* refers to the incremental dollar amount per share that the acquirer offers relative to the target's unaffected share price, expressed as a percentage. As such, it is only relevant for public target companies. In calculating the premium paid relative to a given date, it is important to use the target's unaffected share price so as to isolate the true effect of the purchase offer.

The closing share price on the day prior to the official transaction announcement typically serves as a good proxy for the unaffected share price. However, to isolate for the effects of market gyrations and potential share price "creep" due to rumors or information leakage regarding the deal, the banker examines the offer price per share relative to the target's share price at multiple time intervals prior to transaction announcement (e.g., one trading day, seven calendar days, and 30 calendar days or more).[15]

In the event the seller has publicly announced its intention to pursue "strategic alternatives" or there is a major leak prior to announcement, the target's share

---

[15]Sixty, 90, 180, or an average of a set number of calendar days prior, as well as the 52-week high and low, may also be reviewed.

price may increase in anticipation of a potential takeover. In this case, the target's share price on the day(s) prior to the official transaction announcement is not truly unaffected. Therefore, it is appropriate to examine the premiums paid relative to the target's share price at various intervals prior to such an announcement or leak in addition to the actual transaction announcement.

The formula for calculating the percentage premium paid, as well as an illustrative example, is shown in Exhibit 2.17. In this example, we calculate a 25% premium assuming that the target's shareholders are being offered $20.00 per share for a stock that was trading at an unaffected share price of $16.00.

EXHIBIT 2.17   Calculation of Premium Paid

Synergies   Synergies refer to the expected cost savings, growth opportunities, and other financial benefits that occur as a result of the combination of two businesses. Consequently, the assessment of synergies is most relevant for transactions where a strategic buyer is purchasing a target in a related business.

Synergies represent tangible value to the acquirer in the form of future cash flow and earnings above and beyond what can be achieved by the target on a standalone basis. Therefore, the size and degree of likelihood for realizing potential synergies play an important role for the acquirer in framing the purchase price for a particular target. Theoretically, higher synergies translate into a higher potential price that the acquirer can pay. In analyzing a given comparable acquisition, the amount of announced synergies provides important perspective on the purchase price and multiple paid.

Upon announcement of a material acquisition, public acquirers often provide guidance on the nature and amount of expected synergies. This information is typically communicated via the press release announcing the transaction (see illustrative press release excerpt in Exhibit 2.18) and potentially an investor presentation. Equity research reports also may provide helpful commentary on the value of expected synergies, including the likelihood of realization. Depending on the situation, investors afford varying degrees of credit for announced synergies, as reflected in the acquirer's post-announcement share price.

In precedent transactions, it is helpful to note the announced expected synergies for each transaction where such information is available. However, the transaction multiples are typically shown on the basis of the target's reported LTM financial information (i.e., without adjusting for synergies). For a deeper understanding of a particular multiple paid, the banker may calculate adjusted multiples that reflect

EXHIBIT 2.18   Press Release Excerpt Discussing Synergies in a Strategic Acquisition

CLEVELAND, Ohio – June 30, 2008 – AcquirerCo and TargetCo announced today that they have signed a definitive agreement to merge the two companies…The proposed transaction is expected to provide substantial benefits for shareholders of the combined company and significant value creation through identified highly achievable synergies of $25.0 million in the first year after closing, and $50.0 million annually beginning in 2010. As facilities and operations are consolidated, a substantial portion of cost synergies and capital expenditure savings are expected to come from increased scale. Additional savings are expected to result from combining staff functions and the elimination of a significant amount of SG&A expenses that would be duplicative in the combined company.

expected synergies. This typically involves adding the full effect of expected annual run-rate cost savings synergies (excluding costs to achieve) to an earnings metric in the denominator (e.g., EBITDA).

Exhibit 2.19 shows the calculation of an EV/LTM EBITDA transaction multiple before and after the consideration of expected synergies, assuming a purchase price of $1,200 million, LTM EBITDA of $150 million, and synergies of $30 million.

EXHIBIT 2.19   Synergies-Adjusted Multiple

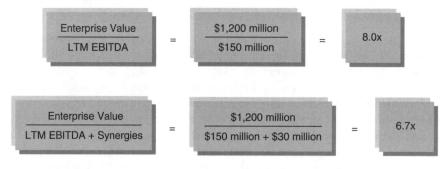

STEP IV. BENCHMARK THE COMPARABLE ACQUISITIONS

As with trading comps, the next level of analysis involves an in-depth study of the selected comparable acquisitions so as to determine those most relevant for valuing the target. As part of this analysis, the banker re-examines the business profile and benchmarks the key financial statistics and ratios for each of the acquired companies, with an eye toward identifying those most comparable to the target. Output sheets, such as those shown in Exhibits 1.53 and 1.54 in Chapter 1, facilitate this analysis.

The transaction multiples and deal information for each selected acquisition are also linked to an output sheet where they can be easily benchmarked against one another and the broader universe (see Exhibit 2.35). Each comparable acquisition is closely examined as part of the final refining of the universe, with the best comparable transactions identified and obvious outliers eliminated. As would be expected, a recently consummated deal involving a direct competitor with a similar financial profile is typically more relevant than, for example, an older transaction from a different point in the business or credit cycle, or for a marginal player in the sector.

A thoughtful analysis weighs other considerations such as market conditions and deal dynamics in conjunction with the target's business and financial profile. For example, a high multiple LBO consummated via an auction process during the credit boom of the mid-2000s would be less relevant for valuing a target in the ensuing period.

STEP V. DETERMINE VALUATION

In precedent transactions, the multiples of the selected comparable acquisitions universe are used to derive an implied valuation range for the target. While standards vary by sector, the key multiples driving valuation in precedent transactions tend to be enterprise value-to-LTM EBITDA and equity value-to-net income (or offer price per share-to-LTM diluted EPS, if public). Therefore, the banker typically uses the means and medians of these multiples from the universe to establish a preliminary valuation range for the target, with the highs and lows also serving as reference points.

As noted earlier, valuation requires a significant amount of art in addition to science. Therefore, while the mean and median multiples provide meaningful valuation guideposts, often the banker focuses on as few as two or three of the best transactions (as identified in Step IV) to establish valuation.

For example, if the banker calculates a mean $7.0\times$ EV/LTM EBITDA multiple for the comparable acquisitions universe, but the most relevant transactions were consummated in the $7.5\times$ to $8.0\times$ area, a $7.0\times$ to $8.0\times$ range might be more appropriate. This would place greater emphasis on the best transactions. The chosen multiple range would then be applied to the target's LTM financial statistics to derive an implied valuation range for the target, using the methodology described in Chapter 1 (see Exhibits 1.35, 1.36, and 1.37).

As with other valuation methodologies, once a valuation range for the target has been established, it is necessary to analyze the output and test conclusions. A common red flag for precedent transactions is when the implied valuation range is significantly lower than the range derived using comparable companies. In this instance, the banker should revisit the assumptions underlying the selection of both the universes of comparable acquisitions and comparable companies, as well as the calculations behind the multiples. However, it is important to note that this may not always represent a flawed analysis. If a particular sector is "in play" or benefiting from a cyclical high, for example, the implied valuation range from comparable companies might be higher than that from precedent transactions. The banker should also examine the results in isolation, using best judgment as well as guidance from a senior colleague to determine whether the results make sense.

KEY PROS AND CONS

Pros

- *Market-based* – analysis is based on actual acquisition multiples and premiums paid for similar companies

- *Current* – recent transactions tend to reflect prevailing M&A, capital markets, and general economic conditions

- *Relativity* – multiples approach provides straightforward reference points across sectors and time periods

- *Simplicity* – key multiples for a few selected transactions can anchor valuation

- *Objectivity* – precedent-based and, therefore, avoids making assumptions about a company's future performance

Cons

- *Market-based* – multiples may be skewed depending on capital markets and/or economic environment at the time of the transaction

- *Time lag* – precedent transactions, by definition, have occurred in the past and, therefore, may not be truly reflective of prevailing market conditions (e.g., the LBO boom in the mid-2000s vs. the ensuing credit crunch)

- *Existence of comparable acquisitions* – in some cases it may be difficult to find a robust universe of precedent transactions

- *Availability of information* – information may be insufficient to determine transaction multiples for many comparable acquisitions

- *Acquirer's basis for valuation* – multiple paid by the buyer may be based on expectations governing the target's future financial performance (which is typically not publicly disclosed) rather than on reported LTM financial information

ILLUSTRATIVE PRECEDENT TRANSACTION ANALYSIS FOR VALUECO

The following section provides a detailed, step-by-step example of how precedent transactions analysis is applied to establish a valuation range for our illustrative target company, ValueCo.

Step I. Select the Universe of Comparable Acquisitions

Screen for Comparable Acquisitions Our screen for comparable acquisitions began by searching M&A databases for past transactions involving companies similar to ValueCo in terms of sector and size. Our initial screen focused on transactions that occurred over the past three years with enterprise value of between $250 million and $3,000 million. At the same time, we examined the acquisition history of ValueCo's comparable companies (as determined in Chapter 1) for relevant transactions.

The comparable companies' public filings (including merger proxies) were helpful for identifying and analyzing past acquisitions and sales of relevant businesses. Research reports for individual companies as well as sector reports also provided valuable information. In total, these resources produced a sizeable list of potential precedent transactions. Upon further scrutiny, we eliminated several transactions where the target's size or business model differed significantly from that of ValueCo.

Examine Other Considerations For each of the selected transactions, we examined the specific deal circumstances, including market conditions and deal dynamics. For example, we discerned whether the acquisition took place during a cyclical high or low in the target's sector as well as the prevailing capital markets conditions. We also determined whether the acquirer was a strategic buyer or a financial sponsor and noted whether the target was sold through an auction process or a negotiated/friendly transaction, and if it was contested. The form of consideration (i.e., cash vs. stock) was also analyzed as part of this exercise. While these deal considerations did not change the list of comparable acquisitions, the context helped us better interpret and compare the acquisition multiples and premiums paid.

By the end of Step I, we established a solid initial list of comparable acquisitions to be further analyzed. Exhibit 2.20 displays basic data about the selected transactions and target companies for easy comparison.

Step II. Locate the Necessary Deal-Related and Financial Information

In Step II, we set out to locate the relevant deal-related and financial information necessary to spread each comparable acquisition. To illustrate this task, we highlighted Pearl Corp.'s ("Pearl") acquisition of Rosenbaum Industries ("Rosenbaum"), the most recent transaction on our list.[16] As this transaction involved a public acquirer

---

[16]Pearl is also a comparable company to ValueCo (see Chapter 1, Exhibits 1.53, 1.54, and 1.55).

EXHIBIT 2.20 Initial List of Comparable Acquisitions

($ in millions)

List of Comparable Acquisitions							
Date Announced	Acquirer	Target	Transaction Type	Target Business Description	Equity Value	Enterprise Value	LTM Sales
11/3/2008	Pearl Corp.	Rosenbaum Industries	Public / Public	Manufactures roofing and related products primarily in North America	$1,700	$2,000	$1,375
10/30/2008	Goodson Corp.	Schneider & Co.	Public / Public	Manufactures, distributes, and markets high-quality ceramic tile products globally	932	1,232	1,045
6/22/2008	Leicht & Co.	ParkCo	Public / Private	Manufactures vinyl, wood-clad, and fiberglass windows and aluminum doors	650	875	798
4/15/2008	Pryor, Inc.	Bress Products	Public / Public	Manufactures engineered wood products for use in commercial and residential construction	1,301	1,326	825
10/1/2007	The Hochberg Group	Whalen Inc.	Sponsor / Private	Manufactures kitchen, bathroom, and plumbing accessories for the home construction and remodeling markets	225	330	255
8/8/2007	Cole Manufacturing	Gordon Inc.	Public / Public	Manufactures and markets carpeting, rugs, and other flooring products and accessories	2,371	2,796	1,989
7/6/2007	Eu-Han Capital	Rughwani International	Sponsor / Public	Manufactures and distributes a variety of exterior building materials for the residential construction market	1,553	2,233	1,917
11/9/2006	The Meisner Group	Kamras Brands	Sponsor / Public	Manufactures interior and exterior doors primarily in North America and Europe	916	936	809
6/21/2006	Domanski Capital	Neren Industries	Sponsor / Public	Manufactures residential building products, including air conditioning and heating products, windows, doors, and siding	1,248	1,798	1,889
3/20/2006	Lanzarone International	Falk & Sons	Public / Private	Manufactures and distributes a wide range of outdoor and indoor lighting products to the commercial, industrial, and residential markets	360	530	588

and a public target, the necessary information was readily accessible via the relevant SEC filings.

8-K/Press Release   Our search for relevant deal information began by locating the 8-K filed upon announcement of the transaction. The 8-K contained the press release announcing the transaction as well as a copy of the definitive agreement as an exhibit. The press release provided an overview of the basic terms of the deal, including the offer price per share, enterprise value, and purchase consideration, as well as a description of both the acquirer and target and a brief description of the transaction rationale (see Exhibit 2.21). The definitive agreement contained the detailed terms and conditions of the transaction.

We also checked to see whether the original transaction changed for any new announced terms. As previously discussed, this is a relatively common occurrence in competitive situations where two or more parties enter into a bidding war for a given target.

EXHIBIT 2.21 Press Release Excerpt from the Announcement of the Pearl/Rosenbaum Transaction

CLEVELAND, Ohio – November 3, 2008 – PEARL CORP. (NYSE: PRL), a manufacturer of siding and windows, announced today that it has entered into a definitive agreement to acquire ROSENBAUM INDUSTRIES (NYSE: JNR), a manufacturer of roofing and related products, for an aggregate consideration of approximately $2.0 billion, including the payment of $20.00 per outstanding share in cash and the assumption of $300.0 million in net debt. The strategic business combination of Pearl and Rosenbaum will create the leading provider of "best-in-class" building products in North America. When completed, Pearl anticipates the combined companies will benefit from a broader product offering, complementary distribution channels, and efficiencies from streamlining facilities.

Proxy Statement (DEFM14A) As Rosenbaum is a public company, its board of directors sought approval for the transaction from Rosenbaum's shareholders via a proxy statement. The proxy statement contained Rosenbaum's most recent basic share count, a detailed background of the merger, discussion of the premium paid, and an excerpt from the fairness opinion, among other items. The background described key events leading up to the transaction announcement and provided us with helpful insight into other deal considerations useful for interpreting purchase price, including buyer/seller dynamics (see excerpt in Exhibit 2.22).

EXHIBIT 2.22 Excerpt from Rosenbaum's Proxy Statement

On June 2, 2008, Rosenbaum's CEO was informed of a financial sponsor's interest in a potential takeover and request for additional information in order to make a formal bid. This unsolicited interest prompted Rosenbaum's board of directors to form a special committee and engage an investment bank and legal counsel to explore strategic alternatives. Upon being contacted by Rosenbaum's advisor, the sponsor submitted a written indication of interest containing a preliminary valuation range of $15.00 to $17.00 per share and outlining a proposed due diligence process. Subsequently, certain media outlets reported that a sale of Rosenbaum was imminent, prompting the company to publicly announce its decision to explore strategic alternatives on August 15, 2008.

One week later, Pearl, a strategic buyer, sent Rosenbaum a preliminary written indication of interest with a price range of $17.00 to $18.00. In addition, Rosenbaum's advisor contacted an additional 5 strategic buyers and 5 financial sponsors, although these parties did not ultimately participate in the formal process. Both the bidding financial sponsor and Pearl were then invited to attend a management presentation and perform due diligence, after which the financial sponsor and Pearl presented formal letters with bids of $18.00 and $20.00 per share in cash, respectively. Pearl's bid, as the highest cash offer, was accepted.

This background highlights the competitive dynamics involved in the process, which helped explain why the multiple paid for Rosenbaum is above the mean of the selected comparable acquisitions (see Exhibit 2.35).

Rosenbaum's 10-K and 10-Q Rosenbaum's 10-K and 10-Q for the period prior to transaction announcement provided us with the financial data necessary to calculate its LTM financial statistics as well as equity value and enterprise value (based on the offer price per share). We also read through the MD&A and notes to the financials for further insight into Rosenbaum's financial performance as well as for information on potential non-recurring items and recent events. *These public filings provided us with the remaining information necessary to calculate the transaction multiples.*

Research Reports   We also read through equity research reports for Pearl and Rosenbaum following the transaction announcement for further color on the circumstances of the deal, including Pearl's strategic rationale and expected synergies.

Investor Presentation   In addition, Pearl posted an investor presentation to its corporate website under an "Investor Relations" link, which confirmed the financial information and multiples calculated in Exhibit 2.23.

Financial Information Service   We used a financial information service to source key historical share price information for Rosenbaum. These data points included the share price on the day prior to the actual transaction announcement, the unaffected share price (i.e., on the day prior to Rosenbaum's announcement of the exploration of strategic alternatives), and the share price at various intervals prior to the unaffected share price. This share price information served as the basis for the premiums paid calculations in Exhibit 2.33.

Step III. Spread Key Statistics, Ratios, and Transaction Multiples

After locating the necessary deal-related and financial information for the selected comparable acquisitions, we created input pages for each transaction, as shown in Exhibit 2.23 for the Pearl/Rosenbaum transaction.

EXHIBIT 2.23 Input Page for the Acquisition of Rosenbaum by Pearl

Acquisition of Rosenbaum Industries by Pearl Corp.
Input Page
($ in millions, except per share data)

General Information

Target	
Ticker	Rosenbaum Industries / JNR
Fiscal Year Ending	Dec-31
Marginal Tax Rate	38.0%

Acquirer	
Ticker	Pearl Corp. / PRL
Fiscal Year Ending	Dec-31

Date Announced	11/3/2008
Date Effective	Pending
Transaction Type	Public / Public
Purchase Consideration	Cash

Calculation of Equity and Enterprise Value

Offer Price per Share	
Cash Offer Price per Share	$20.00
Stock Offer Price per Share	-
Exchange Ratio	-
Pearl Corp. Share Price	-
Offer Price per Share	**$20.00**

Fully Diluted Shares Outstanding	85.000
Implied Equity Value	**$1,700.0**
Plus: Total Debt	325.0
Plus: Preferred Stock	-
Plus: Noncontrolling Interest	-
Less: Cash and Cash Equivalents	(25.0)
Implied Enterprise Value	**$2,000.0**

LTM Transaction Multiples

	Metric	Metric
EV/Sales	1.5x	$1,375.0
EV/EBITDA	8.0x	$250.0
EV/EBIT	9.1x	$220.0
P/E	13.6x	$1.47

Premiums Paid

Transaction Announcement	Unaffected Share Price	Premium
1 Day Prior	$17.39	15.0%
1 Day Prior	$15.38	30.0%
7 Days Prior	$15.75	27.0%
30 Days Prior	$15.04	33.0%

Source Documents

	Period	Date Filed
Rosenbaum Industries 10-K	12/31/2007	2/14/2008
Rosenbaum Industries 10-Q	9/30/2008	10/30/2008
Rosenbaum Industries 8-K		11/3/2008
Rosenbaum Industries DEFM14A		12/15/2008

Reported Income Statement

	FYE 12/31/2007	Prior Stub 9/30/2007	Current Stub 9/30/2008	LTM 9/30/2008
Sales	$1,250.0	$875.0	$1,000.0	$1,375.0
COGS	815.0	570.0	650.0	895.0
Gross Profit	**$435.0**	**$305.0**	**$350.0**	**$480.0**
SG&A	250.0	175.0	200.0	275.0
Other Expense / (Income)	-	-	-	-
EBIT	**$185.0**	**$130.0**	**$150.0**	**$205.0**
Interest Expense	18.8	14.4	14.1	18.4
Pre-tax Income	**$166.2**	**$115.6**	**$135.9**	**$186.6**
Income Taxes	63.2	43.9	51.7	70.9
Noncontrolling Interest	-	-	-	-
Preferred Dividends	-	-	-	-
Net Income	**$103.1**	**$71.6**	**$84.3**	**$115.7**
Effective Tax Rate	*38.0%*	*38.0%*	*38.0%*	*38.0%*
Weighted Avg. Diluted Shares	85.0	85.0	85.0	85.0
Diluted EPS	$1.21	$0.84	$0.99	$1.36

Adjusted Income Statement

	FYE 12/31/2007	Prior Stub 9/30/2007	Current Stub 9/30/2008	LTM 9/30/2008
Reported Gross Profit	$435.0	$305.0	$350.0	$480.0
Non-recurring Items in COGS	-	-	-	-
Adjusted Gross Profit	**$435.0**	**$305.0**	**$350.0**	**$480.0**
% margin	*34.8%*	*34.9%*	*35.0%*	*34.9%*
Reported EBIT	$185.0	$130.0	$150.0	$205.0
Non-recurring Items in COGS	-			-
Other Non-recurring Items	15.0	-	-	15.0
Adjusted EBIT	**$200.0**	**$130.0**	**$150.0**	**$220.0**
% margin	*16.0%*	*14.9%*	*15.0%*	*16.0%*
Depreciation & Amortization	28.0	22.0	24.0	30.0
Adjusted EBITDA	**$228.0**	**$152.0**	**$174.0**	**$250.0**
% margin	*18.2%*	*17.4%*	*17.4%*	*18.2%*
Reported Net Income	$103.1	$71.6	$84.3	$115.7
Non-recurring Items in COGS	-			-
Other Non-recurring Items	15.0	-	-	15.0
Non-operating Non-rec. Items	-			-
Tax Adjustment	(5.7)	-	-	(5.7)
Adjusted Net Income	**$112.4**	**$71.6**	**$84.3**	**$125.0**
% margin	*9.0%*	*8.2%*	*8.4%*	*9.1%*
Adjusted Diluted EPS	**$1.32**	**$0.84**	**$0.99**	**$1.47**

Cash Flow Statement Data

	FYE 12/31/2007	Prior Stub 9/30/2007	Current Stub 9/30/2008	LTM 9/30/2008
Depreciation & Amortization	28.0	22.0	24.0	30.0
% sales	*2.2%*	*2.5%*	*2.4%*	*2.2%*
Capital Expenditures	27.0	20.0	22.0	29.0
% sales	*2.2%*	*2.3%*	*2.2%*	*2.1%*

(1)

Target Description

Manufactures roofing and related products primarily in North America

Acquirer Description

Manufactures and distributes building products in North America and internationally, including roofing, siding, and windows

Comments

The combined company will benefit from a broader product offering, complementary distribution channels, and efficiencies from streamlining facilities.

Calculation of Fully Diluted Shares Outstanding

Basic Shares Outstanding	83.000
Plus: Shares from In-the-Money Options	3.750
Less: Shares Repurchased from Option Proceeds	(1.750)
Net New Shares from Options	2.000
Plus: Shares from Convertible Securities	-
Fully Diluted Shares Outstanding	**85.000**

Options/Warrants

Tranche	Number of Shares	Exercise Price	In-the-Money Shares	Proceeds
Tranche 1	1.500	$5.00	1.500	$7.5
Tranche 2	1.250	10.00	1.250	12.5
Tranche 3	1.000	15.00	1.000	15.0
Tranche 4	-	-	-	-
Tranche 5	-	-	-	-
Total	**3.750**		**3.750**	**$35.0**

Convertible Securities

	Amount	Conversion Price	Conversion Ratio	New Shares
Issue 1	-	-	-	-
Issue 2	-	-	-	-
Issue 3	-	-	-	-
Issue 4	-	-	-	-
Issue 5	-	-	-	-
Total	**-**			**-**

Notes

(1) In Q4 2007, Rosenbaum Industries recorded a $15.0 million pre-tax payment in regards to a litigation settlement (see 2007 10-K MD&A, page 50).

(2) On August 15, 2008, Rosenbaum Industries announced the formation of a special committee to explore strategic alternatives.

Below, we walk through each section of the input sheet in Exhibit 2.23.

General Information   In the "General Information" section of the input page, we entered basic company and transaction information, such as the target's and acquirer's names and fiscal year ends, as well as the transaction announcement and closing dates, transaction type, and purchase consideration. As shown in Exhibit 2.24, Rosenbaum Industries (NYSE:JNR) was acquired by Pearl Corp. (NYSE:PRL) in an all-cash transaction. Both companies have a fiscal year ending December 31. The transaction was announced on November 3, 2008.

EXHIBIT 2.24   General Information Section

General Information	
Target	**Rosenbaum Industries**
Ticker	JNR
Fiscal Year Ending	Dec-31
Marginal Tax Rate	*38.0%*
Acquirer	**Pearl Corp.**
Ticker	PRL
Fiscal Year Ending	Dec-31
Date Announced	11/3/2008
Date Effective	Pending
Transaction Type	Public / Public
Purchase Consideration	Cash

EXHIBIT 2.25   Calculation of Equity and Enterprise Value Section

Calculation of Equity and Enterprise Value	
Offer Price per Share	
Cash Offer Price per Share	$20.00
Stock Offer Price per Share	-
Exchange Ratio	-
Pearl Corp. Share Price	-
Offer Price per Share	**$20.00**
Fully Diluted Shares Outstanding	-
Implied Equity Value	**-**
Implied Enterprise Value	
Plus: Total Debt	-
Plus: Preferred Stock	-
Plus: Noncontrolling Interest	-
Less: Cash and Cash Equivalents	-
Implied Enterprise Value	**-**

= Cash Offer Price per Share + Stock Offer Price per Share
= $20.00 + $0.00

Calculation of Equity and Enterprise Value Under "Calculation of Equity and Enterprise Value," we first entered Pearl's offer price per share of $20.00 in cash to Rosenbaum's shareholders, as disclosed in the 8-K and accompanying press release announcing the transaction (see Exhibit 2.25).

Calculation of Fully Diluted Shares Outstanding As sourced from the most recent proxy statement, Rosenbaum had basic shares outstanding of 83 million. Rosenbaum also had three "tranches" of options, as detailed in its most recent 10-K (see "Options/Warrants" heading in Exhibit 2.26).

At the $20.00 offer price, the three tranches of options are all in-the-money. In calculating fully diluted shares outstanding for precedent transactions, all outstanding in-the-money options and warrants are converted at their weighted average strike prices regardless of whether they are exercisable or not. These three tranches represent 3.75 million shares, which generate total proceeds of $35 million at their respective exercise prices. In accordance with the TSM, these proceeds are assumed to repurchase 1.75 million shares at the $20.00 offer price ($35 million / $20.00), thereby providing net new shares of 2 million. These incremental shares are added to Rosenbaum's basic shares to calculate fully diluted shares outstanding of 85 million.

EXHIBIT 2.26 Calculation of Fully Diluted Shares Outstanding Section

Equity Value The 85 million fully diluted shares outstanding feeds into the "Calculation of Equity and Enterprise Value" section. It is multiplied by the $20.00 offer price per share to produce an equity value of $1,700 million (see Exhibit 2.27).

EXHIBIT 2.27   Equity Value

Calculation of Equity and Enterprise Value	
Offer Price per Share	
Cash Offer Price per Share	$20.00
Stock Offer Price per Share	-
Exchange Ratio	-
Pearl Corp. Share Price	-
Offer Price per Share	**$20.00**
Fully Diluted Shares Outstanding	85.000
Implied Equity Value	**$1,700.0**

= Offer Price per Price x Fully Diluted Shares Outstanding
= $20.00 x 85.0 million

Enterprise Value   Rosenbaum's enterprise value was determined by adding net debt to the calculated equity value. We calculated net debt of $300 million by subtracting cash and cash equivalents of $25 million from total debt of $325 million, as sourced from Rosenbaum's 10-Q for the period ending September 30, 2008. The $300 million was then added to the calculated equity value of $1,700 million to derive an enterprise value of $2,000 million (see Exhibit 2.28).

EXHIBIT 2.28   Enterprise Value

Calculation of Equity and Enterprise Value	
Offer Price per Share	
Cash Offer Price per Share	$20.00
Stock Offer Price per Share	-
Exchange Ratio	-
Pearl Corp. Share Price	-
Offer Price per Share	**$20.00**
Fully Diluted Shares Outstanding	85.000
Implied Equity Value	**$1,700.0**
Implied Enterprise Value	
Plus: Total Debt	325.0
Plus: Preferred Stock	-
Plus: Noncontrolling Interest	-
Less: Cash and Cash Equivalents	(25.0)
Implied Enterprise Value	**$2,000.0**

= Equity Value + Total Debt - Cash
= $1,700.0 million + $325.0 million - $25.0 million

Reported Income Statement   Next, we entered Rosenbaum's income statement information for the prior full year 2007 and YTD 2007 and 2008 periods directly from its most recent 10-K and 10-Q, respectively (see Exhibit 2.29). We also made adjustments for non-recurring items, as appropriate (see Exhibit 2.30).

EXHIBIT 2.29 Rosenbaum's Reported Income Statement Section

Reported Income Statement				
	FYE 12/31/2007	Prior Stub 9/30/2007	Current Stub 9/30/2008	LTM 9/30/2008
Sales	$1,250.0	$875.0	$1,000.0	$1,375.0
COGS	815.0	570.0	650.0	895.0
Gross Profit	$435.0	$305.0	$350.0	$480.0
SG&A	250.0	175.0	200.0	275.0
Other Expense / (Income)	-	-	-	-
EBIT	$185.0	$130.0	$150.0	$205.0
Interest Expense	18.8	14.4	14.1	18.4
Pre-tax Income	$166.2	$115.6	$135.9	$186.6
Income Taxes	63.2	43.9	51.7	70.9
Noncontrolling Interest	-	-	-	-
Preferred Dividends	-	-	-	-
Net Income	$103.1	$71.6	$84.3	$115.7
Effective Tax Rate	*38.0%*	*38.0%*	*38.0%*	*38.0%*
Weighted Avg. Diluted Shares	85.0	85.0	85.0	85.0
Diluted EPS	$1.21	$0.84	$0.99	$1.36

EXHIBIT 2.30 Rosenbaum's Adjusted Income Statement Section

Litigation settlement

Adjusted Income Statement				
	FYE 12/31/2007	Prior Stub 9/30/2007	Current Stub 9/30/2008	LTM 9/30/2008
Reported Gross Profit	$435.0	$305.0	$350.0	$480.0
Non-recurring Items in COGS	-	-	-	-
Adjusted Gross Profit	$435.0	$305.0	$350.0	$480.0
% margin	*34.8%*	*34.9%*	*35.0%*	*34.9%*
Reported EBIT	$185.0	$130.0	$150.0	$205.0
Non-recurring Items in COGS	-	-	-	-
Other Non-recurring Items	15.0	-	-	15.0 (1)
Adjusted EBIT	$200.0	$130.0	$150.0	$220.0
% margin	*16.0%*	*14.9%*	*15.0%*	*16.0%*
Depreciation & Amortization	28.0	22.0	24.0	30.0
Adjusted EBITDA	$228.0	$152.0	$174.0	$250.0
% margin	*18.2%*	*17.4%*	*17.4%*	*18.2%*
Reported Net Income	$103.1	$71.6	$84.3	$115.7
Non-recurring Items in COGS	-	-	-	-
Other Non-recurring Items	15.0	-	-	15.0
Non-operating Non-rec. Items	-	-	-	-
Tax Adjustment	(5.7)	-	-	(5.7)
Adjusted Net Income	$112.4	$71.6	$84.3	$125.0
% margin	*9.0%*	*8.2%*	*8.4%*	*9.1%*
Adjusted Diluted EPS	$1.32	$0.84	$0.99	$1.47

(1) In Q4 2007, Rosenbaum Industries recorded a $15.0 million pre-tax payment in regards to a litigation settlement (see 2007 10-K MD&A, page 50).

= Negative adjustment for pre-tax gain on asset sale x Marginal tax rate
= - $15.0 million x 38.0%

Adjusted Income Statement   A review of Rosenbaum's financial statements and MD&A revealed that it made a $15 million pre-tax payment regarding a litigation settlement in Q4 2007, which we construed as non-recurring. Therefore, we added this charge back to Rosenbaum's reported financials, resulting in adjusted EBITDA, EBIT, and net income of $250 million, $220 million and $125 million, respectively. *These adjusted financials served as the basis for calculating Rosenbaum's transaction multiples in Exhibit 2.32.*

Cash Flow Statement Data   Rosenbaum's D&A and capex information was sourced directly from its cash flow statement, as it appeared in the 10-K and 10-Q (see Exhibit 2.31).

EXHIBIT 2.31   Cash Flow Statement Data Section

Cash Flow Statement Data				
	FYE 12/31/2007	Prior Stub 9/30/2007	Current Stub 9/30/2008	LTM 9/30/2008
Depreciation & Amortization	28.0	22.0	24.0	30.0
% sales	*2.2%*	*2.5%*	*2.4%*	*2.2%*
Capital Expenditures	27.0	20.0	22.0	29.0
% sales	*2.2%*	*2.3%*	*2.2%*	*2.1%*

LTM Transaction Multiples   For the calculation of Rosenbaum's transaction multiples, we applied enterprise value and offer price per share to the corresponding adjusted LTM financial data (see Exhibit 2.32). These multiples were then linked to the precedent transactions output sheet (see Exhibit 2.35) where the multiples for the entire universe are displayed.

EXHIBIT 2.32   LTM Transaction Multiples Section

LTM Transaction Multiples	
EV/Sales	1.5x
Metric	$1,375.0
EV/EBITDA	8.0x
Metric	$250.0
EV/EBIT	9.1x
Metric	$220.0
P/E	13.6x
Metric	$1.47

= Enterprise Value / LTM 9/30/08 EBITDA
= $2,000.0 million / $250.0 million

Enterprise Value-to-LTM EBITDA   For EV/LTM EBITDA, we divided Rosenbaum's enterprise value of $2,000 million by its LTM 9/30/08 adjusted EBITDA of $250 million to provide a multiple of 8.0×. We used the same approach to calculate the LTM EV/sales and EV/EBIT multiples.

Offer Price per Share-to-LTM Diluted Earnings per Share   For P/E, we divided the offer price per share of $20.00 by Rosenbaum's LTM diluted EPS of $1.47 to provide a multiple of 13.6×.

Premiums Paid   The premiums paid analysis for precedent transactions does not apply when valuing private companies such as ValueCo. However, as Rosenbaum was a public company, we performed this analysis for illustrative purposes (see Exhibit 2.33).

EXHIBIT 2.33   Premiums Paid Section

Premiums Paid		
Transaction Announcement		**Premium**
1 Day Prior	$17.39	15.0%
Unaffected Share Price		
1 Day Prior	$15.38	30.0%
7 Days Prior	15.75	27.0%
30 Days Prior	15.04	33.0%

(2)

= Offer Price per Price / Share Price One Day Prior to Announcement - 1
= $20.00 / $16.67 - 1

Notes
(2) On August 15, 2008, Rosenbaum Industries announced the formation of a special committee to explore strategic alternatives.

The $20.00 offer price per share served as the basis for performing the premiums paid analysis, representing a 15% premium to Rosenbaum's share price of $17.39 on the day prior to transaction announcement. However, as shown in Exhibit 2.34, Rosenbaum's share price was directly affected by the announcement that it was exploring strategic alternatives on August 15, 2008 (even though the actual deal wasn't announced until November 3, 2008). Therefore, we also analyzed the unaffected premiums paid on the basis of Rosenbaum's closing share prices of $15.38, $15.75, and $15.04, for the one-, seven-, and 30-calendar-day periods prior to August 15, 2008. This provided us with premiums paid of 30%, 27%, and 33%, respectively, which are more in line with traditional public M&A premiums.

Step IV. Benchmark the Comparable Acquisitions

In Step IV, we linked the key financial statistics and ratios for the target companies (calculated in Step III) to output sheets used for benchmarking purposes (see Chapter 1, Exhibits 1.53 and 1.54, for general templates). The benchmarking sheets helped us determine those targets most comparable to ValueCo from a financial perspective, namely Rosenbaum Industries, Schneider & Co., and ParkCo. At the same time, our analysis in Step I provided us with sufficient information to confirm that these companies were highly comparable to ValueCo from a business perspective.

The relevant transaction multiples and deal information for each of the individual comparable acquisitions were also linked to an output sheet. As shown in Exhibit 2.35, ValueCo's sector experienced robust M&A activity during the 2006 to

EXHIBIT 2.34   Rosenbaum's Annotated Price/Volume Graph

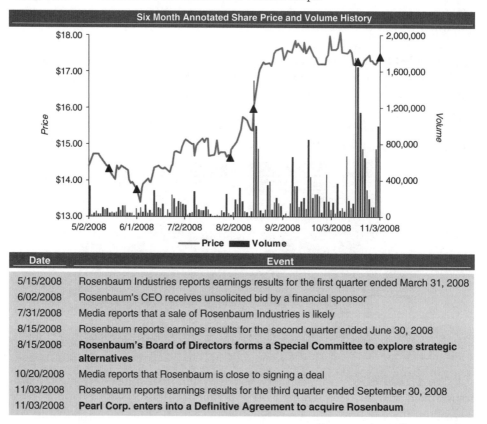

Date	Event
5/15/2008	Rosenbaum Industries reports earnings results for the first quarter ended March 31, 2008
6/02/2008	Rosenbaum's CEO receives unsolicited bid by a financial sponsor
7/31/2008	Media reports that a sale of Rosenbaum Industries is likely
8/15/2008	Rosenbaum reports earnings results for the second quarter ended June 30, 2008
8/15/2008	**Rosenbaum's Board of Directors forms a Special Committee to explore strategic alternatives**
10/20/2008	Media reports that Rosenbaum is close to signing a deal
11/03/2008	Rosenbaum reports earnings results for the third quarter ended September 30, 2008
11/03/2008	**Pearl Corp. enters into a Definitive Agreement to acquire Rosenbaum**

2008 period, which provided us with sufficient relevant data points for our analysis. Consideration of the market conditions and other deal dynamics for each of these transactions further supported our selection of Pearl Corp./Rosenbaum Industries, Goodson Corp./Schneider & Co., and Leicht & Co./ParkCo as the best comparable acquisitions. These multiples formed the primary basis for our selection of the appropriate multiple range for ValueCo.

Step V. Determine Valuation

In ValueCo's sector, companies are typically valued on the basis of EV/EBITDA multiples. Therefore, we employed an LTM EV/EBITDA multiple approach in valuing ValueCo using precedent transactions. We placed particular emphasis on those transactions deemed most comparable, namely the acquisitions of Rosenbaum Industries, Schneider & Co., and ParkCo to frame the range (as discussed in Step IV).

This approach led us to establish a multiple range of 7.0× to 8.0× LTM EBITDA. We then multiplied the endpoints of this range by ValueCo's LTM 9/30/08 EBITDA of $146.7 million to calculate an implied enterprise value range of approximately $1,027 million to $1,173 million (see Exhibit 2.36).

EXHIBIT 2.35 Precedent Transactions Analysis Output Page

ValueCo Corporation
Precedent Transactions Analysis
($ in millions)

Date Announced	Acquirer	Target	Transaction Type	Purchase Consideration	Equity Value	Enterprise Value	Enterprise Value / LTM Sales	Enterprise Value / LTM EBITDA	Enterprise Value / LTM EBIT	LTM EBITDA Margin	Equity Value / LTM Net Income	Premiums Paid — Days Prior to Unaffected 1	7	30
11/3/2008	Pearl Corp.	Rosenbaum Industries	Public / Public	Cash	$1,700	$2,000	1.5x	8.0x	9.1x	18%	13.6x	30%	27%	33%
10/30/2008	Goodson Corp.	Schneider & Co.	Public / Public	Cash / Stock	932	1,232	1.2x	7.6x	8.7x	16%	13.9x	29%	32%	31%
6/22/2008	Leicht & Co.	ParkCo	Public / Private	Cash	650	875	1.1x	7.1x	8.1x	15%	12.0x	NA	NA	NA
4/15/2008	Pryor, Inc.	Bress Products	Public / Public	Stock	1,301	1,326	1.6x	8.5x	12.5x	19%	14.4x	29%	36%	34%
10/1/2007	The Hochberg Group	Whalen Inc.	Sponsor / Private	Cash	225	330	1.3x	7.7x	9.2x	17%	13.3x	NA	NA	NA
8/8/2007	Cole Manufacturing	Gordon Inc.	Public / Public	Stock	2,371	2,796	1.4x	8.0x	10.7x	18%	17.7x	33%	31%	36%
7/6/2007	Eu-Han Capital	Rughwani International	Sponsor / Public	Cash	1,553	2,233	1.2x	7.5x	9.3x	15%	12.4x	38%	42%	43%
11/9/2006	The Meisner Group	Kamras Brands	Sponsor / Public	Cash	916	936	1.2x	7.3x	8.3x	16%	13.1x	34%	35%	36%
6/21/2006	Domanski Capital	Neren Industries	Sponsor / Public	Cash	1,248	1,798	1.0x	7.2x	8.3x	13%	16.0x	35%	37%	39%
3/20/2006	Lanzarone International	Falk & Sons	Public / Private	Cash	360	530	0.9x	6.5x	8.1x	14%	10.6x	NA	NA	NA
Mean							1.2x	7.5x	9.2x	16%	13.7x	33%	34%	36%
Median							1.2x	7.5x	8.9x	16%	13.4x	33%	35%	36%
High							1.6x	8.5x	12.5x	19%	17.7x	38%	42%	43%
Low							0.9x	6.5x	8.1x	13%	10.6x	29%	27%	31%

Source: Company filings

EXHIBIT 2.36 ValueCo's Implied Valuation Range

ValueCo Corporation				
Implied Valuation Range				
($ in millions, LTM 9/30/2008)				

EBITDA	Metric	Multiple Range		Implied Enterprise Value
LTM	$146.7	7.00x –	8.00x	$1,026.7 – $1,173.3

As a final step, we analyzed the valuation range derived from precedent transactions versus that derived from comparable companies. As shown in the football field in Exhibit 2.37, the valuation range derived from precedent transactions is relatively consistent with that derived from comparable companies. The slight premium to comparable companies can be attributed to the premiums paid in M&A transactions.

EXHIBIT 2.37 ValueCo Football Field Displaying Comparable Companies and Precedent Transactions

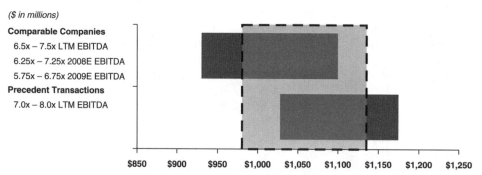

($ in millions)

Comparable Companies
6.5x – 7.5x LTM EBITDA
6.25x – 7.25x 2008E EBITDA
5.75x – 6.75x 2009E EBITDA
Precedent Transactions
7.0x – 8.0x LTM EBITDA

$850 $900 $950 $1,000 $1,050 $1,100 $1,150 $1,200 $1,250

Discounted Cash Flow Analysis

Discounted cash flow analysis ("DCF analysis" or the "DCF") is a fundamental valuation methodology broadly used by investment bankers, corporate officers, university professors, investors, and other finance professionals. It is premised on the principle that the value of a company, division, business, or collection of assets ("target") can be derived from the present value of its projected *free cash flow* (FCF). A company's projected FCF is derived from a variety of assumptions and judgments about its expected financial performance, including sales growth rates, profit margins, capital expenditures, and *net working capital* (NWC) requirements. The DCF has a wide range of applications, including valuation for various M&A situations, IPOs, restructurings, and investment decisions.

The valuation implied for a target by a DCF is also known as its *intrinsic value*, as opposed to its market value, which is the value ascribed by the market at a given point in time. As a result, when performing a comprehensive valuation, a DCF serves as an important alternative to market-based valuation techniques such as comparable companies and precedent transactions, which can be distorted by a number of factors, including market aberrations (e.g., the post-subprime credit crunch). As such, a DCF plays an important role as a check on the prevailing market valuation for a publicly traded company. A DCF is also valuable when there are limited (or no) pure play, peer companies or comparable acquisitions.

In a DCF, a company's FCF is typically projected for a period of five years. The projection period, however, may be longer depending on the company's sector, stage of development, and the underlying predictability of its financial performance. Given the inherent difficulties in accurately projecting a company's financial performance over an extended period of time (and through various business and economic cycles), a *terminal value* is used to capture the remaining value of the target beyond the projection period (i.e., its "going concern" value).

The projected FCF and terminal value are discounted to the present at the target's *weighted average cost of capital* (WACC), which is a discount rate commensurate with its business and financial risks. The present value of the FCF and terminal value are summed to determine an enterprise value, which serves as the basis for the DCF valuation. The WACC and terminal value assumptions typically have a substantial impact on the output, with even slight variations producing meaningful differences in valuation. As a result, a DCF output is viewed in terms of a valuation range based on a range of key input assumptions, rather than as a single value. The impact of these assumptions on valuation is tested using *sensitivity analysis*.

The assumptions driving a DCF are both its primary strength and weakness versus market-based valuation techniques. On the positive side, the use of defensible assumptions regarding financial projections, WACC, and terminal value helps shield the target's valuation from market distortions that occur periodically. In addition, a DCF provides the flexibility to analyze the target's valuation under different scenarios by changing the underlying inputs and examining the resulting impact. On the negative side, a DCF is only as strong as its assumptions. Hence, assumptions that fail to adequately capture the realistic set of opportunities and risks facing the target will also fail to produce a meaningful valuation.

This chapter walks through a step-by-step construction of a DCF, or its science (see Exhibit 3.1). At the same time, it provides the tools to master the art of the DCF, namely the ability to craft a logical set of assumptions based on an in-depth analysis of the target and its key performance drivers. Once this framework is established, we perform an illustrative DCF analysis for our target company, ValueCo.

EXHIBIT 3.1   Discounted Cash Flow Analysis Steps

Step I.   Study the Target and Determine Key Performance Drivers
Step II.   Project Free Cash Flow
Step III.   Calculate Weighted Average Cost of Capital
Step IV.   Determine Terminal Value
Step V.   Calculate Present Value and Determine Valuation

Summary of Discounted Cash Flow Analysis Steps

- **Step I. Study the Target and Determine Key Performance Drivers.** The first step in performing a DCF, as with any valuation exercise, is to study and learn as much as possible about the target and its sector. Shortcuts in this critical area of due diligence may lead to misguided assumptions and valuation distortions later on. This exercise involves determining the key drivers of financial performance (in particular sales growth, profitability, and FCF generation), which enables the banker to craft (or support) a defensible set of projections for the target. Step I is invariably easier when valuing a public company as opposed to a private company due to the availability of information from sources such as SEC filings (e.g., 10-Ks, 10-Qs, and 8-Ks), equity research reports, earnings call transcripts, and investor presentations.

  For private, non-filing companies, the banker often relies upon company management to provide materials containing basic business and financial information. In an organized M&A sale process, this information is typically provided in the form of a CIM (see Chapter 6). In the absence of this information, alternative sources (e.g., company websites, trade journals, and news articles, as well as SEC filings and research reports for public competitors, customers, and suppliers) must be used to learn basic company information and form the basis for developing the assumptions to drive financial projections.

- **Step II. Project Free Cash Flow.** The projection of the target's *unlevered* FCF forms the core of a DCF. Unlevered FCF, which we simply refer to as FCF in this chapter, is the cash generated by a company after paying all cash operating expenses and taxes, as well as the funding of capex and working capital, but prior to the payment of any interest expense.[1] The target's projected FCF is driven by assumptions underlying its future financial performance, including sales growth rates, profit margins, capex, and working capital requirements. Historical performance, combined with third party and/or management guidance, helps in developing these assumptions. The use of realistic FCF projections is critical as it has the greatest effect on valuation in a DCF.

In a DCF, the target's FCF is typically projected for a period of five years, but this period may vary depending on the target's sector, stage of development, and the predictability of its FCF. However, five years is typically sufficient for spanning at least one business/economic cycle and allowing for the successful realization of in-process or planned initiatives. The goal is to project FCF to a point in the future when the target's financial performance is deemed to have reached a "steady state" that can serve as the basis for a terminal value calculation (see Step IV).

- **Step III. Calculate Weighted Average Cost of Capital.** In a DCF, WACC is the rate used to discount the target's projected FCF and terminal value to the present. It is designed to fairly reflect the target's business and financial risks. As its name connotes, WACC represents the "weighted average" of the required return on the invested capital (customarily debt and equity) in a given company. It is also commonly referred to as a company's "discount rate" or "cost of capital." As debt and equity components generally have significantly different risk profiles and tax ramifications, WACC is dependent on capital structure.

- **Step IV. Determine Terminal Value.** The DCF approach to valuation is based on determining the present value of future FCF produced by the target. Given the challenges of projecting the target's FCF indefinitely, a terminal value is used to quantify the remaining value of the target after the projection period. The terminal value typically accounts for a substantial portion of the target's value in a DCF. Therefore, it is important that the target's financial data in the final year of the projection period ("terminal year") represents a steady state or normalized level of financial performance, as opposed to a cyclical high or low.

  There are two widely accepted methods used to calculate a company's terminal value—the exit multiple method (EMM) and the perpetuity growth method (PGM). The EMM calculates the remaining value of the target after the projection period on the basis of a multiple of the target's terminal year EBITDA (or EBIT). The PGM calculates terminal value by treating the target's terminal year FCF as a perpetuity growing at an assumed rate.

- **Step V. Calculate Present Value and Determine Valuation.** The target's projected FCF and terminal value are discounted to the present and summed to calculate its enterprise value. Implied equity value and share price (if relevant) can then be derived from the calculated enterprise value. The present value calculation is performed by multiplying the FCF for each year in the projection period,

---

[1]See Chapter 4: Leveraged Buyouts and Chapter 5: LBO Analysis for a discussion of *levered* free cash flow or cash available for debt repayment.

as well as the terminal value, by its respective *discount factor*. The discount factor represents the present value of one dollar received at a given future date assuming a given discount rate.[2]

As a DCF incorporates numerous assumptions about key performance drivers, WACC, and terminal value, it is used to produce a valuation range rather than a single value. The exercise of driving a valuation range by varying key inputs is called sensitivity analysis. Core DCF valuation drivers such as WACC, exit multiple or perpetuity growth rate, sales growth rates, and margins are the most commonly sensitized inputs. Once determined, the valuation range implied by the DCF should be compared to those derived from other methodologies such as comparable companies, precedent transactions, and LBO analysis (if applicable) as a sanity check.

Once the step-by-step approach summarized above is complete, the final DCF output page should look similar to the one shown in Exhibit 3.2.

---

[2]For example, assuming a 10% discount rate and a one year time horizon, the discount factor is 0.91 (1/(1+10%)^1), which implies that one dollar received one year in the future would be worth $0.91 today.

EXHIBIT 3.2   DCF Analysis Output Page

ValueCo Corporation
Discounted Cash Flow Analysis
($ in millions, except per share data, fiscal year ending December 31)

| | Historical Period | | | CAGR | | Projection Period | | | | | | CAGR |
	2005	2006	2007	('05 - '07)	2008	2009	2010	2011	2012	2013	('08 - '13)
Sales	$780.0	$850.0	$925.0	8.9%	$1,000.0	$1,080.0	$1,144.8	$1,190.6	$1,226.3	$1,263.1	4.8%
% growth	NA	9.0%	8.8%		8.1%	8.0%	6.0%	4.0%	3.0%	3.0%	
EBITDA	$109.2	$123.3	$138.8	12.7%	$150.0	$162.0	$171.7	$178.6	$183.9	$189.5	4.8%
% margin	14.0%	14.5%	15.0%		15.0%	15.0%	15.0%	15.0%	15.0%	15.0%	
Depreciation & Amortization	15.6	17.0	18.5		20.0	21.6	22.9	23.8	24.5	25.3	
EBIT	$93.6	$106.3	$120.3	13.3%	$130.0	$140.4	$148.8	$154.8	$159.4	$164.2	4.8%
% margin	12.0%	12.5%	13.0%		13.0%	13.0%	13.0%	13.0%	13.0%	13.0%	
Taxes	35.6	40.4	45.7		49.4	53.4	56.6	58.8	60.6	62.4	
EBIAT	$58.0	$65.9	$74.6	13.3%	$80.6	$87.0	$92.3	$96.0	$98.8	$101.8	4.8%
Plus: Depreciation & Amortization	15.6	17.0	18.5		20.0	21.6	22.9	23.8	24.5	25.3	
Less: Capital Expenditures	(15.0)	(18.0)	(18.5)		(20.0)	(21.6)	(22.9)	(23.8)	(24.5)	(25.3)	
Less: Increase in Net Working Capital						(8.0)	(6.5)	(4.6)	(3.6)	(3.7)	
Unlevered Free Cash Flow					$79.0	$85.8	$91.4	$95.3	$98.1	
WACC 11.0%											
Discount Period					0.5	1.5	2.5	3.5	4.5	
Discount Factor					0.95	0.86	0.77	0.69	0.63	
Present Value of Free Cash Flow					$75.0	$73.4	$70.4	$66.1	$61.4	

Enterprise Value

Cumulative Present Value of FCF	$346.3
Terminal Value	
Terminal Year EBITDA (2013E)	$189.5
Exit Multiple	7.0x
Terminal Value	$1,326.3
Discount Factor	0.59
Present Value of Terminal Value	$787.1
% of Enterprise Value	69.4%
Enterprise Value	**$1,133.3**

Implied Equity Value and Share Price

Enterprise Value	$1,133.3
Less: Total Debt	(300.0)
Less: Preferred Securities	-
Less: Noncontrolling Interest	25.0
Plus: Cash and Cash Equivalents	50.0
Implied Equity Value	**$858.3**
Fully Diluted Shares Outstanding	50.0
Implied Share Price	**$17.17**

Implied Perpetuity Growth Rate

Terminal Year Free Cash Flow (2013E)	$98.1
WACC	11.0%
Terminal Value	$1,326.3
Implied Perpetuity Growth Rate	**3.0%**

Implied EV/EBITDA

Enterprise Value	$1,133.3
LTM 9/30/2008 EBITDA	146.7
Implied EV/EBITDA	**7.7x**

Enterprise Value

WACC	Exit Multiple				
	6.0x	6.5x	7.0x	7.5x	8.0x
10.0%	1,060	1,119	1,177	1,236	1,295
10.5%	1,040	1,098	1,155	1,213	1,270
11.0%	1,021	1,077	1,133	1,190	1,246
11.5%	1,002	1,057	1,112	1,167	1,222
12.0%	984	1,038	1,091	1,145	1,199

Implied Perpetuity Growth Rate

WACC	Exit Multiple				
	6.0x	6.5x	7.0x	7.5x	8.0x
10.0%	0.9%	1.5%	2.1%	2.6%	3.0%
10.5%	1.3%	2.0%	2.5%	3.0%	3.5%
11.0%	1.7%	2.4%	3.0%	3.5%	3.9%
11.5%	2.2%	2.8%	3.4%	3.9%	4.4%
12.0%	2.6%	3.3%	3.9%	4.4%	4.8%

STEP I. STUDY THE TARGET AND DETERMINE KEY PERFORMANCE DRIVERS

Study the Target

The first step in performing a DCF, as with any valuation exercise, is to study and learn as much as possible about the target and its sector. A thorough understanding of the target's business model, financial profile, value proposition for customers, end markets, competitors, and key risks is essential for developing a framework for valuation. The banker needs to be able to craft (or support) a realistic set of financial projections, as well as WACC and terminal value assumptions, for the target. Performing this task is invariably easier when valuing a public company as opposed to a private company due to the availability of information.

For a public company,[3] a careful reading of its recent SEC filings (e.g., 10-Ks, 10-Qs, and 8-Ks), earnings call transcripts, and investor presentations provides a solid introduction to its business and financial characteristics. To determine key performance drivers, the MD&A sections of the most recent 10-K and 10-Q are an important source of information as they provide a synopsis of the company's financial and operational performance during the prior reporting periods, as well as management's outlook for the company. Equity research reports add additional color and perspective while typically providing financial performance estimates for the future two- or three-year period.

For private, non-filing companies or smaller divisions of public companies (for which segmented information is not provided), company management is often relied upon to provide materials containing basic business and financial information. In an organized M&A sale process, this information is typically provided in the form of a CIM. In the absence of this information, alternative sources must be used, such as company websites, trade journals and news articles, as well as SEC filings and research reports for public competitors, customers, and suppliers. For those private companies that were once public filers, or operated as a subsidiary of a public filer, it can be informative to read through old filings or research reports.

Determine Key Performance Drivers

The next level of analysis involves determining the key drivers of a company's performance (particularly sales growth, profitability, and FCF generation) with the goal of crafting (or supporting) a defensible set of FCF projections. These drivers can be both internal (such as opening new facilities/stores, developing new products, securing new customer contracts, and improving operational and/or working capital efficiency) as well as external (such as acquisitions, end market trends, consumer buying patterns, macroeconomic factors, or even legislative/regulatory changes).

A given company's growth profile can vary significantly from that of its peers within the sector with certain business models and management teams more focused on, or capable of, expansion. Profitability may also vary for companies within a given

---

[3]Including those companies that have outstanding registered debt securities, but do not have publicly traded stock.

sector depending on a multitude of factors including management, brand, customer base, operational focus, product mix, sales/marketing strategy, scale, and technology. Similarly, in terms of FCF generation, there are often meaningful differences among peers in terms of capex (e.g., expansion projects or owned versus leased machinery) and working capital efficiency, for example.

STEP II. PROJECT FREE CASH FLOW

After studying the target and determining key performance drivers, the banker is prepared to project its FCF. As previously discussed, FCF is the cash generated by a company after paying all cash operating expenses and associated taxes, as well as the funding of capex and working capital, but prior to the payment of any interest expense (see Exhibit 3.3). FCF is independent of capital structure as it represents the cash available to all capital providers (both debt and equity holders).

EXHIBIT 3.3 Free Cash Flow Calculation

Earnings Before Interest and Taxes
Less: Taxes (at the Marginal Tax Rate)
Earnings Before Interest After Taxes
Plus: Depreciation & Amortization
Less: Capital Expenditures
Less: Increase/(Decrease) in Net Working Capital
Free Cash Flow

Considerations for Projecting Free Cash Flow

Historical Performance Historical performance provides valuable insight for developing defensible assumptions to project FCF. Past growth rates, profit margins, and other ratios are usually a reliable indicator of future performance, especially for mature companies in non-cyclical sectors. While it is informative to review historical data from as long a time horizon as possible, typically the prior three-year period (if available) serves as a good proxy for projecting future financial performance.

Therefore, as the output in Exhibit 3.2 demonstrates, the DCF customarily begins by laying out the target's historical financial data for the prior three-year period. This historical financial data is sourced from the target's financial statements with adjustments made for non-recurring items and recent events, as appropriate, to provide a normalized basis for projecting financial performance.

Projection Period Length Typically, the banker projects the target's FCF for a period of five years depending on its sector, stage of development, and the predictability of its financial performance. As discussed in Step IV, it is critical to project FCF to a point in the future where the target's financial performance reaches a steady state or normalized level. For mature companies in established industries, five years is often sufficient for allowing a company to reach its steady state. A five-year projection period typically spans at least one business cycle and allows sufficient time for the successful realization of in-process or planned initiatives.

In situations where the target is in the early stages of rapid growth, however, it may be more appropriate to build a longer-term projection model (e.g., ten years or more) to allow the target to reach a steady state level of cash flow. In addition, a longer projection period is often used for businesses in sectors with long-term, contracted revenue streams such as natural resources, satellite communications, or utilities.

Alternative Cases   Whether advising on the buy-side or sell-side of an organized M&A sale process, the banker typically receives five years of financial projections for the target, which is usually labeled "Management Case." At the same time, the banker must develop a sufficient degree of comfort to support and defend these assumptions. Often, the banker makes adjustments to management's projections that incorporate assumptions deemed more probable, known as the "Base Case," while also crafting upside and downside cases.

The development of alternative cases requires a sound understanding of company-specific performance drivers as well as sector trends. The banker enters the various assumptions that drive these cases into assumptions pages (see Chapter 5, Exhibits 5.52 and 5.53), which feed into the DCF output page (see Exhibit 3.2). A "switch" or "toggle" function in the model allows the banker to move between cases without having to re-input the financial data by entering a number or letter (that corresponds to a particular set of assumptions) into a single cell.

Projecting Financial Performance without Management Guidance   In many instances, a DCF is performed without the benefit of receiving an initial set of projections. For publicly traded companies, consensus research estimates for financial statistics such as sales, EBITDA, and EBIT (which are generally provided for a future two- or three-year period) are typically used to form the basis for developing a set of projections. Individual equity research reports may provide additional financial detail, including (in some instances) a full scale two-year (or more) projection model.

For private companies, a robust DCF often depends on receiving financial projections from company management. In practice, however, this is not always possible. Therefore, the banker must develop the skill set necessary to reasonably forecast financial performance in the absence of management projections. In these instances, the banker typically relies upon historical financial performance, sector trends, and consensus estimates for public comparable companies to drive defensible projections.

The remainder of this section provides a detailed discussion of the major components of FCF, as well as practical approaches for projecting FCF *without the benefit of readily available projections or management guidance*.

Projection of Sales, EBITDA, and EBIT

Sales Projections   For public companies, the banker often sources top line projections for the first two or three years of the projection period from consensus estimates. Similarly, for private companies, consensus estimates for peer companies can be used as a proxy for expected sales growth rates provided the trend line is consistent with historical performance and sector outlook.

As equity research normally does not provide estimates beyond a future two- or three-year period (excluding initiating coverage reports), the banker must derive growth rates in the outer years from alternative sources. Without the benefit of management guidance, this typically involves more art than science. Often, industry reports and consulting studies provide estimates on longer-term sector trends and growth rates. In the absence of reliable guidance, the banker typically steps down the growth rates incrementally in the outer years of the projection period to arrive at a reasonable long-term growth rate by the terminal year (e.g., 2% to 4%).

For a highly cyclical business such as a steel or lumber company, however, sales levels need to track the movements of the underlying commodity cycle. Consequently, sales trends are typically more volatile and may incorporate dramatic peak-to-trough swings depending on the company's point in the cycle at the start of the projection period. Regardless of where in the cycle the projection period begins, it is crucial that the terminal year financial performance represents a normalized level as opposed to a cyclical high or low. Otherwise, the company's terminal value, which usually comprises a substantial portion of the overall value in a DCF, will be skewed toward an unrepresentative level. Therefore, in a DCF for a cyclical company, top line projections might peak (or trough) in the early years of the projection period and then decline (or increase) precipitously before returning to a normalized level by the terminal year.

Once the top line projections are established, it is essential to give them a sanity check versus the target's historical growth rates as well as peer estimates and sector/market outlook. Even when sourcing information from consensus estimates, each year's growth assumptions need to be justifiable, whether on the basis of market share gains/declines, end market trends, product mix changes, demand shifts, pricing increases, or acquisitions, for example. Furthermore, the banker must ensure that sales projections are consistent with other related assumptions in the DCF, such as those for capex and working capital. For example, higher top line growth typically requires the support of higher levels of capex and working capital.

COGS and SG&A Projections For public companies, the banker typically relies upon historical COGS[4] (gross margin) and SG&A levels (as a percentage of sales) and/or sources estimates from research to drive the initial years of the projection period, if available. For the outer years of the projection period, it is common to hold gross margin and SG&A as a percentage of sales constant, although the banker may assume a slight improvement (or decline) if justified by company trends or outlook for the sector/market. Similarly, for private companies, the banker usually relies upon historical trends to drive gross profit and SG&A projections, typically holding margins constant at the prior historical year levels. At the same time, the banker may also examine research estimates for peer companies to help craft/support the assumptions and provide insight on trends.

---

[4]For companies with COGS that can be driven on a unit volume/cost basis, COGS is typically projected on the basis of expected volumes sold and cost per unit. Assumptions governing expected volumes and cost per unit can be derived from historical levels, production capacity, and/or sector trends.

In some cases, the DCF may be constructed on the basis of EBITDA and EBIT projections alone, thereby excluding line item detail for COGS and SG&A. This approach generally requires that NWC be driven as a percentage of sales as COGS detail for driving inventory and accounts payable is unavailable (see Exhibits 3.9, 3.10, and 3.11). However, the inclusion of COGS and SG&A detail allows the banker to drive multiple operating scenarios on the basis of gross margins and/or SG&A efficiency.

EBITDA and EBIT Projections   For public companies, EBITDA and EBIT projections for the future two- or three-year period are typically sourced from (or benchmarked against) consensus estimates, if available.[5] These projections inherently capture both gross profit performance and SG&A expenses. A common approach for projecting EBITDA and EBIT for the outer years is to hold their margins constant at the level represented by the last year provided by consensus estimates (if the last year of estimates is representative of a steady state level). As previously discussed, however, increasing (or decreasing) levels of profitability may be modeled throughout the projection period, perhaps due to product mix changes, cyclicality, operating leverage,[6] or pricing power/pressure.

For private companies, the banker looks at historical trends as well as consensus estimates for peer companies for insight on projected margins. In the absence of sufficient information to justify improving or declining margins, the banker may simply hold margins constant at the prior historical year level to establish a baseline set of projections.

Projection of Free Cash Flow

In a DCF analysis, EBIT typically serves as the springboard for calculating FCF (see Exhibit 3.4). To bridge from EBIT to FCF, several additional items need to be determined, including the marginal tax rate, D&A, capex, and changes in net working capital.

EXHIBIT 3.4   EBIT to FCF

EBIT
Less: Taxes (at the Marginal Tax Rate)
EBIAT
Plus: D&A
Less: Capex
Less: Increase/(Decrease) in NWC
FCF

---

[5]If the model is built on the basis of COGS and SG&A detail, the banker must ensure that the EBITDA and EBIT consensus estimates dovetail with those assumptions. This exercise may require some triangulation among the different inputs to ensure consistency.

[6]The extent to which sales growth results in growth at the operating income level; it is a function of a company's mix of fixed and variable costs.

Tax Projections   The first step in calculating FCF from EBIT is to net out estimated taxes. The result is tax-effected EBIT, also known as EBIAT or NOPAT. This calculation involves multiplying EBIT by (1 − t), where "t" is the target's marginal tax rate. A marginal tax rate of 35% to 40% is generally assumed for modeling purposes, but the company's actual tax rate (effective tax rate) in previous years can also serve as a reference point.[7]

Depreciation & Amortization Projections   Depreciation is a non-cash expense that approximates the reduction of the book value of a company's long-term fixed assets or property, plant, and equipment (PP&E) over an estimated *useful life* and reduces reported earnings. Amortization, like depreciation, is a non-cash expense that reduces the value of a company's *definite life* intangible assets and also reduces reported earnings.[8]

Some companies report D&A together as a separate line item on their income statement, but these expenses are more commonly included in COGS (especially for manufacturers of goods) and, to a lesser extent, SG&A. Regardless, D&A is explicitly disclosed in the cash flow statement as well as the notes to a company's financial statements. As D&A is a non-cash expense, it is added back to EBIAT in the calculation of FCF (see Exhibit 3.4). Hence, while D&A decreases a company's reported earnings, it does not decrease its FCF.

Depreciation   Depreciation expenses are typically scheduled over several years corresponding to the useful life of each of the company's respective asset classes. The *straight-line depreciation* method assumes a uniform depreciation expense over the estimated useful life of an asset. For example, an asset purchased for $100 million that is determined to have a ten-year useful life would be assumed to have an annual depreciation expense of $10 million per year for ten years. Most other depreciation methods fall under the category of *accelerated depreciation*, which assumes that an asset loses most of its value in the early years of its life (i.e., the asset is depreciated on an accelerated schedule allowing for greater deductions earlier on).

For DCF modeling purposes, depreciation is often projected as a percentage of sales or capex based on historical levels as it is directly related to a company's capital spending, which, in turn, tends to support top line growth. An alternative approach is to build a detailed PP&E schedule[9] based on the company's existing depreciable net PP&E base and incremental capex projections. This approach involves assuming

---

[7]It is important to understand that a company's effective tax rate, or the rate that it actually pays in taxes, often differs from the marginal tax rate due to the use of tax credits, non-deductible expenses (such as government fines), deferred tax asset valuation allowances, and other company-specific tax policies.

[8]D&A for GAAP purposes typically differs from that for federal income taxes. For example, federal government tax rules generally permit a company to depreciate assets on a more accelerated basis than GAAP. These differences create deferred liabilities. Due to the complexity of calculating tax D&A, the banker typically uses GAAP D&A as a proxy for tax D&A.

[9]A schedule for determining a company's PP&E for each year in the projection period on the basis of annual capex (additions) and depreciation (subtractions). PP&E for a particular year in the projection period is the sum of the prior year's PP&E plus the projection year's capex less the projection year's depreciation.

an average remaining life for current depreciable net PP&E as well as a depreciation period for new capex. While more technically sound than the "quick-and-dirty" method of projecting depreciation as a percentage of sales or capex, building a PP&E schedule generally does not yield a substantially different result.

For a DCF constructed on the basis of EBITDA and EBIT projections, depreciation (and amortization) can simply be calculated as the difference between the two. In this scenario however, the banker must ensure that the implied D&A is consistent with historical levels as well as capex projections.[10] Regardless of which approach is used, the banker often makes a simplifying assumption that depreciation and capex are in line by the final year of the projection period so as to ensure that the company's PP&E base remains steady in perpetuity. Otherwise, the company's valuation would be influenced by an expanding or diminishing PP&E base, which would not be representative of a steady state business.

Amortization   Amortization differs from depreciation in that it reduces the value of definite life intangible assets as opposed to tangible assets. Definite life intangible assets include contractual rights such as non-compete clauses, copyrights, licenses, patents, trademarks, or other intellectual property, as well as information technology and customer lists, among others. These intangible assets are amortized according to a determined or useful life.[11]

Like depreciation, amortization can be projected as a percentage of sales or by building a detailed schedule based upon a company's existing intangible assets. However, amortization is often combined with depreciation as a single line item within a company's financial statements. Therefore, it is more common to simply model amortization with depreciation as part of one line-item (D&A).

Assuming depreciation and amortization are combined as one line item, D&A is projected in accordance with one of the approaches described under the "Depreciation" heading (e.g., as a percentage of sales or capex, through a detailed schedule, or as the difference between EBITDA and EBIT).

Capital Expenditures Projections   Capital expenditures are the funds that a company uses to purchase, improve, expand, or replace physical assets such as buildings, equipment, facilities, machinery, and other assets. Capex is an expenditure as opposed to an expense. It is capitalized on the balance sheet once the expenditure is made and then expensed over its useful life as depreciation through the company's income statement. As opposed to depreciation, capital expenditures represent actual cash outflows and, consequently, must be subtracted from EBIAT in the calculation of FCF (in the year in which the purchase is made).

Historical capex is disclosed directly on a company's cash flow statement under the investing activities section and also discussed in the MD&A section of a public

---

[10]When using consensus estimates for EBITDA and EBIT, the difference between the two may imply a level of D&A that is not defensible. This situation is particularly common when there are a different number of research analysts reporting values for EBITDA than for EBIT.

[11]Indefinite life intangible assets, most notably goodwill (value paid in excess over the book value of an asset), are not amortized. Rather, goodwill is held on the balance sheet and tested annually for impairment.

company's 10-K and 10-Q. Historical levels generally serve as a reliable proxy for projecting future capex. However, capex projections may deviate from historical levels in accordance with the company's strategy, sector, or phase of operations. For example, a company in expansion mode might have elevated capex levels for some portion of the projection period, while one in harvest or cash conservation mode might limit its capex.

For public companies, future planned capex is often discussed in the MD&A of its 10-K. Research reports may also provide capex estimates for the future two- or three-year period. In the absence of specific guidance, capex is generally driven as a percentage of sales in line with historical levels due to the fact that top line growth typically needs to be supported by growth in the company's asset base.

Change in Net Working Capital Projections   Net working capital is typically defined as non-cash current assets ("current assets") less non-interest-bearing current liabilities ("current liabilities"). It serves as a measure of how much cash a company needs to fund its operations on an ongoing basis. All of the necessary components to determine a company's NWC can be found on its balance sheet. Exhibit 3.5 displays the main current assets and current liabilities line items.

EXHIBIT 3.5   Current Assets and Current Liabilities Components

Current Assets	Current Liabilities
■ Accounts Receivable (A/R)	■ Accounts Payable (A/P)
■ Inventory	■ Accrued Liabilities
■ Prepaid Expenses and Other Current Assets	■ Other Current Liabilities

The formula for calculating NWC is shown in Exhibit 3.6.

EXHIBIT 3.6   Calculation of Net Working Capital

$$\text{NWC} = \frac{(\text{Accounts Receivable} + \text{Inventory} + \text{Prepaid Expenses and Other Current Assets})}{less}$$
$$(\text{Accounts Payable} + \text{Accrued Liabilities} + \text{Other Current Liabilities})$$

The change in NWC from year to year is important for calculating FCF as it represents an annual source or use of cash for the company. An increase in NWC over a given period (i.e., when current assets increase by more than current liabilities) is a use of cash. This is typical for a growing company, which tends to increase its spending on inventory to support sales growth. Similarly, A/R tends to increase in line with sales growth, which represents a use of cash as it is incremental cash that has not yet been collected. Conversely, an increase in A/P represents a source of cash as it is money that has been retained by the company as opposed to paid out.

As an increase in NWC is a use of cash, it is subtracted from EBIAT in the calculation of FCF. If the net change in NWC is negative (source of cash), then that value is added back to EBIAT. The calculation of a year-over-year (YoY) change in NWC is shown in Exhibit 3.7.

EXHIBIT 3.7   Calculation of a YoY Change in NWC

$$\Delta \text{ NWC } = \boxed{\text{NWC}_n - \text{NWC}_{(n-1)}}$$

where: n = the most recent year
              (n − 1) = the prior year

A "quick-and-dirty" shortcut for projecting YoY changes in NWC involves projecting NWC as a percentage of sales at a designated historical level and then calculating the YoY changes accordingly. This approach is typically used when a company's detailed balance sheet and COGS information is unavailable and working capital ratios cannot be determined. A more granular and recommended approach (where possible) is to project the individual components of both current assets and current liabilities for each year in the projection period. NWC and YoY changes are then calculated accordingly.

A company's current assets and current liabilities components are typically projected on the basis of historical ratios from the prior year level or a three-year average. In some cases, the company's trend line, management guidance, or sector trends may suggest improving or declining working capital efficiency ratios, thereby impacting FCF projections. In the absence of such guidance, the banker typically assumes constant working capital ratios in line with historical levels throughout the projection period.[12]

Current Assets

Accounts Receivable   Accounts receivable refers to amounts owed to a company for its products and services sold on credit. A/R is customarily projected on the basis of days sales outstanding (DSO), as shown in Exhibit 3.8.

EXHIBIT 3.8   Calculation of DSO

$$\text{DSO } = \boxed{\dfrac{\text{A/R}}{\text{Sales}} \times 365}$$

DSO provides a gauge of how well a company is managing the collection of its A/R by measuring the number of days it takes to collect payment after the sale of a product or service. For example, a DSO of 30 implies that the company, on average, receives payment 30 days after an initial sale is made. The lower a company's DSO, the faster it receives cash from credit sales.

---

[12]For the purposes of the DCF, working capital ratios are generally measured on an annual basis.

An increase in A/R represents a use of cash. Hence, companies strive to minimize their DSO so as to speed up their collection of cash. Increases in a company's DSO can be the result of numerous factors, including customer leverage or renegotiation of terms, worsening customer credit, poor collection systems, or change in product mix, for example. This increase in the cash cycle decreases short-term liquidity as the company has less cash on hand to fund short-term business operations and meet current debt obligations.

Inventory Inventory refers to the value of a company's raw materials, work in progress, and finished goods. It is customarily projected on the basis of days inventory held (DIH), as shown in Exhibit 3.9.

EXHIBIT 3.9 Calculation of DIH

$$DIH = \frac{Inventory}{COGS} \times 365$$

DIH measures the number of days it takes a company to sell its inventory. For example, a DIH of 90 implies that, on average, it takes 90 days for the company to turn its inventory (or approximately four "inventory turns" per year, as discussed in more detail below). An increase in inventory represents a use of cash. Therefore, companies strive to minimize DIH and turn their inventory as quickly as possible so as to minimize the amount of cash it ties up. Additionally, idle inventory is susceptible to damage, theft, or obsolescence due to newer products or technologies.

An alternate approach for measuring a company's efficiency at selling its inventory is the inventory turns ratio. As depicted in the Exhibit 3.10, inventory turns measures the number of times a company turns over its inventory in a given year. As with DIH, inventory turns is used together with COGS to project future inventory levels.

EXHIBIT 3.10 Calculation of Inventory Turns

$$Inventory\ Turns = COGS / Inventory$$

Prepaid Expenses and Other Current Assets Prepaid expenses are payments made by a company before a product has been delivered or a service has been performed. For example, insurance premiums are typically paid upfront although they cover a longer term period (e.g., six months or a year). Prepaid expenses and other current assets are typically projected as a percentage of sales in line with historical levels. As with A/R and inventory, an increase in prepaid expenses and other current assets represents a use of cash.

Current Liabilities

Accounts Payable Accounts payable refers to amounts owed by a company for products and services already purchased. A/P is customarily projected on the basis of days payable outstanding (DPO), as shown in Exhibit 3.11.

EXHIBIT 3.11 Calculation of DPO

$$DPO = \frac{A/P}{COGS} \times 365$$

   DPO measures the number of days it takes for a company to make payment on its outstanding purchases of goods and services. For example, a DPO of 30 implies that the company takes 30 days on average to pay its suppliers. The higher a company's DPO, the more time it has available to use its cash on hand for various business purposes before paying outstanding bills.

   An increase in A/P represents a source of cash. Therefore, as opposed to DSO, companies aspire to maximize or "push out" (within reason) their DPO so as to increase short-term liquidity.

Accrued Liabilities and Other Current Liabilities   Accrued liabilities are expenses such as salaries, rent, interest, and taxes that have been incurred by a company but not yet paid. As with prepaid expenses and other current assets, accrued liabilities and other current liabilities are typically projected as a percentage of sales in line with historical levels. As with A/P, an increase in accrued liabilities and other current liabilities represents a source of cash.

Free Cash Flow Projections   Once all of the above items have been projected, annual FCF for the projection period is relatively easy to calculate in accordance with the formula first introduced in Exhibit 3.3. The projection period FCF, however, represents only a portion of the target's value. The remainder is captured in the terminal value, which is discussed in Step IV.

STEP III. CALCULATE WEIGHTED AVERAGE COST OF CAPITAL

WACC is a broadly accepted standard for use as the discount rate to calculate the present value of a company's projected FCF and terminal value. It represents the weighted average of the required return on the invested capital (customarily debt and equity) in a given company. As debt and equity components have different risk profiles and tax ramifications, WACC is dependent on a company's "target" capital structure.

   WACC can also be thought of as an opportunity cost of capital or what an investor would expect to earn in an alternative investment with a similar risk profile. Companies with diverse business segments may have different costs of capital for their various businesses. In these instances, it may be advisable to conduct a DCF using a "sum of the parts" approach in which a separate DCF analysis is performed for each distinct business segment, each with its own WACC. The values for each business segment are then summed to arrive at an implied enterprise valuation for the entire company.

The formula for the calculation of WACC is shown in Exhibit 3.12.

EXHIBIT 3.12 Calculation of WACC

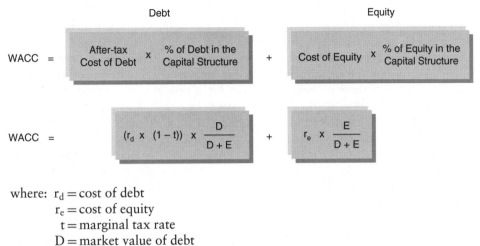

where: r_d = cost of debt
r_e = cost of equity
t = marginal tax rate
D = market value of debt
E = market value of equity

A company's capital structure or total capitalization is comprised of two main components, debt and equity (as represented by $D + E$). The rates—r_d (return on debt) and r_e (return on equity)—represent the company's market cost of debt and equity, respectively. As its name connotes, the ensuing weighted average cost of capital is simply a weighted average of the company's cost of debt (tax-effected) and cost of equity based on an assumed or "target" capital structure.

Below we demonstrate a step-by-step process for calculating WACC, as outlined in Exhibit 3.13.

EXHIBIT 3.13 Steps for Calculating WACC

Step III(a): Determine Target Capital Structure
Step III(b): Estimate Cost of Debt (r_d)
Step III(c): Estimate Cost of Equity (r_e)
Step III(d): Calculate WACC

Step III(a): Determine Target Capital Structure

WACC is predicated on choosing a target capital structure for the company that is consistent with its long-term strategy. This target capital structure is represented by the debt-to-total capitalization ($D/(D+E)$) and equity-to-total capitalization ($E/(D+E)$) ratios (see Exhibit 3.12). In the absence of explicit company guidance on target capital structure, the banker examines the company's current and historical debt-to-total capitalization ratios as well as the capitalization of its peers. Public comparable companies provide a meaningful benchmark for target capital structure as it is assumed that their management teams are seeking to maximize shareholder value.

In the finance community, the approach used to determine a company's target capital structure may differ from firm to firm. For public companies, existing capital structure is generally used as the target capital structure as long as it is comfortably within the range of the comparables. If it is at the extremes of, or outside, the range, then the mean or median for the comparables may serve as a better representation of the target capital structure. For private companies, the mean or median for the comparables is typically used. Once the target capital structure is chosen, it is assumed to be held constant throughout the projection period.

The graph in Exhibit 3.14 shows the impact of capital structure on a company's WACC. When there is no debt in the capital structure, WACC is equal to the cost of equity. As the proportion of debt in the capital structure increases, WACC gradually decreases due to the tax deductibility of interest expense. WACC continues to decrease up to the point where the *optimal capital structure*[13] is reached. Once this threshold is surpassed, the cost of potential financial distress (i.e., the negative effects of an over-leveraged capital structure, including the increased probability of insolvency) begins to override the tax advantages of debt. As a result, both debt and equity investors demand a higher yield for their increased risk, thereby driving WACC upward beyond the optimal capital structure threshold.

EXHIBIT 3.14   Optimal Capital Structure

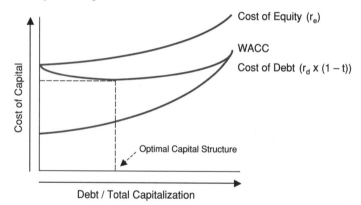

Step III(b): Estimate Cost of Debt (r_d)

A company's cost of debt reflects its credit profile at the target capital structure, which is based on a multitude of factors including size, sector, outlook, cyclicality, credit ratings, credit statistics, cash flow generation, financial policy, and acquisition strategy, among others. Assuming the company is currently at its target capital structure, cost of debt is generally derived from the blended yield on its outstanding debt instruments, which may include a mix of public and private debt. In the event

---

[13]The financing mix that minimizes WACC, thereby maximizing a company's theoretical value.

the company is <u>not</u> currently at its target capital structure, the cost of debt must be derived from peer companies.

For publicly traded bonds, cost of debt is determined on the basis of the *current yield*[14] on all outstanding issues. For private debt, such as revolving credit facilities and term loans,[15] the banker typically consults with an in-house debt capital markets (DCM) specialist to ascertain the current yield. Market-based approaches such as these are generally preferred as the current yield on a company's outstanding debt serves as the best indicator of its <u>expected cost of debt and reflects the risk</u> of <u>default</u>.

In the absence of current market data (e.g., for companies with debt that is not actively traded), an alternative approach is to calculate the company's weighted average cost of debt on the basis of the at-issuance coupons of its current debt maturities. This approach, however, is not always accurate as it is backward-looking and may not reflect the company's cost of raising debt capital under prevailing market conditions. A preferred, albeit more time-consuming, approach in these instances is to approximate a company's cost of debt based on its current (or implied) credit ratings at the target capital structure and the cost of debt for comparable credits, typically with guidance from an in-house DCM professional.

Once determined, the cost of debt is tax-effected at the company's marginal tax rate as interest payments are tax deductible.

Step III(c): Estimate Cost of Equity (r_e)

Cost of equity is the <u>required annual rate of return that a company's equity</u> investors expect to receive (including dividends). Unlike the cost of debt, which can be deduced from a company's outstanding maturities, a company's cost of equity is not readily observable in the market. To calculate the expected return on a company's equity, the banker typically employs a formula known as the capital asset pricing model (CAPM).

Capital Asset Pricing Model CAPM is based on the premise that equity investors need to be compensated for their assumption of systematic risk in the form of a risk premium, or the amount of market return in excess of a stated risk-free rate. Systematic risk is the risk related to the overall market, which is also known as non-diversifiable risk. A company's level <u>of systematic risk</u> depends on the covariance of its share price with movements in the overall market, as measured by its *beta* (β) (discussed later in this section).

---

[14]Technically, a bond's current yield is calculated as the annual coupon on the par value of the bond divided by the current price of the bond. However, callable bond yields are typically quoted at the yield-to-worst call (YTW). A callable bond has a call schedule (defined in the bond's indenture) that lists several call dates and their corresponding call prices. The YTW is the lowest calculated yield when comparing all of the possible yield-to-calls from a bond's call schedule given the initial offer price or current trading price of the bond.

[15]See Chapter 4: Leveraged Buyouts for additional information on term loans and other debt instruments.

By contrast, unsystematic or "specific" risk is company- or sector-specific and can be avoided through diversification. Hence, equity investors are not compensated for it (in the form of a premium). As a general rule, the smaller the company and the more specified its product offering, the higher its unsystematic risk.

The formula for the calculation of CAPM is shown in Exhibit 3.15.

EXHIBIT 3.15   Calculation of CAPM

Cost of Equity (r_e)   =   Risk-Free Rate + Levered Beta x Market Risk Premium

Cost of Equity (r_e)   = $r_f + \beta_L \times (r_m - r_f)$

where: r_f = risk-free rate
            β_L = levered beta
            r_m = expected return on the market
            $r_m - r_f$ = market risk premium

Risk-Free Rate (r_f)   The risk-free rate is the expected rate of return obtained by investing in a "riskless" security. U.S. government securities such as T-bills, T-notes, and T-bonds[16] are accepted by the market as "risk-free" because they are backed by the full faith of the U.S. federal government. Interpolated yields[17] for government securities can be located on Bloomberg[18] as well as the U.S. Department of Treasury website,[19] among others. The actual risk-free rate used in CAPM varies with the prevailing yields for the chosen security.

Investment banks may differ on accepted proxies for the appropriate risk-free rate, with some using the yield on the 10-year U.S. Treasury note and others preferring the yield on longer-term Treasuries. The general goal is to use as long dated an instrument as possible to match the expected life of the company (assuming a going concern), but practical considerations also need to be taken into account. Due to the moratorium on the issuance of 30-year Treasury bonds[20] and shortage of securities

---

[16]T-bills are non-interest-bearing securities issued with maturities of 3 months, 6 months, and 12 months at a discount to face value. T-notes and bonds, by contrast, have a stated coupon and pay semiannual interest. T-notes are issued with maturities of between one and ten years, while T-bonds are issued with maturities of more than ten years.

[17]Yields on nominal Treasury securities at "constant maturity" are interpolated by the U.S. Treasury from the daily yield curve for non-inflation-indexed Treasury securities. This curve, which relates the yield on a security to its time-to-maturity, is based on the closing market bid yields on actively traded Treasury securities in the over-the-counter market.

[18]Bloomberg function: "ICUR {# years} <GO>." For example, the interpolated yield for a 10-year Treasury note can be obtained from Bloomberg by typing "ICUR10," then pressing <GO>.

[19]Located under "Daily Treasury Yield Curve Rates."

[20]The 30-year Treasury bond was discontinued on February 18, 2002, and reintroduced on February 9, 2006.

with 30-year maturities, Ibbotson Associates ("Ibbotson")[21] uses an interpolated yield for a 20-year bond as the basis for the risk-free rate.[22,23]

Market Risk Premium ($r_m - r_f$ or mrp) The market risk premium is the spread of the expected market return[24] over the risk-free rate. Finance professionals, as well as academics, often differ over which historical time period is most relevant for observing the market risk premium. Some believe that more recent periods, such as the last ten years or the post-World War II era are more appropriate, while others prefer to examine the pre-Great Depression era to the present.

Ibbotson tracks data on the equity risk premium dating back to 1926. Depending on which time period is referenced, the premium of the market return over the risk-free rate ($r_m - r_f$) may vary substantially. For the 1926 to 2007 period, Ibbotson calculates a market risk premium of 7.1%.[25]

Many investment banks have a firm-wide policy governing market risk premium in order to ensure consistency in valuation work across their various projects and departments. The equity risk premium employed on Wall Street typically ranges from approximately 4% to 8%. Consequently, it is important for the banker to consult with senior colleagues for guidance on the appropriate market risk premium to use in the CAPM formula.

Beta (β) Beta is a measure of the covariance between the rate of return on a company's stock and the overall market return (systematic risk), with the S&P 500 traditionally used as a proxy for the market. As the S&P 500 has a beta of 1.0, a stock with a beta of 1.0 should have an expected return equal to that of the market. A stock with a beta of less than 1.0 has lower systematic risk than the market, and a stock with a beta greater than 1.0 has higher systematic risk. Mathematically, this is captured in the CAPM, with a higher beta stock exhibiting a higher cost of equity; and vice versa for lower beta stocks.

A public company's historical beta may be sourced from financial information resources such as Bloomberg,[26] FactSet, or Thomson Reuters. Recent historical equity returns (i.e., over the previous two-to-five years), however, may not be a reliable indicator of future returns. Therefore, many bankers prefer to use a

---

[21] Morningstar acquired Ibbotson Associates in March 2006. Ibbotson Associates is a leading authority on asset allocation, providing products and services to help investment professionals obtain, manage, and retain assets. Morningstar's annual *Ibbotson® SBBI® (Stocks, Bonds, Bills, and Inflation) Valuation Yearbook* is a widely used reference for cost of capital input estimations for U.S.-based businesses.

[22] Bloomberg function: "ICUR20" <GO>.

[23] While there are currently no 20-year Treasury bonds issued by the U.S. Treasury, as long as there are bonds being traded with at least 20 years to maturity, there will be a proxy for the yield on 20-year Treasury bonds.

[24] The S&P 500® is typically used as the proxy for the return on the market.

[25] Expected risk premium for equities is based on the difference of historical arithmetic mean returns for the 1926 to 2007 period. Arithmetic annual returns are independent of one another. Geometric annual returns are dependent on the prior year's returns.

[26] Bloomberg function: Ticker symbol <Equity> BETA <GO>.

predicted beta (e.g., provided by MSCI Barra[27]) whenever possible as it is forward-looking.

The exercise of calculating WACC for a private company involves deriving beta from a group of publicly traded peer companies that may or may not have similar capital structures to one another or the target. To neutralize the effects of different capital structures (i.e., remove the influence of leverage), the banker must *unlever* the beta for each company in the peer group to achieve the *asset beta* ("unlevered beta"). The formula for unlevering beta is shown in Exhibit 3.16.

EXHIBIT 3.16   Unlevering Beta

$$\beta_U = \frac{\beta_L}{\left(1 + \dfrac{D}{E} \times (1 - t)\right)}$$

where: β_U = unlevered beta
β_L = levered beta
D/E = debt-to-equity[28] ratio
t = marginal tax rate

After calculating the unlevered beta for each company, the banker determines the average unlevered beta for the peer group.[29] This average unlevered beta is then *relevered* using the company's target capital structure and marginal tax rate. The formula for relevering beta is shown in Exhibit 3.17.

EXHIBIT 3.17   Relevering Beta

$$\beta_L = \beta_U \times \left(1 + \frac{D}{E} \times (1 - t)\right)$$

where: D/E = <u>target</u> debt-to-equity ratio

The resulting levered beta serves as the beta for calculating the private company's cost of equity using the CAPM. Similarly, for a public company that is not currently at its target capital structure, its asset beta must be calculated and then relevered at the target D/E.

---

[27]MSCI Barra is a leading provider of investment decision support tools and supplies predicted betas for most public companies among other products and services. MSCI Barra uses a proprietary multi-factor risk model, known as the Multiple-Horizon U.S. Equity Model™, which relies on market information, fundamental data, regressions, historical daily returns, and other risk analyses to predict beta. MSCI Barra betas can be obtained from Alacra, among other financial information services.

[28]Market value of equity.

[29]Average unlevered beta may be calculated on a market-cap weighted basis.

Size Premium (SP)   The concept of a size premium is based on empirical evidence suggesting that smaller sized companies are riskier and, therefore, should have a higher cost of equity. This phenomenon, which to some degree contradicts the CAPM, relies on the notion that smaller companies' risk is not entirely captured in their betas given limited trading volumes of their stock, making covariance calculations inexact. Therefore, the banker may choose to add a size premium to the CAPM formula for smaller companies to account for the perceived higher risk and, therefore, expected higher return (see Exhibit 3.18). Ibbotson provides size premia for companies based on their market capitalization, tiered in deciles.

EXHIBIT 3.18   CAPM Formula Adjusted for Size Premium

$$r_e \ = \ r_f \ + \ \beta_L \ \times \ (r_m - r_f) \ + \ SP$$

where: SP = size premium

Step III(d): Calculate WACC

Once all of the above steps are completed, the various components are entered into the formula in Exhibit 3.19 to calculate the company's WACC. Given the numerous assumptions involved in determining a company's WACC and its sizeable impact on valuation, its key inputs are typically sensitized to produce a WACC range (see Exhibit 3.49). This range is then used in conjunction with other sensitized inputs, such as exit multiple, to produce a valuation range for the target.

EXHIBIT 3.19   WACC Formula

$$WACC \ = \ (r_d \times (1-t)) \times \frac{D}{D+E} \ + \ r_e \times \frac{E}{D+E}$$

STEP IV. DETERMINE TERMINAL VALUE

The DCF approach to valuation is based on determining the present value of all future FCF produced by a company. As it is infeasible to project a company's FCF indefinitely, the banker uses a terminal value to capture the value of the company beyond the projection period. As its name suggests, terminal value is typically calculated on the basis of the company's FCF (or a proxy such as EBITDA) in the final year of the projection period.

The terminal value typically accounts for a substantial portion of a company's value in a DCF, sometimes as much as three-quarters or more. Therefore, it is important that the company's terminal year financial data represents a steady state level of financial performance, as opposed to a cyclical high or low. Similarly, the underlying assumptions for calculating the terminal value must be carefully examined and sensitized.

There are two widely accepted methods used to calculate a company's terminal value—the exit multiple method and the perpetuity growth method. Depending on the situation and company being valued, the banker may use one or both methods, with each serving as a check on the other.

Exit Multiple Method

The EMM calculates the remaining value of a company's FCF produced after the projection period on the basis of a multiple of its terminal year EBITDA (or EBIT). This multiple is typically based on the current LTM trading multiples for comparable companies. As current multiples may be affected by sector or economic cycles, it is important to use both a normalized trading multiple and EBITDA. The use of a peak or trough multiple and/or an un-normalized EBITDA level can produce a skewed result. This is especially important for companies in cyclical industries.

As the exit multiple is a critical driver of terminal value, and hence overall value in a DCF, the banker subjects it to sensitivity analysis. For example, if the selected exit multiple range based on comparable companies is 6.5x to 7.5x, a common approach would be to create a valuation output table premised on exit multiples of 6.0x, 6.5x, 7.0x, 7.5x, and 8.0x (see Exhibit 3.32). The formula for calculating terminal value using the EMM is shown in Exhibit 3.20.

EXHIBIT 3.20   Exit Multiple Method

$$\text{Terminal Value} = \text{EBITDA}_n \times \text{Exit Multiple}$$

where: n = terminal year of the projection period

Perpetuity Growth Method

The PGM calculates terminal value by treating a company's terminal year FCF as a perpetuity growing at an assumed rate. As the formula in Exhibit 3.21 indicates, this method relies on the WACC calculation performed in Step III and requires the banker to make an assumption regarding the company's long-term, sustainable growth rate ("perpetuity growth rate"). The perpetuity growth rate is typically chosen on the basis of the company's expected long-term industry growth rate, which generally tends to be within a range of 2% to 4% (i.e., nominal GDP growth). As with the exit multiple, the perpetuity growth rate is also sensitized to produce a valuation range.

EXHIBIT 3.21   Perpetuity Growth Method

$$\text{Terminal Value} = \frac{\text{FCF}_n \times (1 + g)}{(r - g)}$$

Capitalization rate = (r - g)

where: FCF = unlevered free cash flow

   n = terminal year of the projection period

   g = perpetuity growth rate

   r = WACC

The PGM is often used in conjunction with the EMM, with each serving as a sanity check on the other. For example, if the implied perpetuity growth rate, as derived from the EMM is too high or low (see Exhibits 3.22(a) and 3.22(b)), it could be an indicator that the exit multiple assumptions are unrealistic.

EXHIBIT 3.22(a)   Implied Perpetuity Growth Rate (End-of-Year Discounting)

$$\text{Implied Perpetuity Growth Rate} = \frac{((\text{Terminal Value}^{(a)} \times \text{WACC}) - \text{FCF}_{\text{Terminal Year}})}{(\text{Terminal Value}^{(a)} + \text{FCF}_{\text{Terminal Year}})}$$

EXHIBIT 3.22(b)   Implied Perpetuity Growth Rate (Mid-Year Discounting, see Exhibit 3.26)

$$\text{Implied Perpetuity Growth Rate} = \frac{((\text{Terminal Value}^{(a)} \times \text{WACC}) - \text{FCF}_{\text{Terminal Year}} \times (1 + \text{WACC})^{0.5})}{(\text{Terminal Value}^{(a)} + \text{FCF}_{\text{Terminal Year}} \times (1 + \text{WACC})^{0.5})}$$

[a] Terminal Value calculated using the EMM.

Similarly, if the implied exit multiple from the PGM (see Exhibits 3.23(a) and 3.23(b)) is not in line with normalized trading multiples for the target or its peers, the perpetuity growth rate should be revisited.

EXHIBIT 3.23(a)   Implied Exit Multiple (End-of-Year Discounting)

$$\text{Implied Exit Multiple} = \frac{\text{Terminal Value}^{(a)}}{\text{EBITDA}_{\text{Terminal Year}}}$$

EXHIBIT 3.23(b)   Implied Exit Multiple (Mid-Year Discounting, see Exhibit 3.26)

$$\text{Implied Exit Multiple} = \frac{\text{Terminal Value}^{(a)} \times (1 + \text{WACC})^{0.5}}{\text{EBITDA}_{\text{Terminal Year}}}$$

[a] Terminal Value calculated using the PGM.

STEP V. CALCULATE PRESENT VALUE AND DETERMINE VALUATION

Calculate Present Value

Calculating present value centers on the notion that a dollar today is worth more than a dollar tomorrow, a concept known as the time value of money. This is due to the fact that a dollar earns money through investments (capital appreciation) and/or interest (e.g., in a money market account). In a DCF, a company's projected FCF and terminal value are discounted to the present at the company's WACC in accordance with the time value of money.

The present value calculation is performed by multiplying the FCF for each year in the projection period and the terminal value by its respective discount factor. The discount factor is the fractional value representing the present value of one dollar received at a future date given an assumed discount rate. For example, assuming a 10% discount rate, the discount factor for one dollar received at the end of one year is 0.91 (see Exhibit 3.24).

EXHIBIT 3.24 Discount Factor

$$\text{Discount Factor} = \frac{1}{(1 + \text{WACC})^n}$$

$$0.91 = \frac{\$1.00}{(1 + 10\%)^1}$$

where: n = year in the projection period

The discount factor is applied to a given future financial statistic to determine its present value. For example, given a 10% WACC, FCF of $100 million at the end of the first year of a company's projection period (Year 1) would be worth $91 million today (see Exhibit 3.25).

EXHIBIT 3.25 Present Value Calculation Using a Year-End Discount Factor

$$\text{PV of FCF}_n = \text{FCF}_n \times \text{Discount Factor}_n$$

$$\$91 \text{ million} = \$100 \text{ million} \times 0.91$$

where: n = year in the projection period

Mid-Year Convention To account for the fact that annual FCF is usually received throughout the year rather than at year-end, it is typically discounted in accordance with a *mid-year convention*. Mid-year convention assumes that a company's FCF is received evenly throughout the year, thereby approximating a steady (and more realistic) FCF generation.[30]

The use of a mid-year convention results in a slightly higher valuation than year-end discounting due to the fact that FCF is received sooner. As Exhibit 3.26 depicts, if one dollar is received evenly over the course of the first year of the projection period rather than at year-end, the discount factor is calculated to be 0.95 (assuming a 10% discount rate). Hence, $100 million received throughout Year 1 would be worth $95 million today in accordance with a mid-year convention, as opposed to $91 million using the year-end approach in Exhibit 3.25.

EXHIBIT 3.26   Discount Factor Using a Mid-Year Convention

$$\text{Discount Factor} = \frac{1}{(1 + WACC)^{(n - 0.5)}}$$

$$0.95 = \frac{\$1.00}{(1 + 10\%)^{0.5}}$$

where: n = year in the projection period, and
0.5 = is subtracted from n in accordance with a mid-year convention

Terminal Value Considerations   When employing a mid-year convention for the projection period, mid-year discounting is also applied for the terminal value under the PGM, as the banker is discounting perpetual future FCF assumed to be received throughout the year. The EMM, however, which is typically based on the LTM trading multiples of comparable companies for a calendar year end EBITDA (or EBIT), uses year-end discounting.

Determine Valuation

Calculate Enterprise Value   A company's projected FCF and terminal value are each discounted to the present and summed to provide an enterprise value. Exhibit 3.27 depicts the DCF calculation of enterprise value for a company with a five-year projection period, incorporating a mid-year convention and the EMM.

EXHIBIT 3.27   Enterprise Value Using Mid-Year Discounting

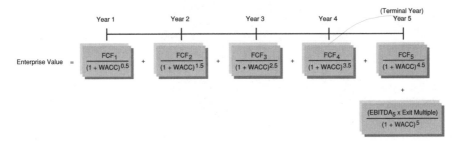

---

[30]May not be appropriate for highly seasonal businesses.

Derive Implied Equity Value   To derive implied equity value, the company's net debt, preferred stock, and noncontrolling interest are subtracted from the calculated enterprise value (see Exhibit 3.28).

EXHIBIT 3.28   Equity Value

Implied Equity Value = Enterprise Value – Net Debt + Preferred Stock + Noncontrolling Interest

Derive Implied Share Price   For publicly traded companies, implied equity value is divided by the company's fully diluted shares outstanding to calculate an implied share price (see Exhibit 3.29).

EXHIBIT 3.29   Share Price

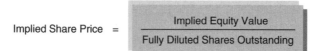

$$\text{Implied Share Price} = \frac{\text{Implied Equity Value}}{\text{Fully Diluted Shares Outstanding}}$$

The existence of in-the-money options and warrants, however, creates a *circular reference* in the basic formula shown in Exhibit 3.29 between the company's fully diluted shares outstanding count and implied share price. In other words, equity value per share is dependent on the number of fully diluted shares outstanding, which, in turn, is dependent on the implied share price. This is remedied in the model by activating the *iteration* function in Microsoft Excel (see Exhibit 3.30).

EXHIBIT 3.30   Iteration Function in Microsoft Excel

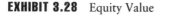

Once the iteration function is activated, the model is able to iterate between the cell determining the company's implied share price (see shaded area "A" in

Exhibit 3.31) and those cells determining whether each option tranche is in-the-money (see shaded area "B" in Exhibit 3.31). At an assumed enterprise value of $1,000 million, implied equity value of $775 million, 50 million basic shares outstanding, and the options data shown in Exhibit 3.31, we calculate an implied share price of $15.00.

EXHIBIT 3.31   Calculation of Implied Share Price

($ in millions, except per share data; shares in millions)

Calculation of Implied Share Price	
Enterprise Value	$1,000.0
Less: Total Debt	(250.0)
Less: Preferred Securities	-
Less: Noncontrolling Interest	(25.0)
Plus: Cash and Cash Equivalents	50.0
Implied Equity Value	**$775.0**

Options/Warrants

Tranche	Number of Shares	Exercise Price	In-the-Money Shares	Proceeds	
Options 1	1.250	$2.50	1.250	3.1	In-the-money options are dependent on implied share price...
Options 2	1.000	7.50	1.000	7.5	= IF (Exercise Price < Implied Share Price, then display Number of Shares, otherwise display 0)
Options 3	0.750	12.50	0.750	9.4	= IF ($2.50 < $15.00, 1.250, 0)
Options 4	0.500	17.50	-	-	= Exercise Price x In-the-Money Shares
Options 5	0.250	25.00	-	-	= $12.50 x 0.750
Total	**3.750**		**3.000**	**$20.0**	

Basic Shares Outstanding	50.000	= - Total Options Proceeds / Implied Share Price = ($20.0) million / $15.00
Plus: Shares from In-the-Money Options	3.000	
Less: Shares Repurchased	(1.333)	Shares repurchased are dependent on implied share price...
Net New Shares from Options	**1.667**	
Plus: Shares from Convertible Securities	-	= Implied Equity Value / Fully Diluted Shares = $775.0 million / 51.667
Fully Diluted Shares Outstanding	**51.667**	
Implied Share Price	**$15.00**	Implied share price is dependent on in-the-money options...

Perform Sensitivity Analysis

The DCF incorporates numerous assumptions, each of which can have a sizeable impact on valuation. As a result, the DCF output is viewed in terms of a valuation range based on a series of key input assumptions, rather than as a single value. The exercise of deriving a valuation range by varying key inputs is called sensitivity analysis.

Sensitivity analysis is a testament to the notion that valuation is as much an art as a science. Key valuation drivers such as WACC, exit multiple, and perpetuity growth rate are the most commonly sensitized inputs in a DCF. The banker may also perform additional sensitivity analysis on key financial performance drivers, such as sales growth rates and profit margins (e.g., EBITDA or EBIT). Valuation outputs produced by sensitivity analysis are typically displayed in a data table, such as that shown in Exhibit 3.32.

The center shaded portion of the sensitivity table in Exhibit 3.32 displays an enterprise value range of $926 million to $1,077 million assuming a WACC range of 9.5% to 10.5% and an exit multiple range of 6.5x to 7.5x. As the exit multiple increases, enterprise value increases accordingly; conversely, as the discount rate increases, enterprise value decreases.

EXHIBIT 3.32 Sensitivity Analysis

Linked to the model output for enterprise value
(cell containing $1,000 value in DCF model)

	Enterprise Value				
			Exit Multiple		
	6.0x	6.5x	7.0x	7.5x	8.0x
9.0%	926	983	1,041	1,099	1,156
9.5%	908	964	1,020	1,077	1,133
10.0%	890	945	$1,000	1,055	1,110
10.5%	873	926	980	1,034	1,088
11.0%	856	908	961	1,014	1,066

WACC (row label for the 9.0%–11.0% column)

Table [?][X]

Row input cell: 7.0x

Column input cell: 10.0%

[OK] [Cancel]

The sensitivity analysis above can be performed in MS Excel using the following process:
- create an output table similar to the format above
- input the WACC and exit multiple ranges
- link the top left corner (shaded for presentation purposes) to the model output for enterprise value (cell containing $1,000 value in DCF model)
- highlight entire data table
- select Data, Table from the menu and the input box to the left will appear on the screen
- link the "Row input cell:" to the cell containing the exit multiple driver of 7.0x in the DCF model
- link the "Column input cell:" to the cell containing the WACC driver of 10.0% in the DCF model
- click the "OK" button and the data table will populate

As with comparable companies and precedent transactions, once a DCF valuation range is determined, it should be compared to the valuation ranges derived from other methodologies. If the output produces notably different results, it is advisable to revisit the assumptions and fine-tune, if necessary. Common missteps that can skew the DCF valuation include the use of unrealistic financial projections (which generally has the largest impact),[31] WACC, or terminal value assumptions. A substantial difference in the valuation implied by the DCF versus other methodologies, however, does not necessarily mean the analysis is flawed. Multiples-based valuation methodologies may fail to account for company-specific factors that may imply a higher or lower valuation.

---

[31]This is a common pitfall in the event that management projections (Management Case) are used without independently analyzing and testing the underlying assumptions.

KEY PROS AND CONS

Pros

- *Cash flow-based* – reflects value of projected FCF, which represents a more fundamental approach to valuation than using multiples-based methodologies

- *Market independent* – more insulated from market aberrations such as bubbles and distressed periods

- *Self-sufficient* – does not rely entirely upon truly comparable companies or transactions, which may or may not exist, to frame valuation; a DCF is particularly important when there are limited or no "pure play" public comparables to the company being valued

- *Flexibility* – allows the banker to run multiple financial performance scenarios, including improving or declining growth rates, margins, capex requirements, and working capital efficiency

Cons

- *Dependence on financial projections* – accurate forecasting of financial performance is challenging, especially as the projection period lengthens

- *Sensitivity to assumptions* – relatively small changes in key assumptions, such as growth rates, margins, WACC, or exit multiple, can produce meaningfully different valuation ranges

- *Terminal value* – the present value of the terminal value can represent as much as three-quarters or more of the DCF valuation, which decreases the relevance of the projection period's annual FCF

- *Assumes constant capital structure* – basic DCF does not provide flexibility to change the company's capital structure over the projection period

ILLUSTRATIVE DISCOUNTED CASH FLOW ANALYSIS FOR VALUECO

The following section provides a detailed, step-by-step construction of a DCF analysis and illustrates how it is used to establish a valuation range for our target company, ValueCo. As discussed in the Introduction, ValueCo is a private company for which we are provided detailed historical financial information. However, for our illustrative DCF analysis, we assume that no management projections were provided in order to cultivate the ability to develop financial projections with limited information. We do, however, assume that we were provided with basic information on ValueCo's business and operations.

Step I. Study the Target and Determine Key Performance Drivers

As a first step, we reviewed the basic company information provided on ValueCo. This foundation, in turn, allowed us to study ValueCo's sector in greater detail, including the identification of key competitors (and comparable companies), customers, and suppliers. Various trade journals and industry studies, as well as SEC filings and research reports of public comparables, were particularly important in this respect.

From a financial perspective, ValueCo's historical financials provided a basis for developing our initial assumptions regarding future performance and projecting FCF. We used consensus estimates of public comparables to provide further guidance for projecting ValueCo's Base Case growth rates and margin trends.

Step II. Project Free Cash Flow

Historical Financial Performance

We began the projection of ValueCo's FCF by laying out its income statement through EBIT for the three-year historical and LTM periods (see Exhibit 3.33). We also entered ValueCo's historical capex and working capital data. The historical period provided important perspective for developing defensible Base Case projection period financials.

As shown in Exhibit 3.33, ValueCo's historical period includes financial data for 2005 to 2007 as well as for LTM 9/30/08. The company's sales and EBITDA grew at an 8.9% and 12.7% CAGR, respectively, over the 2005 to 2007 period. In addition, ValueCo's EBITDA margin was in the 14% to 15% range over this period and average capex as a percentage of sales was 2%. The historical working capital levels and ratios are also shown in Exhibit 3.33. ValueCo's average DSO, DIH, and DPO for the 2005 to 2007 period were 59.5, 74.4, and 47.7 days, respectively. For the LTM period, ValueCo's EBITDA margin was 15% and capex as a percentage of sales was 2%.

Projection of Sales, EBITDA and EBIT

Sales Projections We projected ValueCo's top line growth for the first three years of the projection period on the basis of consensus research estimates for public comparable companies. Using the average projected sales growth rate for ValueCo's

EXHIBIT 3.33   ValueCo Summary Historical Operating and Working Capital Data

($ in millions)

ValueCo Summary Historical Operating and Working Capital Data					
	Fiscal Year Ending December 31			CAGR	LTM
	2005A	2006A	2007A	('05 - '07)	9/30/2008A
Operating Data					
Sales	**$780.0**	**$850.0**	**$925.0**	8.9%	**$977.8**
% growth	NA	9.0%	8.8%		NA
Cost of Goods Sold	471.9	512.1	555.0		586.7
% sales	60.5%	60.3%	60.0%		60.0%
Gross Profit	**$308.1**	**$337.9**	**$370.0**	9.6%	**$391.1**
% margin	39.5%	39.8%	40.0%		40.0%
Selling, General & Administrative	198.9	214.6	231.3		244.4
% sales	25.5%	25.3%	25.0%		25.0%
EBITDA	**$109.2**	**$123.3**	**$138.8**	12.7%	**$146.7**
% margin	14.0%	14.5%	15.0%		15.0%
Depreciation & Amortization	15.6	17.0	18.5		19.6
% sales	2.0%	2.0%	2.0%		2.0%
EBIT	**$93.6**	**$106.3**	**$120.3**	13.3%	**$127.1**
% margin	12.0%	12.5%	13.0%		13.0%
				3-year Average	
Capex	$15.0	$18.0	$18.5		19.6
% sales	1.9%	2.1%	2.0%	2.0%	2.0%
Working Capital Data					
Current Assets					
Accounts Receivable	$123.2	$141.1	$152.6		
DSO	57.7	60.6	60.2	59.5	
Inventory	$94.6	$104.0	$115.6		
DIH	73.2	74.1	76.0	74.4	
Prepaid Expenses and Other	$7.1	$8.5	$9.3		
% sales	0.9%	1.0%	1.0%	1.0%	
Current Liabilities					
Accounts Payable	$65.2	$66.0	$69.4		
DPO	50.4	47.0	45.6	47.7	
Accrued Liabilities	$69.9	$83.2	$92.5		
% sales	9.0%	9.8%	10.0%	9.6%	
Other Current Liabilities	$15.6	$20.4	$23.1		
% sales	2.0%	2.4%	2.5%	2.3%	

closest peers, we arrived at 2009E, 2010E, and 2011E YoY growth rates of 8%, 6%, and 4%, respectively, which are consistent with its historical rates.[32] These growth rate assumptions (as well as the assumptions for all of our model inputs) formed the basis for the Base Case financial projections and were entered into an assumptions page that drives the DCF model (see Chapter 5, Exhibits 5.52 and 5.53).

As the projections indicate, Wall Street expects ValueCo's peers (and, by inference, we expect ValueCo) to continue to experience steady growth in 2009E

---

[32]We also displayed ValueCo's full year 2008E financial data, for which we have reasonable comfort given its proximity at the end of Q3 2008. For the purposes of the DCF valuation, we used 2009E as the first full year of projections. An alternative approach is to include the "stub" period FCF (i.e., for Q4 2008E) in the projection period and adjust the discounting for a quarter year.

EXHIBIT 3.34 ValueCo Historical and Projected Sales

($ in millions)	Historical Period			CAGR		Projection Period					CAGR
	2005	2006	2007	('05 - '07)	2008	2009	2010	2011	2012	2013	('08 - '13)
Sales	$780.0	$850.0	$925.0	8.9%	$1,000.0	$1,080.0	$1,144.8	$1,190.6	$1,226.3	$1,263.1	4.8%
% growth	NA	9.0%	8.8%		8.1%	8.0%	6.0%	4.0%	3.0%	3.0%	

before gradually declining through 2011E. Beyond 2011E, in the absence of additional company-specific information or guidance, we decreased ValueCo's growth to a sustainable long-term rate of 3% for the remainder of the projection period.

COGS and SG&A Projections   As shown in Exhibit 3.35, we held COGS and SG&A constant at the prior historical year levels of 60% and 25% of sales, respectively. Accordingly, ValueCo's gross profit margin remains at 40% throughout the projection period.

EXHIBIT 3.35 ValueCo Historical and Projected COGS and SG&A

($ in millions)	Historical Period			CAGR		Projection Period					CAGR
	2005	2006	2007	('05 - '07)	2008	2009	2010	2011	2012	2013	('08 - '13)
Sales	$780.0	$850.0	$925.0	8.9%	$1,000.0	$1,080.0	$1,144.8	$1,190.6	$1,226.3	$1,263.1	4.8%
% growth	NA	9.0%	8.8%		8.1%	8.0%	6.0%	4.0%	3.0%	3.0%	
COGS	471.9	512.1	555.0		600.0	648.0	686.9	714.4	735.8	757.9	
% sales	60.5%	60.3%	60.0%		60.0%	60.0%	60.0%	60.0%	60.0%	60.0%	
Gross Profit	$308.1	$337.9	$370.0	9.6%	$400.0	$432.0	$457.9	$476.2	$490.5	$505.2	4.8%
% margin	39.5%	39.8%	40.0%		40.0%	40.0%	40.0%	40.0%	40.0%	40.0%	
SG&A	198.9	214.6	231.3		250.0	270.0	286.2	297.6	306.6	315.8	
% sales	25.5%	25.3%	25.0%		25.0%	25.0%	25.0%	25.0%	25.0%	25.0%	

EBITDA Projections   In the absence of guidance or management projections for EBITDA, we simply held ValueCo's margins constant throughout the projection period at prior historical year levels. These constant margins fall out naturally due to the fact that we froze COGS and SG&A as a percentage of sales at 2007 levels. As shown in Exhibit 3.36, ValueCo's EBITDA margins remain constant at 15% throughout the projection period. We also examined the consensus estimates for ValueCo's peer group, which provided comfort that the assumption of constant EBITDA margins was justifiable.

EXHIBIT 3.36 ValueCo Historical and Projected EBITDA

($ in millions)	Historical Period			CAGR		Projection Period					CAGR
	2005	2006	2007	('05 - '07)	2008	2009	2010	2011	2012	2013	('08 - '13)
Sales	$780.0	$850.0	$925.0	8.9%	$1,000.0	$1,080.0	$1,144.8	$1,190.6	$1,226.3	$1,263.1	4.8%
% growth	NA	9.0%	8.8%		8.1%	8.0%	6.0%	4.0%	3.0%	3.0%	
COGS	471.9	512.1	555.0		600.0	648.0	686.9	714.4	735.8	757.9	
% sales	60.5%	60.3%	60.0%		60.0%	60.0%	60.0%	60.0%	60.0%	60.0%	
Gross Profit	$308.1	$337.9	$370.0	9.6%	$400.0	$432.0	$457.9	$476.2	$490.5	$505.2	4.8%
% margin	39.5%	39.8%	40.0%		40.0%	40.0%	40.0%	40.0%	40.0%	40.0%	
SG&A	198.9	214.6	231.3		250.0	270.0	286.2	297.6	306.6	315.8	
% sales	25.5%	25.3%	25.0%		25.0%	25.0%	25.0%	25.0%	25.0%	25.0%	
EBITDA	$109.2	$123.3	$138.8	12.7%	$150.0	$162.0	$171.7	$178.6	$183.9	$189.5	4.8%
% margin	14.0%	14.5%	15.0%		15.0%	15.0%	15.0%	15.0%	15.0%	15.0%	

EBIT Projections   To drive EBIT projections, we held D&A as a percentage of sales constant at the 2007 level of 2%. We gained comfort that these D&A levels were appropriate as they were consistent with historical data as well as our capex projections (see Exhibit 3.39). EBIT was then calculated in each year of the projection period by subtracting D&A from EBITDA (see Exhibit 3.37). As previously discussed, an

For A/R, inventory, and A/P, respectively, these ratios are DSO of 60.2, DIH of 76.0, and DPO of 45.6. For prepaid expenses and other current assets, accrued liabilities, and other current liabilities, the percentage of sales levels are 1%, 10%, and 2.5%, respectively. For ValueCo's Base Case financial projections, we conservatively did not assume any improvements in working capital efficiency during the projection period.

As depicted in the callouts in Exhibit 3.40, using ValueCo's 2007 ratios, we projected 2008E NWC to be $100 million. To determine the 2009E YoY change in NWC, we then subtracted this value from ValueCo's 2009E NWC of $108 million. The $8 million difference is a use of cash and is, therefore, subtracted from EBIAT, resulting in a reduction of ValueCo's 2009E FCF. Hence, it is shown in Exhibit 3.41 as a negative value.

EXHIBIT 3.41 ValueCo's Projected Changes in Net Working Capital

($ in millions)		Projection Period				
	2008	**2009**	**2010**	**2011**	**2012**	**2013**
Total Current Assets	$300.0	$324.0	$343.4	$357.2	$367.9	$378.9
Less: Total Current Liabilities	200.0	216.0	229.0	238.1	245.3	252.6
Net Working Capital	**$100.0**	**$108.0**	**$114.5**	**$119.1**	**$122.6**	**$126.3**
(Increase) / Decrease in NWC		($8.0)	($6.5)	($4.6)	($3.6)	($3.7)

= Total Current Assets$_{2008E}$ - Total Current Liabilities$_{2008E}$
= $300.0 million - $200.0 million

= Net Working Capital$_{2008E}$ - Net Working Capital$_{2009E}$
= $100.0 million - $108.0 million

The methodology for determining ValueCo's 2009E NWC was then applied in each year of the projection period. Each annual change in NWC was added to the corresponding annual EBIAT (with increases in NWC expressed as negative values) to calculate annual FCF.

A potential shortcut to the detailed approach outlined in Exhibits 3.40 and 3.41 is to bypass projecting individual working capital components and simply project NWC as a percentage of sales in line with historical levels. For example, we could have used ValueCo's 2007 NWC percentage of sales ratio of 10% to project its NWC for each year of the projection period. We would then have simply calculated YoY changes in ValueCo's NWC and made the corresponding subtractions from EBIAT.

Free Cash Flow Projections Having determined all of the above line items, we calculated ValueCo's annual projected FCF, which increases from $79 million in 2009E to $98.1 million in 2013E (see Exhibit 3.42).

EXHIBIT 3.42 ValueCo Projected FCF

($ in millions)	Historical Period			CAGR	2008	Projection Period					CAGR
	2005	2006	2007	('05 - '07)		2009	2010	2011	2012	2013	('08 - '13)
Sales	$780.0	$850.0	$925.0	8.9%	$1,000.0	$1,080.0	$1,144.8	$1,190.6	$1,226.3	$1,263.1	4.8%
% growth	NA	9.0%	8.8%		8.1%	8.0%	6.0%	4.0%	3.0%	3.0%	
COGS	471.9	512.1	555.0		600.0	648.0	686.9	714.4	735.8	757.9	
% sales	60.5%	60.3%	60.0%		60.0%	60.0%	60.0%	60.0%	60.0%	60.0%	
Gross Profit	$308.1	$337.9	$370.0	9.6%	$400.0	$432.0	$457.9	$476.2	$490.5	$505.2	4.8%
% margin	39.5%	39.8%	40.0%		40.0%	40.0%	40.0%	40.0%	40.0%	40.0%	
SG&A	198.9	214.6	231.3		250.0	270.0	286.2	297.6	306.6	315.8	
% sales	25.5%	25.3%	25.0%		25.0%	25.0%	25.0%	25.0%	25.0%	25.0%	
EBITDA	$109.2	$123.3	$138.8	12.7%	$150.0	$162.0	$171.7	$178.6	$183.9	$189.5	4.8%
% margin	14.0%	14.5%	15.0%		15.0%	15.0%	15.0%	15.0%	15.0%	15.0%	
D&A	15.6	17.0	18.5		20.0	21.6	22.9	23.8	24.5	25.3	
% of sales	2.0%	2.0%	2.0%		2.0%	2.0%	2.0%	2.0%	2.0%	2.0%	
EBIT	$93.6	$106.3	$120.3	13.3%	$130.0	$140.4	$148.8	$154.8	$159.4	$164.2	4.8%
% margin	12.0%	12.5%	13.0%		13.0%	13.0%	13.0%	13.0%	13.0%	13.0%	
Taxes						53.4	56.6	58.8	60.6	62.4	
EBIAT						$87.0	$92.3	$96.0	$98.8	$101.8	4.8%
Plus: D&A						21.6	22.9	23.8	24.5	25.3	
Less: Capex						(21.6)	(22.9)	(23.8)	(24.5)	(25.3)	
Less: Inc. in NWC						(8.0)	(6.5)	(4.6)	(3.6)	(3.7)	
Unlevered Free Cash Flow						**$79.0**	**$85.8**	**$91.4**	**$95.3**	**$98.1**	

Step III. Calculate Weighted Average Cost of Capital

Below, we demonstrate the step-by-step calculation of ValueCo's WACC, which we determined to be 11%.

Step III(a): Determine Target Capital Structure Our first step was to determine ValueCo's target capital structure. For private companies, the target capital structure is generally extrapolated from peers. As ValueCo's peers have an average (mean) D/E of 42.9%—or debt-to-total capitalization (D/(D+E)) of 30%—we used this as our target capital structure (see Exhibit 3.45).

Step III(b): Estimate Cost of Debt We estimated ValueCo's long-term cost of debt based on the current yield on its existing term loan, the only outstanding debt instrument in its capital structure (see Exhibit 3.43).[33] The term loan, which for illustrative purposes we assumed is trading at par, is priced at a spread of 300 basis points (bps)[34] to LIBOR[35] (L+300 bps). Based on LIBOR of 300 bps, we estimated ValueCo's cost of debt at 6% (or approximately 3.7% on an after-tax basis).

---

[33] Alternatively, ValueCo's cost of debt could be extrapolated from that of its peers. We took comfort with using the current yield on ValueCo's existing term loan because its current capital structure is in line with its peers.

[34] A basis point is a unit of measure equal to 1/100th of 1% (100 bps = 1%).

[35] The London Interbank Offered Rate (LIBOR) is the rate of interest at which banks can borrow funds from other banks, in marketable size, in the London interbank market.

EXHIBIT 3.43   ValueCo Capitalization

($ in millions)	Amount	% of Total Capitalization	Maturity	Coupon
Cash and Cash Equivalents	$25.0			
Revolving Credit Facility	-	- %	2010	L+275 bps
Term Loan	300.0	30.0%	2011	L+300 bps
Total Debt	**$300.0**	**30.0%**		
Shareholders' Equity	700.0	70.0%		
Total Capitalization	**$1,000.0**	**100.0%**		
Net Debt	$275.0			

Step III(c): Estimate Cost of Equity   We calculated ValueCo's cost of equity in accordance with the CAPM formula shown in Exhibit 3.44.

EXHIBIT 3.44   CAPM Formula

$$r_e \; = \; r_f + \beta_L \times (r_m - r_f) + SP$$

Determine Risk-free Rate and Market Risk Premium   We assumed a risk-free rate (r_f) of 4%, based on the interpolated yield of the 20-year Treasury bond. For the market risk premium ($r_m - r_r$), we used the arithmetic mean of 7.1% in accordance with Ibbotson (for the 1926–2007 period).

Determine the Average Unlevered Beta of ValueCo's Comparable Companies   As ValueCo is a private company, we extrapolated beta from its closest comparables (see Chapter 1). We began by sourcing predicted levered betas for each of ValueCo's closest comparables.[36] We then entered the market values for each comparable company's debt[37] and equity, and calculated the D/E ratios accordingly. This information, in conjunction with the marginal tax rate assumptions, enabled us to unlever the individual betas and calculate an average unlevered beta for the peer group (see Exhibit 3.45).

EXHIBIT 3.45   Average Unlevered Beta

= 1.25 / (1 + (55.0%) x (1 - 38.0%))
= Predicted Levered Beta / (1 + (Debt/Equity) x (1 - t))

Comparable Companies Unlevered Beta

Company	Predicted Levered Beta	Market Value of Debt	Market Value of Equity	Debt/ Equity	Marginal Tax Rate	Unlevered Beta
Adler Industries	1.11	$575.0	$2,600.0	22.1%	38.0%	0.98
Lanzarone International	1.08	515.0	1,750.0	29.4%	38.0%	0.91
Lajoux Global	1.35	715.0	1,050.0	68.1%	38.0%	0.95
Momper Corp.	1.25	550.0	1,000.0	55.0%	38.0%	0.93
McMenamin & Co.	1.19	250.0	630.0	39.7%	38.0%	0.96
Mean	1.20			42.9%		0.95
Median	1.19			39.7%		0.95

---

[36] An alternate approach is to use historical betas (e.g., from Bloomberg), or both historical and predicted betas, and then show a range of outputs.

[37] For simplicity, we assumed that the market value of debt was equal to the book value.

For example, based on Momper Corp.'s predicted levered beta of 1.25, D/E of 55%, and a marginal tax rate of 38%, we calculated an unlevered beta of 0.93. We performed this calculation for each of the selected comparable companies and then calculated an average unlevered beta of 0.95 for the group.

Relever Average Unlevered Beta at ValueCo's Capital Structure   We then relevered the average unlevered beta of 0.95 at ValueCo's previously determined target capital structure of 42.9% D/E, using its marginal tax rate of 38%. This provided a levered beta of 1.20 (see Exhibit 3.46).

EXHIBIT 3.46   ValueCo Relevered Beta

| = Mean Unlevered Beta x (1 + (Target Debt/Equity) x (1 - Target Marginal Tax Rate) |
| = 0.95 x (1 + (42.9%) x (1 - 38.0%)) |

ValueCo Relevered Beta

	Mean Unlevered Beta	Target Debt/ Equity	Target Marginal Tax Rate	Relevered Beta
Relevered Beta	0.95	42.9%	38.0%	1.20

| = Debt-to-Total Capitalization / Equity-to-Total Capitalization |
| = 30.0% / 70.0% |

Calculate Cost of Equity   Using the CAPM, we calculated a cost of equity for ValueCo of 14.1% (see Exhibit 3.47), which is higher than the expected return on the market (calculated as 11.1% based on a risk-free rate of 4% and a market risk premium of 7.1%). This relatively high cost of equity was driven by the relevered beta of 1.20, versus 1.0 for the market as a whole, as well as a size premium of 1.65%.[38]

EXHIBIT 3.47   ValueCo Cost of Equity

Cost of Equity	
Risk-free Rate	4.0%
Market Risk Premium	7.1%
Levered Beta	1.20
Size Premium	1.65%
Cost of Equity	**14.1%**

| = Risk-free Rate + (Levered Beta x Market Risk Premium) + Size Premium |
| = 4.0% + (1.20 x 7.1%) + 1.65% |

---

[38]Ibbotson estimates a size premium of 1.65% for companies in the Low-Cap Decile for market capitalization.

Step III(d): Calculate WACC   We now have determined all of the components necessary to calculate ValueCo's WACC. These inputs were entered into the formula in Exhibit 3.12, resulting in a WACC of 11%. Exhibit 3.48 displays each of the assumptions and calculations for determining ValueCo's WACC.

As previously discussed, the DCF is highly sensitive to WACC, which itself is dependent on numerous assumptions governing target capital structure, cost of debt, and cost of equity. Therefore, a sensitivity analysis is typically performed on key WACC inputs to produce a WACC range. In Exhibit 3.49, we sensitized target capital structure and pre-tax cost of debt to produce a WACC range of approximately 10.5% to 11.5% for ValueCo.

EXHIBIT 3.48   ValueCo WACC Calculation

EXHIBIT 3.49 ValueCo Weighted Average Cost of Capital Analysis

ValueCo Corporation
Weighted Average Cost of Capital Analysis
($ in millions)

WACC Calculation

Target Capital Structure

Debt-to-Total Capitalization	30.0%
Equity-to-Total Capitalization	70.0%

Cost of Debt

Cost of Debt	6.0%
Tax Rate	38.0%
After-tax Cost of Debt	3.7%

Cost of Equity

Risk-free Rate[1]	4.0%
Market Risk Premium[2]	7.1%
Levered Beta	1.20
Size Premium[3]	1.65%
Cost of Equity	14.1%

WACC	**11.0%**

Comparable Companies Unlevered Beta

Company	Predicted Levered Beta[4]	Market Value of Debt	Market Value of Equity	Debt/ Equity	Marginal Tax Rate	Unlevered Beta
Adler Industries	1.11	$575.0	$2,600.0	22.1%	38.0%	0.98
Lanzarone International	1.08	515.0	1,750.0	29.4%	38.0%	0.91
Lajoux Global	1.35	715.0	1,050.0	68.1%	38.0%	0.95
Momper Corp.	1.25	550.0	1,000.0	55.0%	38.0%	0.93
McMenamin & Co.	1.19	250.0	630.0	39.7%	38.0%	0.96
Mean	1.20			42.9%		0.95
Median	1.19			39.7%		0.95

ValueCo Relevered Beta

	Mean Unlevered Beta	Target Debt/ Equity	Target Marginal Tax Rate	Relevered Beta
Relevered Beta	0.95	42.9%	38.0%	1.20

WACC Sensitivity Analysis

		Pre-tax Cost of Debt			
Debt-to-Total Capitalization	5.00%	5.50%	6.00%	6.50%	7.00%
10.0%	11.9%	11.9%	11.9%	11.9%	12.0%
20.0%	11.3%	11.4%	11.5%	11.5%	11.6%
30.0%	10.8%	10.9%	11.0%	11.1%	11.2%
40.0%	10.3%	10.4%	10.6%	10.7%	10.8%
50.0%	9.8%	10.0%	10.1%	10.3%	10.4%

(1) Interpolated yield on 20-year U.S. Treasury
(2) Obtained from *Ibbotson SBBI Valuation Yearbook*
(3) Low-Cap Decile size premium based on market capitalization, per Ibbotson
(4) Sourced from Barra

Step IV. Determine Terminal Value

Exit Multiple Method   We used the LTM EV/EBITDA trading multiples for ValueCo's closest public comparable companies as the basis for calculating terminal value in accordance with the EMM. These companies tend to trade in a range of 6.5x to 7.5x LTM EBITDA. Multiplying ValueCo's terminal year EBITDA of $189.5 million by the 7.0x midpoint of this range provided a terminal value of $1,326.3 million (see Exhibit 3.50).

EXHIBIT 3.50   Exit Multiple Method

($ in millions)

Calculation of Terminal Value using EMM	
Terminal Year EBITDA (2013E)	$189.5
Exit Multiple	7.0x
Terminal Value	**$1,326.3**

= EBITDA$_{\text{Terminal Year}}$ x Exit Multiple
= $189.5 million x 7.0x

We then solved for the perpetuity growth rate implied by the exit multiple of 7.0x EBITDA. Given the terminal year FCF of $98.1 million and 11% midpoint of the selected WACC range, and adjusting for the use of a mid-year convention for the PGM terminal value, we calculated an implied perpetuity growth rate of 3% (see Exhibit 3.51).

EXHIBIT 3.51   Implied Perpetuity Growth Rate

($ in millions)

Implied Perpetuity Growth Rate	
Terminal Year Free Cash Flow (2013E)	$98.1
Discount Rate	11.0%
Terminal Value	1,326.3
Implied Perpetuity Growth Rate	**3.0%**

= ((EMM Terminal Value x WACC) - FCF$_{\text{Terminal Year}}$ x $(1 + \text{WACC})^{0.5}$) / (EMM Terminal Value + FCF$_{\text{Terminal Year}}$)
= (($1,326.3 million) x 11.0%) - $98.1 million x $(1 + 11.0\%)^{0.5}$) / ($1,326.3 million + $98.1 million x $(1 + 11.0\%)^{0.5}$)

Perpetuity Growth Method   We selected a perpetuity growth rate range of 2% to 4% to calculate ValueCo's terminal value using the PGM. Using a perpetuity growth rate midpoint of 3%, WACC midpoint of 11%, and terminal year FCF of $98.1 million, we calculated a terminal value of $1,263.4 million for ValueCo (see Exhibit 3.52).

EXHIBIT 3.52   Perpetuity Growth Rate

($ in millions)

Calculation of Terminal Value using PGM	
Terminal Year Free Cash Flow (2013E)	$98.1
WACC	11.0%
Perpetuity Growth Rate	3.0%
Terminal Value	**$1,263.4**

= $FCF_{Terminal\ Year}$ x (1 + Perpetuity Growth Rate) / (WACC - Perpetuity Growth Rate)
= $98.1 million x (1 + 3.0%) / (11.0% - 3.0%)

The terminal value of $1,263.4 million calculated using the PGM implied a 7.0x exit multiple, adjusting for year-end discounting using the EMM (see Exhibit 3.53). This is consistent with our assumptions using the EMM approach in Exhibit 3.50.

EXHIBIT 3.53   Implied Exit Multiple

($ in millions)

Implied Exit Multiple	
Terminal Value	$1,263.4
Terminal Year EBITDA (2013E)	189.5
WACC	11.0%
Implied Exit Multiple	**7.0x**

= PGM Terminal Value x $(1 + WACC)^{0.5}$ / $EBITDA_{Terminal\ Year}$
= $1,263.4 million x $(1 + 11.0\%)^{0.5}$ / $189.5 million

Step V. Calculate Present Value and Determine Valuation

Calculate Present Value

ValueCo's projected annual FCF and terminal value were discounted to the present using the selected WACC midpoint of 11% (see Exhibit 3.54). We used a mid-year convention to discount projected FCF. For the terminal value calculated using the EMM, however, we used year-end discounting.

EXHIBIT 3.54   Present Value Calculation

$= 1 / ((1 + WACC)^{(n - .05)})$
$= 1 / ((1 + 11.0\%)^{(4.5)})$
Note: Mid-Year Convention applied

($ in millions)

		Projection Period				
		2009	**2010**	**2011**	**2012**	**2013**
Unlevered Free Cash Flow		$79.0	$85.8	$91.4	$95.3	$98.1
WACC	11.0%					
Discount Period		0.5	1.5	2.5	3.5	4.5
Discount Factor		0.95	0.86	0.77	0.69	0.63
Present Value of Free Cash Flow		**$75.0**	**$73.4**	**$70.4**	**$66.1**	**$61.4**

= Unlevered FCF$_{2009E}$ x Discount Factor
= $79.0 million x 0.95

= Exit Year EBITDA x Exit Multiple
= $189.5 million x 7.0x

Terminal Value	
Terminal Year EBITDA (2013E)	$189.5
Exit Multiple	7.0x
Terminal Value	**$1,326.3**
Discount Factor	0.59
Present Value of Terminal Value	**$787.1**

$= 1 / ((1 + WACC)^n)$
$= 1 / ((1 + 11.0\%)^5)$
Note: Year-End Discounting applied for Exit Multiple Method

Determine Valuation

Calculate Enterprise Value   The results of the present value calculations for the projected FCF and terminal value were summed to produce an enterprise value of $1,133.3 million for ValueCo (see Exhibit 3.55). The enterprise value is comprised of $346.3 million from the present value of the projected FCF and $787.1 million from the present value of the terminal value. This implies that ValueCo's terminal value represents 69.4% of the enterprise value.

EXHIBIT 3.55   Enterprise Value

($ in millions)

Enterprise Value	
Present Value of Free Cash Flow	**$346.3**

= Sum(FCF$_{2009-2013}$, discounted at 11.0%)
= Sum($75.0 million : $61.4 million)

Terminal Value	
Terminal Year EBITDA (2013E)	$189.5
Exit Multiple	7.0x
Terminal Value	**$1,326.3**
Discount Factor	0.59
Present Value of Terminal Value	**$787.1**
% of Enterprise Value	*69.4%*
Enterprise Value	**$1,133.3**

= Terminal Value x Discount Factor
= $1,326.3 million x 0.59

= PV of Terminal Value / Enterprise Value
= $787.1 million / $1,133.3 million

= PV of FCF$_{2009-2013}$ + PV of Terminal Value
= $346.3 million + $787.1 million

Derive Equity Value   We then calculated an implied equity value of $858.3 million for ValueCo by subtracting its net debt of $275 million ($300 million of debt – $25 million of cash) from enterprise value of $1,133.3 million (Exhibit 3.56). If ValueCo were a publicly traded company, we would then have divided the implied equity value by its fully diluted shared outstanding to determine an implied share price (see Exhibits 3.2 and 3.31).

EXHIBIT 3.56   Equity Value

Implied Equity Value and Share Price	
Enterprise Value	$1,133.3
Less: Total Debt	(300.0)
Less: Preferred Securities	-
Less: Noncontrolling Interest	-
Plus: Cash and Cash Equivalents	25.0
Implied Equity Value	**$858.3**
= Enterprise Value - Total Debt + Cash and Cash Equivalents	
= $1,133.3 million - $300.0 million + $25.0 million	

DCF Output Page   Exhibit 3.57 displays a typical DCF output page for ValueCo using the EMM.

EXHIBIT 3.57 ValueCo DCF Analysis Output Page

ValueCo Corporation
Discounted Cash Flow Analysis
($ in millions, fiscal year ending December 31)

Operating Scenario: 1
Mid-Year Convention: Y

Operating Scenario — Base

	Historical Period			CAGR		Projection Period					CAGR
	2005	2006	2007	('05 - '07)	2008	2009	2010	2011	2012	2013	('08 - '13)
Sales	$780.0	$850.0	$925.0	8.9%	$1,000.0	$1,080.0	$1,144.8	$1,190.6	$1,226.3	$1,263.1	4.8%
% growth	NA	9.0%	8.8%		8.1%	8.0%	6.0%	4.0%	3.0%	3.0%	
Cost of Goods Sold	471.9	512.1	555.0		600.0	648.0	686.9	714.4	735.8	757.9	
Gross Profit	$308.1	$337.9	$370.0	9.6%	$400.0	$432.0	$457.9	$476.2	$490.5	$505.2	4.8%
% margin	39.5%	39.8%	40.0%		40.0%	40.0%	40.0%	40.0%	40.0%	40.0%	
Selling, General & Administrative	198.9	214.6	231.3		250.0	270.0	286.2	297.6	306.6	315.8	
EBITDA	$109.2	$123.3	$138.8	12.7%	$150.0	$162.0	$171.7	$178.6	$183.9	$189.5	4.8%
% margin	14.0%	14.5%	15.0%		15.0%	15.0%	15.0%	15.0%	15.0%	15.0%	
Depreciation & Amortization	15.6	17.0	18.5		20.0	21.6	22.9	23.8	24.5	25.3	
EBIT	$93.6	$106.3	$120.3	13.3%	$130.0	$140.4	$148.8	$154.8	$159.4	$164.2	4.8%
% margin	12.0%	12.5%	13.0%		13.0%	13.0%	13.0%	13.0%	13.0%	13.0%	
Taxes	35.6	40.4	45.7		49.4	53.4	56.6	58.8	60.6	62.4	
EBIAT	$58.0	$65.9	$74.6	13.3%	$80.6	$87.0	$92.3	$96.0	$98.8	$101.8	4.8%
Plus: Depreciation & Amortization	15.6	17.0	18.5		20.0	21.6	22.9	23.8	24.5	25.3	
Less: Capital Expenditures	(15.0)	(18.0)	(18.5)		(20.0)	(21.6)	(22.9)	(23.8)	(24.5)	(25.3)	
Less: Increase in Net Working Capital					(20.0)	(8.0)	(6.5)	(4.6)	(3.6)	(3.7)	
Unlevered Free Cash Flow						$79.0	$85.8	$91.4	$95.3	$98.1	
WACC	11.0%					0.5	1.5	2.5	3.5	4.5	
Discount Period						0.5	1.5	2.5	3.5	4.5	
Discount Factor						0.95	0.86	0.77	0.69	0.63	
Present Value of Free Cash Flow						$75.0	$73.4	$70.4	$66.1	$61.4	

Enterprise Value

Cumulative Present Value of FCF	$346.3
Terminal Value	
Terminal Year EBITDA (2013E)	$189.5
Exit Multiple	7.0x
Terminal Value	$1,326.3
Discount Factor	0.59
Present Value of Terminal Value	$787.1
% of Enterprise Value	69.4%
Enterprise Value	$1,133.3

Implied Equity Value and Share Price

Enterprise Value	$1,133.3
Less: Total Debt	(300.0)
Less: Preferred Securities	-
Less: Noncontrolling Interest	-
Plus: Cash and Cash Equivalents	25.0
Implied Equity Value	$858.3

Implied Perpetuity Growth Rate

Terminal Year Free Cash Flow (2013E)	$98.1
WACC	11.0%
Terminal Value	$1,326.3
Implied Perpetuity Growth Rate	3.0%

Implied EV/EBITDA

Enterprise Value	$1,133.3
LTM 9/30/2008 EBITDA	146.7
Implied EV/EBITDA	7.7x

Enterprise Value

WACC	Exit Multiple				
	6.0x	6.5x	7.0x	7.5x	8.0x
10.0%	1,060	1,119	1,177	1,236	1,295
10.5%	1,040	1,098	1,155	1,213	1,270
11.0%	1,021	1,077	1,133	1,190	1,246
11.5%	1,002	1,057	1,112	1,167	1,222
12.0%	984	1,038	1,091	1,145	1,199

Implied Perpetuity Growth Rate

WACC	Exit Multiple				
	6.0x	6.5x	7.0x	7.5x	8.0x
10.0%	0.9%	1.5%	2.1%	2.6%	3.0%
10.5%	1.3%	2.0%	2.5%	3.0%	3.5%
11.0%	1.7%	2.4%	3.0%	3.5%	3.9%
11.5%	2.2%	2.8%	3.4%	3.9%	4.4%
12.0%	2.6%	3.3%	3.9%	4.4%	4.8%

155

EXHIBIT 3.58 ValueCo Sensitivity Analysis

ValueCo Corporation
Sensitivity Analysis
($ in millions)

Enterprise Value

WACC	Exit Multiple				
	6.0x	6.5x	7.0x	7.5x	8.0x
10.0%	1,060	1,119	1,177	1,236	1,295
10.5%	1,040	1,098	1,155	1,213	1,270
11.0%	1,021	1,077	$1,133	1,190	1,246
11.5%	1,002	1,057	1,112	1,167	1,222
12.0%	984	1,038	1,091	1,145	1,199

Implied Equity Value

WACC	Exit Multiple				
	6.0x	6.5x	7.0x	7.5x	8.0x
10.0%	785	844	902	961	1,020
10.5%	765	823	880	938	995
11.0%	746	802	$858	915	971
11.5%	727	782	837	892	947
12.0%	709	763	816	870	924

Implied Perpetuity Growth Rate

WACC	Exit Multiple				
	6.0x	6.5x	7.0x	7.5x	8.0x
10.0%	0.9%	1.5%	2.1%	2.6%	3.0%
10.5%	1.3%	2.0%	2.5%	3.0%	3.5%
11.0%	1.7%	2.4%	3.0%	3.5%	3.9%
11.5%	2.2%	2.8%	3.4%	3.9%	4.4%
12.0%	2.6%	3.3%	3.9%	4.4%	4.8%

Implied Enterprise Value / LTM EBITDA

WACC	Exit Multiple				
	6.0x	6.5x	7.0x	7.5x	8.0x
10.0%	7.2x	7.6x	8.0x	8.4x	8.8x
10.5%	7.1x	7.5x	7.9x	8.3x	8.7x
11.0%	7.0x	7.3x	7.7x	8.1x	8.5x
11.5%	6.8x	7.2x	7.6x	8.0x	8.3x
12.0%	6.7x	7.1x	7.4x	7.8x	8.2x

PV of Terminal Value as % of Enterprise Value

WACC	Exit Multiple				
	6.0x	6.5x	7.0x	7.5x	8.0x
10.0%	66.6%	68.4%	69.9%	71.4%	72.7%
10.5%	66.3%	68.1%	69.7%	71.1%	72.4%
11.0%	66.1%	67.9%	69.4%	70.9%	72.2%
11.5%	65.8%	67.6%	69.2%	70.6%	72.0%
12.0%	65.6%	67.3%	68.9%	70.4%	71.7%

Perform Sensitivity Analysis

We then performed a series of sensitivity analyses on WACC and exit multiple for several key outputs, including enterprise value, equity value, implied perpetuity growth rate, implied EV/LTM EBITDA, and PV of terminal value as a percentage of enterprise value (see Exhibit 3.58).

We also sensitized key financial assumptions, such as sales growth rates and EBIT margins, to analyze the effects on enterprise value. This sensitivity analysis provided helpful perspective on our assumptions and enabled us to study the potential value creation or erosion resulting from outperformance or underperformance versus the Base Case financial projections. For example, as shown in Exhibit 3.59, an increase in ValueCo's annual sales growth rates and EBIT margins by 50 bps each results in an increase of $38.3 million in enterprise value to $1,171.6 million versus $1,133.3 million.

EXHIBIT 3.59 Sensitivity Analysis on Sales Growth Rates and EBIT Margins

		Enterprise Value				
		Annual Sales Growth Rate Inc. / (Dec.)				
		(1.0%)	(0.5%)	0.0%	0.5%	1.0%
Annual EBIT Margin Inc. / (Dec.)	(1.0%)	1,059	1,082	1,105	1,129	1,153
	(0.5%)	1,073	1,096	1,119	1,143	1,167
	0.0%	1,087	1,110	$1,133	1,157	1,182
	0.5%	1,100	1,124	1,147	1,172	1,196
	1.0%	1,114	1,138	1,162	1,186	1,211

After completing the sensitivity analysis, we proceeded to determine ValueCo's ultimate DCF valuation range. To derive this range, we focused on the shaded portion of the exit multiple / WACC data table (see top left corner of Exhibit 3.58). Based on an exit multiple range of 6.5x to 7.5x and a WACC range of 10.5% to 11.5%, we calculated an enterprise value range of approximately $1,057 million to $1,213 million for ValueCo.

We then added this range to our "football field" and compared it to the derived valuation ranges from our comparable companies analysis and precedent transactions analysis performed in Chapters 1 and 2 (see Exhibit 3.60).

EXHIBIT 3.60 ValueCo Football Field Displaying Comparable Companies, Precedent Transactions, and DCF Analysis

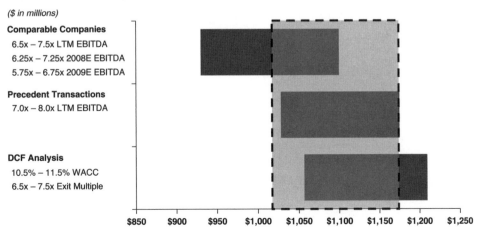

($ in millions)

Comparable Companies
6.5x – 7.5x LTM EBITDA
6.25x – 7.25x 2008E EBITDA
5.75x – 6.75x 2009E EBITDA

Precedent Transactions
7.0x – 8.0x LTM EBITDA

DCF Analysis
10.5% – 11.5% WACC
6.5x – 7.5x Exit Multiple

$850 $900 $950 $1,000 $1,050 $1,100 $1,150 $1,200 $1,250

Leveraged Buyouts

Leveraged Buyouts

A leveraged buyout (LBO) is the acquisition of a company, division, business, or collection of assets ("target") using debt to finance a large portion of the purchase price. The remaining portion of the purchase price is funded with an equity contribution by a financial sponsor ("sponsor"). LBOs are used by sponsors to acquire a broad range of businesses, including both public and private companies, as well as their divisions and subsidiaries. The sponsor's ultimate goal is to realize an acceptable return on its equity investment upon exit, typically through a sale or IPO of the target. Sponsors have historically sought a 20%+ annualized return and an investment exit within five years.[1]

In a traditional LBO, debt has typically comprised 60% to 70% of the financing structure, with equity comprising the remaining 30% to 40% (see Exhibit 4.12). The disproportionately high level of debt incurred by the target is supported by its projected free cash flow[2] and asset base, which enables the sponsor to contribute a small equity investment relative to the purchase price. The ability to leverage the relatively small equity investment is important for sponsors to achieve acceptable returns. The use of leverage provides the additional benefit of tax savings realized due to the tax deductibility of interest expense.

Companies with stable and predictable cash flow, as well as substantial assets, generally represent attractive LBO candidates due to their ability to support larger quantities of debt. Strong cash flow is needed to service periodic interest payments and reduce debt over the life of the investment. In addition, a strong asset base increases the amount of *bank debt* available to the borrower (the least expensive source of debt financing) by providing greater comfort to lenders regarding the likelihood of principal recovery in the event of a bankruptcy. When the credit markets are particularly robust, however, credit providers are increasingly

---

[1] Depending on the long-term structural effects of the subprime mortgage crisis and ensuing credit crunch, including the ability to raise debt at historical levels, these long-established benchmarks may be revisited.

[2] The "free cash flow" term ("levered free cash flow" or "cash available for debt repayment") used in LBO analysis differs from the "unlevered free cash flow" term used in DCF analysis as it includes the effects of leverage.

willing to focus more on cash flow generation and less on the strength of the asset base.

During the time from which the sponsor acquires the target until its exit ("investment horizon"), cash flow is used primarily to service and repay debt, thereby increasing the equity portion of the capital structure. At the same time, the sponsor aims to improve the financial performance of the target and grow the existing business (including through future "bolt-on" acquisitions), thereby increasing enterprise value and further enhancing potential returns. An appropriate LBO financing structure must balance the target's ability to service and repay debt with its need to use cash flow to manage and grow the business.

The successful closing of an LBO relies upon the sponsor's ability to obtain the requisite financing needed to acquire the target. Investment banks traditionally play a critical role in this respect, primarily as arrangers/underwriters of the debt used to fund the purchase price.[3] They typically compete with one another to provide a financing commitment for the sponsor's preferred financing structure in the form of legally binding letters ("financing" or "commitment" papers). The commitment letters promise funding for the debt portion of the purchase price in exchange for various fees and subject to specific conditions, including the sponsor's contribution of an acceptable level of cash equity.[4]

The debt used in an LBO is raised through the issuance of various types of loans, securities, and other instruments that are classified based on their *security* status as well as their *seniority* in the capital structure. The condition of the prevailing debt capital markets plays a key role in determining leverage levels, as well as the cost of financing and key terms. The equity portion of the financing structure is usually sourced from a pool of capital ("fund") managed by the sponsor. Sponsors' funds range in size from tens of millions to tens of billions of dollars.

Due to the proliferation of private investment vehicles (e.g., private equity firms and hedge funds) in the mid-2000s and their considerable pools of capital, LBOs became an increasingly large part of the capital markets and M&A landscape. Bankers who advise on LBO financings are tasked with helping to craft a marketable financing structure that enables the sponsor to meet its investment objectives and return thresholds, while providing the target with sufficient financial flexibility and cushion needed to operate and grow the business. Investment banks also provide buy-side and sell-side M&A advisory services to sponsors on LBO transactions. Furthermore, LBOs provide a multitude of subsequent opportunities for investment banks to provide their services after the close of the original transaction, most notably for future buy-side M&A activity, refinancing opportunities, and traditional exit events such as a sale of the target or an IPO.

This chapter provides an overview of the fundamentals of leveraged buyouts as depicted in the main categories shown in Exhibit 4.1.

---

[3]The term "investment bank" is used broadly to refer to financial intermediaries that perform corporate finance and M&A advisory services, as well as capital markets underwriting activities.

[4]These letters are typically highly negotiated among the sponsor, the banks providing the financing, and their respective legal counsels before they are executed.

EXHIBIT 4.1   LBO Fundamentals

- Key Participants
- Characteristics of a Strong LBO Candidate
- Economics of LBOs
- Primary Exit/Monetization Strategies
- LBO Financing: Structure
- LBO Financing: Primary Sources
- LBO Financing: Selected Key Terms

KEY PARTICIPANTS

This section provides an overview of the key participants in an LBO (see Exhibit 4.2).

EXHIBIT 4.2   Key Participants

- Financial Sponsors
- Investment Banks
- Bank and Institutional Lenders
- Bond Investors
- Target Management

Financial Sponsors

The term "financial sponsor" refers to traditional private equity (PE) firms, merchant banking divisions of investment banks, hedge funds, venture capital funds, and special purpose acquisition companies (SPACs), among other investment vehicles. PE firms, hedge funds, and venture capital funds raise the vast majority of their investment capital from third-party investors, which include public and corporate pension funds, insurance companies, endowments and foundations, sovereign wealth funds, and wealthy families/individuals. Sponsor partners and investment professionals may also invest their own money in particular investment opportunities.

This capital is organized into funds that are usually established as limited partnerships. Limited partnerships are typically structured as a fixed-life investment vehicle, in which the general partner (GP, i.e., the sponsor) manages the fund on a day-to-day basis and the limited partners (LPs) serve as passive investors.[5] These vehicles are considered "blind pools" in that the LPs subscribe without specific knowledge of the investment(s) that the sponsor plans to make.[6] However, sponsors are often limited

---

[5]To compensate the GP for management of the fund, LPs typically pay 1% to 2% per annum on committed funds as a management fee. In addition, once the LPs have received the return of every dollar of committed capital plus the required investment return threshold, the sponsor typically receives a 20% "carry" on every dollar of investment profit.

[6]LPs generally hold the capital they invest in a given fund until it is called by the GP in connection with a specific investment.

in the amount of the fund's capital that can be invested in any particular business, typically no more then 10% to 20%.

Sponsors vary greatly in terms of fund size, focus, and investment strategy. The size of a sponsor's fund(s), which can range from tens of millions to tens of billions of dollars (based on its ability to raise capital), helps dictate its investment parameters. Some firms specialize in specific sectors (such as industrials or media, for example) while others focus on specific situations (such as distressed companies/turnarounds, roll-ups, or corporate divestitures). Many are simply generalists that look at a broad spectrum of opportunities across multiple industries and investment strategies. These firms are staffed accordingly with investment professionals that fit their strategy, many of whom are former investment bankers. They also typically employ (or engage the services of) operational professionals and industry experts, such as former CEOs and other company executives, who consult and advise the sponsor on specific transactions.

In evaluating an investment opportunity, the sponsor performs detailed due diligence on the target, typically through an organized M&A sale process (see Chapter 6). Due diligence is the process of learning as much as possible about all aspects of the target (e.g., business, sector, financial, accounting, tax, legal, regulatory, and environmental) to discover, confirm, or discredit information critical to the sponsor's investment thesis. Sponsors use due diligence findings to develop a financial model and support purchase price assumptions (including a preferred financing structure), often hiring accountants, consultants, and industry and other functional experts to assist in the process. Larger and/or specialized sponsors typically engage operating experts, many of whom are former senior industry executives, to assist in diligence and potentially the eventual management of acquired companies.

Investment Banks

Investment banks play a key role in LBOs, both as a provider of financing and as a strategic M&A advisor. Sponsors rely heavily on investment banks to help develop and market an optimal financing structure. They may also engage investment banks as buy-side M&A advisors in return for sourcing deals and/or for their expertise, relationships, and in-house resources. On the sell-side, sponsors typically engage bankers as M&A advisors (and potentially as *stapled financing* providers[7]) to market their portfolio companies to prospective buyers through an organized sale process.

Investment banks perform thorough due diligence on LBO targets (usually alongside their sponsor clients) and go through an extensive internal credit process in order to validate the target's business plan. They also must gain comfort with the target's ability to service a highly leveraged capital structure and their ability to market the structure to the appropriate investors. Investment banks work closely with their sponsor clients to determine an appropriate financing structure for a particular

---

[7]The investment bank running an auction process (or sometimes a "partner" bank) may offer a pre-packaged financing structure, typically for prospective financial buyers, in support of the target being sold. This is commonly referred to as stapled financing ("staple"). See Chapter 6: M&A Sale Process for additional information.

transaction.[8] Once the sponsor chooses the preferred financing structure for an LBO (often a compilation of the best terms from proposals solicited from several banks), the deal team presents it to the bank's internal credit committee(s) for final approval.

Following credit committee approval, the investment banks are able to provide a financing commitment to support the sponsor's bid.[9] This commitment offers funding for the debt portion of the transaction under proposed terms and conditions (including worst case maximum interest rates ("caps")) in exchange for various fees[10] and subject to specific conditions, including the sponsor's contribution of an acceptable level of cash equity. This is also known as an *underwritten* financing, which traditionally has been required for LBOs due to the need to provide certainty of closing to the seller (including financing).[11] These letters also typically provide for a marketing period during which the banks seek to syndicate their commitments to investors prior to funding the transaction.

For the bank debt, each arranger[12] expects to hold a certain dollar amount of the revolving credit facility in its loan portfolio, while seeking to syndicate the remainder along with any term loan(s). As underwriters of the *high yield bonds* or *mezzanine debt*,[13] the investment banks attempt to sell the entire offering to investors without committing to hold any securities on their balance sheets. However, in an underwritten financing, the investment banks typically commit to provide a *bridge loan* for these securities to provide assurance that sufficient funding will be available to finance and close the deal.

Bank and Institutional Lenders

Bank and institutional lenders are the capital providers for the bank debt in an LBO financing structure. Although there is often overlap between them, traditional bank lenders provide capital for revolvers and amortizing term loans, while institutional lenders provide capital for longer tenored, limited amortization term loans.

---

[8]Alternatively, the banks may be asked to commit to a financing structure already developed by the sponsor.

[9]The financing commitment includes: a *commitment letter* for the bank debt and a bridge facility (to be provided by the lender in lieu of a bond financing if the capital markets are not available at the time the acquisition is consummated); an *engagement letter*, in which the sponsor engages the investment banks to underwrite the bonds on behalf of the issuer; and a *fee letter*, which sets forth the various fees to be paid to the investment banks in connection with the financing. Traditionally, in an LBO, the sponsor has been required to provide certainty of financing and, therefore, had to pay for a bridge financing commitment even if it was unlikely that the bridge would be funded.

[10]The fees associated with the commitment compensate the banks for their underwriting role and the risk associated with the pledge to fund the transaction in the event that a syndication to outside investors is not achievable.

[11]The credit crunch has resulted in certain sellers loosening this requirement and accepting bids with financing conditions.

[12]The primary investment banks responsible for marketing the bank debt, including the preparation of marketing materials and running the syndication, are referred to as "Lead Arrangers" or "Bookrunners."

[13]The lead investment banks responsible for marketing the high yield bonds or mezzanine debt are referred to as "Bookrunners."

Bank lenders typically consist of commercial banks, savings and loan institutions, finance companies, and the investment banks serving as arrangers. The institutional lender base is largely comprised of hedge funds, pension funds, prime funds, insurance companies, and structured vehicles such as collateralized debt obligation funds (CDOs).[14]

Like investment banks, lenders perform due diligence and undergo an internal credit process before participating in an LBO financing. This involves analyzing the target's business and credit profile (with a focus on projected cash flow generation and credit statistics) to gain comfort that they will receive full future interest payments and principal repayment at maturity. Lenders also look to mitigate downside risk by requiring covenants and collateral coverage. Prior experience with a given credit, sector, or particular sponsor is also factored into the decision to participate. To a great extent, however, lenders rely on the diligence performed (and materials prepared) by the lead arrangers.

As part of their diligence process, prospective lenders attend a group meeting known as a "bank meeting," which is organized by the lead arrangers.[15] In a bank meeting, the target's senior management team gives a detailed slideshow presentation about the company and its investment merits, followed by an overview of the offering by the lead arrangers and a Q&A session. At the bank meeting, prospective lenders receive a hard copy of the presentation, as well as a confidential information memorandum (CIM or "bank book") prepared by management and the lead arrangers.[16] As lenders go through their internal credit processes and make their final investment decisions, they conduct follow-up diligence that often involves requesting additional information and analysis from the company.

Bond Investors

Bond investors are the purchasers of the high yield bonds issued as part of the LBO financing structure. They generally include high yield mutual funds, hedge funds, pension funds, insurance companies, distressed debt funds, and CDOs.

As part of their investment assessment and decision-making process, bond investors attend one-on-one meetings, known as "roadshow presentations," during

---

[14]CDOs are asset-backed securities ("securitized") backed by interests in pools of assets, usually some type of debt obligation. When the interests in the pool are loans, the vehicle is called a collateralized loan obligation (CLO). When the interests in the pool are bonds, the vehicle is called a collateralized bond obligation (CBO).

[15]For particularly large or complex transactions, the target's management may present to lenders on a one-on-one basis.

[16]The bank book is a comprehensive document that contains a detailed description of the transaction, investment highlights, company, and sector, as well as preliminary term sheets and historical and projected financials. In the event that publicly registered bonds are contemplated as part of the offering, two versions of the CIM are usually created—a public version and a private version (or private supplement). The public version, which excludes financial projections and forward-looking statements, is distributed to lenders who intend to purchase bonds or other securities that will eventually be registered with the SEC. The private version, on the other hand, includes financial projections as it is used by investors that intend to invest solely in the company's unregistered debt (i.e., bank debt). Both the bank meeting presentation and bank book are typically available to lenders through an online medium.

which senior executives present the investment merits of the company and the proposed transaction. A roadshow is typically a one- to two-week process (depending on the size and scope of the transaction), where bankers from the lead underwriting institution (and generally an individual from the sponsor team) accompany the target's management on meetings with potential investors. These meetings may also be conducted as breakfasts or luncheons with groups of investors. The typical U.S. roadshow includes stops in the larger financial centers such as New York, Boston, Los Angeles, and San Francisco, as well as smaller cities throughout the country.[17,18]

Prior to the roadshow meeting, bond investors receive a preliminary offering memorandum (OM), which is a legal document containing much of the target's business, industry, and financial information found in the bank book. The preliminary OM, however, must satisfy a higher degree of legal scrutiny and disclosure (including risk factors[19]). Unlike bank debt, most bonds are eventually registered with the SEC (so they can be traded on an exchange) and are therefore subject to regulation under the Securities Act of 1933 and the Securities Exchange Act of 1934.[20] The preliminary OM also contains detailed information on the bonds, including a preliminary term sheet (excluding pricing) and a description of notes (DON).[21] Once the roadshow concludes and the bonds have been priced, the final terms are inserted into the document, which is then distributed to bond investors as the final OM.

Target Management

Management plays a crucial role in the marketing of the target to potential buyers (see Chapter 6) and lenders alike, working closely with the bankers on the preparation of marketing materials and financial information. Management also serves as the primary face of the company and must articulate the investment merits of the transaction to these constituents. Consequently, in an LBO, a strong management team can create tangible value by driving favorable financing terms and pricing, as well as providing sponsors with comfort to stretch on valuation.

From a structuring perspective, management typically holds a meaningful equity interest in the post-LBO company through "rolling" its existing equity or investing in the business alongside the sponsor at closing. Several layers of management typically also have the opportunity to participate (on a post-closing basis) in a stock option-based compensation package, generally tied to an agreed upon set of financial targets for the company.[22] This structure provides management with meaningful economic

---

[17]For example, roadshow schedules often include stops in Philadelphia, Baltimore, Minneapolis, Milwaukee, Chicago, and Houston, as well as various cities throughout New Jersey and Connecticut, in accordance with where the underwriters believe there will be investor interest.
[18]European roadshows include primary stops in London, Paris, and Frankfurt, as well as secondary stops typically in Milan, Edinburgh, Zurich, and Amsterdam.
[19]A discussion of the most significant factors that make the offering speculative or risky.
[20]Laws that set forth requirements for securities listed on public exchanges, including registration and periodic disclosures of financial status, among others.
[21]The DON contains an overview of the material provisions of the bond indenture including key definitions, terms, and covenants.
[22]These option incentives may comprise up to 15% of the equity value of the company (and are realized by management upon a sale or IPO).

incentives to improve the company's performance as they share in the equity upside. As a result, management and sponsor interests are aligned in pursuing superior performance. The broad-based equity incentive program outlined above is often a key differentiating factor versus a public company structure.

Management Buyout   An LBO originated and led by a target's existing management team is referred to as a management buyout (MBO). Often, an MBO is effected with the help of an equity partner, such as a financial sponsor, who provides capital support and access to debt financing through established investment banking relationships. The basic premise behind an MBO is that the management team believes it can create more value running the company on its own than under current ownership. The MBO structure also serves to eliminate the conflict between management and the board of directors/shareholders as owner-managers are able to run the company as they see fit.

Public company management may be motivated by the belief that the market is undervaluing the company, SEC and Sarbanes-Oxley (SOX)[23] compliance is too burdensome and costly (especially for smaller companies), and/or the company could operate more efficiently as a private entity. LBO candidates with sizeable management ownership are generally strong MBO candidates. Another common MBO scenario involves a buyout by the management of a division or subsidiary of a larger corporation who believe they can run the business better separate from the parent.

CHARACTERISTICS OF A STRONG LBO CANDIDATE

Financial sponsors as a group are highly flexible investors that seek attractive investment opportunities across a broad range of sectors, geographies, and situations. While there are few steadfast rules, certain common traits emerge among traditional LBO candidates, as outlined in Exhibit 4.3.

EXHIBIT 4.3   Characteristics of a Strong LBO Candidate

- Strong Cash Flow Generation
- Leading and Defensible Market Positions
- Growth Opportunities
- Efficiency Enhancement Opportunities
- Low Capex Requirements
- Strong Asset Base
- Proven Management Team

---

[23]The Sarbanes-Oxley Act of 2002 enacted substantial changes to the securities laws that govern public companies and their officers and directors in regards to corporate governance and financial reporting. Most notably, Section 404 of SOX requires public registrants to establish and maintain "Internal Controls and Procedures," which can consume significant internal resources, time, commitment, and expense.

During due diligence, the sponsor studies and evaluates an LBO candidate's key strengths and risks. Often, LBO candidates are identified among non-core or underperforming divisions of larger companies, neglected or troubled companies with turnaround potential, or companies in fragmented markets as platforms for a roll-up strategy.[24] In many instances, the target is simply a solidly performing company with a compelling business model, defensible competitive position, and strong growth opportunities. For a publicly traded LBO candidate, a sponsor may perceive the target as undervalued by the market or recognize opportunities for growth and efficiency not being exploited by current management. Regardless of the situation, the target only represents an attractive LBO opportunity if it can be purchased at a price and utilizing a financing structure that provides sufficient returns with a viable exit strategy.

Strong Cash Flow Generation

The ability to generate strong, predictable cash flow is critical for LBO candidates given the highly leveraged capital structure. Debt investors require a business model that demonstrates the ability to support periodic interest payments and debt repayment over the life of the loans and securities. Business characteristics that support the predictability of robust cash flow increase a company's attractiveness as an LBO candidate. For example, many strong LBO candidates operate in a mature or niche business with stable customer demand and end markets. They often feature a strong brand name, established customer base, and/or long-term sales contracts, all of which serve to increase the predictability of cash flow. Prospective buyers and financing providers seek to confirm a given LBO candidate's cash flow generation during due diligence to gain the requisite level of comfort with the target management's projections. Cash flow projections are usually stress-tested (sensitized) based on historical volatility and potential future business and economic conditions to ensure the ability to support the LBO financing structure under challenging circumstances.

Leading and Defensible Market Positions

Leading and defensible market positions generally reflect entrenched customer relationships, brand name recognition, superior products and services, a favorable cost structure, and scale advantages, among other attributes. These qualities create barriers to entry and increase the stability and predictability of a company's cash flow. Accordingly, the sponsor spends a great deal of time during due diligence seeking assurance that the target's market positions are secure (and can potentially be expanded). Depending on the sponsor's familiarity with the sector, consultants may be hired to perform independent studies analyzing market share and barriers to entry.

Growth Opportunities

Sponsors seek companies with growth potential, both organically and through potential future bolt-on acquisitions. Profitable top line growth at above-market rates

---

[24] A roll-up strategy involves consolidating multiple companies in a given market or sector to create an entity with increased size, scale, and efficiency.

helps drive outsized returns, generating greater cash available for debt repayment while also increasing EBITDA and enterprise value. Growth also enhances the speed and optionality for exit opportunities. For example, a strong growth profile is particularly important if the target is designated for an eventual IPO exit.

Companies with robust growth profiles have a greater likelihood of driving EBITDA "multiple expansion"[25] during the sponsor's investment horizon, which further enhances returns. Moreover, as discussed in Chapter 1, larger companies tend to benefit from their scale, market share, purchasing power, and lower risk profile, and are often rewarded with a premium valuation relative to smaller peers, all else being equal. In some cases, the sponsor opts not to maximize the amount of debt financing at purchase. This provides greater flexibility to pursue a growth strategy that may require future incremental debt to make acquisitions or build new facilities, for example.

Efficiency Enhancement Opportunities

While an ideal LBO candidate should have a strong fundamental business model, sponsors seek opportunities to improve operational efficiencies and generate cost savings. Traditional cost-saving measures include lowering corporate overhead, streamlining operations, reducing headcount, rationalizing the supply chain, and implementing new management information systems. The sponsor may also seek to source new (or negotiate better) terms with existing suppliers and customers. These initiatives are a primary focus for the consultants and industry experts hired by the sponsor to assist with due diligence and assess the opportunity represented by establishing "best practices" at the target. Their successful implementation often represents substantial value creation that accrues to equity value at a multiple of each dollar saved (given an eventual exit).

At the same time, sponsors must be careful not to jeopardize existing sales or attractive growth opportunities. Extensive cuts in marketing, capex, or research & development, for example, may hurt customer retention, new product development, or other growth initiatives. Such moves could put the company at risk of deteriorating sales and profitability.

Low Capex Requirements

All else being equal, low capex requirements enhance a company's cash flow generation capabilities. As a result, the best LBO candidates tend to have limited capital investment needs. However, a company with substantial capex requirements may still represent an attractive investment opportunity if it has a strong growth profile, high profit margins, and the business strategy is validated during due diligence.

During due diligence, the sponsor and its advisors focus on differentiating those expenditures deemed necessary to continue operating the business ("maintenance capex") from those that are discretionary ("growth capex"). Maintenance capex is capital required to sustain existing assets (typically PP&E) at their current output

---

[25]Selling the target for a higher multiple of EBITDA upon exit (i.e., purchasing the target for 7.0x EBITDA and selling it for 8.0x EBITDA).

levels. Growth capex is primarily used to purchase new assets or expand the existing asset base. Therefore, growth capex can potentially be reduced or eliminated in the event that economic conditions or operating performance decline.

Strong Asset Base

A strong asset base pledged as collateral against a loan benefits lenders by increasing the likelihood of principal recovery in the event of bankruptcy (and liquidation). This, in turn, increases their willingness to provide debt to the target. The target's asset base is particularly important in the leveraged loan market, where the value of the assets helps dictate the amount of bank debt available (see "LBO Financing" sections for additional information). A strong asset base also tends to signify high barriers to entry because of the substantial capital investment required, which serves to deter new entrants in the target's markets. At the same time, a company with little or no assets can still be an attractive LBO candidate provided it generates sufficient cash flow.

Proven Management Team

A proven management team serves to increase the attractiveness (and value) of an LBO candidate. Talented management is critical in an LBO scenario given the need to operate under a highly leveraged capital structure with ambitious performance targets. Prior experience operating under such conditions, as well as success in integrating acquisitions or implementing restructuring initiatives, is highly regarded by sponsors.

For LBO candidates with strong management, the sponsor usually seeks to keep the existing team in place post-acquisition. It is customary for management to retain, invest, or be granted a meaningful equity stake so as to align their incentives under the new ownership structure with that of the sponsor. Alternatively, in those instances where the target's management is weak, sponsors seek to add value by making key changes to the existing team or installing a new team altogether to run the company. In either circumstance, a strong management team is crucial for driving company performance going forward and helping the sponsor meet its investment objectives.

ECONOMICS OF LBOs

Returns Analysis – Internal Rate of Return

Internal rate of return (IRR) is the primary metric by which sponsors gauge the attractiveness of a potential LBO, as well as the performance of their existing investments. IRR measures the total return on a sponsor's equity investment, including any additional equity contributions made, or dividends received, during the investment horizon. It is defined as the discount rate that must be applied to the sponsor's cash outflows and inflows during the investment horizon in order to produce a net present value (NPV) of zero. Although the IRR calculation can be performed with a financial calculator or by using the IRR function in Microsoft Excel, it is important to understand the supporting math. Exhibit 4.4 displays the equation for calculating IRR, assuming a five-year investment horizon.

EXHIBIT 4.4 IRR Timeline

While multiple factors affect a sponsor's ultimate decision to pursue a potential acquisition, comfort with meeting acceptable IRR thresholds is critical. Sponsors typically target superior returns relative to alternative investments for their LPs, with a 20%+ threshold historically serving as a widely held "rule of thumb." This threshold, however, may increase or decrease depending on market conditions, the perceived risk of an investment, and other factors specific to the situation.

The primary IRR drivers include the target's projected financial performance,[26] purchase price, and financing structure (particularly the size of the equity contribution), as well as the exit multiple and year. As would be expected, a sponsor seeks to minimize the price paid and equity contribution while gaining a strong degree of confidence in the target's future financial performance and the ability to exit at a sufficient valuation.

In Exhibit 4.5, we assume that a sponsor contributes $250 million of equity (cash outflow) at the end of Year 0 as part of the LBO financing structure and receives equity proceeds upon sale of $750 million (cash inflow) at the end of Year 5. This scenario produces an IRR of 24.6%, as demonstrated by the NPV of zero.

EXHIBIT 4.5 IRR Timeline Example

Returns Analysis – Cash Return

In addition to IRR, sponsors also examine returns on the basis of a multiple of their cash investment ("cash return"). For example, assuming a sponsor contributes $250 million of equity and receives equity proceeds of $750 million at the end of the investment horizon, the cash return is 3.0x (assuming no additional investments or dividends during the period). However, unlike IRR, the cash return approach does not factor in the time value of money.

---

[26]Based on the sponsor's model. See Chapter 5: LBO Analysis for additional information.

How LBOs Generate Returns

LBOs generate returns through a combination of debt repayment and growth in enterprise value. Exhibit 4.6 depicts how each of these scenarios independently increases equity value, assuming a sponsor purchases a company for $1,000 million, using $750 million of debt financing (75% of the purchase price) and an equity contribution of $250 million (25% of the purchase price). In each scenario, the returns are equivalent on both an IRR and cash return basis.

EXHIBIT 4.6 How LBOs Generate Returns

Scenario I In Scenario I, we assume that the target generates cumulative free cash flow of $500 million, which is used to repay debt during the investment horizon. Debt repayment increases equity value on a dollar-for-dollar basis. Assuming the sponsor sells the target for $1,000 million at exit, the value of the sponsor's equity investment increases from $250 million at purchase to $750 million even though there is no growth in the company's enterprise value. This scenario produces an IRR of 24.6% (assuming a five-year investment horizon) with a cash return of 3.0x.

Scenario II In Scenario II, we assume that the target does not repay any debt during the investment horizon. Rather, all cash generated by the target (after the payment of interest expense) is reinvested into the business and the sponsor realizes 50% growth in enterprise value by selling the target for $1,500 million after five years. This enterprise value growth can be achieved through EBITDA growth (e.g., organic growth, acquisitions, or streamlining operations) and/or achieving EBITDA multiple expansion.

As the debt represents a fixed claim on the business, the incremental $500 million of enterprise value accrues entirely to equity value. As in Scenario I, the value of the sponsor's equity investment increases from $250 million to $750 million, but this time without any debt repayment. Consequently, Scenario II produces an IRR and cash return equivalent to those in Scenario I (i.e., 24.6% and 3.0x, respectively).

How Leverage is Used to Enhance Returns

The concept of using leverage to enhance returns is fundamental to understanding LBOs. Assuming a fixed enterprise value at exit, using a higher percentage of debt in the financing structure (and a correspondingly smaller equity contribution) generates higher returns. Exhibit 4.7 illustrates this principle by analyzing comparative returns of an LBO financed with 25% debt versus an LBO financed with 75% debt. A higher level of debt provides the additional benefit of greater tax savings realized due to the tax deductibility of a higher amount of interest expense.

EXHIBIT 4.7   How Leverage is Used to Enhance Returns

75% Equity Contribution / 25% Debt		25% Equity Contribution / 75% Debt	
Assumptions		**Assumptions**	
Purchase Price	$1,000.0	Purchase Price	$1,000.0
Equity Contribution	750.0	Equity Contribution	250.0
Cost of Debt	8.0%	Cost of Debt [a]	8.0%
Cumulative FCF (after debt service)	250.0	Cumulative FCF (after debt service) [b]	117.9
Sale Price (Year 5)	$1,500.0	Sale Price (Year 5)	$1,500.0
Equity Value and Returns		**Equity Value and Returns**	
Equity Contribution	$750.0	Equity Contribution	$250.0
Increases to Equity Value:		*Increases to Equity Value:*	
Increase in Enterprise Value	500.0	Increase in Enterprise Value	500.0
Decrease in Debt from Repayment	250.0	Decrease in Debt from Repayment	117.9
Equity Value At Exit	**$1,500.0**	**Equity Value At Exit**	**$867.9**
IRR	14.9%	**IRR**	28.3%
Cash Return	2.0x	**Cash Return**	3.5x

[a]In practice, the higher leverage in Scenario IV would require a higher blended cost of debt by investors versus Scenario III. For simplicity, we assume a constant cost of debt in this example.

[b]Reduced FCF in Scenario IV versus Scenario III reflects the incremental interest expense associated with the additional $500 million of debt, which results in less cash available for debt repayment.

While increased leverage may be used to generate enhanced returns, there are certain clear trade-offs. As discussed in Chapter 3, higher leverage increases the company's risk profile (and probability of financial distress), limiting financial flexibility and making the company more susceptible to business or economic downturns.

Scenario III   In Scenario III, we assume a sponsor purchases the target for $1,000 million using $250 million of debt (25% of the purchase price) and contributing $750 million of equity (75% of the purchase price). After five years, the target is sold for $1,500 million, thereby resulting in a $500 million increase in enterprise value ($1,500 million sale price – $1,000 million purchase price).

During the five-year investment horizon, we assume that the target generates annual free cash flow after the payment of interest expense of $50 million ($250 million on a cumulative basis), which is used for debt repayment. As shown in the timeline in Exhibit 4.8, the target completely repays the $250 million of debt by the end of Year 5.

By the end of the five-year investment horizon, the sponsor's original $750 million equity contribution is worth $1,500 million as there is no debt remaining in the capital structure. This scenario generates an IRR of 14.9% and a cash return of approximately 2.0x after five years.

EXHIBIT 4.8   Scenario III Debt Repayment Timeline

($ in millions)

Scenario III - 75% Debt / 25% Equity						
	Year 0	Year 1	Year 2	Year 3	Year 4	Year 5
Equity Contribution	($750.0)					
Total Debt, beginning balance		$250.0	$200.0	$150.0	$100.0	$50.0
Free Cash Flow[(a)]		$50.0	$50.0	$50.0	$50.0	$50.0
Total Debt, ending balance	**$250.0**	**$200.0**	**$150.0**	**$100.0**	**$50.0**	-
Sale Price						$1,500.0
Less: Total Debt						(250.0)
Plus: Cumulative Free Cash Flow						250.0
Equity Value at Exit						**$1,500.0**
IRR						14.9%
Cash Return						2.0x

= Beginning Debt Balance$_{Year\,1}$ - Free Cash Flow$_{Year\,1}$
= $250.0 million - $50.0 million

[(a)]Annual free cash flow is post debt service on the $250 million of debt. Also known as levered free cash flow or cash available for debt repayment (see Chapter 5).

Scenario IV   In Scenario IV, we assume that a sponsor buys the same target for $1,000 million, but uses $750 million of debt (75% of the purchase price) and contributes $250 million of equity (25% of the purchase price). As in Scenario III, we assume the target is sold for $1,500 million at the end of Year 5. However, annual free cash flow is reduced due to the incremental annual interest expense on the $500 million of additional debt.

As shown in Exhibit 4.9, under Scenario IV, the additional $500 million of debt ($750 million – $250 million) creates incremental interest expense of $40 million ($24 million after-tax) in Year 1. This is calculated as the $500 million difference multiplied by an 8% assumed cost of debt and then tax-effected at a 40% assumed marginal tax rate. For each year of the projection period, we calculate incremental interest expense as the difference between total debt (beginning balance) in Scenario III versus Scenario IV multiplied by 8% (4.8% after tax).

By the end of Year 5, the sponsor's original $250 million equity contribution is worth $867.9 million ($1,500 million sale price − $632.1 million of debt remaining in the capital structure). This scenario generates an IRR of 28.3% and a cash return of approximately 3.5x after five years.

EXHIBIT 4.9   Scenario IV Debt Repayment Timeline[a]

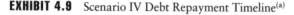

| = Total Debt, beginning balance$_{Year\,5}$ - Free Cash Flow, ending$_{Year\,5}$ |
| = $653.1 million - $21.0 million |

| = (Scenario IV Total Debt, beginning balance$_{Year\,1}$ - |
| Scenario III Total Debt, beginning balance$_{Year\,1}$) x Cost of Debt |
| = ($750.0 million - $250.0 million) x 8.0% |

($ in millions)

Scenario IV - 25% Debt / 75% Equity

	Year 0	Year 1	Year 2	Year 3	Year 4	Year 5
Equity Contribution	($250.0)					
Total Debt, beginning balance		$750.0	$724.0	$699.2	$675.5	$653.1
Free Cash Flow, beginning[b]		50.0	50.0	50.0	50.0	50.0
Incremental Interest Expense		40.0	41.9	43.9	46.0	48.3
Interest Tax Savings		(16.0)	(16.8)	(17.6)	(18.4)	(19.3)
Free Cash Flow, ending		**$26.0**	**$24.8**	**$23.6**	**$22.4**	**$21.0**
Total Debt, ending balance	**$750.0**	**$724.0**	**$699.2**	**$675.5**	**$653.1**	**$632.1**
Sale Price						$1,500.0
Less: Total Debt						(750.0)
Plus: Cumulative Free Cash Flow						117.9
Equity Value at Exit						**$867.9**

| = - Incremental Interest Expense$_{Year\,2}$ x Marginal Tax Rate |
| = ($41.9) million x 40.0% |

| IRR | 28.3% |
| **Cash Return** | 3.5x |

[a] Employs a beginning year as opposed to an average debt balance approach to calculating interest expense (see Chapter 5).
[b] Post debt service on the $250 million of debt in Scenario III.

PRIMARY EXIT/MONETIZATION STRATEGIES

Most sponsors aim to exit or monetize their investments within a five-year holding period in order to provide timely returns to their LPs. These returns are typically realized via a sale to another company (commonly referred to as a "strategic sale"), a sale to another sponsor, or an IPO. Sponsors may also extract a return prior to exit through a dividend recapitalization. The ultimate decision regarding when to monetize an investment, however, depends on the performance of the target as well as prevailing market conditions. In some cases, such as when the target has performed particularly well or market conditions are favorable, the exit or monetization may occur within a year or two. Alternatively, the sponsor may be forced to hold an investment longer than desired as dictated by company performance or the market.

By the end of the investment horizon, ideally the sponsor has increased the target's EBITDA (e.g., through organic growth, acquisitions, and/or increased profitability) and reduced its debt, thereby substantially increasing the target's equity value. The sponsor also seeks to achieve multiple expansion upon exit. There are several strategies aimed at achieving a higher exit multiple, including an increase in the target's size and scale, meaningful operational improvements, a repositioning of the business toward more highly valued industry segments, an acceleration of the target's organic growth rate and/or profitability, and the accurate timing of a cyclical sector or economic upturn.

Below, we discuss the primary LBO exit/monetization strategies for financial sponsors.

Sale of Business

Traditionally, sponsors have sought to sell portfolio companies to strategic buyers, who typically represent the strongest potential bidder due to their ability to realize synergies from the target and, therefore, pay a higher price. Strategic buyers may also benefit from a lower cost of capital and a lower return threshold. The proliferation of private equity funds, however, made exits via a sale to another sponsor increasingly commonplace during the mid-2000s. Moreover, during the strong debt financing markets of this time period, sponsors were able to use high leverage levels and generous debt terms to support purchase prices competitive with (or even in excess of) those offered by strategic buyers.

Initial Public Offering

In an IPO exit, the sponsor sells a portion of its shares in the target to the public. Post-IPO, the sponsor typically retains the largest single equity stake in the target with the understanding that a full exit will come through future follow-on equity offerings or an eventual sale of the company. Therefore, as opposed to an outright sale, an IPO generally does not afford the sponsor full upfront monetization. At the same time, the IPO provides the sponsor with a liquid market for its remaining equity investment while also preserving the opportunity to share in any future upside potential. Furthermore, depending on equity capital market conditions, an IPO may offer a compelling valuation premium to an outright sale.

Dividend Recapitalization

While not a true "exit strategy," a dividend recapitalization ("dividend recap") provides the sponsor with a viable option for monetizing a sizeable portion of its investment prior to exit. In a dividend recap, the target raises proceeds through the issuance of additional debt to pay shareholders a dividend. The incremental indebtedness may be issued in the form of an "add-on" to the target's existing credit facilities and/or bonds, a new security at the HoldCo level,[27] or as part of a complete refinancing of the existing capital structure. A dividend recap provides the sponsor with the added benefit of retaining 100% of its existing ownership position in the target, thus preserving the ability to share in any future upside potential and the option to pursue a sale or IPO at a future date. Depending on the size of the dividend, the sponsor may be able to recoup all of (or more than) its initial equity investment.

---

[27]Debt incurrence and restricted payments covenants in the target's existing operating company level ("OpCo") debt often substantially limit both incremental debt and the ability to pay a dividend to shareholders (see Exhibits 4.22 and 4.23). Therefore, dividend recaps frequently involve issuing a new security at the holding company level ("HoldCo"), which is not subject to the existing OpCo covenants.

LBO FINANCING: STRUCTURE

In a traditional LBO, debt has typically comprised 60% to 70% of the financing structure, with the remainder of the purchase price funded by an equity contribution from a sponsor (or group of sponsors) and rolled/contributed equity from management. Given the inherently high leverage associated with an LBO, the various debt components of the capital structure are usually deemed non-investment grade, or rated 'Ba1' and below by Moody's Investor Service and 'BB+' and below by Standard and Poor's (see Chapter 1, Exhibit 1.23 for a ratings scale). The debt portion of the LBO financing structure may include a broad array of loans, securities, or other debt instruments with varying terms and conditions that appeal to different classes of investors.

We have grouped the primary types of LBO financing sources into the categories shown in Exhibit 4.10, corresponding to their relative ranking in the capital structure.

EXHIBIT 4.10   General Ranking of Financing Sources in an LBO Capital Structure

As a general rule, the higher a given debt instrument ranks in the capital structure hierarchy, the lower its risk and, consequently, the lower its cost of capital to the borrower/issuer. However, cost of capital tends to be inversely related to the flexibility permitted by the applicable debt instrument. For example, bank debt usually represents the least expensive form of LBO financing. At the same time, bank debt is secured by various forms of collateral and governed by *maintenance* covenants that require the borrower to "maintain" a designated credit profile through compliance with certain financial ratios (see Exhibit 4.22).

During the 1999 to 2008 period, the average LBO financing structure varied substantially in terms of leverage levels, purchase multiple, percentage of capital sourced from each class of debt, and equity contribution percentage. As shown in Exhibit 4.11, the average LBO purchase price and leverage multiples increased dramatically during the 2001 to 2007 period. This resulted from changes in the prevailing capital markets conditions and investor landscape, including the proliferation of private investment vehicles (e.g., private equity funds and hedge funds) and structured credit vehicles such as CDOs.

EXHIBIT 4.11 Average LBO Purchase Price Breakdown 1999 – 2008

Source: Standard & Poor's Leveraged Commentary & Data Group
Note: Prior to 2003, excludes media, telecommunications, energy, and utility transactions. Thereafter, all outliers, regardless of the industry, are excluded. 2008 includes deals committed to in 2007 (during the credit boom) that closed in 2008.
Senior debt includes bank debt, 2nd lien debt, senior secured notes, and senior unsecured notes.
Subordinated includes senior and junior subordinated debt.
Equity includes HoldCo debt/seller notes, preferred stock, common stock, and rolled equity.
Other is cash and any other unclassified sources.

However, beginning in the second half of 2007, credit market conditions deteriorated dramatically stemming from the subprime mortgage crisis. As shown in Exhibit 4.11, the average LBO leverage level decreased from 6.1x in 2007 to 5.0x in 2008. Correspondingly, the average LBO's percentage of contributed equity increased from 31% to 39% during the same time period (see Exhibit 4.12).

EXHIBIT 4.12 Average Sources of LBO Proceeds 1999 – 2008

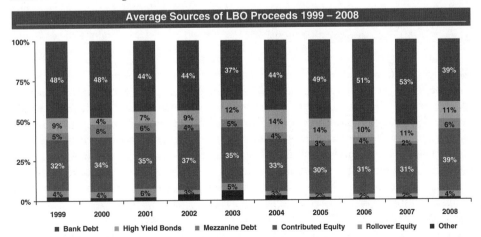

Source: Standard & Poor's Leveraged Commentary & Data Group
Note: Contributed equity includes HoldCo debt/seller notes, preferred stock, and common stock.

Furthermore, the LBO dollar volume and number of closed deals decreased considerably through 2008 versus the unprecedented levels of 2006 and 2007 (see Exhibit 4.13).

EXHIBIT 4.13   Global LBO Volume and Number of Closed Deals 1999 – 2008

Source: Thomson Reuters SDC Platinum
Excludes deals under $250 million in enterprise value.

LBO FINANCING: PRIMARY SOURCES

Bank Debt

EXHIBIT 4.14   Bank Debt

Bank debt is an integral part of the LBO financing structure, consistently serving as a substantial source of capital (as shown in Exhibit 4.12). Also referred to as "senior secured credit facilities," it is typically comprised of a revolving credit facility (which may be borrowed, repaid, and reborrowed) and one or more term loan tranches (which may not be reborrowed once repaid). The revolving credit facility may take the form of a traditional "cash flow" revolver[28] or an asset based lending (ABL) facility.[29] Bank debt is issued in the private market and is therefore not subject to SEC

---

[28]Lenders to the facility focus on the ability of the borrower to cover debt service by generating cash flow.

[29]Lenders to the facility focus on the liquidation value of the assets comprising the facility's borrowing base, typically accounts receivable and inventory (see Exhibit 4.15).

regulations and disclosure requirements.[30] However, it has restrictive covenants that require the borrower to comply with certain provisions and financial tests throughout the life of the facility (see Exhibit 4.22).

Bank debt typically bears interest (payable on a quarterly basis) at a given benchmark rate, usually LIBOR or the Base Rate,[31] plus an applicable margin ("spread") based on the credit of the borrower. This type of debt is often referred to as *floating rate* due to the fact that the borrowing cost varies in accordance with changes to the underlying benchmark rate. In addition, the spread may be adjusted downward (or upward) if it is tied to a performance-based grid based on the borrower's leverage ratio or credit ratings.

Revolving Credit Facility A traditional cash flow revolving credit facility ("revolver") is a line of credit extended by a bank or group of banks that permits the borrower to draw varying amounts up to a specified aggregate limit for a specified period of time. It is unique in that amounts borrowed can be freely repaid and reborrowed during the term of the facility, subject to agreed-upon conditions set forth in a credit agreement[32] (see Exhibit 4.22). The majority of companies utilize a revolver or equivalent lending arrangement to provide ongoing liquidity for seasonal working capital needs, capital expenditures, letters of credit (LC),[33] and other general corporate purposes. A revolver may also be used to fund a portion of the purchase price in an LBO, although it is usually undrawn at close.

Revolvers are typically arranged by one or more investment banks and then syndicated to a group of commercial banks and finance companies. To compensate lenders for making this credit line available to the borrower (which may or may not be drawn upon and offers a less attractive return when unfunded), a nominal annual *commitment fee* is charged on the undrawn portion of the facility.[34]

---

[30] As a private market instrument, bank debt is not subject to the Securities Act of 1933 and the Securities Exchange Act of 1934, which require periodic public reporting of financial and other information.

[31] Base Rate is most often defined as a rate equal to the higher of the prime rate or the Federal Funds rate plus 1/2 of 1%.

[32] The legal contract between the borrower and its lenders that governs bank debt. It contains key definitions, terms, representations and warranties, covenants, events of default, and other miscellaneous provisions.

[33] An LC is a document issued to a specified beneficiary that guarantees payment by an "issuing" lender under the credit agreement. LCs reduce revolver availability.

[34] The fee is assessed on an ongoing basis and accrues daily, typically at an annualized rate up to 50 basis points (bps) depending on the credit of the borrower. For example, an undrawn $100 million revolver would typically have an annual commitment fee of 50 bps or $500,000 ($100 million × 0.50%). Assuming the average daily revolver usage (including the outstanding LC amounts) is $25 million, the annual commitment fee would be $375,000 (($100 million − $25 million) × 0.50%). For any drawn portion of the revolver, the borrower pays interest on that dollar amount at LIBOR or the Base Rate plus a spread. To the extent the revolver's availability is reduced by outstanding LCs, the borrower pays a fee on the dollar amount of undrawn outstanding LCs at the full spread, but does not pay LIBOR or the Base Rate. Banks may also be paid an *up-front fee* upon the initial closing of the revolver and term loan(s) to incentivize participation.

The revolver is generally the least expensive form of capital in the LBO financing structure, typically priced at, or slightly below, the term loan's spread. In return for the revolver's low cost, the borrower must sacrifice some flexibility. For example, lenders generally require a first priority security interest ("lien") on certain assets[35] of the borrower[36] (shared with the term loan facilities) and compliance with various covenants. The first lien provides lenders greater comfort by granting their debt claims a higher priority in the event of bankruptcy relative to obligations owed to second priority and unsecured creditors (see "Security"). The historical market standard for LBO revolvers has been a term ("tenor") of five to six years, with no scheduled reduction to the committed amount of such facilities prior to maturity.

Asset Based Lending Facility   An ABL facility is a type of revolving credit facility that is available to asset intensive companies. ABL facilities are secured by a first priority lien on all current assets (typically accounts receivable and inventory) of the borrower and may include a second priority lien on all other assets (typically PP&E). They are more commonly used by companies with sizeable accounts receivable and inventory and variable working capital needs that operate in seasonal or cyclical businesses. For example, ABL facilities are used by retailers, selected commodity producers and distributors (e.g., chemicals, forest products, and steel), manufacturers, and rental equipment businesses.

ABL facilities are subject to a *borrowing base* formula that limits availability based on "eligible" accounts receivable, inventory, and, in certain circumstances, fixed assets, real estate, or other more specialized assets of the borrower, all of which are pledged as security. The maximum amount available for borrowing under an ABL facility is capped by the size of the borrowing base at a given point in time. While the borrowing base formula varies depending on the individual borrower, a common example is shown in Exhibit 4.15.

EXHIBIT 4.15   ABL Borrowing Base Formula

ABL Borrowing Base   =   85% x Eligible Accounts Receivable + 60%[a] x Eligible Inventory

[a]Based on 85% of appraised net orderly liquidation value (expected net proceeds if inventory is liquidated) as determined by a third party firm.

ABL facilities provide lenders with certain additional protections not found in traditional cash flow revolvers, such as periodic collateral reporting requirements and appraisals. In addition, the assets securing ABLs (such as accounts receivable and inventory) are typically easier to monetize and turn into cash in the event of bankruptcy. As such, the interest rate spread on an ABL facility is lower than that of a cash flow revolver for the same credit. Given their reliance upon a borrowing base as collateral, ABL facilities traditionally have only one "springing" financial

---

[35]For example, in the tangible and intangible assets of the borrower, including capital stock of subsidiaries.

[36]As well as its domestic subsidiaries (in most cases).

covenant.[37] Traditional bank debt, by contrast, has multiple financial maintenance covenants restricting the borrower. The typical tenor of an ABL revolver is five years.

Term Loan Facilities

A term loan ("leveraged loan," when non-investment grade) is a loan with a specified maturity that requires principal repayment ("amortization") according to a defined schedule, typically on a quarterly basis. Like a revolver, a traditional term loan for an LBO financing is structured as a first lien debt obligation[38] and requires the borrower to maintain a certain credit profile through compliance with financial maintenance covenants contained in the credit agreement. Unlike a revolver, however, a term loan is fully funded on the date of closing and once principal is repaid, it cannot be reborrowed. Term loans are classified by an identifying letter such as "A," "B," "C," etc. in accordance with their lender base, amortization schedule, and terms.

Amortizing Term Loans   "A" term loans ("Term Loan A" or "TLA") are commonly referred to as "amortizing term loans" because they typically require substantial principal repayment throughout the life of the loan.[39] Term loans with significant, annual required amortization are perceived by lenders as less risky than those with *de minimus* required principal repayments during the life of the loan due to their shorter average life. Consequently, TLAs are often the lowest priced term loans in the capital structure. TLAs are syndicated to commercial banks and finance companies together with the revolver and are often referred to as "pro rata" tranches because lenders typically commit to equal ("ratable") percentages of the revolver and TLA during syndication. TLAs in LBO financing structures typically have a term that ends simultaneously ("co-terminus") with the revolver.

Institutional Term Loans   "B" term loans ("Term Loan B" or "TLB"), which are commonly referred to as "institutional term loans," are more prevalent than TLAs in LBO financings. They are typically larger in size than TLAs and sold to institutional investors (often the same investors who buy high yield bonds) rather than banks. The institutional investor class prefers non-amortizing loans with longer maturities and higher coupons. As a result, TLBs generally amortize at a nominal rate (e.g., 1% per annum) with a bullet payment at maturity.[40] TLBs are typically structured to have a longer term than the revolver and any TLA as bank lenders prefer to have their debt

---

[37]The traditional springing financial covenant is a *fixed charge coverage ratio* of 1.0x and is tested only if "excess availability" falls below a certain level (usually 10% to 15% of the ABL facility). Excess availability is equal to the lesser of the ABL facility or the borrowing base less, in each case, outstanding amounts under the facility.

[38]*Pari passu* (or on an equal basis) with the revolver, which entitles term loan lenders to an equal right of repayment upon bankruptcy of the borrower.

[39]A mandatory repayment schedule for a TLA issued at the end of 2008 with a six-year maturity might be structured as follows: 2009: 10%, 2010: 10%, 2011: 15%, 2012: 15%, 2013: 25%, 2014: 25%. Another example might be: 2009: 0%, 2010: 0%, 2011: 5%, 2012: 5%, 2013: 10%, 2014: 80%. The amortization schedule is typically set on a quarterly basis.

[40]A large repayment of principal at maturity that is standard among institutional term loans. A typical mandatory amortization schedule for a TLB issued at the end of 2008 with a seven-year maturity would be as follows: 2009: 1%, 2010: 1%, 2011: 1%, 2012: 1%, 2013:

mature before the TLB. Hence, a tenor for TLBs of up to seven (or sometimes seven and one-half years) has historically been market standard for LBOs.

Second Lien Term Loans   The issuance of second lien term loans[41] to finance LBOs became increasingly prevalent during the credit boom of the mid-2000s. A second lien term loan is a floating rate loan that is secured by a second priority security interest in the assets of the borrower. It ranks junior to the first priority security interest in the assets of the borrower benefiting a revolver, TLA, and TLB. In the event of bankruptcy (and liquidation), second lien lenders are entitled to repayment from the proceeds of collateral sales <u>after</u> such proceeds have first been applied to the claims of first lien lenders, but <u>prior to</u> any application to unsecured claims.[42] Unlike first lien term loans, second lien term loans generally do not amortize.

For borrowers, second lien term loans offer an alternative to more traditional junior debt instruments, such as high yield bonds and mezzanine debt. As compared to traditional high yield bonds, for example, second lien term loans provide borrowers with superior prepayment optionality and no ongoing public disclosure requirements. They can also be issued in a smaller size than high yield bonds, which usually have a minimum issuance amount of $125 to $150 million due to investors' desire for trading liquidity. Depending on the borrower and market conditions, second lien term loans may also provide a lower cost-of-capital. However, they typically carry the burden of financial covenants, albeit moderately less restrictive than first lien debt. For investors, which typically include hedge funds and CDOs, second lien term loans offer less risk (due to the secured status) than typical high yield bonds while paying a higher coupon than first lien debt.

High Yield Bonds

EXHIBIT 4.16   High Yield Bonds

High yield bonds are non-investment grade debt securities that obligate the issuer to make interest payments to bondholders at regularly defined intervals (typically on a semiannual basis) and repay principal at a stated maturity date, usually seven to ten years after issuance. As opposed to term loans, high yield bonds are non-amortizing with the entire principal due as a bullet payment at maturity. Due to

---

1%, 2014: 1%, 2015: 94%. Like TLAs, the amortization schedule for B term loans is typically set on a quarterly basis. The sizeable 2015 principal repayment is referred to as a bullet.

[41] High yield bonds can also be structured with a second lien.

[42] Exact terms and rights between first and second lien lenders are set forth in an intercreditor agreement.

their junior, typically unsecured position in the capital structure, longer maturities, and less restrictive *incurrence* covenants as set forth in an indenture (see Exhibit 4.23),[43] high yield bonds feature a higher coupon than bank debt to compensate investors for the greater risk.

High yield bonds typically pay interest at a *fixed rate,* which is priced at issuance on the basis of a spread to a benchmark Treasury. As its name suggests, a fixed rate means that interest rate is constant over the entire maturity. While high yield bonds may be structured with a floating rate coupon, this is not common for LBO financings. High yield bonds are typically structured as senior unsecured, senior subordinated, or, in certain circumstances, senior secured (first lien, second lien, or even third lien).

Traditionally, high yield bonds have been a mainstay in LBO financings. Used in conjunction with bank debt, high yield bonds enable sponsors to substantially increase leverage levels beyond those available in the leveraged loan market alone. This permits sponsors to pay a higher purchase price and/or reduce the equity contribution. Furthermore, high yield bonds afford issuers greater flexibility than bank debt due to their less restrictive incurrence covenants (and absence of maintenance covenants), longer maturities, and lack of mandatory amortization. One offsetting factor, however, is that high yield bonds have non-call features (see Exhibit 4.21) that can negatively impact a sponsor's exit strategy.

Typically, high yield bonds are initially sold to qualified institutional buyers (QIBs)[44] through a private placement under Rule 144A of the Securities Act of 1933. They are then registered with the SEC within one year of issuance so that they can be traded on an open market. The private sale to QIBs expedites the initial sale of the bonds because SEC registration, which involves review of the registration statement by the SEC, can take several weeks or months. Once the SEC review of the documentation is complete, the issuer conducts an exchange offer pursuant to which investors exchange the unregistered bonds for registered securities. Post-registration, the issuer is subject to SEC disclosure requirements (e.g., the filing of 10-Ks, 10-Qs, 8-Ks, etc).

A feature in the high yield market that was prevalent in LBOs during the credit boom of the mid-2000s was the use of a payment-in-kind (PIK) toggle for interest payments.[45] The PIK toggle allows an issuer to choose to pay PIK interest (i.e., in the form of additional notes) instead of cash interest. This optionality provides the issuer with the ability to preserve cash in times of challenging business or economic conditions, especially during the early years of the investment period when leverage

---

[43]The legal contract entered into by an issuer and corporate trustee (who acts on behalf of the bondholders) that defines the rights and obligations of the issuer and its creditors with respect to a bond issue. Similar to a credit agreement for bank debt, an indenture sets forth the covenants and other terms of a bond issue.

[44]As part of Rule 144A, the SEC created another category of financially sophisticated investors known as qualified institutional buyers, or QIBs. Rule 144A provides a safe harbor exemption from federal registration requirements for the resale of restricted securities to QIBs. QIBs generally are institutions or other entities that, in aggregate, own and invest (on a discretionary basis) at least $100 million in securities.

[45]PIK toggle notes are rare (or non-existent) during more normalized credit market conditions.

is highest. If the issuer elects to pay PIK interest in lieu of cash, the coupon typically increases by 75 bps.

Bridge Loans   A bridge loan facility ("bridge") is interim, committed financing provided to the borrower to "bridge" to the issuance of permanent capital, most often high yield bonds (the "take-out" securities). In an LBO, investment banks typically commit to provide funding for the bank debt and a bridge loan facility. The bridge usually takes the form of an unsecured term loan, which is only funded if the take-out securities cannot be issued and sold by the closing of the LBO.

Bridge loans are particularly important for LBO financings due to the sponsor's need to provide certainty of funding to the seller. The bridge financing gives comfort that the purchase consideration will be funded even in the event that market conditions for the take-out securities deteriorate between signing and closing of the transaction (subject to any conditions precedent to closing enumerated in the definitive agreement (see Chapter 6, Exhibit 6.10) or the commitment letter). If funded, the bridge loan can be replaced with the take-out securities at a future date, markets permitting.

In practice, however, the bridge loan is rarely intended to be funded, serving only as a financing of last resort. From the sponsor's perspective, the bridge loan is a potentially costly funding alternative due to the additional fees required to be paid to the arrangers.[46] The interest rate on a bridge loan also typically increases periodically the longer it is outstanding until it hits the caps (maximum interest rate). The investment banks providing the bridge loan also hope that the bridge remains unfunded as it ties up capital and increases exposure to the borrower's credit. To mitigate the risk of funding a bridge, the lead arrangers often seek to syndicate all or a portion of the bridge loan commitment prior to the closing of the transaction.

Mezzanine Debt

EXHIBIT 4.17   Mezzanine Debt

As its name suggests, mezzanine debt refers to a layer of capital that lies between traditional debt and equity. Mezzanine debt is a highly negotiated instrument between the issuer and investors that is tailored to meet the financing needs of the

---

[46]Investment banks are paid a commitment fee for arranging the bridge loan facility regardless of whether the bridge is funded. In the event the bridge is funded, the banks and lenders receive an additional *funding fee*. Furthermore, if the bridge remains outstanding after one year, the borrower also pays a *conversion fee*.

specific transaction and required investor returns. As such, mezzanine debt allows great flexibility in structuring terms conducive to issuer and investor alike.

For sponsors, mezzanine debt provides incremental capital at a cost below that of equity, which enables them to stretch leverage levels and purchase price when alternative capital sources are inaccessible. For example, mezzanine debt may serve to substitute for, or supplement, high yield financing when markets are unfavorable or even inaccessible (e.g., for smaller companies whose size needs are below high yield bond market minimum thresholds). In the United States it is particularly prevalent in middle market transactions.[47]

Typical investors include dedicated mezzanine funds and hedge funds. For the investor, mezzanine debt offers a higher rate of return than traditional high yield bonds and can be structured to offer equity upside potential in the form of detachable warrants that are exchangeable into common stock of the issuer. The interest rate on mezzanine debt typically includes a combination of cash and non-cash PIK payments. Depending on available financing alternatives and market conditions, mezzanine investors typically target a "blended" return (including cash and non-cash components) in the mid-to-high teens (or higher). Maturities for mezzanine debt, like terms, vary substantially, but tend to be similar to those for high yield bonds.[48]

Equity Contribution

The remaining portion of LBO funding comes in the form of an equity contribution by the financial sponsor and rolled/contributed equity by the target's management. The equity contribution percentage typically ranges from approximately 30% to 40% of the LBO financing structure, although this may vary depending on debt market conditions, the type of company, and the purchase multiple paid.[49] For large LBOs, several sponsors may team up to create a consortium of buyers, thereby reducing the amount of each individual sponsor's equity contribution (known as a "club deal").

The equity contribution provides a cushion for lenders and bondholders in the event that the company's enterprise value deteriorates as equity value is eliminated before debt holders lose recovery value. For example, if a sponsor contributes 30% equity to a given deal, lenders gain comfort that the value of the business would have to decline by more than 30% from the purchase price before their principal is jeopardized. Sponsors may also choose to "over-equitize" certain LBOs, such as

---

[47]In Europe, mezzanine debt is used to finance large as well as middle market transactions. It is typically structured as a floating rate loan (with a combination of cash and PIK interest) that benefits from a second or third lien on the same collateral benefiting the bank debt (of the same capital structure). U.S. mezzanine debt, on the other hand, is typically structured with a fixed rate coupon and is contractually subordinated (see Exhibit 4.19), thereby not benefiting from any security.

[48]However, if an LBO financing structure has both high yield bonds and mezzanine debt, the mezzanine debt will typically mature outside the high yield bonds, thereby reducing the risk to the more senior security.

[49]As previously discussed, the commitment papers for the debt financing are typically predicated on a minimum equity contribution by the sponsor.

when they plan to issue incremental debt at a future date to fund acquisitions or growth initiatives for the company.

Rollover/contributed equity by existing company management and/or key shareholders varies according to the situation, but often ranges from approximately 2% to 5% (or more) of the overall equity portion. Management equity rollover/contribution is usually encouraged by the sponsor in order to align incentives.

LBO FINANCING: SELECTED KEY TERMS

Both within and across the broad categories of debt instruments used in LBO financings—which we group into bank debt, high yield bonds, and mezzanine debt—there are a number of key terms that affect risk, cost, flexibility, and investor base. As shown in Exhibit 4.18 and discussed in greater detail below, these terms include *security, seniority, maturity, coupon, call protection,* and *covenants.*

EXHIBIT 4.18   Summary of Selected Key Terms

Security

Security refers to the pledge of, or lien on, collateral that is granted by the borrower to the holders of a given debt instrument. Collateral represents assets, property, and/or securities pledged by a borrower to secure a loan or other debt obligation, which is subject to seizure and/or liquidation in the event of a default.[50] It can include accounts receivable, inventory, PP&E, intellectual property, and securities such as the common stock of the borrower/issuer and its subsidiaries. Depending upon the volatility of the target's cash flow, creditors may require higher levels of collateral coverage as protection.

---

[50]In practice, in the event a material default is not waived by a borrower/issuer's creditors, the borrower/issuer typically seeks protection under Chapter 11 of the Bankruptcy Code to continue operating as a "going concern" while it attempts to restructure its financial obligations. During bankruptcy, while secured creditors are generally stayed from enforcing their remedies, they are entitled to certain protections and rights not provided to unsecured creditors (including the right to continue to receive interest payments). Thus, obtaining collateral can be beneficial to a creditor even if it does not exercise its remedies to foreclose and sell that collateral.

Seniority

Seniority refers to the priority status of a creditor's claims against the borrower/issuer relative to those of other creditors. Generally, seniority is achieved through either *contractual* or *structural subordination.*

Contractual Subordination Contractual subordination refers to the priority status of debt instruments at the same legal entity. It is established through *subordination provisions,* which stipulate that the claims of senior creditors must be satisfied in full before those of junior creditors (generally "senior" status is limited to bank lenders or similar creditors, not trade creditors[51]). In the case of subordinated bonds, the indenture contains the subordination provisions that are relied upon by the senior creditors as "third-party" beneficiaries.[52] Exhibit 4.19 provides an illustrative diagram showing the contractual seniority of multiple debt instruments.

EXHIBIT 4.19 Contractual Subordination

While both senior secured debt and senior unsecured debt have contractually equal debt claims (pari passu), senior secured debt may be considered "effectively" senior to the extent of the value of the collateral securing such debt.

Structural Subordination Structural subordination refers to the priority status of debt instruments at different legal entities within a company. For example, debt obligations at OpCo, where the company's assets are located, are structurally senior to debt obligations at HoldCo[53] so long as such HoldCo obligations do not benefit from a *guarantee* (credit support)[54] from OpCo. In the event of bankruptcy at OpCo, its obligations must be satisfied in full before a distribution or dividend can be made to its sole shareholder (i.e., HoldCo). Exhibit 4.20 provides an illustrative diagram showing the structural seniority of debt instruments at two legal entities.

---

[51] Creditors owed money for goods and services.

[52] When the transaction involves junior debt not governed by an indenture (e.g., privately placed second lien or mezzanine debt), the subordination provisions will generally be included in an intercreditor agreement with the senior creditors.

[53] A legal entity that owns all or a portion of the voting stock of another company/entity, in this case, OpCo.

[54] Guarantees provide credit support by one party for a debt obligation of a third party. For example, a subsidiary with actual operations and assets "guarantees" the debt, meaning that it agrees to use its cash and assets to pay debt obligations on behalf of HoldCo.

EXHIBIT 4.20   Structural Subordination

Debt obligations at the OpCo level are
structurally senior to obligations at the HoldCo level
(so long as the OpCo has not guaranteed any debt at the HoldCo level)

Maturity

The maturity ("tenor" or "term") of a debt obligation refers to the length of time the instrument remains outstanding until the full principal amount must be repaid. Shorter tenor debt is deemed less risky than debt with longer maturities as it is required to be repaid earlier. Therefore, all else being equal, shorter tenor debt carries a lower cost of capital than longer tenor debt of the same credit.

In an LBO, various debt instruments with different maturities are issued to finance the debt portion of the transaction. Bank debt tends to have shorter maturities, often five to six years for revolvers and seven (or sometimes seven and one-half years) for institutional term loans. Historically, high yield bonds have had a maturity of seven to ten years. In an LBO financing structure comprising several debt instruments (e.g., a revolver, institutional term loans, and bonds), the revolver will mature before the institutional term loans, which, in turn, will mature before the bonds.

Coupon

Coupon refers to the annual interest rate ("pricing") paid on a debt obligation's principal amount outstanding. It can be based on either a floating rate (typical for bank debt) or a fixed rate (typical for bonds). Bank debt generally pays interest on a quarterly basis, while bonds generally pay interest on a semiannual basis. The bank debt coupon is typically based on a given benchmark rate, usually LIBOR or the Base Rate, plus a spread based on the credit of the borrower. A high yield bond coupon, however, is generally priced at issuance on the basis of a spread to a benchmark Treasury.

There are a number of factors that affect a debt obligation's coupon, including the type of debt (and its investor class), ratings, security, seniority, maturity, covenants, and prevailing market conditions. In a traditional LBO financing structure, bank debt tends to be the lowest cost of capital debt instrument because it has a higher facility rating, first lien security, higher seniority, a shorter maturity, and more restrictive covenants than high yield bonds.

EXHIBIT 4.22 (*Continued*)

Negative Covenants	Limit the borrower's and its subsidiaries' ability to take certain actions (often subject to certain exceptions or "baskets").[a] Examples of negative covenants include:

- limitations on debt – limits the amount of debt that may be outstanding at any time
- limitations on dividends and stock redemptions – prevents cash from being distributed by the borrower to, or for the benefit of, equity holders
- limitations on liens – prevents pledge of assets as collateral
- limitations on dispositions of assets (including sales/leaseback transactions) – prevents the sale or transfer of assets in excess of an aggregate threshold
- limitations on investments – restricts the making of loans, acquisitions, and other investments (including joint ventures)
- limitations on mergers and consolidations – prohibits a merger or consolidation
- limitations on prepayments of, and amendments to, certain other debt – prohibits the prepayment of certain other debt or any amendments thereto in a manner that would be adverse to lenders
- limitations on transactions with affiliates – restricts the borrower and its subsidiaries from undertaking transactions with affiliated companies that may benefit the affiliate to the detriment of the borrower and its creditors[b]

Financial Maintenance Covenants	Require the borrower to maintain a certain credit profile through compliance with specified financial ratios or tests on a quarterly basis. Examples of financial maintenance covenants include:

- maximum senior secured leverage ratio – prohibits the ratio of senior secured debt-to-EBITDA for the trailing four quarters from exceeding a level set forth in a defined quarterly schedule
- maximum total leverage ratio – prohibits the ratio of total debt-to-EBITDA for the trailing four quarters from exceeding a level set in a defined quarterly schedule
- minimum interest coverage ratio – prohibits the ratio of EBITDA-to-interest expense for the trailing four quarters from falling below a set level as defined in a quarterly schedule
- minimum fixed charge coverage ratio[c] – prohibits the ratio of a measure of cash flow-to-fixed charges from falling below a set level (which may be fixed for the term of the bank debt or adjusted quarterly)
- maximum annual capital expenditures – prohibits the borrower and its subsidiaries from exceeding a set dollar amount of capital expenditures in any given year
- minimum EBITDA – requires the borrower to maintain a minimum dollar amount of EBITDA for the trailing four quarters as set forth in a defined quarterly schedule

---

[a]Baskets ("carve-outs") provide exceptions to covenants that permit the borrower/issuer to take specific actions (e.g., incur specific types and amounts of debt, make certain restricted payments, and sell assets up to a specified amount).

[b]Affiliate transactions must be conducted on an "arms-length" basis (i.e., terms no less favorable than if the counterparty was unrelated).

[c]A fixed charge coverage ratio measures a borrower/issuer's ability to cover its fixed obligations, including debt interest and lease obligations. Although the definition may vary by credit agreement or indenture, fixed charges typically include interest expense, preferred stock dividends, and lease expenses (such as rent). The definition may be structured to include or exclude non-cash and capitalized interest.

High Yield Bond Covenants   Many of the covenants found in a high yield bond indenture are similar to those found in a bank debt credit agreement (see Exhibit 4.23). A key difference, however, is that indentures contain incurrence covenants as opposed to maintenance covenants. Incurrence covenants only prevent the issuer from taking specific actions (e.g., incurring additional debt, making certain investments, paying dividends) in the event it is not in pro forma compliance with a "Ratio Test," or does not have certain "baskets" available to it at the time such action is taken. The Ratio Test is often a coverage test (e.g., a fixed charge coverage ratio), although it may also be structured as a leverage test (e.g., total debt-to-EBITDA) as is common for telecommunications/media companies.

EXHIBIT 4.23   High Yield Bond Covenants

High Yield Covenants	Principal covenants found in high yield bond indentures include:

- limitations on additional debt – ensures that the issuer cannot incur additional debt unless it is in pro forma compliance with the Ratio Test or otherwise permitted by a defined "basket"
- limitations on restricted payments – prohibits the issuer from making certain payments such as dividends, investments, and prepayments of junior debt except for a defined "basket" (subject to certain exceptions)[a]
- limitations on liens (generally senior subordinated notes allow unlimited liens on senior debt otherwise permitted to be incurred) – for senior notes, prohibits the issuer from granting liens on pari passu or junior debt without providing an equal and ratable lien in favor of the senior notes, subject to certain exceptions and/or compliance with a specified "senior secured leverage ratio"
- limitations on asset sales – prevents the issuer from selling assets without using net proceeds to reinvest in the business or reduce indebtedness (subject to certain exceptions)
- limitations on transactions with affiliates – see credit agreement definition
- limitations on mergers, consolidations, or sale of substantially all assets – prohibits a merger, consolidation, or sale of substantially all assets unless the surviving entity assumes the debt of the issuer and can incur $1.00 of additional debt under the Ratio Test
- limitation on layering (specific to indentures for senior subordinated notes) – prevents the issuer from issuing additional subordinated debt ("layering") which is senior to the existing issue
- change of control put (specific to indentures) – provides bondholders with the right to require the issuer to repurchase the notes at a premium of 101% of par in the event of a change in majority ownership of the company or sale of substantially all of the assets of the borrower and its subsidiaries

[a]The restricted payments basket is typically calculated as a small set dollar amount ("starting basket") plus 50% of cumulative consolidated net income of the issuer since issuance of the bonds, plus the amount of new equity issuances by the issuer since issuance of the bonds, plus cash from the sale of unrestricted subsidiaries (i.e., those that do not guarantee the debt).

CHAPTER 5

LBO Analysis

LBO analysis is the core analytical tool used to assess financing structure, investment returns, and valuation in leveraged buyout scenarios. The same techniques can also be used to assess refinancing opportunities and restructuring alternatives for corporate issuers. LBO analysis is a more complex methodology than those previously discussed in this book as it requires specialized knowledge of financial modeling, leveraged debt capital markets, M&A, and accounting. At the center of an LBO analysis is a financial model (the "LBO model"), which is constructed with the flexibility to analyze a given target's performance under multiple financing structures and operating scenarios.

Financing Structure

On the debt financing side, the banker uses LBO analysis to help craft a viable financing structure for the target, which encompasses the amount and type of debt (including key terms outlined in Chapter 4), as well as an equity contribution from a financial sponsor. The model output enables the banker to analyze a given financing structure on the basis of cash flow generation, debt repayment, credit statistics, and investment returns over a projection period.

The analysis of an LBO financing structure is typically spearheaded by an investment bank's leveraged finance and capital market teams (along with a sector coverage team, collectively the "deal team"). The goal is to present a financial sponsor with tailored financing options that maximize returns while remaining marketable to investors. The financing structure must also provide the target with sufficient flexibility and cushion to run its business according to plan.

As discussed in Chapter 4, sponsors typically work closely with financing providers (e.g., investment banks) to determine the financing structure for a particular transaction. Once the sponsor chooses the preferred financing structure (often a compilation of the best terms from proposals solicited from several banks), the deal team presents it to the bank's internal credit committee(s) for approval. Following committee approval, the investment banks typically provide a financing commitment, which is then submitted to the seller and its advisor(s) as part of its final bid package (see Chapter 6).

Valuation

LBO analysis is also an essential component of an M&A toolset. It is used by sponsors, bankers, and other finance professionals to determine an implied valuation range for a given target in a potential LBO sale based on achieving acceptable returns. The valuation output is premised on key variables such as financial projections, purchase price, and financing structure, as well as exit multiple and year. Therefore, sensitivity analysis is performed on these key value drivers to produce a range of IRRs used to frame valuation for the target (see Exhibits 5.42 and 5.43). As discussed in Chapter 4, sponsors have historically used 20%+ IRRs to assess acquisition opportunities and determine valuation accordingly.

In an M&A sell-side advisory context, the banker conducts LBO analysis to assess valuation from the perspective of a financial sponsor. This provides the ability to set sale price expectations for the seller and guide negotiations with prospective buyers accordingly. Similarly, on buy-side engagements, the banker typically performs LBO analysis to help determine a purchase price range. For a strategic buyer, this analysis (along with those derived from other valuation methodologies) is used to frame valuation and bidding strategy by analyzing the price that a competing sponsor bidder might be willing to pay for the target.

The goal of this chapter is to provide a sound introduction to LBO analysis and its broad applications. While there are multiple approaches to performing this analysis (especially with regard to constructing the LBO model), we have designed the steps in Exhibit 5.1 to be as user-friendly as possible. We also perform an illustrative LBO analysis using ValueCo as our LBO target.

EXHIBIT 5.1   LBO Analysis Steps

Step I.   **Locate and Analyze the Necessary Information**
Step II.   **Build the Pre-LBO Model**
           a. Build Historical and Projected Income Statement through EBIT
           b. Input Opening Balance Sheet and Project Balance Sheet Items
           c. Build Cash Flow Statement through Investing Activities
Step III. **Input Transaction Structure**
           a. Enter Purchase Price Assumptions
           b. Enter Financing Structure into Sources and Uses
           c. Link Sources and Uses to Balance Sheet Adjustments Columns
Step IV.   **Complete the Post-LBO Model**
           a. Build Debt Schedule
           b. Complete Pro Forma Income Statement from EBIT to Net Income
           c. Complete Pro Forma Balance Sheet
           d. Complete Pro Forma Cash Flow Statement
Step V.   **Perform LBO Analysis**
           a. Analyze Financing Structure
           b. Perform Returns Analysis
           c. Determine Valuation
           d. Create Transaction Summary Page

Once the above steps are completed, all the essential outputs are linked to a transaction summary page that serves as the cover page of the LBO model (see Exhibit 5.2). This page allows the deal team to quickly review and spot-check the

EXHIBIT 5.2 LBO Model Transaction Summary Page

ValueCo Corporation
Leveraged Buyout Analysis
($ in millions, fiscal year ending December 31)

Financing Structure: Structure 1
Operating Scenario: Base

Transaction Summary

Sources of Funds

	Amount	% of Total Sources	Multiple of EBITDA 9/30/2008	Cumulative	Pricing
Revolving Credit Facility	-	- %	- x	- x	L-325 bps
Term Loan A	-	- %	- x	- x	NA
Term Loan B	450.0	38.8%	3.1x	3.1x	L-350 bps
Term Loan C	-	- %	- x	3.1x	NA
2nd Lien	-	- %	- x	3.1x	NA
Senior Notes	-	- %	- x	3.1x	NA
Senior Subordinated Notes	300.0	25.9%	2.0x	5.1x	10.000%
Equity Contribution	385.0	33.2%	2.6x	7.7x	
Rollover Equity	-	- %	- x	7.7x	
Cash on Hand	25.0	2.2%	0.2x	7.9x	
Total Sources	**$1,160.0**	**100.0%**	**7.9x**	**7.9x**	

Uses of Funds

	Amount	% of Total Uses
Purchase ValueCo Equity	$825.0	71.1%
Repay Existing Debt	300.0	25.9%
Tender / Call Premiums	-	- %
Financing Fees	20.0	1.7%
Other Fees and Expenses	15.0	1.3%
Total Uses	**$1,160.0**	**100.0%**

Purchase Price

Offer Price per Share	-
Fully Diluted Shares	-
Equity Purchase Price	$825.0
Plus: Existing Net Debt	275.0
Enterprise Value	$1,100.0

Transaction Multiples

Enterprise Value / Sales	LTM 9/30/2008	$977.8	1.1x
	2008E	1,000.0	1.1x
Enterprise Value / EBITDA	LTM 9/30/2008	$146.7	7.5x
	2008E	150.0	7.3x

Return Analysis

Exit Year	-
Entry Multiple	$825.0
Exit Multiple	275.0
IRR	$1,100.0
Cash Return	

Options

Financing Structure	
Operating Scenario	
Cash Flow Sweep	
Cash Balance	
Average Interest	
Financing Fees	

Summary Financial Data

		Historical Period			LTM 9/30/2008	Pro forma 2008	Year 1 2009	Year 2 2010	Year 3 2011	Year 4 2012	Year 5 2013	Projection Period Year 6 2014	Year 7 2015	Year 8 2016	Year 9 2017	Year 10 2018
	2005	2006	2007													
Sales	$780.0	$850.0	$925.0	$977.8	$1,000.0	$1,080.0	$1,144.8	$1,190.6	$1,226.3	$1,263.1	$1,301.0	$1,340.0	$1,380.2	$1,421.6	$1,464.3
% growth	NA	9.0%	8.8%	NA	8.1%	8.0%	6.0%	4.0%	3.0%	3.0%	3.0%	3.0%	3.0%	3.0%	3.0%
Gross Profit	$308.1	$337.9	$370.0	$391.1	$400.0	$432.0	$457.9	$476.2	$490.5	$505.2	$520.4	$536.0	$552.1	$568.7	$585.7
% margin	39.5%	39.8%	40.0%	40.0%	40.0%	40.0%	40.0%	40.0%	40.0%	40.0%	40.0%	40.0%	40.0%	40.0%	40.0%
EBITDA	$109.2	$123.3	$138.8	$146.7	$150.0	$162.0	$171.7	$178.6	$183.9	$189.5	$195.1	$201.0	$207.0	$213.2	$219.6
% margin	14.0%	14.5%	15.0%	15.0%	15.0%	15.0%	15.0%	15.0%	15.0%	15.0%	15.0%	15.0%	15.0%	15.0%	15.0%
Capital Expenditures	15.0	18.0	19.6		20.0	21.6	22.9	23.8	24.5	25.3	26.0	26.8	27.6	28.4	29.3
% sales	1.9%	2.1%	2.0%		2.0%	2.0%	2.0%	2.0%	2.0%	2.0%	2.0%	2.0%	2.0%	2.0%	2.0%
Cash Interest Expense					59.9	58.5	55.9	52.7	49.2	45.2	40.0	34.0	30.7	30.7	30.7
Total Interest Expense					62.4	60.9	58.4	55.2	51.7	47.6	42.5	36.2	31.7	31.7	31.7
Free Cash Flow															
EBITDA						$162.0	$171.7	$178.6	$183.9	$189.5	$195.1	$201.0	$207.0	$213.2	$219.6
Less: Cash Interest Expense						(58.5)	(55.9)	(52.7)	(49.2)	(45.2)	(40.0)	(34.0)	(30.7)	(30.7)	(30.7)
Plus: Interest Income						-	-	-	-	-	-	0.0	1.4	4.2	7.1
Less: Income Taxes						(30.2)	(34.4)	(37.9)	(40.9)	(44.3)	(48.1)	(52.5)	(56.7)	(59.8)	(63.0)
Less: Capital Expenditures						(21.6)	(22.9)	(23.8)	(24.5)	(25.3)	(26.0)	(26.8)	(27.6)	(28.4)	(29.3)
Less: Increase in Net Working Capital						(8.0)	(6.5)	(4.6)	(3.6)	(3.7)	(3.8)	(3.9)	(4.0)	(4.1)	(4.3)
Free Cash Flow						$43.7	$52.0	$59.6	$65.7	$71.1	$77.2	$83.9	$89.5	$94.4	$99.6
Cumulative Free Cash Flow						43.7	95.8	155.4	221.1	292.1	369.3	453.2	542.7	637.2	736.7

Capitalization

	Pro forma 2008	Year 1 2009	Year 2 2010	Year 3 2011	Year 4 2012	Year 5 2013	Year 6 2014	Year 7 2015	Year 8 2016	Year 9 2017	Year 10 2018
Cash	-	-	-	-	-	-	-	$3.2	$92.7	$187.2	$286.7
Revolving Credit Facility	-	-	-	-	-	-	-	-	-	-	-
Term Loan B	450.0	406.3	354.2	294.6	228.9	157.9	80.7	-	-	-	-
Other Debt	-	-	-	-	-	-	-	-	-	-	-
Total Senior Secured Debt	**$450.0**	**$406.3**	**$354.2**	**$294.6**	**$228.9**	**$157.9**	**$80.7**	-	-	-	-
Senior Subordinated Notes	300.0	300.0	300.0	300.0	300.0	300.0	300.0	300.0	300.0	300.0	300.0
Total Debt	**$750.0**	**$706.3**	**$654.2**	**$594.6**	**$528.9**	**$457.9**	**$380.7**	**$300.0**	**$300.0**	**$300.0**	**$300.0**
Shareholders' Equity	370.0	419.3	475.3	537.1	603.9	676.2	754.7	840.3	932.8	1,030.4	1,133.1
Total Capitalization	**$1,120.0**	**$1,125.5**	**$1,129.6**	**$1,131.7**	**$1,132.8**	**$1,134.0**	**$1,135.4**	**$1,140.3**	**$1,232.8**	**$1,330.4**	**$1,433.1**
% of Bank Debt Repaid	-	9.7%	21.3%	34.5%	49.1%	64.9%	82.1%	100.0%	100.0%	100.0%	100.0%

Credit Statistics

	Pro forma 2008	Year 1 2009	Year 2 2010	Year 3 2011	Year 4 2012	Year 5 2013	Year 6 2014	Year 7 2015	Year 8 2016	Year 9 2017	Year 10 2018
% Debt / Total Capitalization	67.0%	62.7%	57.9%	52.5%	46.7%	40.4%	33.5%	26.3%	24.3%	22.6%	20.9%
EBITDA / Cash Interest Expense	2.5x	2.8x	3.1x	3.4x	3.7x	4.2x	4.9x	5.9x	6.8x	7.0x	7.2x
(EBITDA - Capex) / Cash Interest Expense	2.2x	2.4x	2.7x	2.9x	3.2x	3.6x	4.2x	5.1x	5.9x	6.0x	6.2x
EBITDA / Total Interest Expense	2.4x	2.7x	2.9x	3.2x	3.6x	4.0x	4.6x	5.6x	6.5x	6.7x	6.9x
(EBITDA - Capex) / Total Interest Expense	2.1x	2.3x	2.5x	2.8x	3.1x	3.4x	4.0x	4.8x	5.7x	5.8x	6.0x
Senior Secured Debt / EBITDA	3.0x	2.5x	2.1x	1.6x	1.2x	0.8x	0.4x	NM	NM	NM	NM
Total Debt / EBITDA	5.0x	4.4x	3.8x	3.3x	2.9x	2.4x	2.0x	1.5x	1.4x	1.4x	1.4x
Net Debt / EBITDA	5.0x	4.4x	3.8x	3.3x	2.9x	2.4x	2.0x	1.5x	1.0x	0.5x	0.1x

Return Analysis (2013)

	2013
Exit Year	7.5x
Entry Multiple	7.5x
Exit Multiple	20%
IRR	2.5x
Cash Return	

analysis and make adjustments to the purchase price, financing structure, operating assumptions, and other key inputs as necessary. It also includes the toggle cells that allow the banker to switch between various financing structures and operating scenarios, among other functions.[1] The fully completed model (including all assumptions pages) is shown in Exhibits 5.46 to 5.54.

STEP I. LOCATE AND ANALYZE THE NECESSARY INFORMATION

When performing LBO analysis, the first step is to collect, organize, and analyze all available information on the target, its sector, and the specifics of the transaction. In an organized sale process, the sell-side advisor provides such detail to prospective buyers, including financial projections that usually form the basis for the initial LBO model (see Chapter 6). This information is typically contained in a CIM, with additional information provided via a management presentation and data room. For public targets, this information is supplemented by SEC filings, research reports, and other public sources as described in previous chapters.

In the absence of a CIM or supplemental company information (e.g., if the target is not being actively sold), the banker must rely upon public sources to perform preliminary due diligence and develop an initial set of financial projections. This task is invariably easier for a public company than a private company (see Chapter 3).

Regardless of whether there is a formal sale process, it is important for the banker to independently verify as much information as possible about the target and its sector. Public filings as well as equity and fixed income research on the target (if applicable) and its comparables are particularly important resources. In their absence, news runs, trade publications, and even a simple internet search on a given company or sector and its competitive dynamics may provide valuable information. Within an investment bank, the deal team also relies on the judgment and experience of its sector coverage bankers to provide insight on the target.

STEP II. BUILD THE PRE-LBO MODEL

In Step II, we provide detailed step-by-step instructions (see Exhibit 5.3) on how to build the standalone ("pre-LBO") operating model for our illustrative target company, ValueCo, assuming that the primary financial assumptions are obtained from a CIM. The pre-LBO model is a basic three-statement financial projection model (income statement, balance sheet, and cash flow statement) that initially excludes the effects of the LBO transaction. The incorporation of the LBO financing structure and the resulting pro forma effects are detailed in Steps III and IV.

---

[1]Toggles may also be created to activate the 100% cash flow sweep, cash balance sweep, average interest expense option, or other deal-specific toggles.

EXHIBIT 5.3   Pre-LBO Model Steps

Step II(a):   Build Historical and Projected Income Statement through EBIT
Step II(b):   Input Opening Balance Sheet and Project Balance Sheet Items
Step II(c):   Build Cash Flow Statement through Investing Activities

---

Step II(a): Build Historical and Projected Income Statement through EBIT

The banker typically begins the pre-LBO model by inputting the target's histori-cal income statement information for the prior three-year period, if available. The historical income statement is generally only built through EBIT, as the target's prior annual interest expense and net income are not relevant given that the target will be recapitalized through the LBO. As with the DCF, historical financial per-formance should be shown on a pro forma basis for non-recurring items and recent events. This provides a normalized basis for projecting and analyzing future financial performance.

Management projections for sales through EBIT, as provided in the CIM, are then entered into an assumptions page (see Exhibit 5.52), which feeds into the projected income statement until other operating scenarios are developed/provided. This scenario is typically labeled as "Management Case." At this point, the line items between EBIT and earnings before taxes (EBT) are intentionally left blank, to be completed once a financing structure is entered into the model and a *debt schedule* is built (see Exhibit 5.29). In ValueCo's case, although it has an existing $300 million term loan (see Exhibit 5.5), it is not necessary to model the associated interest expense (or mandatory amortization) as it will be refinanced as part of the LBO transaction.

From a debt financing perspective, the projection period for an LBO model is typically set at seven to ten years so as to match the maturity of the longest tenored debt instrument in the capital structure. A financial sponsor, however, may only use a five-year projection period in its internal LBO model so as to match its expectations for the anticipated investment horizon.

As a CIM typically only provides five years of projected income statement data,[2] it is common for the banker to freeze the Year 5 growth rate and margin assumptions to frame the outer year projections (in the absence of specific guidance). As shown in ValueCo's pre-LBO income statement (Exhibit 5.4), we held Year 5 sales growth rate, gross margin, and EBITDA margin constant at 3%, 40%, and 15%, respectively, to drive projections in Years 6 through 10.

Additional Cases   In addition to the Management Case, the deal team typically de-velops its own, more conservative operating scenario, known as the "Base Case." The Base Case is generally premised on management assumptions, but with adjustments made based on the deal team's independent due diligence, research, and perspectives.

---

[2]The length of the projection period provided in a CIM (or through another medium) may vary depending on the situation.

EXHIBIT 5.4 ValueCo Pre-LBO Income Statement

($ in millions, fiscal year ending December 31)

Income Statement

	Historical Period				Pro forma 2008	Projection Period									
	2005	2006	2007	LTM 9/30/2008		Year 1 2009	Year 2 2010	Year 3 2011	Year 4 2012	Year 5 2013	Year 6 2014	Year 7 2015	Year 8 2016	Year 9 2017	Year 10 2018
Sales	$780.0	$850.0	$925.0	$977.8	$1,000.0	$1,080.0	$1,144.8	$1,190.6	$1,226.3	$1,263.1	$1,301.0	$1,340.0	$1,380.2	$1,421.6	$1,464.3
% growth	NA	9.0%	8.8%	NA	8.1%	8.0%	6.0%	4.0%	3.0%	3.0%	3.0%	3.0%	3.0%	3.0%	3.0%
Cost of Goods Sold	471.9	512.1	555.0	586.7	600.0	648.0	686.9	714.4	735.8	757.9	780.6	804.0	828.1	853.0	878.6
Gross Profit	$308.1	$337.9	$370.0	$391.1	$400.0	$432.0	$457.9	$476.2	$490.5	$505.2	$520.4	$536.0	$552.1	$568.7	$585.7
% margin	39.5%	39.8%	40.0%	40.0%	40.0%	40.0%	40.0%	40.0%	40.0%	40.0%	40.0%	40.0%	40.0%	40.0%	40.0%
Selling, General & Administrative	198.9	214.6	231.3	244.4	250.0	270.0	286.2	297.6	306.6	315.8	325.2	335.0	345.1	355.4	366.1
% sales	25.5%	25.3%	25.0%	25.0%	25.0%	25.0%	25.0%	25.0%	25.0%	25.0%	25.0%	25.0%	25.0%	25.0%	25.0%
Other Expense / (Income)															
EBITDA	$109.2	$123.3	$138.8	$146.7	$150.0	$162.0	$171.7	$178.6	$183.9	$189.5	$195.1	$201.0	$207.0	$213.2	$219.6
% margin	14.0%	14.5%	15.0%	15.0%	15.0%	15.0%	15.0%	15.0%	15.0%	15.0%	15.0%	15.0%	15.0%	15.0%	15.0%
Depreciation & Amortization	15.6	17.0	18.5	19.6	20.0	21.6	22.9	23.8	24.5	25.3	26.0	26.8	27.6	28.4	29.3
EBIT	$93.6	$106.3	$120.3	$127.1	$130.0	$140.4	$148.8	$154.8	$159.4	$164.2	$169.1	$174.2	$179.4	$184.8	$190.4
% margin	12.0%	12.5%	13.0%	13.0%	13.0%	13.0%	13.0%	13.0%	13.0%	13.0%	13.0%	13.0%	13.0%	13.0%	13.0%
Interest Expense															
Revolving Credit Facility															
Term Loan A															
Term Loan B									TO BE CALCULATED						
Term Loan C															
Existing Term Loan															
2nd Lien															
Senior Notes															
Senior Subordinated Notes															
Commitment Fee on Unused Revolver															
Administrative Agent Fee															
Cash Interest Expense															
Amortization of Deferred Financing Fees															
Total Interest Expense															
Interest Income															
Net Interest Expense															
Earnings Before Taxes						140.4	148.8	154.8	159.4	164.2	169.1	174.2	179.4	184.8	190.4
Income Tax Expense						53.4	56.6	58.8	60.6	62.4	64.3	66.2	68.2	70.2	72.3
Net Income						$87.0	$92.3	$96.0	$98.8	$101.8	$104.9	$108.0	$111.2	$114.6	$118.0
% margin						8.1%	8.1%	8.1%	8.1%	8.1%	8.1%	8.1%	8.1%	8.1%	8.1%

Income Statement Assumptions

	2005	2006	2007	LTM 9/30/2008	Pro forma 2008	Year 1 2009	Year 2 2010	Year 3 2011	Year 4 2012	Year 5 2013	Year 6 2014	Year 7 2015	Year 8 2016	Year 9 2017	Year 10 2018
Sales (% YoY growth)	NA	9.0%	8.8%	NA	8.1%	8.0%	6.0%	4.0%	3.0%	3.0%	3.0%	3.0%	3.0%	3.0%	3.0%
COGS (% margin)	60.5%	60.3%	60.0%	60.0%	60.0%	60.0%	60.0%	60.0%	60.0%	60.0%	60.0%	60.0%	60.0%	60.0%	60.0%
SG&A (% sales)	25.5%	25.3%	25.0%	25.0%	25.0%	25.0%	25.0%	25.0%	25.0%	25.0%	25.0%	25.0%	25.0%	25.0%	25.0%
Other Expense / (Income) (% of sales)	- %	- %	- %	- %	- %	- %	- %	- %	- %	- %	- %	- %	- %	- %	- %
Depreciation & Amortization (% of sales)	2.0%	2.0%	2.0%	2.0%	2.0%	2.0%	2.0%	2.0%	2.0%	2.0%	2.0%	2.0%	2.0%	2.0%	2.0%
Interest Income	2.0%	2.0%	2.0%	2.0%	3.0%	3.0%	3.0%	3.0%	3.0%	3.0%	3.0%	3.0%	3.0%	3.0%	3.0%
Tax Rate	38.0%	38.0%	38.0%	38.0%	38.0%	38.0%	38.0%	38.0%	38.0%	38.0%	38.0%	38.0%	38.0%	38.0%	38.0%

The bank's internal credit committee(s) also requires the deal team to analyze the target's performance under one or more stress cases in order to gain comfort with the target's ability to service and repay debt during periods of duress. Sponsors perform similar analyses to test the durability of a proposed investment. These "Downside Cases" typically present the target's financial performance with haircuts to top line growth, margins, and potentially capex and working capital efficiency. As with the DCF model, a "toggle" function in the LBO model allows the banker to move from case to case without having to re-enter key financial inputs and assumptions. A separate toggle provides the ability to analyze different financing structures.

The operating scenario that the deal team ultimately uses to set covenants and market the transaction to investors is provided by the sponsor (the "Sponsor Case"). Sponsors use information gleaned from due diligence, industry experts, consulting studies, and research reports, as well as their own sector expertise to develop this case. The Sponsor Case, along with the sponsor's preferred financing structure (collectively, the "Sponsor Model"), is shared with potential underwriters as the basis for them to provide commitment letters.[3] The deal team then confirms both the feasibility of the Sponsor Case (based on its own due diligence and knowledge of the target and sector) and the marketability of the sponsor's preferred financing structure (by gaining comfort that there are buyers for the loans and securities given the proposed terms). This task is especially important because the investment banks are being asked to provide a commitment to a financing structure that may not come to market for several months (or potentially longer, depending on regulatory or other approvals required before the transaction can close).

Step II(b): Input Opening Balance Sheet and Project Balance Sheet Items

The opening balance sheet (and potentially projected balance sheet data) for the target is typically provided in the CIM and entered into the pre-LBO model (see Exhibit 5.5, "Opening 2008" heading).[4] In addition to the traditional balance sheet accounts, new line items necessary for modeling the pro forma LBO financing structure are added, such as:

- financing fees (which are amortized) under long-term assets
- detailed line items for the new financing structure under long-term liabilities (e.g., the new revolver, term loan(s), and high yield bonds)

The banker must then build functionality into the model in order to input the new LBO financing structure. This is accomplished by inserting "adjustment" columns to account for the additions and subtractions to the opening balance sheet that result from the LBO (see Exhibits 5.5 and 5.15). The inputs for the adjustment columns, which bridge from the opening balance sheet to the pro forma closing balance sheet,

---

[3]The timing for the sharing of the Sponsor Model depends on the specifics of the particular deal and the investment bank's relationship with the sponsor.

[4]If the banker is analyzing a public company as a potential LBO candidate outside of (or prior to) an organized sale process, the latest balance sheet data from the company's most recent 10-K or 10-Q is typically used.

EXHIBIT 5.5 ValueCo Pre-LBO Balance Sheet

($ in millions, fiscal year ending December 31)

Balance Sheet

Callouts:
- The ending cash balance for each year in the projection period is linked to the balance sheet from the cash flow statement once it is completed.
- Prior to entry of capex assumptions, PP&E only reflects D&A.
- Shareholders' equity is inflated until the financing structure is entered into the model.
- Model will balance once the ending cash balance for each year in the projection period is linked from the cash flow statement.

	Opening 2008	Adjustments +/-	Pro Forma 2008	Year 1 2009	Year 2 2010	Year 3 2011	Year 4 2012	Year 5 2013	Year 6 2014	Year 7 2015	Year 8 2016	Year 9 2017	Year 10 2018
Cash and Cash Equivalents	$25.0		$25.0										
Accounts Receivable	165.0		165.0	178.2	188.9	196.4	202.3	208.4	214.7	221.1	227.7	234.6	241.6
Inventories	125.0		125.0	135.0	143.1	148.8	153.3	157.9	162.6	167.5	172.5	177.7	183.0
Prepaids and Other Current Assets	10.0		10.0	10.8	11.4	11.9	12.3	12.6	13.0	13.4	13.8	14.2	14.6
Total Current Assets	**$325.0**		**$325.0**	**$324.0**	**$343.4**	**$357.2**	**$367.9**	**$378.9**	**$390.3**	**$402.0**	**$414.1**	**$426.5**	**$439.3**
Property, Plant and Equipment, net	650.0		650.0	628.4	605.5	581.7	557.2	531.9	505.9	479.1	451.5	423.0	393.3
Goodwill and Intangible Assets	175.0		175.0	175.0	175.0	175.0	175.0	175.0	175.0	175.0	175.0	175.0	175.0
Other Assets	75.0		75.0	75.0	75.0	75.0	75.0	75.0	75.0	75.0	75.0	75.0	75.0
Deferred Financing Fees													
Total Assets	**$1,225.0**		**$1,225.0**	**$1,202.4**	**$1,198.9**	**$1,188.9**	**$1,175.1**	**$1,160.8**	**$1,146.2**	**$1,131.1**	**$1,115.5**	**$1,099.5**	**$1,083.0**
Accounts Payable	75.0		75.0	81.0	85.9	89.3	92.0	94.7	97.6	100.5	103.5	106.6	109.8
Accrued Liabilities	100.0		100.0	108.0	114.5	119.1	122.6	126.3	130.1	134.0	138.0	142.2	146.4
Other Current Liabilities	25.0		25.0	27.0	28.6	29.8	30.7	31.6	32.5	33.5	34.5	35.5	36.6
Total Current Liabilities	**$200.0**		**$200.0**	**$216.0**	**$229.0**	**$238.1**	**$245.3**	**$252.6**	**$260.2**	**$268.0**	**$276.0**	**$284.3**	**$292.9**
Revolving Credit Facility													
Term Loan A													
Term Loan B													
Term Loan C													
Existing Term Loan	300.0		300.0	300.0	300.0	300.0	300.0	300.0	300.0	300.0	300.0	300.0	300.0
2nd Lien													
Senior Notes													
Senior Subordinated Notes													
Other Debt													
Other Long-Term Liabilities	25.0		25.0	25.0	25.0	25.0	25.0	25.0	25.0	25.0	25.0	25.0	25.0
Total Liabilities	**$525.0**		**$525.0**	**$541.0**	**$554.0**	**$563.1**	**$570.3**	**$577.6**	**$585.2**	**$593.0**	**$601.0**	**$609.3**	**$617.9**
Noncontrolling Interest													
Shareholders' Equity	700.0		700.0	787.0	879.3	975.3	1,074.1	1,175.9	1,280.8	1,388.8	1,500.0	1,614.6	1,732.6
Total Shareholders' Equity	**$700.0**		**$700.0**	**$787.0**	**$879.3**	**$975.3**	**$1,074.1**	**$1,175.9**	**$1,280.8**	**$1,388.8**	**$1,500.0**	**$1,614.6**	**$1,732.6**
Total Liabilities and Equity	**$1,225.0**		**$1,225.0**	**$1,328.0**	**$1,433.4**	**$1,538.4**	**$1,644.4**	**$1,753.5**	**$1,866.0**	**$1,981.8**	**$2,101.1**	**$2,223.9**	**$2,350.5**
Balance Check			0.000										
Net Working Capital	100.0		100.0	108.0	114.5	119.1	122.6	126.3	130.1	134.0	138.0	142.2	146.4
(Increase) / Decrease in Net Working Capital				(8.0)	(6.5)	(4.6)	(3.6)	(3.7)	(3.8)	(3.9)	(4.0)	(4.1)	(4.3)

Table region labels: TO BE LINKED / CALCULATED FROM SOURCES AND USES · TO BE LINKED FROM CASH FLOW STATEMENT · TO BE LINKED FROM DEBT SCHEDULE

Balance Sheet Assumptions

Current Assets													
Days Sales Outstanding (DSO)	60.2		60.2	60.2	60.2	60.2	60.2	60.2	60.2	60.2	60.2	60.2	60.2
Days Inventory Held (DIH)	76.0		76.0	76.0	76.0	76.0	76.0	76.0	76.0	76.0	76.0	76.0	76.0
Prepaid and Other Current Assets (% of sales)	1.0%		1.0%	1.0%	1.0%	1.0%	1.0%	1.0%	1.0%	1.0%	1.0%	1.0%	1.0%

Current Liabilities													
Days Payable Outstanding (DPO)	45.6		45.6	45.6	45.6	45.6	45.6	45.6	45.6	45.6	45.6	45.6	45.6
Accrued Liabilities (% of sales)	10.0%		10.0%	10.0%	10.0%	10.0%	10.0%	10.0%	10.0%	10.0%	10.0%	10.0%	10.0%
Other Current Liabilities (% of sales)	2.5%		2.5%	2.5%	2.5%	2.5%	2.5%	2.5%	2.5%	2.5%	2.5%	2.5%	2.5%

feed from the *sources and uses* of funds in the transaction (see Exhibits 5.14 and 5.15). The banker also inserts a "pro forma" column, which nets the adjustments made to the opening balance sheet and serves as the starting point for projecting the target's post-LBO balance sheet throughout the projection period.

Prior to the entry of the LBO financing structure, the opening and pro forma closing balance sheets are identical. The target's basic balance sheet items—such as current assets, current liabilities, PP&E, other assets, and other long-term liabilities—are projected using the same methodologies discussed in Chapter 3. As with the assumptions for the target's projected income statement items, the banker enters the assumptions for the target's projected balance sheet items into the model through an assumptions page (see Exhibit 5.53), which feeds into the projected balance sheet.

Projected debt repayment is not modeled at this point as the LBO financing structure has yet to be entered into the sources and uses of funds. For ValueCo, which has an existing $300 million term loan, we simply set the projection period debt balances equal to the opening balance amount (see Exhibit 5.5). At this stage, annual excess free cash flow[5] accrues to the ending cash balance for each projection year once the pre-LBO cash flow statement is completed (see Step II(c), Exhibits 5.9 and 5.10). This ensures that the model will balance once the three financial statements are fully linked.

Depending on the availability of information and need for granularity, the banker may choose to build a "short-form" LBO model that suffices for calculating debt repayment and performing a basic returns analysis. A short-form LBO model uses an abbreviated cash flow statement and a debt schedule in place of a full balance sheet with working capital typically calculated as a percentage of sales. The construction of a traditional three-statement model, however, is recommended whenever possible so as to provide the most comprehensive analysis.

Step II(c): Build Cash Flow Statement through Investing Activities

The cash flow statement consists of three sections—operating activities, investing activities, and financing activities.

Operating Activities

Income Statement Links   In building the cash flow statement, all the appropriate income statement items, including net income and non-cash expenses (e.g., D&A, amortization of deferred financing fees), must be linked to the operating activities section of the cash flow statement.

Net income is the first line item in the cash flow statement. It is initially inflated in the pre-LBO model as it excludes the pro forma interest expense and amortization of deferred financing fees associated with the LBO financing structure that have not yet been entered into the model. The amortization of deferred financing fees is a non-cash expense that is added back to net income in the post-LBO cash flow statement. Certain items, such as the annual projected D&A, do not change pro forma for the transaction.

---

[5]The "free cash flow" term used in an LBO analysis differs from that used in a DCF analysis as it includes the effects of leverage.

EXHIBIT 5.6   Income Statement Links

($ in millions, fiscal year ending December 31)

Cash Flow Statement

					Projection Period					
	Year 1 2009	Year 2 2010	Year 3 2011	Year 4 2012	Year 5 2013	Year 6 2014	Year 7 2015	Year 8 2016	Year 9 2017	Year 10 2018
Operating Activities										
Net Income	$87.0	$92.3	$96.0	$98.8	$101.8	$104.9	$108.0	$111.2	$114.6	$118.0
Plus: Depreciation & Amortization	21.6	22.9	23.8	24.5	25.3	26.0	26.8	27.6	28.4	29.3
Plus: Amortization of Financing Fees					TO BE LINKED FROM INCOME STATEMENT					

As shown in Exhibit 5.6, ValueCo's 2009E net income is $87 million, which is $37.8 million higher than the pro forma 2009E net income of $49.3 million after giving effect to the LBO financing structure (see Exhibit 5.31).

Balance Sheet Links   Each YoY change to a balance sheet account must be accounted for by a corresponding addition or subtraction to the appropriate line item on the cash flow statement. As discussed in Chapter 3, an increase in an asset is a use of cash (represented by a negative value on the cash flow statement) and a decrease in an asset represents a source of cash. Similarly, an increase or decrease in a liability account represents a source or use of cash, respectively. The YoY changes in the target's projected working capital items are calculated in their corresponding line items in the operating activities section of the cash flow statement. These amounts do not change pro forma for the LBO transaction. The sum of the target's net income, non-cash expenses, changes in working capital items, and other items (as appropriate) provides the cash flow from operating activities amount.

EXHIBIT 5.7   Balance Sheet Links

($ in millions, fiscal year ending December 31)

Cash Flow Statement

					Projection Period					
	Year 1 2009	Year 2 2010	Year 3 2011	Year 4 2012	Year 5 2013	Year 6 2014	Year 7 2015	Year 8 2016	Year 9 2017	Year 10 2018
Operating Activities										
Net Income	$87.0	$92.3	$96.0	$98.8	$101.8	$104.9	$108.0	$111.2	$114.6	$118.0
Plus: Depreciation & Amortization	21.6	22.9	23.8	24.5	25.3	26.0	26.8	27.6	28.4	29.3
Plus: Amortization of Financing Fees					TO BE LINKED FROM INCOME STATEMENT					
Changes in Working Capital Items										
(Inc.) / Dec. in Accounts Receivable	(13.2)	(10.7)	(7.6)	(5.9)	(6.1)	(6.3)	(6.4)	(6.6)	(6.8)	(7.0)
(Inc.) / Dec. in Inventories	(10.0)	(8.1)	(5.7)	(4.5)	(4.6)	(4.7)	(4.9)	(5.0)	(5.2)	(5.3)
(Inc.) / Dec. in Prepaid and Other Current Assets	(0.8)	(0.6)	(0.5)	(0.4)	(0.4)	(0.4)	(0.4)	(0.4)	(0.4)	(0.4)
Inc. / (Dec.) in Accounts Payable	6.0	4.9	3.4	2.7	2.8	2.8	2.9	3.0	3.1	3.2
Inc. / (Dec.) in Accrued Liabilities	8.0	6.5	4.6	3.6	3.7	3.8	3.9	4.0	4.1	4.3
Inc. / (Dec.) in Other Current Liabilities	2.0	1.6	1.1	0.9	0.9	0.9	1.0	1.0	1.0	1.1
(Inc.) / Dec. in Net Working Capital	(8.0)	(6.5)	(4.6)	(3.6)	(3.7)	(3.8)	(3.9)	(4.0)	(4.1)	(4.3)
Cash Flow from Operating Activities	$100.6	$108.7	$115.2	$119.8	$123.4	$127.1	$130.9	$134.8	$138.9	$143.0

As shown in Exhibit 5.7, ValueCo generates $100.6 million of cash flow from operating activities in 2009E before giving effect to the LBO transaction.

Investing Activities   Capex is typically the key line item under investing activities, although planned acquisitions or divestitures may also be captured in the other investing activities line item. Projected capex assumptions are typically sourced from the CIM and inputted into an assumptions page (see Exhibit 5.52) where they are linked to the cash flow statement. The target's projected net PP&E must incorporate the capex projections (added to PP&E) as well as those for depreciation (subtracted from PP&E). As discussed in Chapter 3, in the event that capex projections are not provided/available, the banker typically projects capex as a fixed percentage of sales at historical levels with appropriate adjustments for cyclical or non-recurring items.

The sum of the annual cash flows provided by operating activities and investing activities provides annual cash flow available for debt repayment, which is commonly referred to as free cash flow (see Exhibit 5.25).

EXHIBIT 5.8   Investing Activities

($ in millions, fiscal year ending December 31)

Cash Flow Statement

					Projection Period					
	Year 1 2009	Year 2 2010	Year 3 2011	Year 4 2012	Year 5 2013	Year 6 2014	Year 7 2015	Year 8 2016	Year 9 2017	Year 10 2018
Investing Activities										
Capital Expenditures	(21.6)	(22.9)	(23.8)	(24.5)	(25.3)	(26.0)	(26.8)	(27.6)	(28.4)	(29.3)
Other Investing Activities	-	-	-	-	-	-	-	-	-	-
Cash Flow from Investing Activities	**($21.6)**	**($22.9)**	**($23.8)**	**($24.5)**	**($25.3)**	**($26.0)**	**($26.8)**	**($27.6)**	**($28.4)**	**($29.3)**
Cash Flow Statement Assumptions										
Capital Expenditures (% of sales)	2.0%	2.0%	2.0%	2.0%	2.0%	2.0%	2.0%	2.0%	2.0%	2.0%

As shown in Exhibit 5.8, we do not make any assumptions for ValueCo's other investing activities line item. Therefore, ValueCo's cash flow from investing activities amount is equal to capex in each year of the projection period.

Financing Activities   The financing activities section of the cash flow statement is constructed to include line items for the (repayment)/drawdown of each debt instrument in the LBO financing structure. It also includes line items for dividends and equity issuance/(stock repurchase). These line items are initially left blank until the LBO financing structure is entered into the model (see Step III) and a detailed debt schedule is built (see Step IV(a)).

EXHIBIT 5.9   Financing Activities

($ in millions, fiscal year ending December 31)

Cash Flow Statement

					Projection Period					
	Year 1 2009	Year 2 2010	Year 3 2011	Year 4 2012	Year 5 2013	Year 6 2014	Year 7 2015	Year 8 2016	Year 9 2017	Year 10 2018
Financing Activities										
Revolving Credit Facility										
Term Loan A										
Term Loan B										
Term Loan C				TO BE LINKED FROM DEBT SCHEDULE						
Existing Term Loan										
2nd Lien										
Senior Notes										
Senior Subordinated Notes										
Other Debt	-	-	-	-	-	-	-	-	-	-
Dividends	-	-	-	-	-	-	-	-	-	-
Equity Issuance / (Repurchase)	-	-	-	-	-	-	-	-	-	-
Cash Flow from Financing Activities	-	-	-	-	-	-	-	-	-	-
Excess Cash for the Period	$79.0	$85.8	$91.4	$95.3	$98.1	$101.1	$104.1	$107.2	$110.4	$113.8
Beginning Cash Balance	25.0	104.0	189.8	281.2	376.5	474.6	575.7	679.8	787.0	897.5
Ending Cash Balance	**$104.0**	**$189.8**	**$281.2**	**$376.5**	**$474.6**	**$575.7**	**$679.8**	**$787.0**	**$897.5**	**$1,011.2**

Excess Cash for the Period accrues to the Ending Cash Balance until the LBO financing structure is entered into the model and the debt schedule is built.

As shown in Exhibit 5.9, prior to giving effect to the LBO transaction, ValueCo's projected excess cash for the period accrues to the ending cash balance in each year of the projection period.

Cash Flow Statement Links to Balance Sheet   Once the cash flow statement is built, the ending cash balance for each year in the projection period is linked to the cash and cash equivalents line item in the balance sheet, thereby fully linking the financial statements of the pre-LBO model.

EXHIBIT 5.10   Cash Flow Statement Links to Balance Sheet

($ in millions, fiscal year ending December 31)

Cash Flow Statement

	Year 1 2009	Year 2 2010	Year 3 2011	Year 4 2012	Year 5 2013	Year 6 2014	Year 7 2015	Year 8 2016	Year 9 2017	Year 10 2018
					Projection Period					
Excess Cash for the Period	$79.0	$85.8	$91.4	$95.3	$98.1	$101.1	$104.1	$107.2	$110.4	$113.8
Beginning Cash Balance	25.0	104.0	189.8	281.2	376.5	474.6	575.7	679.8	787.0	897.5
Ending Cash Balance	$104.0	$189.8	$281.2	$376.5	$474.6	$575.7	$679.8	$787.0	$897.5	$1,011.2

Balance Sheet

	Pro Forma 2008	Year 1 2009	Year 2 2010	Year 3 2011	Year 4 2012	Year 5 2013	Year 6 2014	Year 7 2015	Year 8 2016	Year 9 2017	Year 10 2018
						Projection Period					
Cash and Cash Equivalents	$25.0	$104.0	$189.8	$281.2	$376.5	$474.6	$575.7	$679.8	$787.0	$897.5	$1,011.2

= Ending Cash Balance$_{2009}$
(from Cash Flow Statement)

As shown in Exhibit 5.10, in 2009E, ValueCo generates excess cash for the period of $79 million, which is added to the beginning cash balance of $25 million to produce an ending cash balance of $104 million. This amount is linked to the 2009E cash and cash equivalents line item on the balance sheet.

At this point in the construction of the LBO model, the balance sheet should balance (i.e., total assets are equal to the sum of total liabilities and shareholders' equity) for each year in the projection period. If this is the case, then the model is functioning properly and the transaction structure can be entered into the sources and uses.

If the balance sheet does not balance, then the banker must revisit the steps performed up to this point and correct any input, linking, or calculation errors that are preventing the model from functioning properly. Common missteps include depreciation or capex not being properly linked to PP&E or changes in balance sheet accounts not being properly reflected in the cash flow statement.

STEP III. INPUT TRANSACTION STRUCTURE

EXHIBIT 5.11   Steps to Input the Transaction Structure

Step III(a):   Enter Purchase Price Assumptions
Step III(b):   Enter Financing Structure into Sources and Uses
Step III(c):   Link Sources and Uses to Balance Sheet Adjustments Columns

Step III(a): Enter Purchase Price Assumptions

A purchase price must be assumed for a given target in order to determine the supporting financing structure (debt and equity).

For the illustrative LBO of ValueCo (a private company), we assumed that a sponsor is basing its purchase price and financing structure on ValueCo's LTM

9/30/08 EBITDA of $146.7 million and a year-end transaction close.[6] We also assumed a purchase multiple of 7.5x LTM EBITDA, which is consistent with the multiples paid for similar LBO targets (per the illustrative precedent transactions analysis performed in Chapter 2, see Exhibit 2.33). This results in an enterprise value of $1,100 million and an implied equity purchase price of $825 million after subtracting ValueCo's net debt of $275 million.

EXHIBIT 5.12 Purchase Price Input Section of Assumptions Page 3 (see Exhibit 5.54) – Multiple of EBITDA

($ in millions)

Purchase Price	
Public / Private Target	**2**
Entry EBITDA Multiple	7.5x
LTM 9/30/2008 EBITDA	146.7
Enterprise Value	**$1,100.0**
Less: Total Debt	(300.0)
Less: Preferred Securities	-
Less: Noncontrolling Interest	-
Plus: Cash and Cash Equivalents	25.0
Equity Purchase Price	**$825.0**

> Enter "1" for a public target
> Enter "2" for a private target
> *Our LBO model template automatically updates the labels and calculations for each selection (see Exhibit 5.13)*

For a public company, the equity purchase price is calculated by multiplying the offer price per share by the target's fully diluted shares outstanding.[7] Net debt is then added to the equity purchase price to arrive at an implied enterprise value (see Exhibit 5.13).

EXHIBIT 5.13 Purchase Price Assumptions – Offer Price per Share

($ in millions, except per share data)

Purchase Price	
Public / Private Target	**1**
Offer Price per Share	$16.50
Fully Diluted Shares Outstanding	50.0
Equity Purchase Price	**$825.0**
Plus: Total Debt	300.0
Plus: Preferred Securities	-
Plus: Noncontrolling Interest	-
Less: Cash and Cash Equivalents	(25.0)
Enterprise Value	**$1,100.0**

---

[6]As ValueCo is private, we entered a "2" in the toggle cell for public/private target (see Exhibit 5.12).

[7]In this case, a "1" would be entered in the toggle cell for public/private target (see Exhibit 5.13).

Step III(b): Enter Financing Structure into Sources and Uses

A sources and uses table is used to summarize the flow of funds required to consummate a transaction. The *sources of funds* refer to the total capital used to finance an acquisition. The *uses of funds* refer to those items funded by the capital sources—in this case, the purchase of ValueCo's equity, the repayment of existing debt, and the payment of transaction fees and expenses. Regardless of the number and type of components comprising the sources and uses of funds, the sum of the sources of funds must equal the sum of the uses of funds.

We entered the sources and uses of funds for the multiple financing structures analyzed for the ValueCo LBO into an assumptions page (see Exhibits 5.14 and 5.54).

EXHIBIT 5.14   Financing Structures Input Section of Assumptions Page 3 (see Exhibit 5.54)

($ in millions)

Financing Structures

	Structure				
	1	2	3	4	5
Sources of Funds	Structure 1	Structure 2	Structure 3	Structure 4	Status Quo
Revolving Credit Facility Size	$100.0	$100.0	$100.0	$100.0	-
Revolving Credit Facility Draw	-	-	25.0	-	-
Term Loan A	-	125.0	-	-	-
Term Loan B	450.0	350.0	350.0	425.0	-
Term Loan C	-	-	-	-	-
2nd Lien	-	-	-	-	-
Senior Notes	-	-	150.0	-	-
Senior Subordinated Notes	300.0	300.0	250.0	325.0	-
Equity Contribution	385.0	360.0	385.0	410.0	-
Rollover Equity	-	-	-	-	-
Cash on Hand	25.0	25.0	-	-	-
	-	-	-	-	-
Total Sources of Funds	$1,160.0	$1,160.0	$1,160.0	$1,160.0	-
Uses of Funds					
Equity Purchase Price	$825.0	$825.0	$825.0	$825.0	-
Repay Existing Bank Debt	300.0	300.0	300.0	300.0	-
Tender / Call Premiums	-	-	-	-	-
Financing Fees	20.0	20.0	20.0	20.0	-
Other Fees and Expenses	15.0	15.0	15.0	15.0	-
-	-	-	-	-	-
-	-	-	-	-	-
-	-	-	-	-	-
-	-	-	-	-	-
Total Uses of Funds	$1,160.0	$1,160.0	$1,160.0	$1,160.0	-

Sources of Funds Structure 1 served as our preliminary proposed financing structure for the ValueCo LBO. As shown in Exhibit 5.14, it consists of:

- $450 million term loan B ("TLB")
- $300 million senior subordinated notes ("notes")
- $385 million equity contribution
- $25 million of cash on hand

This preliminary financing structure is comprised of senior secured leverage of 3.1x LTM EBITDA, total leverage of 5.1x, and an equity contribution percentage of approximately 33% (see Exhibit 5.2).

We also contemplated a $100 million undrawn revolving credit facility ("revolver") as part of the financing. While not an actual source of funding for the ValueCo LBO, the revolver provides liquidity to fund anticipated seasonal working capital needs, issuance of letters of credit, and other cash uses at, or post, closing.

Uses of Funds The uses of funds include:

- the purchase of ValueCo's equity for $825 million
- the repayment of ValueCo's existing $300 million term loan[8]
- the payment of total transaction fees and expenses of $35 million (consisting of financing fees of $20 million and other fees and expenses of $15 million)

The total sources and uses of funds are $1,160 million, which is $60 million higher than the implied enterprise value calculated in Exhibit 5.12. This is due to the payment of $35 million of total fees and expenses and the use of $25 million of cash on hand as a funding source.

Step III(c): Link Sources and Uses to Balance Sheet Adjustments Columns

Once the sources and uses of funds are entered into the model, each amount is linked to the appropriate cell in the adjustments columns adjacent to the opening balance sheet (see Exhibit 5.15). Any goodwill that is created, however, needs to be calculated on the basis of equity purchase price and existing book value of equity (see Exhibit 5.20). The equity contribution must also be adjusted to account for any transaction-related fees and expenses (other than financing fees) that are expensed upfront.[9] These adjustments serve to bridge the opening balance sheet to the pro forma closing balance sheet, which forms the basis for projecting the target's balance sheet throughout the projection period.

---

[8]In the event the target has debt being refinanced with associated breakage costs (e.g., call or tender premiums), those expenses are included in the uses of funds.

[9]In accordance with FAS 141(R), M&A transaction costs are expensed as incurred. Debt financing fees, however, continue to be treated as deferred costs and amortized over the life of the associated debt instruments.

EXHIBIT 5.15   Sources and Uses Links to Balance Sheet

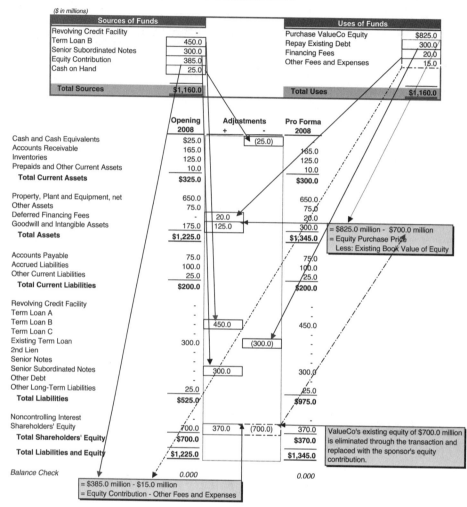

Exhibit 5.16 provides a summary of the transaction adjustments to the opening balance sheet.

Sources of Funds Links   The balance sheet links from the sources of funds to the adjustments columns are fairly straightforward. Each debt capital source corresponds to a like-named line item on the balance sheet and is linked as an addition in the appropriate adjustment column. For the equity contribution, however, the transaction-related fees and expenses must be deducted in the appropriate cell during linkage.

Term Loan B, Senior Subordinated Notes, and Equity Contribution   As shown in Exhibit 5.17, in the ValueCo LBO, the new $450 million TLB, $300 million notes, and $385 million equity contribution ($370 million after deducting $15 million

EXHIBIT 5.16 Balance Sheet Adjustments

($ in millions)

Adjustments	
Additions	**Eliminations**
Assets + $125 million of Goodwill + $20 million of Financing Fees	**Assets** – $25 million of Cash on Hand
Liabilities + $450 million of Term Loan B + $300 million of Senior Subordinated Notes	**Liabilities** – $300 million of Existing Term Loan
Shareholders' Equity + $385 million Sponsor Equity Contribution	**Shareholders' Equity** – $700 million of Existing Shareholders' Equity – $15 million of Other Fees and Expenses

of other fees and expenses) were linked from the sources of funds to their corresponding line items on the balance sheet as an addition under the "+" adjustment column.

EXHIBIT 5.17 Term Loan B, Senior Subordinated Notes, and Equity Contribution

($ in millions)

Balance Sheet

	Opening 2008	Adjustments +	Adjustments –	Pro Forma 2008
Revolving Credit Facility	-			-
Term Loan B	-	450.0		450.0
Existing Term Loan	300.0			300.0
Senior Subordinated Notes	-	300.0		300.0
Other Long-Term Liabilities	25.0			25.0
Total Liabilities	**$525.0**			**$1,275.0**
Noncontrolling Interest	-			-
Shareholders' Equity	700.0	370.0		1,070.0
Total Shareholders' Equity	**$700.0**			**$1,070.0**
Total Liabilities and Equity	**$1,225.0**			**$2,345.0**

= $385.0 million - $15.0 million
= Equity Contribution - Other Fees and Expenses

Cash on Hand As shown in Exhibit 5.18, the $25 million use of cash on hand was linked from the sources of funds as a negative adjustment to the opening cash balance as it is used as a source of funding.

EXHIBIT 5.18 Cash on Hand

($ in millions)

Balance Sheet

	Opening 2008	Adjustments +	Adjustments –	Pro Forma 2008
Cash and Cash Equivalents	$25.0		(25.0)	-

Uses of Funds Links

Purchase ValueCo Equity As shown in Exhibit 5.19, ValueCo's existing shareholders' equity of $700 million, which is included in the $825 million purchase price, was eliminated as a negative adjustment and replaced by the sponsor's equity contribution (less other fees and expenses).

EXHIBIT 5.19   Purchase ValueCo Equity

($ in millions)

Balance Sheet

	Opening 2008	Adjustments +	Adjustments −	Pro Forma 2008
Noncontrolling Interest	-			-
Shareholders' Equity	700.0	370.0	(700.0)	370.0
Total Shareholders' Equity	**$700.0**			**$370.0**

Goodwill Created Goodwill is created from the excess amount paid for a target over its existing book value. For the ValueCo LBO, it is calculated as the equity purchase price of $825 million less book value of $700 million. As shown in Exhibit 5.20, the net value of $125 million is added to the existing goodwill of $175 million, summing to total pro forma goodwill of $300 million.[10] The goodwill created remains on the balance sheet (unamortized) over the life of the investment, but is tested annually for impairment.

EXHIBIT 5.20   Goodwill Created

($ in millions)

Balance Sheet

	Opening 2008	Adjustments +	Adjustments −	Pro Forma 2008
Property, Plant and Equipment, net	650.0			650.0
Goodwill and Intangible Assets	175.0	125.0		300.0

Calculation of Goodwill	
Equity Purchase Price	$825.0
Less: Existing Book Value of Equity	(700.0)
Goodwill Created	**$125.0**
Plus: Existing Goodwill	175.0
Total Goodwill	**$300.0**

---

[10]The allocation of the entire purchase price premium to goodwill is a simplifying assumption for the purposes of this analysis. In an actual transaction, the excess purchase price over the existing book value of equity is allocated to assets, such as PP&E and intangibles, as well as other balance sheet items, to reflect their fair market value at the time of the acquisition. The remaining excess purchase price is then allocated to goodwill. From a cash flow perspective, in a stock sale (see Exhibit 6.10), there is no difference between allocating the entire purchase premium to goodwill as opposed to writing up other assets to fair market value. In an asset sale (see Exhibit 6.10), however, there are differences in cash flows depending on the allocation of goodwill to tangible and intangible assets as the write-up is tax deductible.

Repay Existing Debt   ValueCo's existing $300 million term loan is assumed to be refinanced as part of the new LBO financing structure, which includes $750 million of total funded debt. As shown in Exhibit 5.21, this is performed in the model by linking the repayment of the existing $300 million term loan directly from the uses of funds as a negative adjustment.

EXHIBIT 5.21   Repay Existing Debt

($ in millions)

Balance Sheet				
	Opening 2008	Adjustments +	–	Pro Forma 2008
Revolving Credit Facility	-			-
Term Loan B	-	450.0		450.0
Existing Term Loan	300.0		(300.0)	-

Financing Fees   As opposed to M&A transaction-related fees and expenses, financing fees are a deferred expense and, as such, are not expensed immediately. Therefore, deferred financing fees are capitalized as an asset on the balance sheet, which means they are linked from the uses of funds as an addition to the corresponding line item (see Exhibit 5.22). The financing fees associated with each debt instrument are amortized on a straight line basis over the life of the obligation.[11] As previously discussed, amortization is a non-cash expense and, therefore, must be added back to net income in the operating activities section of the model's cash flow statement in each year of the projection period.

For the ValueCo LBO, we calculated the financing fees associated with the contemplated financing structure to be $20 million. Our illustrative calculation is based on fees of 1.75% for arranging the senior secured credit facilities (the revolver and TLB), 2.25% for underwriting the notes, 1.00% for committing to a bridge loan for the notes, and $0.6 million for other financing fees and expenses.[12]

The left-lead arranger of a revolving credit facility typically serves as the "Administrative Agent"[13] and receives an annual administrative agent fee (e.g., $150,000), which is included in interest expense on the income statement.[14]

Other Fees and Expenses   Other fees and expenses typically include payments for services such as M&A advisory (and potentially a sponsor deal fee), legal,

---

[11]Although financing fees are paid in full to the underwriters at transaction close, they are amortized in accordance with the tenor of the security for accounting purposes. Deferred financing fees from prior financing transactions are typically expensed when the accompanying debt is retired and show up as a one-time charge to the target's net income, thereby reducing retained earnings and shareholders' equity.

[12]Fees are dependent on the debt instrument, market conditions, and specific situation. The fees depicted are for illustrative purposes only and indicative of those used during the mid-2000s.

[13]The bank that monitors the credit facilities including the tracking of lenders, handling of interest and principal payments, and associated back-office administrative functions.

[14]The fee for the first year of the facility is generally paid to the lead arranger at the close of the financing.

accounting, and consulting, as well as other miscellaneous deal-related costs. For the ValueCo LBO, we estimated this amount to be $15 million. Within the context of the LBO sources and uses, this amount is netted upfront against the equity contribution.

EXHIBIT 5.22 Financing Fees

($ in millions)

Balance Sheet

	Opening 2008	Adjustments +	Adjustments −	Pro Forma 2008
Property, Plant and Equipment, net	650.0			650.0
Goodwill and Intangible Assets	175.0	125.0		300.0
Other Assets	75.0			75.0
Deferred Financing Fees	-	20.0		20.0
Total Assets	**$1,225.0**			**$1,345.0**

Calculation of Financing Fees

		Fees	
	Size	(%)	($)
Revolving Credit Facility Size	$100.0	1.75%	$1.8
Term Loan B	450.0	1.75%	7.9
Senior Subordinated Notes	300.0	2.25%	6.8
Senior Subordinated Bridge Facility	300.0	1.00%	3.0
Other Financing Fees & Expenses	-	-	0.6
Total Financing Fees			**$20.0**

STEP IV. COMPLETE THE POST-LBO MODEL

EXHIBIT 5.23   Steps to Complete the Post-LBO Model

Step IV(a):	Build Debt Schedule
Step IV(b):	Complete Pro Forma Income Statement from EBIT to Net Income
Step IV(c):	Complete Pro Forma Balance Sheet
Step IV(d):	Complete Pro Forma Cash Flow Statement

Step IV(a): Build Debt Schedule

The debt schedule is an integral component of the LBO model, serving to layer in the pro forma effects of the LBO financing structure on the target's financial statements.[15] Specifically, the debt schedule enables the banker to:

- complete the pro forma income statement from EBIT to net income

- complete the pro forma long-term liabilities and shareholders' equity sections of the balance sheet

- complete the pro forma financing activities section of the cash flow statement

As shown in Exhibit 5.27, the debt schedule applies free cash flow to make mandatory and optional debt repayments, thereby calculating the annual beginning and ending balances for each debt tranche. The debt repayment amounts are linked to the financing activities section of the cash flow statement and the ending debt balances are linked to the balance sheet. The debt schedule is also used to calculate the annual interest expense for the individual debt instruments, which is linked to the income statement.

The debt schedule is typically constructed in accordance with the security and seniority of the loans, securities, and other debt instruments in the capital structure (i.e., beginning with the revolver, followed by term loan tranches, and bonds). As detailed in the following pages, we began the construction of ValueCo's debt schedule by entering the *forward LIBOR curve*, followed by the calculation of annual projected cash available for debt repayment (free cash flow). We then entered the key terms for each individual debt instrument in the financing structure (i.e., size, term, coupon, and mandatory repayments/amortization schedule, if any).

Forward LIBOR Curve   For floating-rate debt instruments, such as revolving credit facilities and term loans, interest rates are typically based on LIBOR[16] plus a fixed spread. Therefore, to calculate their projected annual interest expense, the banker

---

[15]In lieu of a debt schedule, some LBO model templates use formulas in the appropriate cells in the financing activities section of the cash flow statement and the interest expense line item(s) of the income statement to perform the same functions.

[16]3-month LIBOR is generally used.

must first enter future LIBOR estimates for each year of the projection period. LIBOR for future years is typically sourced from the Forward LIBOR Curve provided by Bloomberg.[17]

EXHIBIT 5.24   Forward LIBOR Curve

($ in millions, fiscal year ending December 31)

Debt Schedule											
						Projection Period					
	Pro forma 2008	Year 1 2009	Year 2 2010	Year 3 2011	Year 4 2012	Year 5 2013	Year 6 2014	Year 7 2015	Year 8 2016	Year 9 2017	Year 10 2018
Forward LIBOR Curve	3.00%	3.00%	3.15%	3.30%	3.60%	4.00%	4.35%	4.80%	4.85%	5.10%	5.25%

As shown in the forward LIBOR curve line item in Exhibit 5.24, LIBOR is expected to increase incrementally throughout the projection period from 300 bps in 2009E to 525 bps by 2018E.[18] The pricing spreads for the revolver and TLB are added to the forward LIBOR in each year of the projection period to calculate their annual interest rates. For example, the 2009E interest rate for ValueCo's revolver, which is priced at L+325 bps, is 6.25% (300 bps LIBOR + 325 bps spread, see Exhibit 5.26).

Cash Available for Debt Repayment (Free Cash Flow)   The annual projected cash available for debt repayment is the sum of the cash flows provided by operating and investing activities on the cash flow statement. It is calculated in a section beneath the forward LIBOR curve inputs. For each year in the projection period, this amount is first used to make mandatory debt repayments on the term loan tranches.[19] The remaining cash flow is used to make optional debt repayments, as calculated in the cash available for optional debt repayment line item (see Exhibit 5.25).

In addition to internally generated free cash flow, existing cash from the balance sheet may be used ("swept") to make incremental debt repayments (see cash from balance sheet line item in Exhibit 5.25). In ValueCo's case, however, there is no cash on the pro forma balance sheet at closing as it is used as part of the transaction funding. In the event the post-LBO balance sheet has a cash balance, the banker may choose to keep a constant minimum level of cash on the balance sheet throughout the projection period by inputting a dollar amount under the "MinCash" heading (see Exhibit 5.25).

As shown in Exhibit 5.25, pro forma for the LBO, ValueCo generates $65.3 million of cash flow from operating activities in 2009E. Netting out ($21.6) million of cash flow from investing activities results in cash available for debt repayment of $43.7 million. After satisfying the $4.5 million mandatory amortization of the TLB, ValueCo has $39.2 million of cash available for optional debt repayment.

---

[17]Bloomberg function: "FWCV," select "US" (if pricing is based on U.S. LIBOR).

[18]Following the onset of the subprime mortgage crisis and the ensuing credit crunch, and the resulting rate cuts by the Federal Reserve, investors have insisted on "LIBOR floors" in many new bank deals. A LIBOR floor guarantees a minimum coupon for investors regardless of how low LIBOR falls. For example, a term loan priced at L+350 bps with a LIBOR floor of 325 bps will have a cost of capital of 6.75% even if the prevailing LIBOR is lower than 325 bps.

[19]Mandatory repayments are determined in accordance with each debt instrument's amortization schedule.

EXHIBIT 5.25 Cash Available for Debt Repayment (Free Cash Flow)

($ in millions, fiscal year ending December 31)

Debt Schedule

						Projection Period					
	Pro forma 2008	Year 1 2009	Year 2 2010	Year 3 2011	Year 4 2012	Year 5 2013	Year 6 2014	Year 7 2015	Year 8 2016	Year 9 2017	Year 10 2018
Forward LIBOR Curve	3.00%	3.00%	3.15%	3.30%	3.60%	4.00%	4.35%	4.80%	4.85%	5.10%	5.25%
Cash Flow from Operating Activities		$65.3	$74.9	$83.4	$90.2	$96.3	$103.2	$110.7	$117.1	$122.9	$128.8
Cash Flow from Investing Activities		(21.6)	(22.9)	(23.8)	(24.5)	(25.3)	(26.0)	(26.8)	(27.6)	(28.4)	(29.3)
Cash Available for Debt Repayment		**$43.7**	**$52.0**	**$59.6**	**$65.7**	**$71.1**	**$77.2**	**$83.9**	**$89.5**	**$94.4**	**$99.6**
Total Mandatory Repayments		(4.5)	(4.5)	(4.5)	(4.5)	(4.5)	(4.5)	(4.5)	-	-	-
Cash From Balance Sheet		-	-	-	-	-	-	-	3.2	92.7	187.2
Cash Available for Optional Debt Repayment		**$39.2**	**$47.5**	**$55.1**	**$61.2**	**$66.6**	**$72.7**	**$79.4**	**$92.7**	**$187.2**	**$286.7**

MinCash

= Cash Flow from Operating Activities $_{2009}$ +
  Cash Flow from Financing Activities $_{2009}$
= $65.3 million + ($21.6) million

= Mandatory Repayments on the Term Loan B,
  calculated as 1% x $450.0 million

= IF (Cash Balance toggle = 1, then sweep cash from the Balance Sheet
  less the Minimum Cash Balance, otherwise display 0)

= Cash Flow for Debt Repayment $_{2012}$ -
  Term Loan B Mandatory Repayment $_{2012}$
= $65.7 million + ($4.5) million

217

Revolving Credit Facility In the "Revolving Credit Facility" section of the debt schedule, the banker inputs the spread, term, and commitment fee associated with the facility (see Exhibit 5.26). The facility's size is linked from an assumptions page where the financing structure is entered (see Exhibits 5.14 and 5.54) and the beginning balance line item for the first year of the projection period is linked from the balance sheet. If no revolver draw is contemplated as part of the LBO financing structure, then the beginning balance is zero.

The revolver's drawdown/(repayment) line item feeds from the cash available for optional debt repayment line item at the top of the debt schedule. In the event the cash available for optional debt repayment amount is negative in any year (e.g., in a downside case), a revolver draw (or use of cash on the balance sheet, if applicable) is required. In the following period, the outstanding revolver debt is then repaid first from any positive cash available for optional debt repayment (i.e., once mandatory repayments are satisfied).

In connection with the ValueCo LBO, we contemplated a $100 million revolver, which is priced at L+325 bps with a term of six years. The revolver is assumed to be undrawn at the close of the transaction and remains undrawn throughout the projection period. Therefore, no interest expense is incurred. ValueCo, however, must pay an annual commitment fee of 50 bps on the undrawn portion of the revolver, translating into an expense of $500,000 ($100 million × 0.50%) per year (see Exhibit 5.26).[20] This amount is included in interest expense on the income statement.

Term Loan Facility In the "Term Loan Facility" section of the debt schedule, the banker inputs the spread, term, and mandatory repayment schedule associated with the facility (see Exhibit 5.27). The facility's size is linked from the sources and uses of funds on the transaction summary page (see Exhibit 5.46). For the ValueCo LBO, we contemplated a $450 million TLB with a coupon of L+350 bps and a term of seven years.

Mandatory Repayments (Amortization) Unlike a revolving credit facility, which only requires repayment at the maturity date of all the outstanding advances, a term loan facility is fully funded at close and has a set amortization schedule as defined in the corresponding credit agreement. While amortization schedules vary per term loan tranche, the standard for TLBs is 1% amortization per year on the principal amount of the loan with a bullet payment of the loan balance at maturity.[21]

As noted in Exhibit 5.27 under the repayment schedule line item, ValueCo's new TLB requires an annual 1% amortization payment equating to $4.5 million ($450 million x 1%).

Optional Repayments A typical LBO model employs a "100% cash flow sweep" that assumes all cash generated by the target after making mandatory debt repayments is applied to the optional repayment of outstanding prepayable debt (typically

---

[20]To the extent the revolver is used, the commitment expense will decline and ValueCo will be charged interest on the amount of the revolver draw at L+325 bps.

[21]Credit agreements typically also have a provision requiring the borrower to prepay term loans in an amount equal to a specified percentage (and definition) of excess cash flow and in the event of specified asset sales and issuances of certain debt or equity.

EXHIBIT 5.26 Revolving Credit Facility Section of Debt Schedule

($ in millions, fiscal year ending December 31)

Debt Schedule

	Pro forma 2008	Projection Period									
		Year 1 2009	Year 2 2010	Year 3 2011	Year 4 2012	Year 5 2013	Year 6 2014	Year 7 2015	Year 8 2016	Year 9 2017	Year 10 2018
Forward LIBOR Curve	3.00%	3.00%	3.15%	3.30%	3.60%	4.00%	4.35%	4.80%	4.85%	5.10%	5.25%
Cash Flow from Operating Activities		$65.3	$74.9	$83.4	$90.2	$96.3	$103.2	$110.7	$117.1	$122.9	$128.8
Cash Flow from Investing Activities		(21.6)	(22.9)	(23.8)	(24.5)	(25.3)	(26.0)	(26.8)	(27.6)	(28.4)	(29.3)
Cash Available for Debt Repayment		**$43.7**	**$52.0**	**$59.6**	**$65.7**	**$71.1**	**$77.2**	**$83.9**	**$89.5**	**$94.4**	**$99.6**
Total Mandatory Repayments		(4.5)	(4.5)	(4.5)	(4.5)	(4.5)	(4.5)	(4.5)			
Cash from Balance Sheet		-	-	-	-	-	-	-	3.2	92.7	187.2
Cash Available for Optional Debt Repayment		**$39.2**	**$47.5**	**$55.1**	**$61.2**	**$66.6**	**$72.7**	**$79.4**	**$92.7**	**$187.2**	**$286.7**

MinCash

Revolving Credit Facility

Revolving Credit Facility Size	$100.0
Spread	3.250%
Term	6 years
Commitment Fee on Unused Portion	0.50%

		Year 1 2009	Year 2 2010	Year 3 2011	Year 4 2012	Year 5 2013	Year 6 2014	Year 7 2015	Year 8 2016	Year 9 2017	Year 10 2018
Beginning Balance											
Drawdown / (Repayment)											
Ending Balance											
Interest Rate		6.25%	6.40%	6.55%	6.85%	7.25%	7.60%	8.05%	8.10%	8.35%	8.50%
Interest Expense											
Commitment Fee		0.5	0.5	0.5	0.5	0.5	0.5	0.5	0.5	0.5	0.5

= Ending Revolver Balance from Pro Forma 2008 Balance Sheet

= Ending Balance from prior year

= LIBOR$_{2009}$ + Spread on Revolver
= 3.00% + 3.25%

= Commitment Fee on Unused Portion x (Revolver Capacity - (Average of Beginning Balance$_{2016}$ and Ending Balance$_{2017}$))
= 0.50% x $100.0 million

= IF (Cash Available for Optional Debt Repayment$_{2018}$ > 0, then sweep the negative value of the minimum of (Cash Available for Optional Debt Repayment$_{2018}$ vs. the Beginning Balance$_{2017}$), otherwise sweep the negative value of the minimum of (Cash Available for Optional Debt Repayment$_{2018}$, $0.0))

= IF (Cash Available for Optional Debt Repayment$_{2018}$ > 0, -MIN(Cash Available for Optional Debt Repayment$_{2018}$, $0.0), -MIN(Cash Available for Optional Debt Repayment$_{2018}$, 0))

EXHIBIT 5.27 Term Loan Facility Section of Debt Schedule

($ in millions, fiscal year ending December 31)

Debt Schedule

	Pro forma 2008		Projection Period								
		Year 1 2009	Year 2 2010	Year 3 2011	Year 4 2012	Year 5 2013	Year 6 2014	Year 7 2015	Year 8 2016	Year 9 2017	Year 10 2018
Forward LIBOR Curve	3.00%	3.00%	3.15%	3.30%	3.60%	4.00%	4.35%	4.80%	4.85%	5.10%	5.25%
Cash Flow from Operating Activities		$65.3	$74.9	$83.4	$90.2	$96.3	$103.2	$110.7	$117.1	$122.9	$128.8
Cash Flow from Investing Activities		(21.6)	(22.9)	(23.8)	(24.5)	(25.3)	(26.0)	(26.8)	(27.6)	(28.4)	(29.3)
Cash Available for Debt Repayment		**$43.7**	**$52.0**	**$59.6**	**$65.7**	**$71.1**	**$77.2**	**$83.9**	**$89.5**	**$94.4**	**$99.6**
Total Mandatory Repayments		(4.5)	(4.5)	(4.5)	(4.5)	(4.5)	(4.5)	(4.5)	-	-	-
Cash from Balance Sheet		-	-	-	-	-	-	3.2	92.7	187.2	
Cash Available for Optional Debt Repayment		**$39.2**	**$47.5**	**$55.1**	**$61.2**	**$66.6**	**$72.7**	**$79.4**	**$92.7**	**$187.2**	**$286.7**

MinCash   -

Term Loan B Facility

Size	$450.0										
Spread	3.500%										
Term	7 years										
Repayment Schedule	1.0% per Annum, Bullet at Maturity										
Beginning Balance		$450.0	$406.3	$354.2	$294.6	$228.9	$157.9	$80.7			
Mandatory Repayments		(4.5)	(4.5)	(4.5)	(4.5)	(4.5)	(4.5)	(4.5)			
Optional Repayments		(39.2)	(47.5)	(55.1)	(61.2)	(66.6)	(72.7)	(76.2)			
Ending Balance		**$406.3**	**$354.2**	**$294.6**	**$228.9**	**$157.9**	**$80.7**				
Interest Rate		6.50%	6.65%	6.80%	7.10%	7.50%	7.85%	8.30%	8.35%	8.60%	8.75%
Interest Expense		27.8	25.3	22.1	18.6	14.5	9.4	3.3			

= Ending Term Loan B Balance from Pro Forma 2008 Balance Sheet

= Interest Rate $_{2008}$ x Average(Beginning Balance $_{2009}$: Ending Balance $_{2009}$)
= 6.50% x Average of $450.0 million and $406.3 million

= The negative of the minimum of ((Cash Flow Available for Optional Debt Repayment $_{2011}$
   vs. Beginning Balance $_{2011}$ + Mandatory Amortization $_{2011}$)
= -MIN($55.1 : $354.2 million + ($4.5) million)

= IF (Beginning Balance $_{2014}$ is greater than 0 and greater than 1% of the principal amount,
   then subtract 1% Mandatory Amortization on the principal amount of the Term Loan B, otherwise display $0.0)
= IF ($157.9 million > 0 and > 1% x $450.0, then 1% x $450.0 million, otherwise display $0.0)

bank debt). For modeling purposes, bank debt is generally repaid in the following order: revolver balance, term loan A, term loan B, etc.[22]

From a credit risk management perspective, ideally the target generates sufficient cumulative free cash flow during the projection period to repay the term loan(s) within their defined maturities. In some cases, however, the borrower may not be expected to repay the entire term loan balance within the proposed tenor and will instead face refinancing risk as the debt matures.

As shown in Exhibit 5.27, in 2009E, ValueCo is projected to generate cash available for debt repayment of $43.7 million. Following the mandatory TLB principal repayment of $4.5 million, ValueCo has $39.2 million of excess free cash flow remaining. These funds are used to make optional debt repayments on the TLB, which is prepayable without penalty. Hence, the beginning year balance of $450 million is reduced to an ending balance of $406.3 million following the combined mandatory and optional debt repayments.

Interest Expense The banker typically employs an average interest expense approach in determining annual interest expense in an LBO model. This methodology accounts for the fact that bank debt is repaid throughout the year rather than at the beginning or end of the year. Annual average interest expense for each debt tranche is calculated by multiplying the average of the beginning and ending debt balances in a given year by its corresponding interest rate.

As shown in Exhibit 5.27, in 2009E, ValueCo's TLB has a beginning balance of $450 million and ending balance of $406.3 million. Using the average debt approach, this implies interest expense of $27.8 million for the TLB in 2009E (($450 million + $406.3 million)/2) x 6.5%). The $27.8 million of interest expense is linked from the debt schedule to the income statement under the corresponding line item for TLB interest expense.

Senior Subordinated Notes In the "Senior Subordinated Notes" section of the debt schedule, the banker inputs the coupon and term associated with the security (see Exhibit 5.28). As with the TLB, the principal amount of the notes is linked from the

EXHIBIT 5.28 Senior Subordinated Notes Section of Debt Schedule

($ in millions, fiscal year ending December 31)

Debt Schedule											
						Projection Period					
	Pro forma 2008	Year 1 2009	Year 2 2010	Year 3 2011	Year 4 2012	Year 5 2013	Year 6 2014	Year 7 2015	Year 8 2016	Year 9 2017	Year 10 2018
Senior Subordinated Notes											
Size	$300.0										
Coupon	10.000%										
Term	10 years										
Beginning Balance		$300.0	$300.0	$300.0	$300.0	$300.0	$300.0	$300.0	$300.0	$300.0	$300.0
Repayment		-	-	-	-	-	-	-	-	-	-
Ending Balance		$300.0	$300.0	$300.0	$300.0	$300.0	$300.0	$300.0	$300.0	$300.0	$300.0
Interest Expense		30.0	30.0	30.0	30.0	30.0	30.0	30.0	30.0	30.0	30.0

= Coupon on Senior Subordinated Notes x Principal Amount
= 10.0% x $300.0

---

[22]Some credit agreements give credit to the borrower for voluntary repayments on a go-forward basis and/or may require pro rata repayment of certain tranches.

sources and uses of funds on the transaction summary page (see Exhibit 5.46). Unlike traditional bank debt, high yield bonds are not prepayable without penalty and do not have a mandatory repayment schedule prior to the bullet payment at maturity. As a result, the model does not assume repayment of the high yield bonds prior to maturity and the beginning and ending balances for each year in the projection period are equal.

For the ValueCo LBO, we contemplated a senior subordinated notes issuance of $300 million with a 10% coupon and a maturity of ten years. The notes are the longest-tenored debt instrument in the financing structure. As the notes do not amortize and there is no optional repayment due to the call protection period (standard in high yield bonds), annual interest expense is simply $30 million ($300 million x 10%).

The completed debt schedule is shown in Exhibit 5.29.

Step IV(b): Complete Pro Forma Income Statement from EBIT to Net Income

The calculated average annual interest expense for each loan, bond, or other debt instrument in the capital structure is linked from the completed debt schedule to its corresponding line item on the income statement (see Exhibit 5.30).[23]

Cash Interest Expense   Cash interest expense refers to a company's actual cash interest and associated financing-related payments in a given year. It is the sum of the average interest expense for each cash-pay debt instrument plus the commitment fee on the unused portion of the revolver and the administrative agent fee.

As shown in Exhibit 5.30, ValueCo is projected to have $58.5 million of cash interest expense in 2009E. This amount decreases to $30.7 million by the end of the projection period after the bank debt is repaid.

Total Interest Expense   Total interest expense is the sum of cash and non-cash interest expense, most notably the amortization of deferred financing fees, which is linked from an assumptions page (see Exhibit 5.54). The amortization of deferred financing fees, while technically not interest expense, is included in total interest expense as it is a financial charge. In a capital structure with a PIK instrument, the non-cash interest portion would also be included in total interest expense and added back to cash flow from operating activities on the cash flow statement.

As shown in Exhibit 5.30, ValueCo has non-cash deferred financing fees of $2.5 million in 2009E. These fees are added to the 2009E cash interest expense of $58.5 million to sum to $60.9 million of total interest expense.

---

[23] At this point, a circular reference centering on interest expense has been created in the model. Interest expense is used to calculate net income and determine cash available for debt repayment and ending debt balances, which, in turn, are used to calculate interest expense. The spreadsheet must be set up to perform the circular calculation (in Microsoft Excel) by selecting Tools, Options, clicking on the "Calculation" tab, checking the box next to "Iteration," and setting the "Maximum iterations" field to 1000 (see Exhibit 3.30).

EXHIBIT 5.29 Debt Schedule

($ in millions, fiscal year ending December 31)

Debt Schedule

	Pro forma 2008	Projection Period									
		Year 1 2009	Year 2 2010	Year 3 2011	Year 4 2012	Year 5 2013	Year 6 2014	Year 7 2015	Year 8 2016	Year 9 2017	Year 10 2018
Forward LIBOR Curve	3.00%	3.00%	3.15%	3.30%	3.60%	4.00%	4.35%	4.80%	4.85%	5.10%	5.25%
Cash Flow from Operating Activities		$65.3	$74.9	$83.4	$90.2	$96.3	$103.2	$110.7	$117.1	$122.9	$128.8
Cash Flow from Investing Activities		(21.6)	(22.9)	(23.8)	(24.5)	(25.3)	(26.0)	(26.8)	(27.6)	(28.4)	(29.3)
Cash Available for Debt Repayment		**$43.7**	**$52.0**	**$59.6**	**$65.7**	**$71.1**	**$77.2**	**$83.9**	**$89.5**	**$94.4**	**$99.6**
Total Mandatory Repayments		(4.5)	(4.5)	(4.5)	(4.5)	(4.5)	(4.5)	(4.5)	-	-	-
Cash from Balance Sheet		-	-	-	-	-	-	-	3.2	92.7	187.2
Cash Available for Optional Debt Repayment		**$39.2**	**$47.5**	**$55.1**	**$61.2**	**$66.6**	**$72.7**	**$79.4**	**$92.7**	**$187.2**	**$286.7**

MinCash -

Revolving Credit Facility

Revolving Credit Facility Size: $100.0
Spread: 3.250%
Term: 6 years
Commitment Fee on Unused Portion: 0.50%

	Pro forma 2008	Year 1 2009	Year 2 2010	Year 3 2011	Year 4 2012	Year 5 2013	Year 6 2014	Year 7 2015	Year 8 2016	Year 9 2017	Year 10 2018
Beginning Balance		-	-	-	-	-	-	-	-	-	-
Drawdown / (Repayment)		-	-	-	-	-	-	-	-	-	-
Ending Balance		-	-	-	-	-	-	-	-	-	-
Interest Rate		6.25%	6.40%	6.55%	6.85%	7.25%	7.60%	8.05%	8.10%	8.35%	8.50%
Interest Expense		-	-	-	-	-	-	-	-	-	-
Commitment Fee		0.5	0.5	0.5	0.5	0.5	0.5	0.5	0.5	0.5	0.5

Term Loan B Facility

Size: $450.0
Spread: 3.500%
Term: 7 years
Repayment Schedule: 1.0% per Annum, Bullet at Maturity

	Pro forma 2008	Year 1 2009	Year 2 2010	Year 3 2011	Year 4 2012	Year 5 2013	Year 6 2014	Year 7 2015	Year 8 2016	Year 9 2017	Year 10 2018
Beginning Balance		$450.0	$406.3	$354.2	$294.6	$228.9	$157.9	$80.7	-	-	-
Mandatory Repayments		(4.5)	(4.5)	(4.5)	(4.5)	(4.5)	(4.5)	(4.5)	-	-	-
Optional Repayments		(39.2)	(47.5)	(55.1)	(61.2)	(66.6)	(72.7)	(76.2)	-	-	-
Ending Balance		**$406.3**	**$354.2**	**$294.6**	**$228.9**	**$157.9**	**$80.7**	**-**	-	-	-
Interest Rate		6.50%	6.65%	6.80%	7.10%	7.50%	7.85%	8.30%	8.35%	8.60%	8.75%
Interest Expense		27.8	25.3	22.1	18.6	14.5	9.4	3.3	-	-	-

Senior Subordinated Notes

Size: $300.0
Coupon: 10.000%
Term: 10 years

	Pro forma 2008	Year 1 2009	Year 2 2010	Year 3 2011	Year 4 2012	Year 5 2013	Year 6 2014	Year 7 2015	Year 8 2016	Year 9 2017	Year 10 2018
Beginning Balance		$300.0	$300.0	$300.0	$300.0	$300.0	$300.0	$300.0	$300.0	$300.0	$300.0
Repayment		-	-	-	-	-	-	-	-	-	-
Ending Balance		**$300.0**	**$300.0**	**$300.0**	**$300.0**	**$300.0**	**$300.0**	**$300.0**	**$300.0**	**$300.0**	**$300.0**
Interest Expense		30.0	30.0	30.0	30.0	30.0	30.0	30.0	30.0	30.0	30.0

EXHIBIT 5.30   Pro Forma Projected Income Statement – EBIT to Net Income

($ in millions, fiscal year ending December 31)

Income Statement

						Projection Period						
	Pro forma 2008	Year 1 2009	Year 2 2010	Year 3 2011	Year 4 2012	Year 5 2013	Year 6 2014	Year 7 2015	Year 8 2016	Year 9 2017	Year 10 2018
EBIT	$130.0	$140.4	$148.8	$154.8	$159.4	$164.2	$169.1	$174.2	$179.4	$184.8	$190.4
% margin	*13.0%*	*13.0%*	*13.0%*	*13.0%*	*13.0%*	*13.0%*	*13.0%*	*13.0%*	*13.0%*	*13.0%*	*13.0%*
Interest Expense											
Revolving Credit Facility	-	-	-	-	-	-	-	-	-	-	-
Term Loan B	29.3	27.8	25.3	22.1	18.6	14.5	9.4	3.3	-	-	-
Senior Subordinated Notes	30.0	30.0	30.0	30.0	30.0	30.0	30.0	30.0	30.0	30.0	30.0
Commitment Fee on Unused Revolver	0.5	0.5	0.5	0.5	0.5	0.5	0.5	0.5	0.5	0.5	0.5
Administrative Agent Fee	0.2	0.2	0.2	0.2	0.2	0.2	0.2	0.2	0.2	0.2	0.2
Cash Interest Expense	$59.9	$58.5	$55.9	$52.7	$49.2	$45.2	$40.0	$34.0	$30.7	$30.7	$30.7
Amortization of Deferred Financing Fees	2.5	2.5	2.5	2.5	2.5	2.5	2.5	2.2	1.0	1.0	1.0
Total Interest Expense	$62.4	$60.9	$58.4	$55.2	$51.7	$47.6	$42.5	$36.2	$31.7	$31.7	$31.7
Interest Income		-	-	-	-	-	-	(0.0)	(1.4)	(4.2)	(7.1)
Net Interest Expense		$60.9	$58.4	$55.2	$51.7	$47.6	$42.5	$36.1	$30.2	$27.5	$24.6
Earnings Before Taxes		79.5	90.4	99.6	107.7	116.6	126.7	138.1	149.2	157.3	165.8
Income Tax Expense		30.2	34.4	37.9	40.9	44.3	48.1	52.5	56.7	59.8	63.0
Net Income		$49.3	$56.1	$61.8	$66.8	$72.3	$78.5	$85.6	$92.5	$97.5	$102.8
% margin		*4.6%*	*4.9%*	*5.2%*	*5.4%*	*5.7%*	*6.0%*	*6.4%*	*6.7%*	*6.9%*	*7.0%*

Net Interest Expense   Net interest expense is calculated by subtracting interest income received on cash held on a company's balance sheet from its total interest expense. In the ValueCo LBO, however, until 2015E (Year 7), when all prepayable debt is repaid and cash begins to build on the balance sheet, there is no interest income as the cash balance is zero. In 2016E, ValueCo is expected to earn interest income of $1.4 million,[24] which is netted against total interest expense of $31.7 million to produce net interest expense of $30.2 million.

Net Income   To calculate ValueCo's net income for 2009E, we subtracted net interest expense of $60.9 million from EBIT of $140.4 million, which resulted in earnings before taxes of $79.5 million. We then multiplied EBT by ValueCo's marginal tax rate of 38% to produce tax expense of $30.2 million, which was netted out of EBT to calculate net income of $49.3 million.

Net income for each year in the projection period is linked from the income statement to the cash flow statement as the first line item under operating activities. It also feeds into the balance sheet as an addition to shareholders' equity in the form of retained earnings.

The completed pro forma income statement is shown in Exhibit 5.31.

Step IV(c): Complete Pro Forma Balance Sheet

Liabilities   The balance sheet is completed by linking the year-end balances for each debt instrument directly from the debt schedule. The remaining non-current and non-debt liabilities, captured in the other long-term liabilities line item, are generally held constant at the prior year level in the absence of specific management guidance.

---

[24] Assumes a 3% interest rate earned on cash (using an average balance method), which is indicative of a short-term money market instrument.

EXHIBIT 5.31 Pro Forma ValueCo Income Statement

($ in millions, fiscal year ending December 31)

Income Statement

	Historical Period				Pro forma 2008	Projection Period									
	2005	2006	2007	LTM 9/30/2008		Year 1 2009	Year 2 2010	Year 3 2011	Year 4 2012	Year 5 2013	Year 6 2014	Year 7 2015	Year 8 2016	Year 9 2017	Year 10 2018
Sales	$780.0	$850.0	$925.0	$977.8	$1,000.0	$1,080.0	$1,144.8	$1,190.6	$1,226.3	$1,263.1	$1,301.0	$1,340.0	$1,380.2	$1,421.6	$1,464.3
% growth	*NA*	*9.0%*	*8.8%*	*NA*	*8.1%*	*8.0%*	*6.0%*	*4.0%*	*3.0%*	*3.0%*	*3.0%*	*3.0%*	*3.0%*	*3.0%*	*3.0%*
Cost of Goods Sold	471.9	512.1	555.0	586.7	600.0	648.0	686.9	714.4	735.8	757.9	780.6	804.0	828.1	853.0	878.6
Gross Profit	$308.1	$337.9	$370.0	$391.1	$400.0	$432.0	$457.9	$476.2	$490.5	$505.2	$520.4	$536.0	$552.1	$568.7	$585.7
% margin	*39.5%*	*39.8%*	*40.0%*	*40.0%*	*40.0%*	*40.0%*	*40.0%*	*40.0%*	*40.0%*	*40.0%*	*40.0%*	*40.0%*	*40.0%*	*40.0%*	*40.0%*
Selling, General & Administrative	198.9	214.6	231.3	244.4	250.0	270.0	286.2	297.6	306.6	315.8	325.2	335.0	345.1	355.4	366.1
% sales	*25.5%*	*25.3%*	*25.0%*	*25.0%*	*25.0%*	*25.0%*	*25.0%*	*25.0%*	*25.0%*	*25.0%*	*25.0%*	*25.0%*	*25.0%*	*25.0%*	*25.0%*
Other Expense / (Income)															
EBITDA	$109.2	$123.3	$138.8	$146.7	$150.0	$162.0	$171.7	$178.6	$183.9	$189.5	$195.1	$201.0	$207.0	$213.2	$219.6
% margin	*14.0%*	*14.5%*	*15.0%*	*15.0%*	*15.0%*	*15.0%*	*15.0%*	*15.0%*	*15.0%*	*15.0%*	*15.0%*	*15.0%*	*15.0%*	*15.0%*	*15.0%*
Depreciation & Amortization	15.6	17.0	18.5	19.6	20.0	21.6	22.9	23.8	24.5	25.3	26.0	26.8	27.6	28.4	29.3
EBIT	$93.6	$106.3	$120.3	$127.1	$130.0	$140.4	$148.8	$154.8	$159.4	$164.2	$169.1	$174.2	$179.4	$184.8	$190.4
% margin	*12.0%*	*12.5%*	*13.0%*	*13.0%*	*13.0%*	*13.0%*	*13.0%*	*13.0%*	*13.0%*	*13.0%*	*13.0%*	*13.0%*	*13.0%*	*13.0%*	*13.0%*
Interest Expense															
Revolving Credit Facility					29.3	27.8	25.3	22.1	18.6	14.5	9.4	3.3	-	-	-
Term Loan B					30.0	30.0	30.0	30.0	30.0	30.0	30.0	30.0	30.0	30.0	30.0
Senior Subordinated Notes					0.5	0.5	0.5	0.5	0.5	0.5	0.5	0.5	0.5	0.5	0.5
Commitment Fee on Unused Revolver					0.2	0.2	0.2	0.2	0.2	0.2	0.2	0.2	0.2	0.2	0.2
Administrative Agent Fee															
Cash Interest Expense					$59.9	$58.5	$55.9	$52.7	$49.2	$45.2	$40.0	$34.0	$30.7	$30.7	$30.7
Amortization of Deferred Financing Fees					2.5	2.5	2.5	2.5	2.5	2.5	2.5	2.2	1.0	1.0	1.0
Total Interest Expense					$62.4	$60.9	$58.4	$55.2	$51.7	$47.6	$42.5	$36.2	$31.7	$31.7	$31.7
Interest Income												(0.0)	(1.4)	(4.2)	(7.1)
Net Interest Expense						$60.9	$58.4	$55.2	$51.7	$47.6	$42.5	$36.1	$30.2	$27.5	$24.6
Earnings Before Taxes						79.5	90.4	99.6	107.7	116.6	126.7	138.1	149.2	157.3	165.8
Income Tax Expense						30.2	34.4	37.9	40.9	44.3	48.1	52.5	56.7	59.8	63.0
Net Income						$49.3	$56.1	$61.8	$66.8	$72.3	$78.5	$85.6	$92.5	$97.5	$102.8
% margin						*4.6%*	*4.9%*	*5.2%*	*5.4%*	*5.7%*	*6.0%*	*6.4%*	*6.7%*	*6.9%*	*7.0%*

Income Statement Assumptions

	2005	2006	2007	LTM	Pro forma 2008	Year 1	Year 2	Year 3	Year 4	Year 5	Year 6	Year 7	Year 8	Year 9	Year 10
Sales (% YoY growth)	NA	9.0%	8.8%	NA	8.1%	8.0%	6.0%	4.0%	3.0%	3.0%	3.0%	3.0%	3.0%	3.0%	3.0%
COGS (% margin)	60.5%	60.3%	60.0%	60.0%	60.0%	60.0%	60.0%	60.0%	60.0%	60.0%	60.0%	60.0%	60.0%	60.0%	60.0%
SG&A (% sales)	25.5%	25.3%	25.0%	25.0%	25.0%	25.0%	25.0%	25.0%	25.0%	25.0%	25.0%	25.0%	25.0%	25.0%	25.0%
Other Expense / (Income) (% of sales)	- %	- %	- %	- %	- %	- %	- %	- %	- %	- %	- %	- %	- %	- %	- %
Depreciation & Amortization (% of sales)	2.0%	2.0%	2.0%	2.0%	2.0%	2.0%	2.0%	2.0%	2.0%	2.0%	2.0%	2.0%	2.0%	2.0%	2.0%
Interest Income					3.0%	3.0%	3.0%	3.0%	3.0%	3.0%	3.0%	3.0%	3.0%	3.0%	3.0%
Tax Rate					38.0%	38.0%	38.0%	38.0%	38.0%	38.0%	38.0%	38.0%	38.0%	38.0%	38.0%

As shown in Exhibit 5.32, during the projection period, ValueCo's $450 million TLB is completely repaid by 2015E. ValueCo's $300 million notes, on the other hand, remain outstanding. In addition, we held the 2008E other long-term liabilities amount constant at $25 million for the length of the projection period.

EXHIBIT 5.32   Pro Forma Total Liabilities Section of Balance Sheet

($ in millions, fiscal year ending December 31)

Balance Sheet

	Opening 2008	Adjustments +	Adjustments -	Pro Forma 2008	Year 1 2009	Year 2 2010	Year 3 2011	Year 4 2012	Year 5 2013	Year 6 2014	Year 7 2015	Year 8 2016	Year 9 2017	Year 10 2018
									Projection Period					
Accounts Payable	75.0			75.0	81.0	85.9	89.3	92.0	94.7	97.6	100.5	103.5	106.6	109.8
Accrued Liabilities	100.0			100.0	108.0	114.5	119.1	122.6	126.3	130.1	134.0	138.0	142.2	146.4
Other Current Liabilities	25.0			25.0	27.0	28.6	29.8	30.7	31.6	32.5	33.5	34.5	35.5	36.6
Total Current Liabilities	**$200.0**			**$200.0**	**$216.0**	**$229.0**	**$238.1**	**$245.3**	**$252.6**	**$260.2**	**$268.0**	**$276.0**	**$284.3**	**$292.9**
Revolving Credit Facility	-			-	-	-	-	-	-	-	-	-	-	-
Term Loan B	-	450.0		450.0	406.3	354.2	294.6	228.9	157.9	80.7	-	-	-	-
Existing Term Loan	300.0		(300.0)	-	-	-	-	-	-	-	-	-	-	-
Senior Subordinated Notes	-	300.0		300.0	300.0	300.0	300.0	300.0	300.0	300.0	300.0	300.0	300.0	300.0
Other Long-Term Liabilities	25.0			25.0	25.0	25.0	25.0	25.0	25.0	25.0	25.0	25.0	25.0	25.0
Total Liabilities	**$525.0**			**$975.0**	**$947.3**	**$908.2**	**$857.7**	**$799.2**	**$735.5**	**$665.9**	**$593.0**	**$601.0**	**$609.3**	**$617.9**

Shareholders' Equity   Pro forma net income, which has now been calculated for each year in the projection period, is added to the prior year's shareholders' equity as retained earnings.

As shown in Exhibit 5.33, at the end of 2008E pro forma for the LBO, ValueCo has $370 million of shareholders' initial equity (representing the sponsor's equity contribution less other fees and expenses). To calculate 2009E shareholders' equity, we added the 2009E net income of $49.3 million, which summed to $419.3 million.

EXHIBIT 5.33   Pro Forma Total Shareholders' Equity Section of Balance Sheet

($ in millions, fiscal year ending December 31)

Balance Sheet

	Opening 2008	Adjustments +	Adjustments -	Pro Forma 2008	Year 1 2009	Year 2 2010	Year 3 2011	Year 4 2012	Year 5 2013	Year 6 2014	Year 7 2015	Year 8 2016	Year 9 2017	Year 10 2018
									Projection Period					
Shareholders' Equity	700.0	370.0	(700.0)	370.0	419.3	475.3	537.1	603.9	676.2	754.7	840.3	932.8	1,030.4	1,133.1
Total Shareholders' Equity	**$700.0**			**$370.0**	**$419.3**	**$475.3**	**$537.1**	**$603.9**	**$676.2**	**$754.7**	**$840.3**	**$932.8**	**$1,030.4**	**$1,133.1**
Total Liabilities and Equity	**$1,225.0**			**$1,345.0**	**$1,366.5**	**$1,383.5**	**$1,394.8**	**$1,403.1**	**$1,411.7**	**$1,420.6**	**$1,433.3**	**$1,533.9**	**$1,639.7**	**$1,751.0**

= $370.0 million + $49.3 million
= Shareholders' Equity$_{2008}$ + Net Income$_{2009}$

The completed pro forma balance sheet is shown in Exhibit 5.34.

Step IV(d): Complete Pro Forma Cash Flow Statement

To complete the cash flow statement, the mandatory and optional repayments for each debt instrument, as calculated in the debt schedule, are linked to the appropriate line items in the financing activities section and summed to produce the annual repayment amounts. The annual pro forma beginning and ending cash balances are then calculated accordingly.

In 2009E, ValueCo is projected to generate $43.7 million of free cash flow. This amount is first used to satisfy the $4.5 million mandatory TLB amortization with the remaining cash used to make an optional repayment of $39.2 million. As

EXHIBIT 5.34 Pro Forma ValueCo Balance Sheet

($ in millions, fiscal year ending December 31)

Balance Sheet

	Opening 2008	Adjustments +	Adjustments −	Pro Forma 2008	Year 1 2009	Year 2 2010	Year 3 2011	Year 4 2012	Year 5 2013	Year 6 2014	Year 7 2015	Year 8 2016	Year 9 2017	Year 10 2018
									Projection Period					
Cash and Cash Equivalents	$25.0		(25.0)	-	-	-	-	-	-	-	$3.2	$92.7	$187.2	$286.7
Accounts Receivable	165.0			165.0	178.2	188.9	196.4	202.3	208.4	214.7	221.1	227.7	234.6	241.6
Inventories	125.0			125.0	135.0	143.1	148.8	153.3	157.9	162.6	167.5	172.5	177.7	183.0
Prepaids and Other Current Assets	10.0			10.0	10.8	11.4	11.9	12.3	12.6	13.0	13.4	13.8	14.2	14.6
Total Current Assets	**$325.0**			**$300.0**	**$324.0**	**$343.4**	**$357.2**	**$367.9**	**$378.9**	**$390.3**	**$405.2**	**$506.8**	**$613.6**	**$726.0**
Property, Plant and Equipment, net	650.0			650.0	650.0	650.0	650.0	650.0	650.0	650.0	650.0	650.0	650.0	650.0
Goodwill and Intangible Assets	175.0	125.0		300.0	300.0	300.0	300.0	300.0	300.0	300.0	300.0	300.0	300.0	300.0
Other Assets	75.0			75.0	75.0	75.0	75.0	75.0	75.0	75.0	75.0	75.0	75.0	75.0
Deferred Financing Fees	-	20.0		20.0	17.5	15.1	12.6	10.2	7.7	5.3	3.1	2.1	1.0	0.0
Total Assets	**$1,225.0**			**$1,345.0**	**$1,366.5**	**$1,383.5**	**$1,394.8**	**$1,403.1**	**$1,411.7**	**$1,420.6**	**$1,433.3**	**$1,533.9**	**$1,639.7**	**$1,751.0**
Accounts Payable	75.0			75.0	81.0	85.9	89.3	92.0	94.7	97.6	100.5	103.5	106.6	109.8
Accrued Liabilities	100.0			100.0	108.0	114.5	119.1	122.6	126.3	130.1	134.0	138.0	142.2	146.4
Other Current Liabilities	25.0			25.0	27.0	28.6	29.8	30.7	31.6	32.5	33.5	34.5	35.5	36.6
Total Current Liabilities	**$200.0**			**$200.0**	**$216.0**	**$229.0**	**$238.1**	**$245.3**	**$252.6**	**$260.2**	**$268.0**	**$276.0**	**$284.3**	**$292.9**
Revolving Credit Facility	-			-	-	-	-	-	-	-	-	-	-	-
Term Loan B	-	450.0		450.0	406.3	354.2	294.6	228.9	157.9	80.7	-	-	-	-
Existing Term Loan	300.0		(300.0)	-	-	-	-	-	-	-	-	-	-	-
Senior Subordinated Notes	-	300.0		300.0	300.0	300.0	300.0	300.0	300.0	300.0	300.0	300.0	300.0	300.0
Other Long-Term Liabilities	25.0			25.0	25.0	25.0	25.0	25.0	25.0	25.0	25.0	25.0	25.0	25.0
Total Liabilities	**$525.0**			**$975.0**	**$947.3**	**$908.2**	**$857.7**	**$799.2**	**$735.5**	**$665.9**	**$593.0**	**$601.0**	**$609.3**	**$617.9**
Noncontrolling Interest	-			-	-	-	-	-	-	-	-	-	-	-
Shareholders' Equity	700.0	370.0	(700.0)	370.0	419.3	475.3	537.1	603.9	676.2	754.7	840.3	932.8	1,030.4	1,133.1
Total Shareholders' Equity	**$700.0**			**$370.0**	**$419.3**	**$475.3**	**$537.1**	**$603.9**	**$676.2**	**$754.7**	**$840.3**	**$932.8**	**$1,030.4**	**$1,133.1**
Total Liabilities and Equity	**$1,225.0**			**$1,345.0**	**$1,366.5**	**$1,383.5**	**$1,394.8**	**$1,403.1**	**$1,411.7**	**$1,420.6**	**$1,433.3**	**$1,533.9**	**$1,639.7**	**$1,751.0**
Balance Check	0.000			0.000	0.000	0.000	0.000	0.000	0.000	0.000	0.000	0.000	0.000	0.000
Net Working Capital	100.0			100.0	108.0	114.5	119.1	122.6	126.3	130.1	134.0	138.0	142.2	146.4
(Increase) / Decrease in Net Working Capital					(8.0)	(6.5)	(4.6)	(3.6)	(3.7)	(3.8)	(3.9)	(4.0)	(4.1)	(4.3)

Balance Sheet Assumptions

Current Assets														
Days Sales Outstanding (DSO)	60.2			60.2	60.2	60.2	60.2	60.2	60.2	60.2	60.2	60.2	60.2	60.2
Days Inventory Held (DIH)	76.0			76.0	76.0	76.0	76.0	76.0	76.0	76.0	76.0	76.0	76.0	76.0
Prepaid and Other Current Assets (% of sales)	1.0%			1.0%	1.0%	1.0%	1.0%	1.0%	1.0%	1.0%	1.0%	1.0%	1.0%	1.0%
Current Liabilities														
Days Payable Outstanding (DPO)	45.6			45.6	45.6	45.6	45.6	45.6	45.6	45.6	45.6	45.6	45.6	45.6
Accrued Liabilities (% of sales)	10.0%			10.0%	10.0%	10.0%	10.0%	10.0%	10.0%	10.0%	10.0%	10.0%	10.0%	10.0%
Other Current Liabilities (% of sales)	2.5%			2.5%	2.5%	2.5%	2.5%	2.5%	2.5%	2.5%	2.5%	2.5%	2.5%	2.5%

shown in Exhibit 5.35, these combined actions are linked to the TLB line item in the financing activities section of the cash flow statement as a $43.7 million use of cash in 2009E.

EXHIBIT 5.35 Pro Forma Financing Activities Section of Cash Flow Statement

($ in millions, fiscal year ending December 31)

Cash Flow Statement

					Projection Period					
	Year 1 2009	Year 2 2010	Year 3 2011	Year 4 2012	Year 5 2013	Year 6 2014	Year 7 2015	Year 8 2016	Year 9 2017	Year 10 2018
Financing Activities										
Revolving Credit Facility	-	-	-	-	-	-	-	-	-	-
Term Loan B	(43.7)	(52.0)	(59.6)	(65.7)	(71.1)	(77.2)	(80.7)	-	-	-
Existing Term Loan	-	-	-	-	-	-	-	-	-	-
Dividends	-	-	-	-	-	-	-	-	-	-
Equity Issuance / (Repurchase)	-	-	-	-	-	-	-	-	-	-
Cash Flow from Financing Activities	($43.7)	($52.0)	($59.6)	($65.7)	($71.1)	($77.2)	($80.7)	-	-	-
Excess Cash for the Period	-	-	-	-	-	-	$3.2	$89.5	$94.4	$99.6
Beginning Cash Balance	-	-	-	-	-	-	-	3.2	92.7	187.2
Ending Cash Balance	-	-	-	-	-	-	$3.2	$92.7	$187.2	$286.7

= Mandatory Repayments $_{2009}$ +
Optional Repayments $_{2009}$
= ($4.5) million + ($39.2) million

As we assumed a 100% cash flow sweep, cash does not build on the balance sheet until the bank debt is fully repaid. Hence, ValueCo's ending cash balance line item remains constant at zero until 2015E when the TLB is completely paid down.[25] As shown in Exhibit 5.10, the ending cash balance for each year in the projection period links to the balance sheet.

The completed pro forma cash flow statement is shown in Exhibit 5.36.

---

[25] While a cash balance of zero may be unrealistic from an operating perspective, it is a relatively common modeling convention.

EXHIBIT 5.36 Pro Forma ValueCo Cash Flow Statement

($ in millions, fiscal year ending December 31)

Cash Flow Statement

					Projection Period					
	Year 1 2009	Year 2 2010	Year 3 2011	Year 4 2012	Year 5 2013	Year 6 2014	Year 7 2015	Year 8 2016	Year 9 2017	Year 10 2018
Operating Activities										
Net Income	$49.3	$56.1	$61.8	$66.8	$72.3	$78.5	$85.6	$92.5	$97.5	$102.8
Plus: Depreciation & Amortization	21.6	22.9	23.8	24.5	25.3	26.0	26.8	27.6	28.4	29.3
Plus: Amortization of Financing Fees	2.5	2.5	2.5	2.5	2.5	2.5	2.2	1.0	1.0	1.0
Changes in Working Capital Items										
(Inc.) / Dec. in Accounts Receivable	(13.2)	(10.7)	(7.6)	(5.9)	(6.1)	(6.3)	(6.4)	(6.6)	(6.8)	(7.0)
(Inc.) / Dec. in Inventories	(10.0)	(8.1)	(5.7)	(4.5)	(4.6)	(4.7)	(4.9)	(5.0)	(5.2)	(5.3)
(Inc.) / Dec. in Prepaid and Other Current Assets	(0.8)	(0.6)	(0.5)	(0.4)	(0.4)	(0.4)	(0.4)	(0.4)	(0.4)	(0.4)
Inc. / (Dec.) in Accounts Payable	6.0	4.9	3.4	2.7	2.8	2.8	2.9	3.0	3.1	3.2
Inc. / (Dec.) in Accrued Liabilities	8.0	6.5	4.6	3.6	3.7	3.8	3.9	4.0	4.1	4.3
Inc. / (Dec.) in Other Current Liabilities	2.0	1.6	1.1	0.9	0.9	0.9	1.0	1.0	1.0	1.1
(Inc.) / Dec. in Net Working Capital	(8.0)	(6.5)	(4.6)	(3.6)	(3.7)	(3.8)	(3.9)	(4.0)	(4.1)	(4.3)
Cash Flow from Operating Activities	**$65.3**	**$74.9**	**$83.4**	**$90.2**	**$96.3**	**$103.2**	**$110.7**	**$117.1**	**$122.9**	**$128.8**
Investing Activities										
Capital Expenditures	(21.6)	(22.9)	(23.8)	(24.5)	(25.3)	(26.0)	(26.8)	(27.6)	(28.4)	(29.3)
Other Investing Activities										
Cash Flow from Investing Activities	**($21.6)**	**($22.9)**	**($23.8)**	**($24.5)**	**($25.3)**	**($26.0)**	**($26.8)**	**($27.6)**	**($28.4)**	**($29.3)**
Financing Activities										
Revolving Credit Facility										
Term Loan B	(43.7)	(52.0)	(59.6)	(65.7)	(71.1)	(77.2)	(80.7)			
Existing Term Loan										
Senior Subordinated Notes										
Dividends										
Equity Issuance / (Repurchase)										
Cash Flow from Financing Activities	**($43.7)**	**($52.0)**	**($59.6)**	**($65.7)**	**($71.1)**	**($77.2)**	**($80.7)**	**-**	**-**	**-**
Excess Cash for the Period								$3.2	$89.5	$94.4	$99.6
Beginning Cash Balance									3.2	92.7	187.2
Ending Cash Balance	**-**	**-**	**-**	**-**	**-**	**-**	**$3.2**	**$92.7**	**$187.2**	**$286.7**
Cash Flow Statement Assumptions	2.0%	2.0%	2.0%	2.0%	2.0%	2.0%	2.0%	2.0%	2.0%	2.0%
Capital Expenditures (% of sales)	2.0%	2.0%	2.0%	2.0%	2.0%	2.0%	2.0%	2.0%	2.0%	2.0%

STEP V. PERFORM LBO ANALYSIS

EXHIBIT 5.37   Steps to Perform LBO Analysis

Step V(a):	Analyze Financing Structure
Step V(b):	Perform Returns Analysis
Step V(c):	Determine Valuation
Step V(d):	Create Transaction Summary Page

Once the LBO model is fully linked and tested, it is ready for use to evaluate various financing structures, gauge the target's ability to service and repay debt, and measure the sponsor's investment returns and other financial effects under multiple operating scenarios. This analysis, in turn, enables the banker to determine an appropriate valuation range for the target.

Step V(a): Analyze Financing Structure

A central part of LBO analysis is the crafting of an optimal financing structure for a given transaction. From an underwriting perspective, this involves determining whether the target's financial projections can support a given leveraged financing structure under various business and economic conditions. The use of realistic and defensible financial projections is critical to assessing whether a given financial structure is viable.

A key credit risk management concern for the underwriters centers on the target's ability to service its annual interest expense and repay all (or a substantial portion) of its bank debt within the proposed tenor. The primary credit metrics used to analyze the target's ability to support a given capital structure include variations of the leverage and coverage ratios outlined in Chapter 1 (e.g., debt-to-EBITDA, debt-to-total capitalization, and EBITDA-to-interest expense). Exhibit 5.38 displays a typical output summarizing the target's key financial data as well as pro forma capitalization and credit statistics for each year in the projection period. This output is typically shown on a transaction summary page (see Exhibit 5.46).

For the ValueCo LBO, we performed our financing structure analysis on the basis of our Base Case financial projections (see Step II) and assumed transaction structure (see Step III). Pro forma for the LBO, ValueCo has a total capitalization of $1,120 million, comprised of the $450 million TLB, $300 million notes, and $370 million of shareholders' equity (the equity contribution less other fees and expenses). This capital structure represents total leverage of 5.1x LTM 9/30/08 EBITDA of $146.7 million, including senior secured leverage of 3.1x. At these levels, ValueCo has a debt-to-total capitalization of 67%, EBITDA-to-interest expense of 2.4x and (EBITDA – capex)-to-interest expense of 2.1x at close.

As would be expected for a company that is projected to grow EBITDA, generate sizeable free cash flow, and repay debt, ValueCo's credit statistics improve significantly over the projection period. By 2015E, ValueCo's TLB is completely repaid as total leverage decreases to 1.5x and senior secured leverage is reduced to zero. In addition, ValueCo's debt-to-total capitalization decreases to 26.3% and EBITDA-to-interest expense increases to 5.9x.

EXHIBIT 5.38 Summary Financial Data, Capitalization, and Credit Statistics

($ in millions, fiscal year ending December 31)

Summary Financial Data

	LTM 9/30/2008	Pro forma 2008	Year 1 2009	Year 2 2010	Year 3 2011	Year 4 2012	Year 5 2013	Year 6 2014	Year 7 2015	Year 8 2016	Year 9 2017	Year 10 2018
							Projection Period					
Sales	$977.8	$1,000.0	$1,080.0	$1,144.8	$1,190.6	$1,226.3	$1,263.1	$1,301.0	$1,340.0	$1,380.2	$1,421.6	$1,464.3
% growth	NA	8.1%	8.0%	6.0%	4.0%	3.0%	3.0%	3.0%	3.0%	3.0%	3.0%	3.0%
Gross Profit	$391.1	$400.0	$432.0	$457.9	$476.2	$490.5	$505.2	$520.4	$536.0	$552.1	$568.7	$585.7
% margin	40.0%	40.0%	40.0%	40.0%	40.0%	40.0%	40.0%	40.0%	40.0%	40.0%	40.0%	40.0%
EBITDA	$146.7	$150.0	$162.0	$171.7	$178.6	$183.9	$189.5	$195.1	$201.0	$207.0	$213.2	$219.6
% margin	15.0%	15.0%	15.0%	15.0%	15.0%	15.0%	15.0%	15.0%	15.0%	15.0%	15.0%	15.0%
Capital Expenditures	19.6	20.0	21.6	22.9	23.8	24.5	25.3	26.0	26.8	27.6	28.4	29.3
% sales	2.0%	2.0%	2.0%	2.0%	2.0%	2.0%	2.0%	2.0%	2.0%	2.0%	2.0%	2.0%
Cash Interest Expense		59.9	58.5	55.9	52.7	49.2	45.2	40.0	34.0	30.7	30.7	30.7
Total Interest Expense		62.4	60.9	58.4	55.2	51.7	47.6	42.5	36.2	31.7	31.7	31.7
Free Cash Flow												
EBITDA			$162.0	$171.7	$178.6	$183.9	$189.5	$195.1	$201.0	$207.0	$213.2	$219.6
Less: Cash Interest Expense			(58.5)	(55.9)	(52.7)	(49.2)	(45.2)	(40.0)	(34.0)	(30.7)	(30.7)	(30.7)
Plus: Interest Income			-	-	-	-	-	-	0.0	1.4	4.2	7.1
Less: Income Taxes			(30.2)	(34.4)	(37.9)	(40.9)	(44.3)	(48.1)	(52.5)	(56.7)	(59.8)	(63.0)
Less: Capital Expenditures			(21.6)	(22.9)	(23.8)	(24.5)	(25.3)	(26.0)	(26.8)	(27.6)	(28.4)	(29.3)
Less: Increase in Net Working Capital			(8.0)	(6.5)	(4.6)	(3.6)	(3.7)	(3.8)	(3.9)	(4.0)	(4.1)	(4.3)
Free Cash Flow			$43.7	$52.0	$59.6	$65.7	$71.1	$77.2	$83.9	$89.5	$94.4	$99.6
Cumulative Free Cash Flow			43.7	95.8	155.4	221.1	292.1	369.3	453.2	542.7	637.2	736.7

Capitalization

	Pro forma 2008	Year 1 2009	Year 2 2010	Year 3 2011	Year 4 2012	Year 5 2013	Year 6 2014	Year 7 2015	Year 8 2016	Year 9 2017	Year 10 2018
Cash								$3.2	$92.7	$187.2	$286.7
Revolving Credit Facility								-	-	-	-
Term Loan B	450.0	406.3	354.2	294.6	228.9	157.9	80.7				
Other Debt							80.7				
Total Senior Secured Debt	$450.0	$406.3	$354.2	$294.6	$228.9	$157.9	$80.7	-	-	-	-
Senior Subordinated Notes	300.0	300.0	300.0	300.0	300.0	300.0	300.0	300.0	300.0	300.0	300.0
Total Debt	$750.0	$706.3	$654.2	$594.6	$528.9	$457.9	$380.7	$300.0	$300.0	$300.0	$300.0
Shareholders' Equity	370.0	419.3	475.3	537.1	603.9	676.2	754.7	840.3	932.8	1,030.4	1,133.1
Total Capitalization	$1,120.0	$1,125.5	$1,129.6	$1,131.7	$1,132.8	$1,134.0	$1,135.4	$1,140.3	$1,232.8	$1,330.4	$1,433.1
% of Bank Debt Repaid	-	9.7%	21.3%	34.5%	49.1%	64.9%	82.1%	100.0%	100.0%	100.0%	100.0%

In Year 7, 100% of ValueCo's bank debt is repaid.

Credit Statistics

	Pro forma 2008	Year 1 2009	Year 2 2010	Year 3 2011	Year 4 2012	Year 5 2013	Year 6 2014	Year 7 2015	Year 8 2016	Year 9 2017	Year 10 2018
% Debt / Total Capitalization	67.0%	62.7%	57.9%	52.5%	46.7%	40.4%	33.5%	26.3%	24.3%	22.6%	20.9%
EBITDA / Cash Interest Expense	2.5x	2.8x	3.1x	3.4x	3.7x	4.2x	4.9x	5.9x	6.8x	7.0x	7.2x
(EBITDA - Capex) / Cash Interest Expense	2.2x	2.4x	2.7x	2.9x	3.2x	3.6x	4.2x	5.1x	5.9x	6.0x	6.2x
EBITDA / Total Interest Expense	2.4x	2.7x	2.9x	3.2x	3.6x	4.0x	4.6x	5.6x	6.5x	6.7x	6.9x
(EBITDA - Capex) / Total Interest Expense	2.1x	2.3x	2.5x	2.8x	3.1x	3.4x	4.0x	4.8x	5.7x	5.8x	6.0x
Senior Secured Debt / EBITDA	3.0x	2.5x	2.1x	1.6x	1.2x	0.8x	0.4x	NM	NM	NM	NM
Total Debt / EBITDA	5.0x	4.4x	3.8x	3.3x	2.9x	2.4x	2.0x	1.5x	1.4x	1.4x	1.4x
Net Debt / EBITDA	5.0x	4.4x	3.8x	3.3x	2.9x	2.4x	2.0x	1.5x	1.0x	0.5x	0.1x

This steady deleveraging and improvement of credit statistics throughout the projection period suggests that ValueCo has the ability to support the contemplated financing structure under the Base Case financial projections.

Step V(b): Perform Returns Analysis

After analyzing the contemplated financing structure from a debt repayment and credit statistics perspective, the banker determines whether it provides sufficient returns to the sponsor given the proposed purchase price and equity contribution. As discussed in Chapter 4, sponsors have historically sought 20%+ IRRs in assessing acquisition opportunities. If the implied returns are too low, both the purchase price and financing structure need to be revisited.

IRRs are driven primarily by the target's projected financial performance, the assumed purchase price and financing structure (particularly the size of the equity contribution), and the assumed exit multiple and year (assuming a sale). Although a sponsor may realize a monetization or exit through various strategies and timeframes (see Chapter 4, "Primary Exit/Monetization Strategies"), a traditional LBO analysis contemplates a full exit via a sale of the entire company in five years.

Return Assumptions   In a traditional LBO analysis, it is common practice to conservatively assume an exit multiple equal to (or below) the entry multiple.

EXHIBIT 5.39   Calculation of Enterprise Value and Equity Value at Exit

($ in millions)

Calculation of Exit Enterprise Value and Equity Value (assumes 7.5x exit multiple and 2013E exit year)	
	Year 5 **2013**
2013E EBITDA	$189.5
Exit EBITDA Multiple	7.5x
Enterprise Value at Exit	**$1,421.0**
Less: Net Debt	
Revolving Credit Facility	-
Term Loan B	157.9
Senior Subordinated Notes	300.0
Total Debt	**$457.9**
Less: Cash and Cash Equivalents	-
Net Debt	**$457.9**
Equity Value at Exit	**$963.1**

As shown in Exhibit 5.39, for ValueCo's LBO analysis, we assumed that the sponsor exits in 2013E (Year 5) at a multiple of 7.5x EBITDA, which is equal to the entry multiple.

In 2013E, ValueCo is projected to generate EBITDA of $189.5 million, translating into an implied enterprise value of $1,421 million at an exit multiple of 7.5x EBITDA. Cumulative debt repayment over the period is $292.1 million (2008E TLB beginning balance of $450 million less 2013E ending balance of $157.9 million), leaving ValueCo with projected 2013E debt of $457.9 million. This debt amount, which is equal to net debt given the zero cash balance, is subtracted from the enterprise value of $1,421 million to calculate an implied equity value of $963.1 million in the exit year.

IRR and Cash Return Calculations Assuming no additional cash inflows (dividends to the sponsor) or outflows (additional investment by the sponsor) during the investment period, IRR and cash return are calculated on the basis of the sponsor's initial equity contribution (outflow) and the assumed equity proceeds at exit (inflow). This concept is illustrated in the timeline shown in Exhibit 5.40.

EXHIBIT 5.40   Investment Timeline

($ in millions)	Pro forma 2008	Year 1 2009	Year 2 2010	Year 3 2011	Year 4 2012	Year 5 2013
Initial Equity Investment	($385.0)					
Dividends / (Investment)	-	-	-	-	-	-
Equity Value at Exit	-	-	-	-	-	963.1
Total	**($385.0)**	**-**	**-**	**-**	**-**	**$963.1**
IRR	20%	=IRR(Initial Equity Investment : Equity Value at Exit) =IRR(($385.0) million : $963.1 million)				
Cash Return	2.5x	= Equity Value at Exit / Initial Equity Investment = $963.1 million / $385.0 million				

The initial equity contribution represents a cash outflow for the sponsor. Hence, it is shown as a negative value on the timeline, as would any additional equity investment by the sponsor, whether for acquisitions or other purposes. On the other hand, cash distributions to the sponsor, such as proceeds received at exit or dividends received during the investment period, are shown as positive values on the timeline.

For the ValueCo LBO, we assumed no cash inflows or outflows during the investment period other than the initial equity contribution and anticipated equity proceeds at exit. Therefore, we calculated an IRR of approximately 20% and a cash return of 2.5x based on $385 million of initial contributed equity and $963.1 million of equity proceeds in 2013E.

Returns at Various Exit Years In Exhibit 5.41, we calculated IRR and cash return assuming an exit at the end of each year in the projection period using the fixed 7.5x EBITDA exit multiple. As we progress through the projection period, equity value increases due to the increasing EBITDA and decreasing net debt. Therefore, the cash return increases as it is a function of the fixed initial equity investment and increasing equity value at exit. In ValueCo's case, however, as the timeline progresses, IRR decreases in accordance with the declining growth rates and the time value of money.

IRR Sensitivity Analysis Sensitivity analysis is critical for analyzing IRRs and framing LBO valuation. IRR can be sensitized for several key value drivers, such as entry and exit multiple, exit year, leverage level, and equity contribution percentage, as well as key operating assumptions such as growth rates and margins (see Chapter 3, Exhibit 3.59).

EXHIBIT 5.41 Returns at Various Exit Years

($ in millions, fiscal year ending December 31)

Returns Analysis

	Pro forma 2008	Year 1 2009	Year 2 2010	Year 3 2011	Year 4 2012	Year 5 2013	Year 6 2014	Year 7 2015	Year 8 2016	Year 9 2017	Year 10 2018
							Projection Period				
Entry EBITDA Multiple	7.5x										
Initial Equity Investment	$385.0										
EBITDA											
Exit EBITDA Multiple	7.5x										
EBITDA		$162.0	$171.7	$178.6	$183.9	$189.5	$195.1	$201.0	$207.0	$213.2	$219.6
Enterprise Value at Exit		**$1,215.0**	**$1,287.9**	**$1,339.4**	**$1,379.6**	**$1,421.0**	**$1,463.6**	**$1,507.5**	**$1,552.8**	**$1,599.3**	**$1,647.3**
Less: Net Debt											
Revolving Credit Facility		-	-	-	-	-	-	-	-	-	-
Term Loan B		406.3	354.2	294.6	228.9	157.9	80.7	-	-	-	-
Senior Subordinated Notes		300.0	300.0	300.0	300.0	300.0	300.0	300.0	300.0	300.0	300.0
Other Debt		-	-	-	-	-	-	-	-	-	-
Total Debt		**$706.3**	**$654.2**	**$594.6**	**$528.9**	**$457.9**	**$380.7**	**$300.0**	**$300.0**	**$300.0**	**$300.0**
Less: Cash and Cash Equivalents		-	-	-	-	-	-	3.2	92.7	187.2	286.7
Net Debt		**$706.3**	**$654.2**	**$594.6**	**$528.9**	**$457.9**	**$380.7**	**$296.8**	**$207.3**	**$112.8**	**$13.3**
Equity Value at Exit		**$508.7**	**$633.7**	**$744.8**	**$850.7**	**$963.1**	**$1,083.0**	**$1,210.7**	**$1,345.5**	**$1,486.5**	**$1,634.0**

Cash Return		1.3x	1.6x	1.9x	2.2x	2.5x	2.8x	3.1x	3.5x	3.9x	4.2x

	Year 1 2009	Year 2 2010	Year 3 2011	Year 4 2012	Year 5 2013	Year 6 2014	Year 7 2015	Year 8 2016	Year 9 2017	Year 10 2018
Initial Equity Investment	($385.0)	($385.0)	($385.0)	($385.0)	($385.0)	($385.0)	($385.0)	($385.0)	($385.0)	($385.0)
Equity Proceeds	$508.7	$633.7	$744.8	$850.7	$963.1	$1,083.0	$1,210.7	$1,345.5	$1,486.5	$1,634.0
IRR	32.1%	28.3%	24.6%	21.9%	20.1%	18.8%	17.8%	16.9%	16.2%	15.6%

As shown in Exhibit 5.42, for the ValueCo LBO, we assumed a fixed leverage level of 5.1x LTM 9/30/08 EBITDA of $146.7 million and a 2013E exit year, while sensitizing entry and exit multiples. For our IRR analysis, we focused on entry and exit multiple combinations that produced an IRR in the 20% area, assuming an equity contribution range of 25% to 35%.

EXHIBIT 5.42 IRR Sensitivity Analysis – Entry and Exit Multiples

			IRR - Assuming Exit in 2013E						
			Exit Multiple						
Enterprise Value	Equity Contribution	Entry Multiple	6.50x	6.75x	7.00x	7.25x	7.50x	7.75x	8.00x
$953.3	23.5%	6.50x	26.6%	28.1%	29.5%	30.9%	32.2%	33.5%	34.7%
990.0	26.2%	6.75x	23.0%	24.5%	25.9%	27.2%	28.5%	29.7%	30.9%
1,026.7	28.7%	7.00x	19.9%	21.4%	22.7%	24.1%	25.3%	26.5%	27.7%
1,063.3	31.0%	7.25x	17.3%	18.7%	20.0%	21.3%	22.6%	23.7%	24.9%
1,100.0	33.2%	7.50x	15.0%	16.4%	17.7%	18.9%	20.1%	21.3%	22.4%
1,136.7	35.2%	7.75x	12.9%	14.3%	15.5%	16.8%	18.0%	19.1%	20.2%
1,173.3	37.2%	8.00x	11.0%	12.4%	13.6%	14.8%	16.0%	17.1%	18.2%

For example, a 7.5x entry and exit multiple provides an IRR of 20.1% while requiring a 33.2% equity contribution given the proposed leverage. A 7.75x entry and exit multiple, however, yields an IRR of 19.1% while requiring an equity contribution of 35.2%. At the low end of the range, a 6.75x entry and exit multiple provides an IRR of 24.5% while requiring a 26.2% equity contribution.

It is also common to perform sensitivity analysis on a combination of exit multiples and exit years. As shown in Exhibit 5.43, we assumed fixed total leverage and entry multiples of 5.1x and 7.5x LTM 9/30/08 EBITDA, respectively, and examined the resulting IRRs for a range of exit years from 2011E to 2015E and exit multiples from 6.5x to 8.5x.

EXHIBIT 5.43 IRR Sensitivity Analysis – Exit Multiple and Exit Year

		IRR - Assuming 7.5x Entry Multiple				
		Exit Year				
		2011	2012	2013	2014	2015
	6.5x	13.7%	14.7%	15.0%	14.9%	14.8%
	7.0x	19.4%	18.5%	17.7%	17.0%	16.3%
Exit Multiple	7.5x	24.6%	21.9%	20.1%	18.8%	17.8%
	8.0x	29.4%	25.1%	22.4%	20.5%	19.1%
	8.5x	33.9%	28.0%	24.5%	22.1%	20.4%

Step V(c): Determine Valuation

As previously discussed, sponsors base their valuation of an LBO target in large part on their comfort with realizing acceptable returns at a given purchase price. This analysis assumes a given set of financial projections, purchase price, and financing structure, as well as exit multiple and year. At the same time, sponsors are guided by the other valuation methodologies discussed in this book.

LBO analysis is also informative for strategic buyers by providing perspective on the price a competing sponsor bidder might be willing to pay for a given target in an organized sale process. This data point allows strategic buyers to frame their bids accordingly. As a result, the banker is expected to employ LBO analysis as a valuation technique while serving as an M&A advisor in both buy-side and sell-side situations.

Traditionally, the valuation implied by LBO analysis is toward the lower end of a comprehensive analysis when compared to other methodologies, particularly precedent transactions and DCF analysis. This is largely due to the constraints imposed by an LBO, including leverage capacity, credit market conditions, and the sponsor's own IRR hurdles. Furthermore, strategic buyers are typically able to realize synergies from the target, thereby enhancing their ability to earn a targeted return on their invested capital at a higher purchase price. However, in robust debt financing environments, such as during the credit boom of the mid-2000s, sponsors were able to compete with strategic buyers on purchase price. The multiples paid in LBO transactions during this period were supported by the use of a high proportion of low-cost debt in the capital structure, translating into a relatively lower overall cost of capital for the target.

EXHIBIT 5.44 ValueCo Football Field Displaying Comparable Companies, Precedent Transactions, DCF Analysis, and LBO Analysis

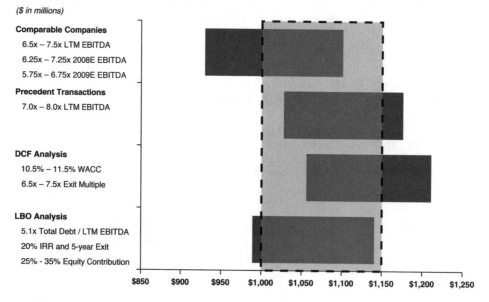

As with the DCF, the implied valuation range for ValueCo was derived from sensitivity analysis output tables (see Exhibit 5.42). For the ValueCo LBO, we focused on a range of entry and exit multiples that produced IRRs in the 20% area, given an equity contribution range of 25% of 35%. This approach led us to determine a valuation range of 6.75x to 7.75x LTM 9/30/08 EBITDA, or approximately $990 million to $1,135 million (see Exhibit 5.44).

Step V(d): Create Transaction Summary Page

Once the LBO model is fully functional, all the essential model outputs are linked to a transaction summary page (see Exhibit 5.46). This page provides an overview of the LBO analysis in a user-friendly format, typically displaying the sources and uses of funds, acquisition multiples, summary returns analysis, and summary financial data, as well as projected capitalization and credit statistics. This format allows the deal team to quickly review and spot-check the analysis and make adjustments to the purchase price, financing structure, operating assumptions, and other key inputs as necessary.

The transaction summary page also typically contains the toggle cells that allow the banker to switch among various financing structures and operating scenarios, as well as activate other functionality. The outputs on this page (and throughout the entire model) change accordingly as the toggle cells are changed.

ILLUSTRATIVE LBO ANALYSIS FOR VALUECO

The following pages display the full LBO model for ValueCo based on the step-by-step approach outlined in this chapter. Exhibit 5.45 lists these pages, which are shown in Exhibits 5.46 to 5.54.

EXHIBIT 5.45   LBO Model Pages

LBO Model
    I.   Transaction Summary
    II. Income Statement
    III. Balance Sheet
    IV. Cash Flow Statement
    V. Debt Schedule
    VI. Returns Analysis

Assumptions Pages
    I.   Assumptions Page 1—Income Statement and Cash Flow Statement
    II. Assumptions Page 2—Balance Sheet
    III. Assumptions Page 3—Financing Structures and Fees

EXHIBIT 5.48 ValueCo LBO Balance Sheet

($ in millions, fiscal year ending December 31)

Balance Sheet

	Opening 2008	Adjustments −	Adjustments +	Pro Forma 2008	Year 1 2009	Year 2 2010	Year 3 2011	Year 4 2012	Year 5 2013		Year 6 2014	Year 7 2015	Year 8 2016	Year 9 2017	Year 10 2018
										Projection Period					
Cash and Cash Equivalents	$25.0	(25.0)		-	-	-	-	-	-		-	$3.2	$92.7	$187.2	$286.7
Accounts Receivable	165.0			165.0	178.2	188.9	196.4	202.3	208.4		214.7	221.1	227.7	234.6	241.6
Inventories	125.0			125.0	135.0	143.1	148.8	153.3	157.9		162.6	167.5	172.5	177.7	183.0
Prepaids and Other Current Assets	10.0			10.0	10.8	11.4	11.9	12.3	12.6		13.0	13.4	13.8	14.2	14.6
Total Current Assets	**$325.0**			**$300.0**	**$324.0**	**$343.4**	**$357.2**	**$367.9**	**$378.9**		**$390.3**	**$405.2**	**$506.8**	**$613.6**	**$726.0**
Property, Plant and Equipment, net	650.0			650.0	650.0	650.0	650.0	650.0	650.0		650.0	650.0	650.0	650.0	650.0
Goodwill and Intangible Assets	175.0		125.0	300.0	300.0	300.0	300.0	300.0	300.0		300.0	300.0	300.0	300.0	300.0
Other Assets	75.0			75.0	75.0	75.0	75.0	75.0	75.0		75.0	75.0	75.0	75.0	75.0
Deferred Financing Fees	-		20.0	20.0	17.5	15.1	12.6	10.2	7.7		5.3	3.1	2.1	1.0	0.0
Total Assets	**$1,225.0**			**$1,345.0**	**$1,366.5**	**$1,383.5**	**$1,394.8**	**$1,403.1**	**$1,411.7**		**$1,420.6**	**$1,433.3**	**$1,533.9**	**$1,639.7**	**$1,751.0**
Accounts Payable	75.0			75.0	81.0	85.9	89.3	92.0	94.7		97.6	100.5	103.5	106.6	109.8
Accrued Liabilities	100.0			100.0	108.0	114.5	119.1	122.6	126.3		130.1	134.0	138.0	142.2	146.4
Other Current Liabilities	25.0			25.0	27.0	28.6	29.8	30.7	31.6		32.5	34.5	34.5	35.5	36.6
Total Current Liabilities	**$200.0**			**$200.0**	**$216.0**	**$229.0**	**$238.1**	**$245.3**	**$252.6**		**$260.2**	**$268.0**	**$276.0**	**$284.3**	**$292.9**
Revolving Credit Facility	-			-	-	-	-	-	-		-	-	-	-	-
Term Loan B	-		450.0	450.0	406.3	354.2	294.6	228.9	157.9		80.7	-	-	-	-
Existing Term Loan	300.0	(300.0)		-	-	-	-	-	-		-	-	-	-	-
Senior Subordinated Notes	-		300.0	300.0	300.0	300.0	300.0	300.0	300.0		300.0	300.0	300.0	300.0	300.0
Other Long-Term Liabilities	25.0			25.0	25.0	25.0	25.0	25.0	25.0		25.0	25.0	25.0	25.0	25.0
Total Liabilities	**$525.0**			**$975.0**	**$947.3**	**$908.2**	**$857.7**	**$799.2**	**$735.5**		**$665.9**	**$593.0**	**$601.0**	**$609.3**	**$617.9**
Noncontrolling Interest	-			-	-	-	-	-	-		-	-	-	-	-
Shareholders' Equity	700.0	(700.0)	370.0	370.0	419.3	475.3	537.1	603.9	676.2		754.7	840.3	932.8	1,030.4	1,133.1
Total Shareholders' Equity	**$700.0**			**$370.0**	**$419.3**	**$475.3**	**$537.1**	**$603.9**	**$676.2**		**$754.7**	**$840.3**	**$932.8**	**$1,030.4**	**$1,133.1**
Total Liabilities and Equity	**$1,225.0**			**$1,345.0**	**$1,366.5**	**$1,383.5**	**$1,394.8**	**$1,403.1**	**$1,411.7**		**$1,420.6**	**$1,433.3**	**$1,533.9**	**$1,639.7**	**$1,751.0**
Balance Check	0.000			0.000	0.000	0.000	0.000	0.000	0.000		0.000	0.000	0.000	0.000	0.000
Net Working Capital	100.0			100.0	108.0	114.5	119.1	122.6	126.3		130.1	134.0	138.0	142.2	146.4
(Increase) / Decrease in Net Working Capital					(8.0)	(6.5)	(4.6)	(3.6)	(3.7)		(3.8)	(3.9)	(4.0)	(4.1)	(4.3)

Balance Sheet Assumptions

Current Assets															
Days Sales Outstanding (DSO)	60.2			60.2	60.2	60.2	60.2	60.2	60.2		60.2	60.2	60.2	60.2	60.2
Days Inventory Held (DIH)	76.0			76.0	76.0	76.0	76.0	76.0	76.0		76.0	76.0	76.0	76.0	76.0
Prepaid and Other Current Assets (% of sales)	1.0%			1.0%	1.0%	1.0%	1.0%	1.0%	1.0%		1.0%	1.0%	1.0%	1.0%	1.0%
Current Liabilities															
Days Payable Outstanding (DPO)	45.6			45.6	45.6	45.6	45.6	45.6	45.6		45.6	45.6	45.6	45.6	45.6
Accrued Liabilities (% of sales)	10.0%			10.0%	10.0%	10.0%	10.0%	10.0%	10.0%		10.0%	10.0%	10.0%	10.0%	10.0%
Other Current Liabilities (% of sales)	2.5%			2.5%	2.5%	2.5%	2.5%	2.5%	2.5%		2.5%	2.5%	2.5%	2.5%	2.5%

EXHIBIT 5.49 ValueCo LBO Cash Flow Statement

($ in millions, fiscal year ending December 31)

Cash Flow Statement

	Projection Period									
	Year 1 2009	Year 2 2010	Year 3 2011	Year 4 2012	Year 5 2013	Year 6 2014	Year 7 2015	Year 8 2016	Year 9 2017	Year 10 2018
Operating Activities										
Net Income	$49.3	$56.1	$61.8	$66.8	$72.3	$78.5	$85.6	$92.5	$97.5	$102.8
Plus: Depreciation & Amortization	21.6	22.9	23.8	24.5	25.3	26.0	26.8	27.6	28.4	29.3
Plus: Amortization of Financing Fees	2.5	2.5	2.5	2.5	2.5	2.5	2.2	1.0	1.0	1.0
Changes in Working Capital Items										
(Inc.) / Dec. in Accounts Receivable	(13.2)	(10.7)	(7.6)	(5.9)	(6.1)	(6.3)	(6.4)	(6.6)	(6.8)	(7.0)
(Inc.) / Dec. in Inventories	(10.0)	(8.1)	(5.7)	(4.5)	(4.6)	(4.7)	(4.9)	(5.0)	(5.2)	(5.3)
(Inc.) / Dec. in Prepaid and Other Current Assets	(0.8)	(0.6)	(0.5)	(0.4)	(0.4)	(0.4)	(0.4)	(0.4)	(0.4)	(0.4)
Inc. / (Dec.) in Accounts Payable	6.0	4.9	3.4	2.7	2.8	2.8	2.9	3.0	3.1	3.2
Inc. / (Dec.) in Accrued Liabilities	8.0	6.5	4.6	3.6	3.7	3.8	3.9	4.0	4.1	4.3
Inc. / (Dec.) in Other Current Liabilities	2.0	1.6	1.1	0.9	0.9	0.9	1.0	1.0	1.0	1.1
(Inc.) / Dec. in Net Working Capital	(8.0)	(6.5)	(4.6)	(3.6)	(3.7)	(3.8)	(3.9)	(4.0)	(4.1)	(4.3)
Cash Flow from Operating Activities	**$65.3**	**$74.9**	**$83.4**	**$90.2**	**$96.3**	**$103.2**	**$110.7**	**$117.1**	**$122.9**	**$128.8**
Investing Activities										
Capital Expenditures	(21.6)	(22.9)	(23.8)	(24.5)	(25.3)	(26.0)	(26.8)	(27.6)	(28.4)	(29.3)
Other Investing Activities	-	-	-	-	-	-	-	-	-	-
Cash Flow from Investing Activities	**($21.6)**	**($22.9)**	**($23.8)**	**($24.5)**	**($25.3)**	**($26.0)**	**($26.8)**	**($27.6)**	**($28.4)**	**($29.3)**
Financing Activities										
Revolving Credit Facility	-	-	-	-	-	-	-			
Term Loan B	(43.7)	(52.0)	(59.6)	(65.7)	(71.1)	(77.2)	(80.7)			
Existing Term Loan	-	-	-	-	-	-	-			
Senior Subordinated Notes	-	-	-	-	-	-	-			
Dividends	-	-	-	-	-	-	-			
Equity Issuance / (Repurchase)	-	-	-	-	-	-	-			
Cash Flow from Financing Activities	**($43.7)**	**($52.0)**	**($59.6)**	**($65.7)**	**($71.1)**	**($77.2)**	**($80.7)**	**-**	**-**	**-**
Excess Cash for the Period	-	-	-	-	-	-	$3.2	$89.5	$94.4	$99.6
Beginning Cash Balance	-	-	-	-	-	-	-	3.2	92.7	187.2
Ending Cash Balance	**-**	**-**	**-**	**-**	**-**	**-**	**$3.2**	**$92.7**	**$187.2**	**$286.7**
Cash Flow Statement Assumptions										
Capital Expenditures (% of sales)	2.0%	2.0%	2.0%	2.0%	2.0%	2.0%	2.0%	2.0%	2.0%	2.0%

EXHIBIT 5.50 ValueCo LBO Debt Schedule

($ in millions, fiscal year ending December 31)

Debt Schedule

| | Pro forma 2008 | Projection Period | | | | | | | | | |
		Year 1 2009	Year 2 2010	Year 3 2011	Year 4 2012	Year 5 2013	Year 6 2014	Year 7 2015	Year 8 2016	Year 9 2017	Year 10 2018
Forward LIBOR Curve	3.00%	3.00%	3.15%	3.30%	3.60%	4.00%	4.35%	4.80%	4.85%	5.10%	5.25%
Cash Flow from Operating Activities		$65.3	$74.9	$83.4	$90.2	$96.3	$103.2	$110.7	$117.1	$122.9	$128.8
Cash Flow from Investing Activities		(21.6)	(22.9)	(23.8)	(24.5)	(25.3)	(26.0)	(26.8)	(27.6)	(28.4)	(29.3)
Cash Available for Debt Repayment		$43.7	$52.0	$59.6	$65.7	$71.1	$77.2	$83.9	$89.5	$94.4	$99.6
Total Mandatory Repayments		(4.5)	(4.5)	(4.5)	(4.5)	(4.5)	(4.5)	(4.5)	-	-	-
Cash from Balance Sheet		-	-	-	-	-	-	-	3.2	92.7	187.2
Cash Available for Optional Debt Repayment		$39.2	$47.5	$55.1	$61.2	$66.6	$72.7	$79.4	$92.7	$187.2	$286.7

Revolving Credit Facility

Revolving Credit Facility Size	$100.0										
Spread	3.250%										
Term	6 years										
Commitment Fee on Unused Portion	0.50%										

MinCash -

		Year 1 2009	Year 2 2010	Year 3 2011	Year 4 2012	Year 5 2013	Year 6 2014	Year 7 2015	Year 8 2016	Year 9 2017	Year 10 2018
Beginning Balance		-	-	-	-	-	-	-	-	-	-
Drawdown / (Repayment)		-	-	-	-	-	-	-	-	-	-
Ending Balance		-	-	-	-	-	-	-	-	-	-
Interest Rate		6.25%	6.40%	6.55%	6.85%	7.25%	7.60%	8.05%	8.10%	8.35%	8.50%
Interest Expense		-	-	-	-	-	-	-	-	-	-
Commitment Fee		0.5	0.5	0.5	0.5	0.5	0.5	0.5	0.5	0.5	0.5

Term Loan B Facility

Size	$450.0										
Spread	3.500%										
Term	7 years										
Repayment Schedule	1.0% per Annum, Bullet at Maturity										

		Year 1 2009	Year 2 2010	Year 3 2011	Year 4 2012	Year 5 2013	Year 6 2014	Year 7 2015	Year 8 2016	Year 9 2017	Year 10 2018
Beginning Balance		$450.0	$406.3	$354.2	$294.6	$228.9	$157.9	$80.7	-	-	-
Mandatory Repayments		(4.5)	(4.5)	(4.5)	(4.5)	(4.5)	(4.5)	(4.5)	-	-	-
Optional Repayments		(39.2)	(47.5)	(55.1)	(61.2)	(66.6)	(72.7)	(76.2)	-	-	-
Ending Balance		$406.3	$354.2	$294.6	$228.9	$157.9	$80.7	-	-	-	-
Interest Rate		6.50%	6.65%	6.80%	7.10%	7.50%	7.85%	8.30%	8.35%	8.60%	8.75%
Interest Expense		27.8	25.3	22.1	18.6	14.5	9.4	3.3	-	-	-

Senior Subordinated Notes

Size	$300.0										
Coupon	10.000%										
Term	10 years										

		Year 1 2009	Year 2 2010	Year 3 2011	Year 4 2012	Year 5 2013	Year 6 2014	Year 7 2015	Year 8 2016	Year 9 2017	Year 10 2018
Beginning Balance		$300.0	$300.0	$300.0	$300.0	$300.0	$300.0	$300.0	$300.0	$300.0	$300.0
Repayment		-	-	-	-	-	-	-	-	-	-
Ending Balance		$300.0	$300.0	$300.0	$300.0	$300.0	$300.0	$300.0	$300.0	$300.0	$300.0
Interest Expense		30.0	30.0	30.0	30.0	30.0	30.0	30.0	30.0	30.0	30.0

EXHIBIT 5.51 ValueCo LBO Returns Analysis

($ in millions, fiscal year ending December 31)

Returns Analysis

	Pro forma 2008	Projection Period									
		Year 1 2009	Year 2 2010	Year 3 2011	Year 4 2012	Year 5 2013	Year 6 2014	Year 7 2015	Year 8 2016	Year 9 2017	Year 10 2018
Entry EBITDA Multiple	7.5x										
Initial Equity Investment	$385.0										
EBITDA		$162.0	$171.7	$178.6	$183.9	$189.5	$195.1	$201.0	$207.0	$213.2	$219.6
Exit EBITDA Multiple	7.5x										
Enterprise Value at Exit		$1,215.0	$1,287.9	$1,339.4	$1,379.6	$1,421.0	$1,463.6	$1,507.5	$1,552.8	$1,599.3	$1,647.3
Less: Net Debt											
Revolving Credit Facility		-	-	-	-	-	-	-	-	-	-
Term Loan B		406.3	354.2	294.6	228.9	157.9	80.7	-	-	-	-
Senior Subordinated Notes		300.0	300.0	300.0	300.0	300.0	300.0	300.0	300.0	300.0	300.0
Other Debt		-	-	-	-	-	-	-	-	-	-
Total Debt		$706.3	$654.2	$594.6	$528.9	$457.9	$380.7	$300.0	$300.0	$300.0	$300.0
Less: Cash and Cash Equivalents		-	-	-	-	-	3.2	92.7	187.2	286.7	
Net Debt		$706.3	$654.2	$594.6	$528.9	$457.9	$380.7	$296.8	$207.3	$112.8	$13.3
Equity Value at Exit		$508.7	$633.7	$744.8	$850.7	$963.1	$1,083.0	$1,210.7	$1,345.5	$1,486.5	$1,634.0

Cash Return

	Year 1 2009	Year 2 2010	Year 3 2011	Year 4 2012	Year 5 2013	Year 6 2014	Year 7 2015	Year 8 2016	Year 9 2017	Year 10 2018
	1.3x	1.6x	1.9x	2.2x	2.5x	2.8x	3.1x	3.5x	3.9x	4.2x
Initial Equity Investment	($385.0)	($385.0)	($385.0)	($385.0)	($385.0)	($385.0)	($385.0)	($385.0)	($385.0)	($385.0)
Equity Proceeds	$508.7	$633.7	$744.8	$850.7	$963.1	$1,083.0	$1,210.7	$1,345.5	$1,486.5	$1,634.0

IRR

	Year 1 2009	Year 2 2010	Year 3 2011	Year 4 2012	Year 5 2013	Year 6 2014	Year 7 2015	Year 8 2016	Year 9 2017	Year 10 2018
	32.1%	28.3%	24.6%	21.9%	20.1%	18.8%	17.8%	16.9%	16.2%	15.6%

IRR - Assuming Exit in 2013E

Entry Multiple	Exit Multiple						
	6.50x	6.75x	7.00x	7.25x	7.50x	7.75x	8.00x
6.50x	26.6%	28.1%	29.5%	30.9%	32.2%	33.5%	34.7%
6.75x	23.0%	24.5%	25.9%	27.2%	28.5%	29.7%	30.9%
7.00x	19.9%	21.4%	22.7%	24.1%	25.3%	26.5%	27.7%
7.25x	17.3%	18.7%	20.0%	21.3%	22.6%	23.7%	24.9%
7.50x	15.0%	16.4%	17.7%	18.9%	20.1%	21.3%	22.4%
7.75x	12.9%	14.3%	15.5%	16.8%	18.0%	19.1%	20.2%
8.00x	11.0%	12.4%	13.6%	14.8%	16.0%	17.1%	18.2%

EXHIBIT 5.52   ValueCo LBO Assumptions Page 1

Assumptions Page 1 - Income Statement and Cash Flow Statement

		Projection Period									
		Year 1 2009	Year 2 2010	Year 3 2011	Year 4 2012	Year 5 2013	Year 6 2014	Year 7 2015	Year 8 2016	Year 9 2017	Year 10 2018
Income Statement Assumptions											
Sales (% growth)											
Base	1	8.0%	6.0%	4.0%	3.0%	3.0%	3.0%	3.0%	3.0%	3.0%	3.0%
Sponsor	2	10.0%	8.0%	6.0%	4.0%	3.0%	3.0%	3.0%	3.0%	3.0%	3.0%
Management	3	12.0%	10.9%	8.0%	6.0%	4.0%	4.0%	4.0%	4.0%	4.0%	4.0%
Downside 1	4	5.0%	4.0%	3.0%	3.0%	3.0%	3.0%	3.0%	3.0%	3.0%	3.0%
Downside 2	5	2.0%	2.0%	2.0%	2.0%	2.0%	2.0%	2.0%	2.0%	2.0%	2.0%
Cost of Goods Sold (% sales)											
Base	1	60.0%	60.0%	60.0%	60.0%	60.0%	60.0%	60.0%	60.0%	60.0%	60.0%
Sponsor	2	60.0%	60.0%	60.0%	60.0%	60.0%	60.0%	60.0%	60.0%	60.0%	60.0%
Management	3	59.0%	59.0%	59.0%	59.0%	59.0%	59.0%	59.0%	59.0%	59.0%	59.0%
Downside 1	4	61.0%	61.0%	61.0%	61.0%	61.0%	61.0%	61.0%	61.0%	61.0%	61.0%
Downside 2	5	62.0%	62.0%	62.0%	62.0%	62.0%	62.0%	62.0%	62.0%	62.0%	62.0%
SG&A (% sales)											
Base	1	25.0%	25.0%	25.0%	25.0%	25.0%	25.0%	25.0%	25.0%	25.0%	25.0%
Sponsor	2	25.0%	25.0%	25.0%	25.0%	25.0%	25.0%	25.0%	25.0%	25.0%	25.0%
Management	3	24.0%	24.0%	24.0%	24.0%	24.0%	24.0%	24.0%	24.0%	24.0%	24.0%
Downside 1	4	26.0%	25.0%	25.0%	25.0%	25.0%	25.0%	25.0%	25.0%	25.0%	25.0%
Downside 2	5	27.0%	26.0%	26.0%	26.0%	26.0%	26.0%	26.0%	26.0%	26.0%	26.0%
Depreciation & Amortization (% sales)											
Base	1	2.0%	2.0%	2.0%	2.0%	2.0%	2.0%	2.0%	2.0%	2.0%	2.0%
Sponsor	2	2.0%	2.0%	2.0%	2.0%	2.0%	2.0%	2.0%	2.0%	2.0%	2.0%
Management	3	2.0%	2.0%	2.0%	2.0%	2.0%	2.0%	2.0%	2.0%	2.0%	2.0%
Downside 1	4	2.0%	2.0%	2.0%	2.0%	2.0%	2.0%	2.0%	2.0%	2.0%	2.0%
Downside 2	5	2.0%	2.0%	2.0%	2.0%	2.0%	2.0%	2.0%	2.0%	2.0%	2.0%
Interest Income											
Base	1	3.0%	3.0%	3.0%	3.0%	3.0%	3.0%	3.0%	3.0%	3.0%	3.0%
Sponsor	2	3.0%	3.0%	3.0%	3.0%	3.0%	3.0%	3.0%	3.0%	3.0%	3.0%
Management	3	3.0%	3.0%	3.0%	3.0%	3.0%	3.0%	3.0%	3.0%	3.0%	3.0%
Downside 1	4	3.0%	3.0%	3.0%	3.0%	3.0%	3.0%	3.0%	3.0%	3.0%	3.0%
Downside 2	5	3.0%	3.0%	3.0%	3.0%	3.0%	5.0%	5.0%	5.0%	5.0%	5.0%
Cash Flow Statement Assumptions											
Capital Expenditures (% sales)											
Base	1	2.0%	2.0%	2.0%	2.0%	2.0%	2.0%	2.0%	2.0%	2.0%	2.0%
Sponsor	2	2.0%	2.0%	2.0%	2.0%	2.0%	2.0%	2.0%	2.0%	2.0%	2.0%
Management	3	2.0%	2.0%	2.0%	2.0%	2.0%	2.0%	2.0%	2.0%	2.0%	2.0%
Downside 1	4	2.5%	2.5%	2.5%	2.5%	2.5%	2.5%	2.5%	2.5%	2.5%	2.5%
Downside 2	5	2.5%	2.5%	2.5%	2.5%	2.5%	2.5%	2.5%	2.5%	2.5%	2.5%

EXHIBIT 5.53 ValueCo LBO Assumptions Page 2

		Projection Period									
		Year 1 2009	Year 2 2010	Year 3 2011	Year 4 2012	Year 5 2013	Year 6 2014	Year 7 2015	Year 8 2016	Year 9 2017	Year 10 2018
Current Assets											
Days Sales Outstanding (DSO)											
Base	1	60.2	60.2	60.2	60.2	60.2	60.2	60.2	60.2	60.2	60.2
Sponsor	2	60.2	60.2	60.2	60.2	60.2	60.2	60.2	60.2	60.2	60.2
Management	3	65.0	65.0	65.0	65.0	65.0	65.0	65.0	65.0	65.0	65.0
Downside 1	4	59.0	59.0	59.0	59.0	59.0	59.0	59.0	59.0	59.0	59.0
Downside 2	5	57.7	57.7	57.7	57.7	57.7	57.7	57.7	57.7	57.7	57.7
Days Inventory Held (DIH)											
Base	1	76.0	76.0	76.0	76.0	76.0	76.0	76.0	76.0	76.0	76.0
Sponsor	2	76.0	76.0	76.0	76.0	76.0	76.0	76.0	76.0	76.0	76.0
Management	3	76.0	76.0	76.0	76.0	76.0	76.0	76.0	76.0	76.0	76.0
Downside 1	4	80.0	80.0	80.0	80.0	80.0	80.0	80.0	80.0	80.0	80.0
Downside 2	5	82.0	82.0	82.0	82.0	82.0	82.0	82.0	82.0	82.0	82.0
Prepaids and Other Current Assets (% sales)											
Base	1	1.0%	1.0%	1.0%	1.0%	1.0%	1.0%	1.0%	1.0%	1.0%	1.0%
Sponsor	2	1.0%	1.0%	1.0%	1.0%	1.0%	1.0%	1.0%	1.0%	1.0%	1.0%
Management	3	1.0%	1.0%	1.0%	1.0%	1.0%	1.0%	1.0%	1.0%	1.0%	1.0%
Downside 1	4	1.0%	1.0%	1.0%	1.0%	1.0%	1.0%	1.0%	1.0%	1.0%	1.0%
Downside 2	5	1.0%	1.0%	1.0%	1.0%	1.0%	1.0%	1.0%	1.0%	1.0%	1.0%
Current Liabilities											
Days Payable Outstanding (DPO)											
Base	1	45.6	45.6	45.6	45.6	45.6	45.6	45.6	45.6	45.6	45.6
Sponsor	2	45.6	45.6	45.6	45.6	45.6	45.6	45.6	45.6	45.6	45.6
Management	3	47.0	47.0	47.0	47.0	47.0	47.0	47.0	47.0	47.0	47.0
Downside 1	4	42.5	42.5	42.5	42.5	42.5	42.5	42.5	42.5	42.5	42.5
Downside 2	5	40.0	40.0	40.0	40.0	40.0	40.0	40.0	40.0	40.0	40.0
Accrued Liabilities (% sales)											
Base	1	10.0%	10.0%	10.0%	10.0%	10.0%	10.0%	10.0%	10.0%	10.0%	10.0%
Sponsor	2	10.0%	10.0%	10.0%	10.0%	10.0%	10.0%	10.0%	10.0%	10.0%	10.0%
Management	3	10.0%	10.0%	10.0%	10.0%	10.0%	10.0%	10.0%	10.0%	10.0%	10.0%
Downside 1	4	10.0%	10.0%	10.0%	10.0%	10.0%	10.0%	10.0%	10.0%	10.0%	10.0%
Downside 2	5	10.0%	10.0%	10.0%	10.0%	10.0%	10.0%	10.0%	10.0%	10.0%	10.0%
Other Current Liabilities (% sales)											
Base	1	2.5%	2.5%	2.5%	2.5%	2.5%	2.5%	2.5%	2.5%	2.5%	2.5%
Sponsor	2	2.5%	2.5%	2.5%	2.5%	2.5%	2.5%	2.5%	2.5%	2.5%	2.5%
Management	3	2.5%	2.5%	2.5%	2.5%	2.5%	2.5%	2.5%	2.5%	2.5%	2.5%
Downside 1	4	2.5%	2.5%	2.5%	2.5%	2.5%	2.5%	2.5%	2.5%	2.5%	2.5%
Downside 2	5	2.5%	2.5%	2.5%	2.5%	2.5%	2.5%	2.5%	2.5%	2.5%	2.5%

EXHIBIT 5.54 ValueCo LBO Assumptions Page 3

($ in millions)

Financing Structures

Sources of Funds	Structure 1 (1)	Structure 2 (2)	Structure 3 (3)	Structure 4 (4)	Status Quo (5)
Revolving Credit Facility Size	$100.0	$100.0	$100.0	$100.0	$100.0
Revolving Credit Facility Draw	-	25.0	25.0	25.0	-
Term Loan A	-	125.0	-	-	-
Term Loan B	450.0	350.0	350.0	425.0	-
Term Loan C	-	-	-	-	-
2nd Lien	-	-	150.0	-	-
Senior Notes	300.0	300.0	250.0	325.0	-
Senior Subordinated Notes	385.0	360.0	385.0	410.0	-
Equity Contribution	-	-	-	-	-
Rollover Equity	-	-	-	-	-
Cash on Hand	25.0	25.0	-	-	-
Total Sources of Funds	**$1,160.0**	**$1,160.0**	**$1,160.0**	**$1,160.0**	**$1,160.0**

Uses of Funds	Structure 1	Structure 2	Structure 3	Structure 4	Status Quo
Equity Purchase Price	$825.0	$825.0	$825.0	$825.0	-
Repay Existing Bank Debt	300.0	300.0	300.0	300.0	-
Tender / Call Premiums	-	-	-	-	-
Financing Fees	20.0	20.0	20.0	20.0	-
Other Fees and Expenses	15.0	15.0	15.0	15.0	-
Total Uses of Funds	**$1,160.0**	**$1,160.0**	**$1,160.0**	**$1,160.0**	**$1,160.0**

Purchase Price

Public / Private Target

Entry EBITDA Multiple	7.5x
LTM 9/30/2008 EBITDA	146.7
Enterprise Value	**$1,100.0**
Less: Total Debt	(300.0)
Less: Preferred Securities	-
Less: Minority Interest	-
Plus: Cash and Cash Equivalents	25.0
Equity Purchase Price	**$825.0**

Calculation of Fully Diluted Shares Outstanding

Offer Price per Share	-
Basic Shares Outstanding	
Plus: Shares from In-the-Money Options	
Less: Shares Repurchased	
Net New Shares from Options	
Plus: Shares from Convertible Securities	
Fully Diluted Shares Outstanding	

Outstanding Options/Warrants

Tranche	Number of Shares	Exercise Price	In-the-Money Shares	Proceeds
Tranche 1	-	-	-	-
Tranche 2	-	-	-	-
Tranche 3	-	-	-	-
Tranche 4	-	-	-	-
Tranche 5	-	-	-	-
Total			-	-

Convertible Securities

	Amount	Conversion Price	Conversion Ratio	New Shares
Issue 1	-	-	-	-
Issue 2	-	-	-	-
Issue 3	-	-	-	-
Issue 4	-	-	-	-
Issue 5	-	-	-	-
Total				-

Financing Fees

Structure 1

	Size	Fees (%)	Fees ($)
Revolving Credit Facility Size	$100.0	1.750%	$1.8
Term Loan A	-	1.750%	-
Term Loan B	450.0	1.750%	7.9
Term Loan C	-		
2nd Lien	-		
Senior Notes		2.250%	
Senior Subordinated Notes	300.0	2.250%	6.8
Senior Bridge Facility		1.000%	
Senior Subordinated Bridge Facility	300.0	1.000%	3.0
Other Financing Fees & Expenses			0.6
Total Financing Fees			**$20.0**

Amortization of Financing Fees

	Term	Year 1 2009	Year 2 2010	Year 3 2011	Year 4 2012	Year 5 2013	Year 6 2014	Year 7 2015	Year 8 2016	Year 9 2017	Year 10 2018
Revolving Credit Facility Size	6	$0.3	$0.3	$0.3	$0.3	$0.3	$0.3	-	-	-	-
Term Loan A	7	1.1	1.1	1.1	1.1	1.1	1.1	1.1	-	-	-
Term Loan B	-	-	-	-	-	-	-	-	-	-	-
Term Loan C	-	-	-	-	-	-	-	-	-	-	-
2nd Lien	-	-	-	-	-	-	-	-	-	-	-
Senior Notes	10	0.7	0.7	0.7	0.7	0.7	0.7	0.7	0.7	0.7	0.7
Senior Subordinated Notes	10	0.3	0.3	0.3	0.3	0.3	0.3	0.3	0.3	0.3	0.3
Senior Bridge Facility	10	0.1	0.1	0.1	0.1	0.1	0.1	0.1	0.1	0.1	0.1
Senior Subordinated Bridge Facility	10	0.1	0.1	0.1	0.1	0.1	0.1	0.1	0.1	0.1	0.1
Other Financing Fees & Expenses											
Annual Amortization		$2.5	$2.5	$2.5	$2.5	$2.5	$2.5	$2.2	$1.0	$1.0	$1.0
Administrative Agent Fee		0.2	0.2	0.2	0.2	0.2	0.2	0.2	0.2	0.2	0.2

Mergers & Acquisitions

CHAPTER 6

M&A Sale Process

The sale of a company, division, business, or collection of assets ("target") is a major event for its owners (shareholders), management, employees, and other stakeholders. It is an intense, time-consuming process with high stakes, usually spanning several months. Consequently, the seller typically hires an investment bank and its team of trained professionals ("sell-side advisor") to ensure that key objectives are met and a favorable result is achieved. In many cases, a seller turns to its bankers for a comprehensive financial analysis of the various strategic alternatives available to the target. These include a sale of all or part of the business, a recapitalization, an initial public offering, or a continuation of the status quo.

Once the decision to sell has been made, the sell-side advisor seeks to achieve the optimal mix of value maximization, speed of execution, and certainty of completion among other deal-specific considerations for the selling party. Accordingly, it is the sell-side advisor's responsibility to identify the seller's priorities from the onset and craft a tailored sale process. If the seller is relatively indifferent toward confidentiality, timing, and potential business disruption, the advisor may consider running a *broad auction* reaching out to as many potential interested parties as reasonably possible. This process, which is relatively neutral toward prospective buyers, is designed to maximize competitive dynamics and heighten the probability of finding the one buyer willing to offer the best value.

Alternatively, if speed, confidentiality, a particular transaction structure, and/or cultural fit are a priority for the seller, then a *targeted auction,* where only a select group of potential buyers are approached, or even a *negotiated sale* with a single party, may be more appropriate. Generally, an auction requires more upfront organization, marketing, process points, and resources than a negotiated sale with a single party. Consequently, this chapter focuses primarily on the auction process.

From an analytical perspective, a sell-side assignment requires the deal team to perform a comprehensive valuation of the target using those methodologies discussed in this book. In addition, to assess the potential purchase price that specific public strategic buyers may be willing to pay for the target, accretion/(dilution) analysis is performed. These valuation analyses are used to frame the seller's price expectations, set guidelines for the range of acceptable bids, evaluate offers received, and ultimately guide negotiations of the final purchase price. Furthermore, for public targets (and certain private targets, depending on the situation) the sell-side advisor or an additional investment bank may be called upon to provide a fairness opinion.

In discussing the process by which companies are bought and sold in the marketplace, we provide greater context to the topics discussed earlier in this book. In a sale process, theoretical valuation methodologies are ultimately tested in the market based on what a buyer will actually pay for the target (see Exhibit 6.1). An effective sell-side advisor seeks to push the buyer(s) toward, or through, the upper endpoint of the implied valuation range for the target. On a fundamental level, this involves properly positioning the business or assets and tailoring the sale process to maximize its value.

AUCTIONS

An auction is a staged process whereby a target is marketed to multiple prospective buyers ("buyers" or "bidders"). A well-run auction is designed to have a substantial positive impact on value (price and terms) received by the seller due to a variety of factors related to the creation of a competitive environment. This environment encourages bidders to put forth their best offer on both price and terms, and helps increase speed of execution by encouraging quick action by buyers.

An auction provides a level of comfort that the market has been tested as well as a strong indicator of inherent value (supported by a fairness opinion, if required). At the same time, the auction process may have potential drawbacks, including information leakage into the market from bidders, negative impact on employee morale, possible collusion among bidders, reduced negotiating leverage once a "winner" is chosen (thereby encouraging re-trading[1]), and "taint" in the event of a failed auction.

A successful auction requires significant dedicated resources, experience, and expertise. Upfront, the deal team establishes a solid foundation through the preparation of compelling marketing materials, identification of potential deal issues, coaching of management, and selection of an appropriate group of prospective buyers. Once the auction commences, the sell-side advisor is entrusted with running as effective a process as possible, which involves the execution of a wide range of duties and functions in a tightly coordinated manner.

To ensure a successful outcome, investment banks commit a team of bankers that is responsible for the day-to-day execution of the transaction. Auctions also require significant time and attention from key members of the target's management team, especially on the production of marketing materials and facilitation of buyer due diligence (e.g., management presentations, site visits, data room population, and responses to specific buyer inquiries). It is the deal team's responsibility, however, to alleviate as much of this burden from the management team as possible.

In the later stages of an auction, a senior member of the sell-side advisory team typically negotiates directly with prospective buyers with the goal of encouraging them to put forth their best offer. As a result, sellers seek investment banks with extensive negotiation experience, sector expertise, and buyer relationships to run these auctions.

There are two primary types of auctions—broad and targeted.

- **Broad Auction:** As its name implies, a broad auction maximizes the universe of prospective buyers approached. This may involve contacting dozens of potential bidders, comprising both strategic buyers (potentially including direct competitors) and financial sponsors. By casting as wide a net as possible, a broad auction is designed to maximize competitive dynamics, thereby increasing the likelihood

---

[1] Refers to the practice of replacing an initial bid with a lower one at a later date.

EXHIBIT 6.1 Valuation Paradigm

	Implied Valuation Range			Actual Price Paid
Comparable Companies Analysis	Precedent Transactions Analysis	Discounted Cash Flow Analysis	Leveraged Buyout Analysis	M&A Sale Process
Description				
• Valuation based on the current trading multiples of peer companies	• Valuation based on the multiples paid for peer companies in past M&A transactions	• Valuation based on the present value of projected free cash flow	• Valuation based on the price a financial sponsor would likely pay	• Determines the ultimate price a buyer is willing to pay
Common Value Drivers				

• Sector performance and outlook
• Company performance
  - size, margins, and growth profile
  - historical and projected financial performance
• Company positioning
  - market share
  - ability to differentiate products/services
  - quality of management
• General economic and capital markets conditions				

Unique Value Drivers				

• Relative performance to peer companies	• M&A market conditions
	• Deal specific situation
	• Premium paid for control
	• Level of synergies
		• Free Cash Flow
		• Cost of capital
		• Terminal Value
			• Credit market conditions
			• Free Cash Flow
			• Ability to leverage
			• Debt repayment
			• Cost of capital
			• Required returns
				• Process dynamics
				  - auction vs. negotiated sale
				  - number of parties in process
				  - level of information disclosure
				  - "trophy" / must own asset
				• Buyer appetite
				  - strategic vs. sponsor
				  - desire/ability to pay
				  - amount needed to "win"
				• Pro forma impact to buyer
				  - financial effects
				  - pro forma leverage
				  - returns thresholds

of finding the best possible offer. This type of process typically involves more upfront organization and marketing due to the larger number of buyer participants in the early stages of the process. It is also more difficult to maintain confidentiality as the process is susceptible to leakage to the public (including customers, suppliers, and competitors), which, in turn, can increase the potential for business disruption.[2]

- *Targeted Auction:* A targeted auction focuses on a few clearly defined buyers that have been identified as having a strong strategic fit and/or desire, as well as the financial capacity, to purchase the target. This process is more conducive to maintaining confidentiality and minimizing business disruption to the target. At the same time, there is greater risk of "leaving money on the table" by excluding a potential bidder that may be willing to pay a higher price.

Exhibit 6.2 provides a summary of the potential advantages and disadvantages of each process.

EXHIBIT 6.2   Advantages and Disadvantages of Broad and Targeted Auctions

	Broad	Targeted
Advantages	■ Heightens competitive dynamics ■ Maximizes probability of achieving maximum sale price ■ Helps to ensure that all likely bidders are approached ■ Limits potential buyers' negotiating leverage ■ Enhances board's comfort that it has satisfied its fiduciary duty to maximize value	■ Higher likelihood of preserving confidentiality ■ Reduces business disruption ■ Reduces the potential of a failed auction by signaling desire to select a "partner" ■ Maintains perception of competitive dynamics ■ Serves as a "market check" for board in discharge of its fiduciary duties
Disadvantages	■ Difficult to preserve confidentiality ■ Greatest risk of business disruption ■ Some prospective buyers may decline participation in broad auctions ■ Unsuccessful outcome can create perception of an undesirable asset ("taint") ■ Risk that industry competitors may participate just to gain access to sensitive information or key executives	■ Potentially excludes non-obvious, but credible, buyers ■ Potential to leave "money on the table" if certain buyers are excluded ■ Lesser degree of competition ■ May afford buyers more leverage in negotiations ■ Provides less market data on which board can rely to satisfy itself that value has been maximized

---

[2]In some circumstances, the auction is actually made public by the seller to encourage all interested buyers to come forward and state their interest in the target.

Auction Structure

The traditional auction is structured as a two-round bidding process that generally spans from three to six months (or longer) from the decision to sell until the signing of a definitive purchase/sale agreement ("definitive agreement") with the winning bidder (see Exhibit 6.3). The timing of the post signing ("closing") period depends on a variety of factors not specific to an auction, such as regulatory approvals and/or third-party consents, financing, and shareholder approval. The entire auction process consists of multiple stages and discrete milestones within each of these stages. There are numerous variations within this structure that allow the sell-side advisor to customize, as appropriate, for a given situation.

EXHIBIT 6.3 Stages of an Auction Process

		Stages of an Auction Process		
Organization and Preparation	**First Round**	**Second Round**	**Negotiations**	**Closing**
■ Identify seller objectives and determine appropriate sale process ■ Perform sell-side advisor due diligence and preliminary valuation analysis ■ Select buyer universe ■ Prepare marketing materials ■ Prepare confidentiality agreement	■ Contact prospective buyers ■ Negotiate and execute confidentiality agreements with interested parties ■ Distribute CIM and initial bid procedures letter ■ Prepare management presentation ■ Set up data room ■ Prepare stapled financing package (if applicable) ■ Receive initial bids and select buyers to proceed to second round	■ Conduct management presentations ■ Facilitate site visits ■ Provide data room access ■ Distribute final bid procedures letter and draft definitive agreement ■ Receive final bids	■ Evaluate final bids ■ Negotiate with preferred buyer(s) ■ Select winning bidder ■ Render fairness opinion (if required) ■ Receive board approval and execute definitive agreement ("signing")	■ Obtain necessary approvals ■ Financing and closing
2 – 4 weeks	4 – 6 weeks	6 – 8 weeks	2 – 6 weeks (may include a third "mini round")	4 – 8 weeks +

ORGANIZATION AND PREPARATION

- Identify Seller Objectives and Determine Appropriate Sale Process
- Perform Sell-Side Advisor Due Diligence and Preliminary Valuation Analysis
- Select Buyer Universe
- Prepare Marketing Materials
- Prepare Confidentiality Agreement

Identify Seller Objectives and Determine Appropriate Sale Process

At the onset of an auction, the sell-side advisor works with the seller to identify its objectives, determine the appropriate sale process to conduct, and develop a process roadmap. The advisor must first gain a clear understanding of the seller's priorities so as to tailor the process accordingly. Perhaps the most basic decision is how many prospective buyers to approach (i.e., whether to run a broad or targeted auction).

As previously discussed, while a broad auction may be more appealing to a seller in certain circumstances, a targeted auction may better satisfy certain "softer" needs, such as speed to transaction closing, heightened confidentiality, and less risk of business disruption. Furthermore, the target's board of directors must also take into account its fiduciary duties in deciding whether to conduct a broad or targeted auction.[3] At this point, the deal team drafts a detailed process timeline and roadmap, including target dates for significant milestones, such as launch, receipt of initial and final bids, contract signing, and deal closing.

Perform Sell-Side Advisor Due Diligence and Preliminary Valuation Analysis

Sale process preparation begins with extensive due diligence on the part of the sell-side advisor. This typically begins with an in-depth session with target management. The sell-side advisor must have a comprehensive understanding of the target's business and the management team's vision prior to drafting marketing materials and communicating with prospective buyers. Due diligence facilitates the advisor's ability to properly position the target and articulate its investment merits. It also allows for the identification of potential buyer concerns on issues ranging from growth sustainability, margin trends, and customer concentration to environmental matters, contingent liabilities, and labor relations.

---

[3]In Delaware (which generally sets the standards upon which many states base their corporate law), when the sale of control or the break-up of a company has become inevitable, the directors have the duty to obtain the highest price reasonably available. There is no statutory or judicial "blueprint" for an appropriate sale or auction process. Directors enjoy some latitude in this regard, so long as the process is designed to satisfy the directors' duties by ensuring that they have reasonably informed themselves about the company's value.

A key portion of sell-side diligence centers on ensuring that the sell-side advisor understands and provides perspective on the assumptions that drive management's financial model. This diligence is particularly important as the model forms the basis for the valuation work that will be performed by prospective buyers. Therefore, the sell-side advisor must approach the target's financial projections from a buyer's perspective and gain comfort with the numbers, trends, and key assumptions driving them.

An effective sell-side advisor understands the valuation methodologies that buyers will use in their analysis (e.g., comparable companies, precedent transactions, DCF analysis, and LBO analysis) and performs this work beforehand to establish a valuation range benchmark. For specific public buyers, accretion/(dilution) analysis is also performed to assess their ability to pay. Ultimately, however, the target's implied valuation based on these methodologies needs to be weighed against market appetite. Furthermore, the actual value received in a transaction must be viewed in both terms of price and terms negotiated in the definitive agreement.

In the event a stapled financing package is being provided, a separate financing deal team is formed (either at the sell-side advisor's institution or another bank) to begin conducting due diligence in parallel with the sell-side team. Their analysis is used to craft a generic pre-packaged financing structure to support the purchase of the target.[4] The initial financing package terms are used as guideposts to derive an implied LBO analysis valuation.

Select Buyer Universe

The selection of an appropriate group of prospective buyers, and compilation of corresponding contact information, is a critical part of the organization and preparation stage. At the extreme, the omission or inclusion of a potential buyer (or buyers) can mean the difference between a successful or failed auction. Sell-side advisors are selected in large part on the basis of their sector knowledge, including their relationships with, and insights on, prospective buyers. Correspondingly, the deal team is expected to both identify the appropriate buyers and effectively market the target to them.

In a broad auction, the buyer list typically includes a mix of strategic buyers and financial sponsors. The sell-side advisor evaluates each buyer on a broad range of criteria pertinent to its likelihood and ability to acquire the target at an acceptable value. When evaluating strategic buyers, the banker looks first and foremost at strategic fit, including potential synergies. Financial capacity or "ability to pay"—which is typically dependent on size, balance sheet strength, access to financing, and risk appetite—is also closely scrutinized. Other factors play a role in assessing potential strategic bidders, such as cultural fit, M&A track record, existing management's role going forward, relative and pro forma market position (including antitrust concerns), and effects on existing customer and supplier relationships.

---

[4]Ultimately, buyers who require financing to complete a deal will typically work with multiple banks to ensure they are receiving the most favorable financing package (debt quantum, pricing, and terms) available in the market.

When evaluating potential financial sponsor buyers, key criteria include investment strategy/focus, sector expertise, fund size,[5] track record, fit within existing investment portfolio, fund life cycle,[6] and ability to obtain financing. As part of this process, the deal team looks for sponsors with existing portfolio companies that may serve as an attractive combination candidate for the target. In many cases, a strategic buyer is able to pay a higher price than a sponsor due to the ability to realize synergies and a lower cost of capital. Depending on the prevailing capital markets conditions, a strategic buyer may also present less financing risk than a sponsor.

Once the sell-side advisor has compiled a list of prospective buyers, it presents them to the seller for final sign-off.

Prepare Marketing Materials

Marketing materials often represent the first formal introduction of the target to prospective buyers. They are essential for sparking buyer interest and creating a favorable first impression. Effective marketing materials present the target's investment highlights in a succinct manner, while also providing supporting evidence and basic operational, financial, and other essential business information. The two main marketing documents for the first round of an auction process are the *teaser* and confidential information memorandum (CIM). The sell-side advisors take the lead on producing these materials with substantial input from management. Legal counsel also reviews these documents, as well as the management presentation, for various potential legal concerns (e.g., antitrust[7]).

Teaser The teaser is the first marketing document presented to prospective buyers. It is designed to inform buyers and generate sufficient interest for them to do further work and potentially submit a bid. The teaser is generally a brief one- or two-page synopsis of the target, including a company overview, investment highlights, and summary financial information. It also contains contact information for the bankers running the sell-side process so that interested parties may respond.

Teasers vary in terms of format and content in accordance with the target, sector, sale process, advisor, and potential seller sensitivities. For public companies, Regulation FD concerns govern the content of the teaser (i.e., no material non-public information) as well as the nature of the buyer contacts themselves.[8] Exhibit 6.4 displays an illustrative teaser template as might be presented to prospective buyers.

---

[5] Refers to the total size of the fund as well as remaining equity available for investment.

[6] As set forth in the agreement between the fund's GP and LPs, refers to how long the fund will be permitted to seek investments prior to entering a harvest and distribution phase.

[7] Typically, counsel closely scrutinizes any discussion of a business combination (i.e., in a strategic transaction) as marketing materials will be subjected to scrutiny by antitrust authorities in connection with their regulatory review.

[8] The initial buyer contact or teaser can put a public company "in play" and may constitute the selective disclosure of material information (i.e., that the company is for sale).

EXHIBIT 6.4 Sample Teaser

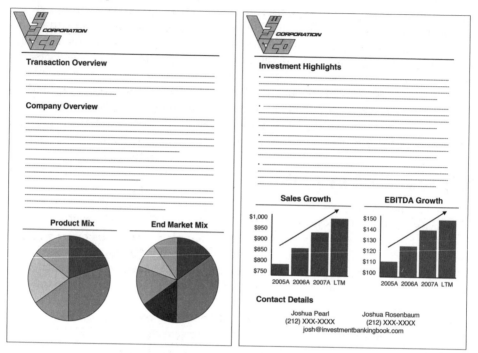

Confidential Information Memorandum The CIM is a detailed written description of the target (often 50+ pages) that serves as the primary marketing document for the target in an auction. The deal team, in collaboration with the target's management, spends significant time and resources drafting the CIM before it is deemed ready for distribution to prospective buyers. In the event the seller is a financial sponsor (e.g., selling a portfolio company), the sponsor's investment professionals typically also provide input.

Like teasers, CIMs vary in terms of format and content depending on situation-specific circumstances. There are, however, certain generally accepted guidelines for content, as reflected in Exhibit 6.5. The CIM typically contains an executive summary, investment considerations, and detailed information about the target, as well as its sector, customers and suppliers (often presented on an anonymous basis), operations, facilities, management, and employees. A modified version of the CIM may be prepared for designated strategic buyers, namely competitors with whom the seller may be concerned about sharing certain sensitive information.

Financial Information The CIM contains a detailed financial section presenting historical and projected financial information with accompanying narrative explaining both past and expected future performance (MD&A). This data forms the basis for the preliminary valuation analysis performed by prospective buyers.

Consequently, the deal team spends a great deal of time working with the target's CFO, treasurer, and/or finance team (and division heads, as appropriate) on the CIM's financial section. This process involves normalizing the historical financials (e.g., for acquisitions, divestitures, and other one-time and/or extraordinary items) and crafting an accompanying MD&A. The sell-side advisor also helps develop a set of projections, typically five years in length, as well as supporting assumptions and narrative. Given the importance of the projections in framing valuation, prospective buyers subject them to intense scrutiny. Therefore, the sell-side advisor must gain sufficient comfort that the numbers are realistic and defensible in the face of potential buyer skepticism.

In some cases, the CIM provides additional financial information to help guide buyers toward potential growth/acquisition scenarios for the target. For example, the sell-side advisor may work with management to compile a list of potential acquisition opportunities for inclusion in the CIM (typically on an anonymous basis), including their incremental sales and EBITDA contributions. This information is designed to provide potential buyers with perspective on the potential upside represented by using the target as a growth platform so they can craft their bids accordingly.

EXHIBIT 6.5 Sample Confidential Information Memorandum Table of Contents

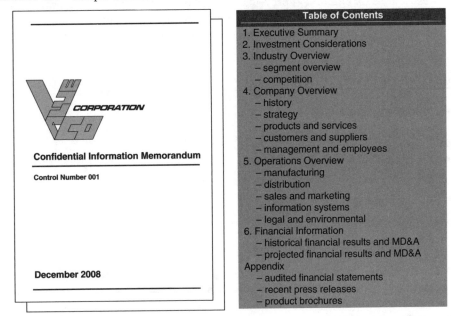

Prepare Confidentiality Agreement

A confidentiality agreement (CA) is a legally binding contract between the target and each prospective buyer that governs the sharing of confidential company information. The CA is typically drafted by the target's counsel and distributed to prospective buyers along with the teaser, with the understanding that the receipt of more detailed information is conditioned on execution of the CA.

A typical CA includes provisions governing the following:

- *Use of information* – states that all information furnished by the seller, whether oral or written, is considered proprietary information and should be treated as confidential and used solely to make a decision regarding the proposed transaction

- *Term* – designates the time period during which the confidentiality restrictions remain in effect[9]

- *Permitted disclosures* – outlines under what limited circumstances the prospective buyer is permitted to disclose the confidential information provided; also prohibits disclosure that the two parties are in negotiations

- *Return of confidential information* – mandates the return or destruction of all provided documents once the prospective buyer exits the process

- *Non-solicitation/no hire* – prevents prospective buyers from soliciting to hire (or hiring) target employees for a designated time period

- *Standstill agreement*[10] – for public targets, precludes prospective buyers from making unsolicited offers or purchases of the target's shares, or seeking to control/influence the target's management, board of directors, or policies

- *Restrictions on clubbing* – prevents prospective buyers from collaborating with each other or with outside financial sponsors/equity providers without the prior consent of the target (in order to preserve a competitive environment)

FIRST ROUND

- Contact Prospective Buyers

- Negotiate and Execute Confidentiality Agreements with Interested Parties

- Distribute Confidential Information Memorandum and Initial Bid Procedures Letter

- Prepare Management Presentation

- Set up Data Room

- Prepare Stapled Financing Package (if applicable)

- Receive Initial Bids and Select Buyers to Proceed to Second Round

Contact Prospective Buyers

The first round begins with the contacting of prospective buyers, which marks the formal launch of the auction process. This typically takes the form of a scripted phone call to each prospective buyer by a senior member of the sell-side advisory team (and/or the coverage banker that maintains the relationship with the particular buyer), followed by the delivery of the teaser and CA.[11] The sell-side advisor generally keeps a detailed record of all interactions with prospective buyers, called a contact log, which is used as a tool to monitor a buyer's activity level and provide a record of the process.

---

[9]Typically one-to-two years for financial sponsors and potentially longer for strategic buyers.
[10]May also be crafted as a separate legal document outside of the CA.
[11]In some cases, the CA must be signed prior to receipt of any information, including the teaser, depending on seller sensitivity.

Negotiate and Execute Confidentiality Agreement with Interested Parties

Upon receipt of the CA, a prospective buyer presents the document to its legal counsel for review. In the likely event there are comments, the buyer's counsel and seller's counsel negotiate the CA with input from their respective clients. Following execution of the CA, the sell-side advisor is legally able to distribute the CIM and *initial bid procedures letter* to a prospective buyer.[12]

Distribute Confidential Information Memorandum and Initial Bid Procedures Letter

Prospective buyers are typically given several weeks to review the CIM,[13] study the target and its sector, and conduct preliminary financial analysis prior to submitting their initial non-binding bids. During this period, the sell-side advisor maintains a dialogue with the prospective buyers, often providing additional color, guidance, and materials, as appropriate, on a case-by-case basis.

Depending on their level of interest, prospective buyers may also engage investment banks (as M&A buy-side advisors and/or financing providers), other external financing sources, and consultants at this stage. Buy-side advisors play a critical role in helping their client, whether a strategic buyer or a financial sponsor, assess the target from a valuation perspective and determine a competitive initial bid price. Financing sources help assess both the buyer's and target's ability to support a given capital structure and provide their clients with data points on amounts, terms, and availability of financing. This financing data is used to help frame the valuation analysis performed by the buyer. Consultants provide perspective on key business and market opportunities, as well as potential risks and areas of operational improvement for the target.

Initial Bid Procedures Letter   The initial bid procedures letter, which is typically sent out to prospective buyers following distribution of the CIM, states the date and time by which interested parties must submit their written, non-binding preliminary indications of interest ("first round bids"). It also defines the exact information that should be included in the bid, such as:

- Indicative purchase price (typically presented as a range) and form of consideration (cash vs. stock mix)[14]

- Key assumptions to arrive at the stated purchase price

- Structural and other considerations

- Information on financing sources

---

[12]Calls are usually commenced one-to-two weeks prior to the CIM being printed to allow sufficient time for the negotiation of CAs. Ideally, the sell-side advisor prefers to distribute the CIMs simultaneously to provide all prospective buyers an equal amount of time to consider the investment prior to the bid due date.

[13]Each CIM is given a unique control number that is used to track each party that receives a copy.

[14]For acquisitions of private companies, buyers are typically asked to bid assuming the target is both cash and debt free.

- Treatment of management and employees

- Timing for completing a deal and diligence that must be performed

- Key conditions to signing and closing

- Required approvals

- Buyer contact information

Prepare Management Presentation

The management presentation is typically structured as a slideshow with accompanying hardcopy handout. The sell-side advisor takes the lead on preparing these materials with substantial input from management. In parallel, the sell-side advisor works with the management team to determine the speaker lineup for the presentation, as well as key messages, and the preparation of answers for likely questions. Depending on the management team, the rehearsal process for the presentations ("dry runs") may be intense and time-consuming. The management presentation slideshow needs to be completed by the start of the second round when the actual meetings with buyers begin.

The presentation format generally maps to that of the CIM, but is more crisp and concise. It also tends to contain an additional level of detail, analysis, and insight more conducive to an interactive session with management and later-stage due diligence. A typical management presentation outline is shown in Exhibit 6.6.

EXHIBIT 6.6   Sample Management Presentation Outline

Set up Data Room

The data room serves as the hub for the buyer due diligence that takes place in the second round of the process. It is a location, typically online, where comprehensive, detailed information about the target is stored, catalogued, and made available to pre-screened bidders.[15] A well-organized data room facilitates buyer due diligence, helps keep the sale process on schedule, and inspires confidence in bidders. While most data rooms follow certain basic guidelines, they may vary greatly in terms of content and accessibility depending on the company and confidentiality concerns.

Data rooms generally contain a broad base of essential company information, documentation, and analyses. In essence, the data room is designed to provide a comprehensive set of information relevant for buyers to make an informed investment decision about the target, such as detailed financial reports, industry reports, and consulting studies. It also contains detailed company-specific information such as customer and supplier lists, labor contracts, purchase contracts, description and terms of outstanding debt, lease and pension contracts, and environmental compliance certification (see Exhibit 6.7). At the same time, the content must reflect any concerns over sharing sensitive data for competitive reasons.[16]

The data room also allows the buyer (together with its legal counsel, accountants, and other advisors) to perform more detailed confirmatory due diligence prior to consummating a transaction. This due diligence includes reviewing charters/bylaws, outstanding litigation, regulatory information, environmental reports, and property deeds, for example. It is typically conducted only after a buyer has decided to seriously pursue the acquisition.

The sell-side bankers work closely with the target's legal counsel and selected employees to organize, populate, and manage the data room. While the data room is continuously updated and refreshed with new information throughout the auction, the aim is to have a basic data foundation in place by the start of the second round. Access to the data room is typically granted to those buyers that move forward after first round bids, prior to, or coinciding with, their attendance at the management presentation.

Prepare Stapled Financing Package

The investment bank running the auction process (or sometimes a "partner" bank) may prepare a "pre-packaged" financing structure in support of the target being sold. The staple, which is targeted toward sponsors, was a mainstay in auction processes during the LBO boom of the mid-2000s. Although prospective buyers are not required to use the staple, historically it has positioned the sell-side advisor to play a role in the deal's financing. Often, however, buyers seek their own financing

---

[15]Prior to the establishment of web-based data retrieval systems, data rooms were physical locations (i.e., offices or rooms, usually housed at the target's law firm) where file cabinets or boxes containing company documentation were set up. Today, however, most data rooms are online sites where buyers can view all the necessary documentation remotely. Among other benefits, the online process facilitates the participation of a greater number of prospective buyers as data room documents can be reviewed simultaneously by different parties. They also enable the seller to customize the viewing, downloading, and printing of various data and documentation for specific buyers.

[16]Sensitive information (e.g., customer, supplier, and employment contracts) is generally withheld from competitor bidders until later in the process.

EXHIBIT 6.7   General Data Room Index

Data Room Index	
1. Organization and Structure ■ Corporate organizational chart ■ Board of directors meeting minutes **2. Financial Information** ■ Audited financial statements ■ Financial model **3. Operational Overview** ■ Contracts and agreements ■ Machinery and equipment leases **4. Research and Development** ■ List of current programs ■ List of completed programs **5. Suppliers** ■ Top 10 suppliers ■ Supplier agreements **6. Products and Markets** ■ Top 10 competitors ■ Market consulting reports **7. Sales and Marketing** ■ Top 10 customers ■ Customer agreements **8. Intellectual Property** ■ List of patents, trademarks, and copyrights ■ Software license agreements	**9. Management and Employee Matters** ■ Employment agreements/benefits ■ Employee options details **10. Property Overview** ■ Summary of owned/leased real estate ■ Deeds, mortgage documents, and leases **11. Insurance** ■ List of insurance policies ■ List of insurance claims **12. Environmental Matters** ■ List of environmental issues ■ Compliance certificates **13. Litigation** ■ List of pending or threatened litigation ■ List of judgments and settlements **14. Legal Documentation** ■ Charters; by-laws ■ Governmental regulations and filings **15. Debt** ■ List of outstanding debt ■ Credit agreements and indentures **16. Regulation** ■ List of appropriate regulatory agencies ■ List of any necessary permits

sources to match or "beat" the staple. Alternatively, certain buyers may choose to use less leverage than provided by the staple.

To avoid a potential conflict of interest, the investment bank running the M&A sell-side sets up a separate financing team distinct from the sell-side advisory team to run the staple process. This financing team is tasked with providing an objective assessment of the target's leverage capacity. They conduct due diligence and financial analysis separately from (but often in parallel with) the M&A team and craft a viable financing structure that is presented to the bank's internal credit committee for approval. This financing package is then presented to the seller for sign-off, after which it is offered to prospective buyers as part of the sale process.

The basic terms of the staple are typically communicated verbally to buyers in advance of the first round bid date so they can use that information to help frame their bids. Staple term sheets and/or actual financing commitments are not provided until later in the auction's second round, prior to submission of final bids. Those investment banks without debt underwriting capabilities (e.g., middle market or boutique investment banks) may pair up with a partner bank capable of providing a staple, if requested by the client.

While buyers are not obligated to use the staple, it is designed to send a strong signal of support from the sell-side bank and provide comfort that the necessary financing will be available to buyers for the acquisition. The staple may also compress the timing between the start of the auction's second round and signing of a definitive agreement by eliminating duplicate buyer financing due diligence. To some extent, the staple may serve to establish a valuation floor for the target by setting a leverage level that can be used as the basis for extrapolating a purchase price. For example, a staple offering debt financing equal to 4.5x LTM EBITDA with a 25% minimum equity contribution would imply a purchase price of at least 6.0x LTM EBITDA.

Receive Initial Bids and Select Buyers to Proceed to Second Round

On the first round bid date, the sell-side advisor receives the initial indications of interest from prospective buyers. Over the next few days, the deal team conducts a thorough analysis of the bids received, assessing indicative purchase price as well as key terms and other stated conditions. There may also be dialogue with certain buyers at this point, typically focused on seeking clarification on key bid points.

An effective sell-side advisor is able to discern which bids are "real" (i.e., less likely to be re-traded). Furthermore, it may be apparent that certain bidders are simply trying to get a free look at the target without any serious intent to consummate a transaction. As previously discussed, the advisor's past deal experience and specific knowledge of the given sector and buyer universe is key in this respect.

Once this analysis is completed, the bid information is then summarized and presented to the seller along with a recommendation on which buyers to invite to the second round (see Exhibit 6.8 for sample graphical presentation of purchase price ranges from bidders). The final decision regarding which buyers should advance, however, is made by the seller in consultation with its advisors.

Valuation Perspectives – Strategic Buyers vs. Financial Sponsors   As discussed in Chapters 4 and 5, financial sponsors use LBO analysis and the implied IRRs and cash returns, together with guidance from the other methodologies discussed in this book, to frame their purchase price range. The CIM financial projections and an initial assumed financing structure (e.g., a staple, if provided, or indicative terms from a financing provider) form the basis for the sponsor in formulating a first round bid. The sell-side advisor performs its own LBO analysis in parallel to assess the sponsor bids.

While strategic buyers also rely on the fundamental methodologies discussed in this book to establish a valuation range for a potential acquisition target, they typically employ additional techniques. For example, public strategics use accretion/(dilution) analysis to measure the pro forma effects of the transaction on earnings, assuming a given purchase price and financing structure. The acquirer's EPS pro forma for the transaction is compared to its EPS on a standalone basis. If the pro forma EPS is higher than the standalone EPS, the transaction is said to be *accretive*; conversely, if the pro forma EPS is lower, the transaction is said to be *dilutive*.

Accretion/(Dilution) Analysis   As a general rule, public companies are reluctant to pursue dilutive transactions due to the potential detrimental effect on their share price. Therefore, a given public buyer's perception of valuation and corresponding bid price is often guided by EPS accretion/(dilution) analysis. Maximum accretive effects are achieved by minimizing purchase price, sourcing the least expensive form

EXHIBIT 6.8   First Round Bids Summary

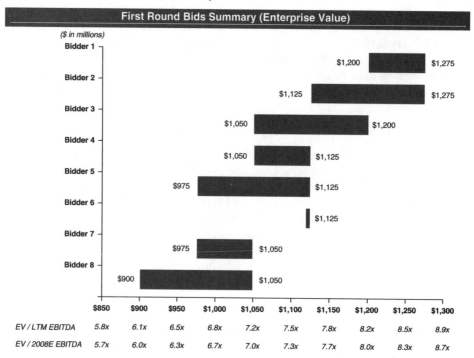

of financing, and identifying significant achievable synergies. However, while certain transactions may not be accretive on day one, they may create escalating value over time. Hence, buyers evaluate the accretive/(dilutive) effects of a transaction on a forward-looking basis taking into account the target's future expected earnings, including growth prospects and other combination effects such as synergies.

From the sell-side advisory perspective, the banker typically performs accretion/(dilution) analysis for the public strategics in the process to assess their ability to pay. This requires making assumptions regarding each specific acquirer's financing mix and cost, as well as synergies. Exhibit 6.9 provides a basic example of how the accretion/(dilution) analysis is performed for an illustrative acquisition of ValueCo by a strategic buyer, StrategicCo. The breakeven pre-tax synergies line item enables the sell-side advisor to assess the maximum price a given strategic buyer can afford to pay based on an assumed financing structure and expected synergies. This information can then be used by the sell-side advisor in negotiations to persuade the buyer to increase its bid.

Based on the various assumptions outlined in Exhibit 6.9, StrategicCo's contemplated purchase of ValueCo for $1,100 million would be accretive by $0.17 per share (or 6% versus standalone EPS) in Year 1. As indicated in the breakeven pre-tax synergies/(cushion) line item, StrategicCo has a cushion of $33.9 million synergies before the deal hits the breakeven accretion/(dilution) point. This means that StrategicCo only needs $16.1+ million in synergies for the deal to be accretive. Assuming the annual synergies of $50 million are achievable, this suggests that StrategicCo can afford to pay higher than the proposed $1,100 million purchase price.

EXHIBIT 6.9   Accretion/(Dilution) Analysis[a]

Acquisition of ValueCo by StrategicCo
50% Stock / 50% Cash Consideration
Accretion / (Dilution) Analysis
($ in millions, except per share data)

= StrategicCo EBIT$_{2009E}$ + ValueCo EBIT$_{2009E}$ + Synergies	= Debt Financing x Cost of Debt
= $500.0 million + $140.4 million + $50.0 million	= $550.0 million x 8.0%

Assumptions

Purchase Price		Financing	
Purchase Price	$1,100.0	Shares Issued by StrategicCo	25.0
% Stock Consideration	50.0%	Debt Financing	$550.0
% Cash Consideration	50.0%	Cost of Debt	8.0%

	Projection Period		
	Year 1 2009	Year 2 2010	Year 3 2011
StrategicCo EBIT	$500.0	$530.0	$551.2
ValueCo EBIT	140.4	148.8	154.8
Synergies	50.0	50.0	50.0
Pro Forma Combined EBIT	**$690.4**	**$728.8**	**$756.0**
Standalone Net Interest Expense	50.0	50.0	50.0
Incremental Net Interest Expense	44.0	44.0	44.0
Earnings Before Taxes	**$596.4**	**$634.8**	**$662.0**
Income Tax Expense @ 38.0%	226.6	241.2	251.6
Pro Forma Combined Net Income	**$369.8**	**$393.6**	**$410.4**
StrategicCo Standalone Net Income	**$279.0**	**$297.6**	**$310.7**
Standalone Fully Diluted Shares Outstanding	100.0	100.0	100.0
Net New Shares Issued in Transaction	25.0	25.0	25.0
Pro Forma Fully Diluted Shares Outstanding	**125.0**	**125.0**	**125.0**
Pro Forma Combined Diluted EPS	$2.96	$3.15	$3.28
StrategicCo Standalone Diluted EPS	2.79	2.98	3.11
Accretion / (Dilution) - $	**$0.17**	**$0.17**	**$0.18**
Accretion / (Dilution) - %	**6.0%**	**5.8%**	**5.7%**
Accretive / Dilutive	*Accretive*	*Accretive*	*Accretive*
Breakeven Pre-Tax Synergies / (Cushion)	(33.9)	(34.8)	(35.5)

= Pro Forma Net Income $_{2009E}$ / Pro Forma Fully Diluted Shares $_{2009E}$
= $369.8 million / 125.0 million

= StrategicCo Standalone Net Income$_{2010E}$ / Standalone Fully Diluted Shares
= $297.6 million / 100.0 million

= Pro Forma Combined Diluted EPS $_{2009E}$ - StrategicCo Standalone Diluted EPS $_{2009E}$
= $2.96 - $2.79

= Pro Forma Combined Diluted EPS$_{2010E}$ / StrategicCo Standalone Diluted EPS$_{2010E}$ - 1
= $3.15 / $2.98 - 1

= - (EPS Accretion/(Dilution) $_{2011E}$ x Pro Forma Fully Diluted Shares) / (1 - Tax Rate)
= - ($0.18 x 125.0 million / (1 - 38.0%)

[a]For simplicity, we do not assume additional transaction-related D&A resulting from writing-up tangible or intangible assets, or additional expenses related to financing fees.

SECOND ROUND

- Conduct Management Presentations
- Facilitate Site Visits
- Provide Data Room Access
- Distribute Final Bid Procedures Letter and Draft Definitive Agreement
- Receive Final Bids

The second round of the auction centers on facilitating the prospective buyers' ability to conduct detailed due diligence and analysis so they can submit strong, final (and ideally) binding bids by the set due date. The diligence process is meant to be exhaustive, typically spanning several weeks, depending on the target's size, sector, geographies, and ownership. The length and nature of the diligence process often differs based on the buyer's profile. A strategic buyer that is a direct competitor of the target, for example, may already have in-depth knowledge of the business and therefore focus on a limited scope of company-specific information.[17] For a financial sponsor that is unfamiliar with the target and its sector, however, due diligence may take longer. As a result, sponsors often seek professional advice from hired consultants, operational advisors, and other industry experts to assist in their due diligence.

The sell-side advisor plays a central role during the second round by coordinating management presentations and facility site visits, monitoring the data room, and maintaining regular dialogue with prospective buyers. During this period, each prospective buyer is afforded time with senior management, a cornerstone of the due diligence process. The buyers also comb through the target's data room, visit key facilities, conduct follow-up diligence sessions with key company officers, and perform detailed financial and industry analyses. Prospective buyers are given sufficient time to complete their due diligence, secure financing, craft a final bid price and structure, and submit a markup of the draft definitive agreement. At the same time, the sell-side advisor seeks to maintain a competitive atmosphere and keep the process moving by limiting the time available for due diligence, access to management, and ensuring bidders move in accordance with the established schedule.

Conduct Management Presentations

The management presentation typically marks the formal kickoff of the second round, often spanning a full business day. At the presentation, the target's management team presents each prospective buyer with a detailed overview of the company, ranging from basic business, industry, and financial information to competitive positioning, future strategy, growth opportunities, synergies (if appropriate), and financial projections. The core team presenting typically consists of the target's CEO, CFO, and key division heads or other operational executives, as appropriate. The

---

[17]Due diligence in these instances may be complicated by the need to limit the prospective buyers' access to highly sensitive information that the seller is unwilling to provide.

presentation is intended to be interactive with Q&A encouraged and expected. It is customary for prospective buyers to bring their investment banking advisors and financing sources, as well as industry and/or operational consultants, to the management presentation so they can conduct their due diligence in parallel and provide insight.

The management presentation is often the buyer's first meeting with management. Therefore, this forum represents a unique opportunity to gain a deeper understanding of the business and its future prospects directly from the individuals who know the company best. Furthermore, the management team itself typically represents a substantial portion of the target's value proposition and is, therefore, a core diligence item. The presentation is also a chance for prospective buyers to gain a sense of "fit" between themselves and management.

Facilitate Site Visits

Site visits are an essential component of buyer due diligence, providing a firsthand view of the target's operations. Often, the management presentation itself takes place at, or near, a key company facility and includes a site visit as part of the agenda. Prospective buyers may also request visits to multiple sites to better understand the target's business and assets. The typical site visit involves a guided tour of a key target facility, such as a manufacturing plant, distribution center, and/or sales office. The guided tours are generally led by the local manager of the given facility, often accompanied by a sub-set of senior management and a member of the sell-side advisory team. They tend to be highly interactive as key buyer representatives, together with their advisors and consultants, use this opportunity to ask detailed questions about the target's operations. In many cases, the seller does not reveal the true purpose of the site visit as employees outside a selected group of senior managers are often unaware a sale process is underway.

Provide Data Room Access

In conjunction with the management presentation and site visits, prospective buyers are provided access to the data room. As outlined in Exhibit 6.7, the data room contains detailed information about all aspects of the target (e.g., business, financial, accounting, tax, legal, insurance, environmental, information technology, and property). Serious bidders dedicate significant resources to ensure their due diligence is as thorough as possible. They often enlist a full team of accountants, attorneys, consultants, and other functional specialists to conduct a comprehensive investigation of company data. Through rigorous data analysis and interpretation, the buyer seeks to identify the key opportunities and risks presented by the target, thereby framing the acquisition rationale and investment thesis. This process also enables the buyer to identify those outstanding items and issues that should be satisfied prior to submitting a formal bid and/or specifically relating to the seller's proposed definitive agreement.

Some online data rooms allow users to download documents, while others only permit screenshots (that may or may not be printable). Similarly, for physical data rooms, some sellers allow photocopying of documents, while others may only permit transcription. Data room access may be tailored to individual bidders or even specific members of the bidder teams (e.g., limited to legal counsel only). For example, strategic buyers that compete directly with the target may be restricted from viewing sensitive competitive information (e.g., customer and supplier contracts), at least until the later stages when the preferred bidder is selected. The sell-side advisor monitors data room access throughout the process, including the viewing of specific items. This enables them to track buyer interest and activity, draw conclusions, and take action accordingly.

As prospective buyers pore through the data, they identify key issues, opportunities, and risks that require follow-up inquiry. The sell-side advisor plays an active role in this respect, channeling follow-up due diligence requests to the appropriate individuals at the target and facilitating an orderly and timely response.

Distribute Final Bid Procedures Letter and Draft Definitive Agreement

During the second round, the *final bid procedures letter* is distributed to the remaining prospective buyers often along with the draft definitive agreement. As part of their final bid package, prospective buyers submit a markup of the draft definitive agreement together with a cover letter detailing their proposal in response to the items outlined in the final bid procedures letter.

Final Bid Procedures Letter   Similar to the initial bid procedures letter in the first round, the final bid procedures letter outlines the exact date and guidelines for submitting a final, legally binding bid package. As would be expected, however, the requirements for the final bid are more stringent, including:

- Purchase price details, including the exact dollar amount of the offer and form of purchase consideration (e.g., cash versus stock)[18]

- Markup of the draft definitive agreement provided by the seller in a form that the buyer would be willing to sign

- Evidence of committed financing and information on financing sources

- Attestation to completion of due diligence (or very limited confirmatory due diligence required)

- Attestation that the offer is binding and will remain open for a designated period of time

- Required regulatory approvals and timeline for completion

- Board of directors approvals (if appropriate)

- Estimated time to sign and close the transaction

- Buyer contact information

---

[18]Like the initial bid procedures letter, for private targets, the buyer is typically asked to bid assuming the target is both cash and debt free. If the target is a public company, the bid will be expressed on a per share basis.

Definitive Agreement   The definitive agreement is a legally binding contract between a buyer and seller detailing the terms and conditions of the sale transaction. In an auction, the first draft is prepared by the seller's legal counsel in collaboration with the seller and its bankers. It is distributed to prospective buyers (and their legal counsel) during the second round—often toward the end of the diligence process. The buyer's counsel then provides specific comments on the draft document (largely informed by the buyer's second round diligence efforts) and submits it as part of the final bid package.

Ideally, the buyer is required to submit a form of revised definitive agreement that it would be willing to sign immediately if the bid is accepted. Often, the buyer's and seller's legal counsel pre-negotiate certain terms in an effort to obtain the most definitive, least conditional revised definitive agreement possible prior to submission to the seller. This aids the seller in evaluating the competing contract terms. Sometimes, however, a prospective buyer refuses to devote legal resources to a specific markup of the definitive agreement until it is informed it has won the auction, instead simply providing an "issues list" in the interim. This can be risky for the seller because it may encourage re-trading on contract terms or tougher negotiations on the agreement after a prospective buyer is identified as the leading or "winning bidder."

Definitive agreements involving public and private companies differ in terms of content, although the basic format of the document is the same, containing an overview of the transaction structure/deal mechanics, representations and warranties, pre-closing commitments (including covenants), closing conditions, termination provisions, and indemnities (if applicable),[19] as well as associated disclosure schedules and exhibits.[20] Exhibit 6.10 provides an overview of some of the key sections of a definitive agreement.

---

[19]Indemnities are generally only included for the sale of private companies or divisions/assets of public companies.

[20]Frequently, the seller's disclosure schedules, which qualify the representations and warranties made by the seller in the definitive agreement and provide other vital information to making an informed bid, are circulated along with the draft definitive agreement.

EXHIBIT 6.10   Key Sections of a Definitive Agreement

Transaction Structure/Deal Mechanics	■ Transaction structure (e.g., merger, stock sale, asset sale)[a] ■ Price and terms (e.g., form of consideration, earn-outs, adjustment to price) ■ Treatment of the target's stock and options (if a merger) ■ Identification of assets and liabilities being transferred (if an asset deal)

Representations and Warranties	■ The buyer and seller make representations ("reps") to each other about their ability to engage in the transaction, and the seller makes reps about the target's business. In a stock-for-stock transaction, the buyer also makes reps about its own business. Examples include:
	  – financial statements must fairly present the current financial position
	  – no material adverse changes (MACs)[b]
	  – all material contracts have been disclosed
	  – availability of funds (usually requested from a financial sponsor)
	■ Reps and warranties serve several purposes:
	  – assist the buyer in due diligence
	  – help assure the buyer it is getting what it thinks it is paying for
	  – baseline for closing condition (see "bring-down" condition below)
	  – baseline for indemnification

Pre-Closing Commitments (Including Covenants)	■ Assurances that the target will operate in the ordinary course between signing and closing, and will not take value-reducing actions or change the business. Examples include:
	  – restrictions on paying special dividends
	  – restrictions on making capital expenditures in excess of an agreed budget
	■ Mutual commitment for the buyer and seller to use their "best efforts" to consummate the transaction, including obtaining regulatory approvals.
	  – the buyer and seller may agree on a maximum level of compromise that the buyer is required to accept from regulatory authorities before it is permitted to walk away from the deal

Other Agreements	■ "No-shop" and other deal protections ■ Treatment of employees post-closing ■ Tax matters (such as the allocation of pre-closing and post-closing taxes within the same tax year) ■ Commitment of the buyer to obtain third-party financing, if necessary, and of the seller to cooperate in obtaining such financing

(Continued)

EXHIBIT 6.10 *(Continued)*

Closing Conditions	■ A party is not required to close the transaction unless the conditions to such party's obligations are satisfied.[c] Key conditions include:
	  – accuracy of the other party's reps and warranties as of the closing date (known as the "bring-down" condition)[d]
	  – compliance by the other party with all of its affirmative covenants
	  – receipt of antitrust clearance and other regulatory approvals
	  – receipt of shareholder approval, if required
	  – absence of injunction

Termination Provisions	■ Circumstances under which one party may terminate the agreement rather than complete the deal. Examples include:
	  – failure to obtain regulatory or shareholder approvals
	  – permanent injunction (i.e., a court order blocking the deal)
	  – seller exercises fiduciary termination (i.e., the right to take a better offer)
	  – deal has not closed by specified outside date ("drop dead date")
	■ In some circumstances, one party may owe a termination fee ("breakup fee") to the other party. Examples include:
	  – if the seller terminates the deal to take a better offer, the seller pays a breakup fee to the buyer
	  – if the seller terminates because the buyer can not come up with financing, the buyer may owe a breakup fee to the seller

Indemnification	■ Typically, in private deals only (public shareholders do not provide indemnities in public deals), the parties will indemnify each other for breaches of the representations and warranties. As a practical matter, it is usually the buyer that is seeking indemnity from the seller.[e] For example:
	  – The seller represents that it has no environmental liability. However, post-closing, a $100 million environmental problem is discovered. If the buyer had an indemnification against environmental liabilities, the seller would be required to pay the buyer $100 million (less any negotiated "deductible").
	■ Indemnification rights are often limited in several respects:
	  – time during which a claim can be made
	  – cap on maximum indemnity
	  – losses that the buyer must absorb before making a claim (a deductible)

(Continued)

EXHIBIT 6.10   (*Continued*)

[a]An acquisition of a company can be effected in several different ways, depending on the particular tax, legal, and other preferences. In a basic *merger* transaction, the acquirer and target merge into one surviving entity. More often, a subsidiary of the acquirer is formed, and that subsidiary merges with the target (with the resulting merged entity becoming a wholly-owned subsidiary of the acquirer). In a basic *stock sale* transaction, the acquirer (or a subsidiary thereof) acquires 100% of the capital stock (or other equity interests) of the target. In a basic *asset sale* transaction, the acquirer (or a subsidiary thereof) purchases all, or substantially all, of the assets of the target and, depending on the situation, may assume all, or some of, the liabilities of the target associated with the acquired assets. In an asset sale, the target survives the transaction and may choose to either continue operations or dissolve after distributing the proceeds from the sale to its equity holders.

[b]Also called material adverse effect (MAE). This is a highly negotiated provision in the definitive agreement, which may permit a buyer to avoid closing the transaction in the event that a substantial adverse situation is discovered after signing or a detrimental post-signing event occurs that affects the target. As a practical matter, it has proven difficult for buyers in recent years to establish that a MAC has occurred such that the buyer is entitled to terminate the deal.

[c]Receipt of financing is usually not a condition to closing, although this may be subject to change in accordance with market conditions.

[d]The representations usually need to be true only to some forgiving standard, such as "true in all material respects" or, more commonly: "true in all respects except for such inaccuracies that, taken together, do not amount to a material adverse effect." Material adverse effect, one of the most negotiated provisions in the entire agreement, has been interpreted by the courts to mean, in most circumstances, a very significant problem that is likely to be lasting rather than short-term.

[e]As the buyer only makes very limited reps and warranties in the definitive agreement, it is rare that any indemnification payments are ever paid by a buyer to a seller.

Receive Final Bids

Upon conclusion of the second round, prospective buyers submit their final bid packages to the sell-side advisor by the date indicated in the final bid procedures letter. These bids are expected to be final with minimal conditionality, or "outs," such as the need for additional due diligence or firming up of financing commitments. In practice, the sell-side advisor works with viable buyers throughout the second round to firm up their bids as much as possible before submission.

NEGOTIATIONS

- Evaluate Final Bids
- Negotiate with Preferred Buyer(s)
- Select Winning Bidder
- Render Fairness Opinion (if required)
- Receive Board Approval and Execute Definitive Agreement

Evaluate Final Bids

The sell-side advisor works together with the seller and its legal counsel to conduct a thorough analysis of the price, structure, and conditionality of the final bids. Purchase price is assessed within the context of the first round bids and the target's recent financial performance, as well as the valuation work performed by the sell-side advisors. The deemed binding nature of each final bid, or lack thereof, is also carefully weighed in assessing its strength. For example, a bid with a superior headline offer price, but significant conditionality, may be deemed weaker than a firmer bid at a lower price. Once this analysis is completed, the seller selects a preferred party or parties with whom to negotiate a definitive agreement.

Negotiate with Preferred Buyer(s)

Often, the sell-side advisor recommends that the seller negotiates with two (or more) parties, especially if the bid packages are relatively close and/or there are issues with the higher bidder's markup of the definitive agreement. Skillful negotiation on the part of the sell-side advisor at this stage can meaningfully improve the final bid terms. While tactics vary broadly, the advisor seeks to maintain a level playing field so as not to advantage one bidder over another and maximize the competitiveness of the final stage of the process. During these final negotiations, the advisor works intensely with the bidders to clear away any remaining confirmatory diligence items (if any) while firming up key terms in the definitive agreement (including price), with the goal of driving one bidder to differentiate itself.

Select Winning Bidder

The sell-side advisor and legal counsel negotiate a final definitive agreement with the winning bidder, which is then presented to the target's board of directors for approval. Not all auctions result in a successful sale. The seller normally reserves the right to reject any and all bids as inadequate at every stage of the process. Similarly, each prospective buyer has the right to withdraw from the process at any time prior to the execution of a binding definitive agreement. An auction that fails to produce a sale is commonly referred to as a "busted" or "failed" process.

Render Fairness Opinion

In response to a proposed offer for a public company, the target's board of directors typically requires a fairness opinion to be rendered as one item for their consideration before making a recommendation on whether to accept the offer and approve the execution of a definitive agreement. For public companies selling divisions or subsidiaries, a fairness opinion may be requested by the board of directors depending on the size and scope of the business being sold. The board of directors of a private company may also require a fairness opinion to be rendered in certain circumstances, especially if the stock of the company is broadly held (i.e., there are a large number of shareholders).

As the name connotes, a fairness opinion is a letter opining on the "fairness" (from a financial point of view) of the consideration offered in a transaction. The opinion letter is supported by detailed analysis and documentation providing an overview of the sale process run (including number of parties contacted and range of bids received), as well as an objective valuation of the target. The valuation analysis typically includes comparable companies, precedent transactions, DCF analysis, and LBO analysis (if applicable), as well as other relevant industry and share price performance benchmarking analyses, including premiums paid (if the target is publicly traded). The supporting analysis also contains a summary of the target's financial performance, including both historical and projected financials, along with key drivers and assumptions on which the valuation is based. Relevant industry information and trends supporting the target's financial assumptions and projections may also be included.

Prior to the delivery of the fairness opinion to the board of directors, the sell-side advisory team must receive approval from its internal fairness opinion committee.[21] In a public deal, the fairness opinion and supporting analysis is publicly disclosed and described in detail in the relevant SEC filings (see Chapter 2). Once rendered, the fairness opinion is one consideration for the target's board of directors as they exercise their broader business judgment seeking to fulfill their fiduciary duties with respect to the proposed transaction.

Receive Board Approval and Execute Definitive Agreement

Once the seller's board of directors votes to approve the deal, the definitive agreement is executed by the buyer and seller. A formal transaction announcement agreed to by both parties is made with key deal terms disclosed depending on the situation (see Chapter 2). The two parties then proceed to satisfy all of the closing conditions to the deal, including regulatory and shareholder approvals.

CLOSING

- Obtain Necessary Approvals
- Financing and Closing

Obtain Necessary Approvals

Regulatory Approval   The primary regulatory approval requirement for the majority of U.S. M&A transactions is made in accordance with the Hart-Scott-Rodino

---

[21]Historically, the investment bank serving as sell-side advisor to the target has typically rendered the fairness opinion. This role was supported by the fact that the sell-side advisor was best positioned to opine on the offer on the basis of its extensive due diligence and intimate knowledge of the target, the process conducted, and detailed financial analyses already performed. In recent years, however, the ability of the sell-side advisor to objectively evaluate the target has come under increased scrutiny. This line of thinking presumes that the sell-side advisor has an inherent bias toward consummating a transaction when a significant portion of the advisor's fee is based on the closing of the deal and/or if a stapled financing is provided by the advisor's firm to the winning bidder. As a result, some sellers hire a separate investment bank/boutique to render the fairness opinion from an "independent" perspective that is not contingent on the closing of the transaction.

Antitrust Improvements Act of 1976 (the "HSR Act").[22] Depending on the size of the transaction, the HSR Act requires both parties to an M&A transaction to file respective notifications and report forms with the Federal Trade Commission (FTC) and Antitrust Division of the Department of Justice (DOJ). Companies with significant foreign operations may require approval from comparable foreign regulatory authorities such as the Competition Bureau (Canada) and European Commission (European Union).

The HSR filing is typically made directly following the execution of a definitive agreement. If there are minimal or no antitrust concerns, the parties can consummate the transaction after a 30-day (15-day in the case of tender offers) waiting period has been observed (unless the regulator agrees to shorten this period). Transactions with complex antitrust issues can take considerably longer to clear or may result in a deal not closing because one or more agencies challenge the deal or require undesirable conditions to be met (e.g., the divestiture of a line of business).

Shareholder Approval

One-Step Merger   In a "one-step" merger transaction for public companies, target shareholders vote on whether to approve or reject the proposed transaction at a formal shareholder meeting pursuant to relevant state law. Prior to this meeting, a proxy statement is distributed to shareholders describing the transaction, parties involved, and other important information.[23] U.S. public acquirers listed on a major exchange may also need to obtain shareholder approval if stock is being offered as a form of consideration and the new shares issued represent over 20% of the acquirer's pre-deal common shares outstanding. Shareholder approval is typically determined by a majority vote, or 50.1% of the voting stock. Some companies, however, may have corporate charters, or are incorporated in states, that require higher approval levels for certain events, including change of control transactions.

In a one-step merger, the timing from the signing of a definitive agreement to closing may take as little as six weeks, but often takes longer (perhaps three or four months) depending on the size and complexity of the transaction. Typically, the main driver of the timing is the SEC's decision on whether to comment on the public disclosure documents. If the SEC determines to comment on the public disclosure, it can often take six weeks or more to receive comments, respond, and obtain the SEC's approval of the disclosure (sometimes, several months). Additionally, regulatory approvals, such as antitrust, banking, or insurance, can impact the timing of the closing.[24]

Following the SEC's approval, the documents are mailed to shareholders and a meeting is scheduled to approve the deal, which typically adds a month or more to

---

[22]Depending on the industry (e.g., banking, insurance, and telecommunications), other regulatory approvals may be necessary.

[23]For public companies, the SEC requires that a proxy statement includes specific information as set forth in Schedule 14A. These information requirements, as relevant in M&A transactions, generally include a summary term sheet, background of the transaction, recommendation of the board(s), fairness opinion(s), summary financial and pro forma data, and the definitive agreement, among many other items either required or deemed pertinent for shareholders to make an informed decision on the transaction.

[24]Large transactions in highly regulated industries, such as telecommunications, can often take more than a year to close because of the lengthy regulatory review.

the timetable. Certain transactions, such as a management buyout or a transaction in which the buyer's shares are being issued to the seller (and, therefore, registered with the SEC), increase the likelihood of an SEC review.

Two-Step Tender Process   Alternatively, a public acquisition can be structured as a "two-step" tender offer[25] on either a negotiated or unsolicited basis, followed by a merger. In Step I of the two-step process, the tender offer is made directly to the target's public shareholders with the target's approval pursuant to a definitive agreement.[26] The tender offer is conditioned, among other things, on sufficient acceptances to ensure that the buyer will acquire a majority (or supermajority, as appropriate) of the target's shares within 20 business days of launching the offer. If the buyer only succeeds in acquiring a majority (or supermajority, as appropriate) of the shares in the tender offer, it would then have to complete the shareholder meeting and approval mechanics in accordance with a "one-step" merger (with approval assured because of the buyer's majority ownership). However, if the requisite threshold of tendered shares is reached as designed (typically 90%), the acquirer can subsequently consummate a back-end "short form" merger (Step II) to squeeze out the remaining public shareholders without needing to obtain shareholder approval.

In a squeeze out scenario, the entire process can be completed much quicker than in a one-step merger. If the requisite level of shares are tendered, the merger becomes effective shortly afterward (e.g., the same day or within a couple of days). In total, the transaction can be completed in as few as five weeks. However, if the buyer needs to access the public capital markets to finance the transaction, the timing advantage of a tender offer would most likely be lost as such transactions typically take approximately 75 to 90 days to arrange post-signing.

Financing and Closing

In parallel with obtaining all necessary approvals and consents as defined in the definitive agreement, the buyer proceeds to source the necessary capital to fund and close the transaction. This financing process timing may range from relatively instantaneous (e.g., the buyer has necessary cash-on-hand or revolver availability) to several weeks or months for funding that requires access to the capital markets (e.g., bank, bond, and/or equity financing). In the latter scenario, the buyer begins the marketing process for the financing following the signing of the definitive agreement so as to be ready to fund expeditiously once all of the conditions to closing in the definitive agreement are satisfied. The acquirer may also use bridge financing to fund and close the transaction prior to raising permanent debt or equity capital. Once the financing is received and conditions to closing in the definitive agreement are met, the transaction is funded and closed.

---

[25] A tender offer is an offer to purchase shares for cash. An acquirer can also effect an exchange offer, pursuant to which the target's shares are exchanged for shares of the acquirer.
[26] Although the tender offer documents are also filed with the SEC and subject to its scrutiny, as a practical matter, the SEC's comments on tender offer documents rarely interfere with, or extend, the timing of the tender offer.

NEGOTIATED SALE

While auctions were prevalent as a sell-side mechanism during the LBO boom of the mid-2000s, a substantial portion of M&A activity is conducted through negotiated transactions. In contrast to an auction, a negotiated sale centers on a direct dialogue with a single prospective buyer. In a negotiated sale, the seller understands that it may have less leverage than in an auction where the presence of multiple bidders throughout the process creates competitive tension. Therefore, the seller and buyer typically reach agreement upfront on key deal terms such as price, structure, and governance matters (e.g., board of directors / management composition).

Negotiated sales are particularly compelling in situations involving a natural strategic buyer with clear synergies and strategic fit. As discussed in Chapter 2, synergies enable the buyer to justify paying a purchase price higher than that implied by a target's standalone valuation. For example, when synergies are added to the existing cash flows in a DCF analysis, they increase the implied valuation accordingly. Similarly, for a multiples-based approach, such as precedent transactions, adding the expected annual run-rate synergies to an earnings metric in the denominator serves to decrease the implied multiple paid.

A negotiated sale is often initiated by the buyer, whether as the culmination of months or years of research, direct discussion between buyer and seller executives, or as a move to preempt an auction ("preemptive bid"). The groundwork for a negotiated sale typically begins well in advance of the actual process. The buyer often engages the seller (or vice versa, as the case may be) on an informal basis with an eye toward assessing the situation. These phone calls or meetings generally involve a member of the prospective buyer's senior management directly communicating with a member of the target's senior management. Depending on the outcome of these initial discussions, the two parties may choose to execute a CA to facilitate the exchange of additional information necessary to further evaluate the potential transaction.

In many negotiated sales, the banker plays a critical role as the idea generator and/or intermediary before a formal process begins. For example, a proactive banker might propose ideas to a client on potential targets with accompanying thoughts and analysis on strategic benefits, valuation, financing structure, pro forma financial effects, and approach tactics. Ideally, the banker has contacts on the target's board of directors or with the target's senior management and can arrange an introductory meeting between key buyer and seller principals. The banker also plays an important role in advising on tactical points at the initial stage, such as timing and script for introductory conversations.

Many of the key negotiated sale process points mirror those of an auction, but on a compressed timetable. The sell-side advisory team still needs to conduct extensive due diligence on the target, position the target's story, understand and provide perspective on management's projection model, anticipate and address buyer concerns, and prepare selected marketing materials (e.g., a fulsome management presentation). The sell-side advisory team must also set up and monitor a data room and coordinate access to management, site visits, and follow-up due diligence. Furthermore, throughout the process, the sell-side advisor is responsible for regular interface with the prospective buyer, including negotiating key deal terms. As a means of keeping pressure on the buyer and discouraging a re-trade (as well as contingency planning), the sell-side advisor may preserve the threat of launching an auction in the event the two parties cannot reach an agreement.

In some cases, a negotiated sale may move faster than an auction as much of the upfront preparation, buyer contact, and marketing is bypassed. This is especially true if a strategic buyer is in the same business as the target, requiring less sector and company-specific education and thereby potentially accelerating to later stage due diligence. A negotiated sale process is typically more flexible than an auction process and can be customized as there is only a single buyer involved. However, depending on the nature of the buyer and seller, as well as the size, profile, and type of transaction, a negotiated sale can be just as intense as an auction. Furthermore, the upfront process during which key deal terms are agreed upon by both sides may be lengthy and contested, requiring multiple iterations over an extended period of time.

In a negotiated sale, ideally the seller realizes fair and potentially full value for the target while avoiding the potential risks and disadvantages of an auction. As indicated in Exhibit 6.11, these may include business disruption, confidentiality breaches, and potential issues with customers, suppliers, and key employees, as well as the potential stigma of a failed process. The buyer, for its part, avoids the time and risk of a process that showcases the target to numerous parties, potentially including competitors.

EXHIBIT 6.11 Advantages and Disadvantages of a Negotiated Sale

	Negotiated Sale
Advantages	■ Highest degree of confidentiality ■ Generally less disruptive to business than an auction; flexible deal timeline/deadlines ■ Typically fastest timing to signing ■ Minimizes "taint" perception if negotiations fail ■ May be the only basis on which a particular buyer will participate in a sale process
Disadvantages	■ Limits seller negotiating leverage and competitive tension ■ Potential to leave "money on the table" if other buyers would have been willing to pay more ■ Still requires significant management time to satisfy buyer due diligence needs ■ Depending on buyer, may require sharing of sensitive information with competitor without certainty of transaction close ■ Provides less market data on which the target's board of directors can rely to satisfy itself that value has been maximized

Bibliography and Recommended Reading

Almeida, Heitor, and Thomas Philippon. "The Risk-Adjusted Cost of Financial Distress." *Journal of Finance* 62 (2007): 2557–2586.

Alti, Aydogan. "How Persistent Is the Impact of Market Timing on Capital Structure?" *Journal of Finance* 61 (2006): 1681–1710.

Altman, Edward I., ed. *The High-Yield Debt Market: Investment Performance and Economic Impact*. New York: Beard Books, 1998.

Andrade, Gregor, and Steven Kaplan. "How Costly is Financial (Not Economic) Distress? Evidence from Highly Leveraged Transactions that Became Distressed." *Journal of Finance* 53 (1998): 1443–1493.

Baginski, Stephen P., and John M. Hassell. *Management Decisions and Financial Accounting Reports*. 2nd ed. Mason, OH: South-Western College Publishing, 2004.

Bahnson, Paul R., Brian P. McAllister, and Paul B.W. Miller. "Noncontrolling Interest: Much More Than a Name Change." *Journal of Accountancy* (2008).

Baker, Malcolm, and Jeffrey Wurgler. "Market Timing and Capital Structure." *Journal of Finance* 57 (2002): 1–32.

Barnhill Jr., Theodore, Mark Shenkman, and William Maxwell. *High Yield Bonds: Market Structure, Valuation, and Portfolio Strategies*. New York: McGraw-Hill, 1999.

Barr, Alistair. "Big Leveraged Buyouts Won't Return for Year or More: Lee Equity." *MarketWatch*, April 8, 2008.

Bierman Jr., Harold. *Private Equity: Transforming Public Stock Into Private Equity to Create Value*. Hoboken, NJ: John Wiley & Sons, 2003.

Boot, Arnoud W. A., Radhakrishnan Goplan, and Anjan V. Thakor. "Market Liquidity, Investor Participation, and Managerial Autonomy: Why Do Firms Go Private?" *Journal of Finance* 63 (2008): 2013–2059.

Bruner, Robert F. *Applied Mergers and Acquisitions*. Hoboken, NJ: John Wiley & Sons, 2004.

Calamos, John P. *Convertible Securities: The Latest Instruments, Portfolio Strategies, and Valuation Analysis*. Rev. ed. New York: McGraw-Hill, 1998.

Carey, Dennis, Robert J. Aiello, Michael D. Watkins, Robert G. Eccles, and Alfred Rappaport. *Harvard Business Review on Mergers & Acquisitions*. Boston: Harvard Business School Press, 2001.

Carney, William J. *Corporate Finance: Principles and Practice*. New York: Foundation Press, 2004.

Carney, William J. *Mergers and Acquisitions: Case and Materials*. New York: Foundation Press, 2000.

Chava, Sudheer, and Michael R. Roberts. "How Does Financing Impact Investment? The Role of Debt Covenants." *Journal of Finance* 63 (2008): 2085–2121.

Chisholm, Andrew. *An Introduction to Capital Markets: Products, Strategies, Participants.* West Sussex, UK: John Wiley & Sons, 2002.

Clements, Philip J., and Philip W. Wisler. *The Standard & Poor's Guide to Fairness Opinions.* New York: McGraw-Hill, 2005.

Copeland, Tom, Tim Koller, Marc Goedhart, and David Wessels. *Valuation: Measuring and Managing the Value of Companies.* 4th ed. Hoboken, NJ: John Wiley & Sons, 2005.

Damodaran, Aswath. *Damodaran on Valuation: Security Analysis for Investment and Corporate Finance.* 2nd ed. Hoboken, NJ: John Wiley & Sons, 2006.

Damodaran, Aswath. *Investment Valuation: Tools and Techniques for Determining the Value of Any Asset.* 2nd ed. New York: John Wiley & Sons, 2002.

Datta, Sudip, Mai Iskandar-Datta, and Kartik Raman. "Managerial Stock Ownership and the Maturity Structure of Corporate Debt." *Journal of Finance* 60 (2005): 2333–2350.

Downes, John, and Jordan Elliot Goodman. *Dictionary of Finance and Investment Terms.* 7th ed. Hauppauge, NY: Barron's Educational Series, 2006.

Ergungor, O. Emre. "Dividends." Federal Reserve Bank of Cleveland, Economic Commentary. 2004.

Evans, Frank C., and David M. Bishop. *Valuation for M&A: Building Value in Private Companies.* New York: John Wiley & Sons, 2001.

Fabozzi, Frank J. *The Handbook of Fixed Income Securities.* 6th ed. New York: McGraw-Hill, 2000.

Fama, Eugene F., and Kenneth R. French. "The Value Premium and the CAPM." *Journal of Finance* 61 (2006): 2163–2185.

Fang, Lily Hua. "Investment Bank Reputation and the Price and Quality of Underwriting Services." *Journal of Finance* 60 (2005): 2729–2761.

Feldman, Stanley J. *Principles of Private Firm Valuation.* Hoboken, NJ: John Wiley & Sons, 2005.

Ferguson, Joy. "LBOs Sponsor-to-Sponsor Deals Raise Eyebrows." *High Yield Report*, August 9, 2004.

Frankel, Michael E. S. *Mergers and Acquisitions Basics: The Key Steps of Acquisitions, Divestitures, and Investments.* Hoboken, NJ: John Wiley & Sons, 2005.

Gaughan, Patrick A. *Mergers, Acquisitions, and Corporate Restructurings.* 4th ed. Hoboken, NJ: John Wiley & Sons, 2007.

Gaughan, Patrick A. *Mergers: What Can Go Wrong and How to Prevent It.* Hoboken, NJ: John Wiley & Sons, 2005.

Gilson, Stuart. "Transactions Costs and Capital Structure Choice: Evidence from Financially Distressed Firms." *Journal of Finance* 52 (1997): 161–196.

Goetzmann, William N., and Roger G. Ibbotson. *The Equity Risk Premium: Essays and Explorations.* New York: Oxford University Press, 2006.

Graham, John R. "How Big Are the Tax Benefits of Debt?" *Journal of Finance* 55 (2000): 1901–1941.

Greenwald, Bruce C. N., Judd Kahn, Paul D. Sonkin, and Michael van Biema. *Value Investing: From Graham to Buffett and Beyond.* Hoboken, NJ: John Wiley & Sons, 2004.

Grinblatt, Mark, and Sheridan Titman. *Financial Markets and Corporate Strategy.* New York: McGraw-Hill, 2008.

Gu, Zhaoyang, and Ting Chen. "Analysts' Treatment of Nonrecurring Items in Street Earnings." Carnegie Mellon University (2004): 1–52.

Haas, Jeffrey J. *Corporate Finance in a Nutshell*. St. Paul, MN: Thomson West, 2003.

Hennessy, Christopher A., and Toni M. Whited. "Debt Dynamics." *Journal of Finance* 60 (2005): 1129–1165.

Hooke, Jeffrey C. *M&A: A Practical Guide to Doing the Deal*. New York: John Wiley & Sons, 1996.

Ibbotson, Roger G., and Rex Sinquefield. *Ibbotson SBBI 2008 Valuation Yearbook*. Chicago: Morningstar, 2007.

Kaback, Hoffer. "Behind the Art of M&A with Bruce Wasserstein." *Directors & Boards*, Spring 1999.

Kaplan, Steven N., and Antoinette Schoar. "Private Equity Performance: Returns, Persistence, and Capital Flows." *Journal of Finance* 60 (2005): 1791–1823.

Kieso, Donald E., Jerry J. Weygandt, and Terry D. Warfield. *Intermediate Accounting*. 12th ed. Hoboken, NJ: John Wiley & Sons, 2007.

Kisgen, Darren J. "Credit Ratings and Capital Structure." *Journal of Finance* 61 (2006): 1035–1072.

Koons, Cynthia. "Strong Loan Market Allowing Riskier Debt." *MarketWatch*, February 14, 2007.

Lajoux, Alexandra Reed. *The Art of M&A Integration: A Guide to Merging Resources, Processes, and Responsibilities*. 2nd ed. New York: McGraw-Hill, 2005.

Lajoux, Alexandra Reed, and Charles M. Elson. *The Art of M&A: Financing and Refinancing*. New York: McGraw-Hill, 1999.

Lajoux, Alexandra Reed, and H. Peter Nesvold. *The Art of M&A Structuring: Techniques for Mitigating Financial, Tax, and Legal Risk*. New York: McGraw-Hill, 2004.

Lajoux, Alexandra Reed, and J. Fred Weston. *The Art of M&A Due Diligence*. New York: McGraw-Hill, 2000.

Latham & Watkins. *The Book of Jargon*. New York: June 2008.

Leary, Mark T., and Michael R. Roberts. "Do Firms Rebalance Their Capital Structure?" *Journal of Finance* 60 (2005): 2575–2619.

Leland, Hayne E. "Corporate Debt Value, Bond Covenants, and Optimal Capital Structure." *Journal of Finance* 49 (1994): 1213–1252.

Leland, Hayne E. "Financial Synergies and the Optimal Scope of the Firm: Implications for Mergers, Spinoffs, and Structured Finance." *Journal of Finance* 62 (2007): 765–808.

Lerner, Josh, Felda Hardymon, and Ann Leamon. *Venture Capital and Private Equity: A Casebook*. Hoboken, NJ: John Wiley & Sons, 2007.

Liaw, K. Thomas. *The Business of Investment Banking: A Comprehensive Overview*. Hoboken, NJ: John Wiley & Sons, 2005.

Liaw, K. Thomas. *Capital Markets*. Mason, OH: Thomson South-Western, 2003.

Luo, Yuanzhi. "Do Insiders Learn from Outsiders? Evidence from Mergers and Acquisitions." *Journal of Finance* 60 (2005): 1951–1982.

Marren, Joseph H. *Mergers & Acquisitions: A Valuation Handbook*. New York: McGraw-Hill, 1992.

Metrick, Andrew, and Ayako Yasuda. "The Economics of Private Equity Funds," (working paper, Yale University). February 22, 2007.

Miller, Hazel (Orrick, Herrington & Sutcliffe LLP). "2005: Another Strong Year for the Financing of LBOs." *Financier Worldwide*, February 2006.

Mitchell, Mark, Todd Pulvino, and Erik Stafford. "Price Pressure around Mergers." *Journal of Finance* 60 (2004): 31–63.

McCafferty, Joseph. "The Buyout Binge." *CFO Magazine*, April 1, 2007.

Oesterle, Dale A. *Mergers and Acquisitions in a Nutshell*. St. Paul, MN: Thomson West, 2006.

Pereiro, Luis E. *Valuation of Companies in Emerging Markets*. New York: John Wiley & Sons, 2002.

Pratt, Shannon P. *Business Valuation Discounts and Premiums*. New York: John Wiley & Sons, 2001.

Pratt, Shannon P., and Roger J. Grabowski. *Cost of Capital: Estimation and Applications*. 3rd ed. Hoboken, NJ: John Wiley & Sons, 2008.

Rajan, Arvind, Glen McDermott, and Ratul Roy. *The Structured Credit Handbook*. Hoboken, NJ: John Wiley & Sons, 2007.

Reed, Stanley Foster, Alexandra Lajoux, and H. Peter Nesvold. *The Art of M&A: A Merger Acquisition Buyout Guide*. 4th ed. New York: McGraw-Hill, 2007.

Rickertsen, Rick, and Robert E. Gunther. *Buyout: The Insider's Guide to Buying Your Own Company*. New York: AMACOM, 2001.

Rhodes-Kropf, Matthew, and S. Viswanathan. "Market Valuation and Merger Waves." *Journal of Finance* 59 (2004): 2685–2718.

Rosenbloom, Arthur H., ed. *Due Diligence for Global Deal Making: The Definitive Guide to Cross-Border Mergers and Acquisitions (M&A), Joint Ventures, Financings, and Strategic Alliances*. Princeton: Bloomberg Press, 2002.

Rubino, Robert, and Timothy Shoyer. "Why Today's Borrowers & Investors Lean Toward Second Liens." *Bank Loan Report*, March 8, 2004.

Ross, Stephen A., Randolph W. Westerfield, and Jeffrey Jaffe. *Corporate Finance*. 6th ed. New York: McGraw-Hill, 2002.

Salter, Malcolm S., and Joshua N. Rosenbaum. *OAO Yukos Oil Company*. Boston: Harvard Business School Publishing, 2001.

Schneider, Arnold. *Managerial Accounting: Manufacturing and Service Applications*. 5th ed. Mason, OH: Cengage Learning, 2009.

Schwert, G. William. "Hostility in Takeovers: In the Eyes of the Beholder?" *Journal of Finance* 55 (2000): 2599–2640.

Scott, David L. *Wall Street Words: An A to Z Guide to Investment Terms for Today's Investor*. 3rd ed. Boston: Houghton Mifflin, 2003.

Siegel, Jeremy J. *Stocks for the Long Run*. 4th ed. New York: McGraw-Hill, 2007.

Sherman, Andrew J., and Milledge A. Hart. *Mergers & Acquisitions From A to Z*. 2nd ed. New York: AMACOM, 2006.

Slee, Robert T. "Business Owners Choose a Transfer Value." *Journal of Financial Planning* 17, no. 6 (2004): 86–91.

Slee, Robert T. *Private Capital Markets: Valuation, Capitalization, and Transfer of Private Business Interests*. Hoboken, NJ: John Wiley & Sons, 2004.

Standard and Poor's/Leveraged Commentary & Data. *A Guide to the Loan Market*. October 2007.

Standard and Poor's/Leveraged Commentary & Data. *High Yield Bond Market Primer.* 2007.

Strebulaev, Ilya A. "Do Tests of Capital Structure Theory Mean What They Say?" *Journal of Finance* 62 (2007): 1747–1787.

Thompson, Samuel C. Jr. *Business Planning for Mergers and Acquisitions: Corporate, Securities, Tax, Antitrust, International, and Related Aspects.* 3rd ed. Durham, NC: Carolina Academic Press, 2007.

Wasserstein, Bruce. *Big Deal: Mergers and Acquisitions in the Digital Age.* New York: Warner Books, 2001.

White, Gerald I., Ashwinpaul C. Sondhi, and Dov Fried. *The Analysis and Use of Financial Statements.* 3rd ed. New York: John Wiley & Sons, 2002.

Yago, Glenn, and Susanne Trimbath. *Beyond Junk Bonds: Expanding High Yield Markets.* New York: Oxford University Press, 2003.

Yasuda, Ayako. "Do Bank Relationships Affect the Firm's Underwriter Choice in the Corporate-Bond Underwriting Market?" *Journal of Finance* 60 (2005): 1259–1292.